EMOTION

We will have to decide whether we want to continue our relationship. ~~You told me~~ a You still see very hostile and get irritated whenever we try to discuss anything at all. Unless we can begin to communicate I don't see how we can relate to one another. You still seem to be angry most of the time and to control me by your anger. You have always been unable to get your thoughts together enough to figure out what is bothering you. Perhaps, also, this is why you were unable to commit yourself to me or love me, though you said you did. It was as if I could not break through your walls and that ~~would~~ you would not let yourself love me — yet you seemed to ~~desperately~~ need love.

Your use of sex power ~~with~~ withholding and refusals was humiliating to me for all these years as you know. I don't know how you could feel justified in treating me this way. I would never be angry or hostile toward you and never held out on you, but surrendered in every way to you. I can't really blame you because I think it must be hard to be in the state you were and are in but I wish

EMOTION
the method of philosophical therapy

Warren Shibles

University of Wisconsin – Whitewater

THE LANGUAGE PRESS
Box 342 Whitewater, Wisconsin 53190

ISBN 0-912386-07-X (Hardcover)

ISBN 0-912386-08-8 (Paperback)

Library of Congress Catalog Card Number 72-82991

By the same author:

Metaphor: An Annotated Bibliography and History Whitewater, Wisc., The Language Press 1971

Philosophical Pictures Dubuque, Iowa: Kendall-Hunt 1969 (revised 1972)

Wittgenstein, Language and Philosophy Kendall-Hunt 1969 (1971)

Models of Ancient Greek Philosophy London: Vision Press (New York: Humanities) 1971

An Analysis of Metaphor The Hague: Mouton (New York: Humanities) 1971

Essays on Metaphor The Language Press 1972

Death: An Interdisciplinary Analysis The Language Press 1974

Printed in the United States of America

Contents

An Analysis of Love
Appendix
II Imagery and Visual Perception

Emotions: The Problem

James Hillman (1961) wrote, "From all the evidence at hand the concept of emotion has become central to the issues of our time."

People often value emotions as perhaps the greatest part of life. The problem of how emotions work may well be the most important issue man has to solve. Some think that emotions are misleading fictions which do not exist as such and others, especially the average man, think they do exist as internal states or entities of some sort. This conflict needs to be resolved. If patients are to be cured of "emotional disorder" we must first determine what an emotion is. Everyone faces so-called emotional problems all the time. His personality and all of his actions consist of emotional factors. There is no use in attempting to find a form of government which can best meet our needs until we clearly determine what our emotions and needs are. If we are confused about emotions that confusion has undesirable consequences for our ability to cure the "emotionally disturbed" (psychotics and neurotics), and for social and personal relations with one another, etc. One cannot adequately cope with social problems such as war, violence or hatred unless one is clear about emotions. This age is characterized by alienation, and many writers on love state that very few people are capable of genuine love. Also perhaps the majority of people are only partially capable of full erotic love. La Rochefoucould states, "It is with true love as it is with ghosts, everyone talks of it, but few have seen it." In the various disciplines we find that, in fact, man was and still is confused about what emotions are. Consider the following admissions regarding emotions:

1

The *Encyclopaedia Britannica* (1955) states,

"Our knowledge of the topic, emotion, is much less complete than our knowledge of the other topics in the field of psychology."

C. Morgan in *Physiological Psychology* (1965) states,

"Emotion has been the subject of considerable theorizing, perhaps because it has been so difficult to understand."

David Rapaport in *Emotions and Memory* (1959) says,

"A dynamic solution of the problem of emotions has not been reached. One reason may be that the psychic forces are still obscure entities."

G. Mandler wrote in *New Directions in Psychology I*, (1962),

"The analysis of emotion has lagged behind other apparently less appealing topics. We know more today about verbal learning, psychophysical scaling, and discrimination in the rat, for example, than about the determinants of emotional behavior."

In 1928 the Wittenberg Symposium was held to investigate emotions and the results were published in *Feelings and Emotions*. In this work E. Claparede states,

"The psychology of affective processes is the most confused chapter in all psychology. Here it is that the greatest differences appear from one psychologist to another. They are in agreement neither on the facts nor on the words." (p. 124)

In the same book H. Langfeld states,

"The general subject of feeling, and to a certain extent also that of the emotions, form perhaps the most unsatisfactory chapter in the systematic psychology of the present day."

Brown and Farber (1951) wrote,

"No genuine order can be discerned within this field. Instead, examination of current treatments of emotion reveals a discouraging state of confusion and uncertainty. Substantial advances have been made in recent years with respect to theories of learning and motivation, but the phenomena of emotion have not, as a rule, been considered in the formulations and remain a tangle of unrelated facts."

Less recent accounts of emotions reveal the same prevailing inability to cope with the concept of emotion.

Alexander Shand wrote,

"The psychology of the emotions, notwithstanding some recent advance, is still perhaps the most backward part of science," and "The psychology of the feelings can give us no answer to these questions: it has long remained the most unprofitable part of science."

Descartes (1596-1650) stated in *Passions of the Soul,*

"There is nothing in which the defective nature of the sciences which we have received from the ancients appears more clearly than in what they have written on the passions." (p. 331)

J. Senault in *The Use of the Passions* (trans. 1649) wrote,

"As there is no man so temperate but that he sometimes experienceth the violence of Passions, and that the disorder thereof is a fate from which very few can fence themselves; so it is the Subject whereupon Philosophers have most exercised their brains, and is the part of Moral Philosophy which hath oftenest been examined; But if I may speak my sense with freedom, and if I may be permitted to censure my Masters, I am of the opinion, that there is no point in the whole body of Philosophy, that hath been treated of with more ostentation and less of profit . . . "

There is in all this some agreement. It is agreed that emotion terms, though thought to be intelligible in everyday usage, are rather vague. They need to be examined and no theory has yet been shown to be adequate to the task. The following is an attempt to provide a clarification of the concept of emotion in light of contemporary knowledge, especially that of contemporary philosophical psychology. It will be shown how we can prevent and eliminate negative emotions and learn to induce positive emotions. This theory will be used to revise much of what is presently believed about emotions. The acquisition of such knowledge can radically change one's character and personality.

4

By showing that emotions are based on reason, the philosopher's arguments and clarifications become relevant. Rational, irrational, negative and positive, as used in this book do not refer to absolutes but are meant mainly as relative and descriptive terms which should be reduced to concrete methods and instances and specific contexts. A negative emotion is not a bad emotion as such, although we do not usually enjoy being angry. I have, nevertheless, retained a common usage here of speaking of negative and positive emotions and rational and irrational statements but with no intention of dictating what is to be negative or rational. On the other hand, numerous specific instances are offered.

Sources:

J. Brown and I. Farber *"Emotions Conceptualized as Intervening Variables"* Psychological Bulletin (1951) pp. 465-495

E. Claparede *"Feelings and Emotions"* Feelings and Emotions (The Wittenberg Symposium) Martin Reymert, ed., Worcester, Mass.: Clark University Press 1928

Rene Descartes *"The Passions of the Soul"* The Philosophical Works of Descartes Haldane and Ross, trans. New York: Dover Vol 1, 1955

"Emotion" Encyclopaedia Britannica 1955

James Hillman Emotion Evanston, Illinois: Northwestern University Press 1961

Herbert Langfeld *"The Role of Feeling and Emotion in Aesthetics"* Feelings and Emotions (1928) pp. 346-354

G. Mandler *"Emotion"* New Directions in Psychology I R. Brown, et al., eds., New York: Holt, Rinehart and Winston (1962) pp. 267-339

Clifford Morgan Physiological Psychology third edition, New York: McGraw-Hill 1965, chapter 11 *"Emotion"* pp. 306-338

David Rapaport Emotions and Memory New York: International Universities Press 1959

J. Senault The Use of the Passions London 1649

Alexander Shand *"Character and Emotions"* Mind N. S 5, 18 (April 1896) pp. 203-226

Emotion as Open-Context

One may say, "My father does not really love me," and he may carry this belief to his father holding it against him. The astonished father may point out that he provided for the child in every way that he knew how, yet receives the response, "Yes, but you did not really love me." Here is a situation analogous to the question, "I see all of the buildings and functions involved here but where is the university?" The answer is, of course, "You have seen it, that is it?" The child is looking for some internal state, or is involved in a logical confusion. He seems to think love is something over and beyond all acts which one can perform. This may be because his problem is that he is unhappy and wishes to find someone or something outside of himself to blame. He then finds he can blame an idealistic and obscure, transcendental "love" which supposedly exists in and of itself.

Something must count for or against an emotion for it to be or not be an emotion. There must be some paradigm case or example which serves as a criterion. To love someone is to perform an act of some kind, e.g., speak to someone in a certain way, do certain things for the person, have certain feelings or desires concerning a person, etc. "If you really loved me, you wouldn't have done that," suggests only that love involves certain acts, not that love must be something over and above the acts and feelings involved. That is, for each use of love there is some paradigm case which shows what love means in that circumstance. "I love ice cream," reports a taste for an object; "I love him," may report a high regard for his acting ability. Emotion words are elliptical statements referring to or implying certain examples or paradigms.

5

However, the paradigms suggested by emotion terms are often obscure, confused, misleading or simply not known. Put a different way, emotion terms are open-context terms with a loosely limited range of customary substitution instances. "Love your neighbor," may mean:

1) Say kind things to him.
2) Help him as much as possible.
3) Be affectionate toward him.
4) Do not disturb your neighbor.
5) Respect your neighbor's legal rights.
6) Be friendly toward your neighbor.
7) Do nothing to harm your neighbor, etc.

Just what "Love your neighbor" means is not clear. It could mean all, none, or only some of the above possible substitution instances. It is open-context in this sense. One might even mean by "love your neighbor" to keep hands off and to mind one's own business.

One may believe that he loves someone and utter statements to that effect. Still he may not know what substitution instances count for "I love you," here. He may not be able to say why he loves someone. What he does say is often beside the point or not the "real" reason, e.g., "She is witty," "She is a beautiful person," etc. There are many witty, beautiful people that he is not in love with. He may then say he loves her but not know exactly why, or what substitution instances or paradigm cases his notion of love implies. He often finds he can only describe his love in terms of metaphors, as poets do. Lovers are regarded as madmen. Lovesickness was once treated as a medical disease to be cured by a physician. The point here is simply that he does not know what exactly love involves. It is something one "falls in" and perhaps later "falls out of" again. "Why is it that you no longer love her? She is still witty and beautiful." The feeling of love may be gone because he found out more things about her or himself. He found out more clearly what he meant by love. He may have regarded her only in an erotic way and so he did not love her but only erotic aspects. But at first he may not have had a clear idea at all as to why he loved her except for a certain feeling he experienced which blinded him to her other qualities.

Asking why one has an emotion can in one sense be like asking why one has a feeling. This is the case in which the paradigm or substitution instance for an emotion is a feeling. To ask why one has a feeling is like asking why one sees. We normally just do see. But even if love is conceived of only as a feeling we can ask why we have that feeling. The feeling may be based on a false belief or be due to intake of drugs or alcohol. We may question the cause of the feeling as well as the object of the feeling. The cause need not be the same as the object. Also we may change our beliefs such that we can eliminate the feeling or promote and develop it. Poetry and metaphor are said to enrich feeling and emotion.

In another sense a feeling may be regarded as an ineffable "object" about which we cannot ask further or relate to other things. It is something or other we "have" not something we can clearly describe. It is like seeing. But "feeling" is not just "had," insomuch as it is a word and so a category gaining its meaning and reference in language.

One may be in love yet not know what he means by it. In addition a person may sincerely say "I love her," yet do nothing but harm to her, without contradiction. It is not contradictory to state, "I am going to kill you because I love you." Love here is an open-context term having many possible substitution instances. To say "I love you," is in itself to say very little. One often finds this out in practice.

Similarly one may assert that he hates someone and not know why, or find that he hates someone because of a false belief that that person said something damaging. Until the mistake is discovered one may find he dislikes everything about the person. There are endless paradigms and substitution instances possible here, though we in fact, or descriptively usually allow only certain things to count as substitution instances for an emotion. Some of these instances may be confused and so might be rejected, and one may stipulate new substitution instances. The poet and novelist often create new emotions or new aspects of emotions in just this way.

If one does not have or cannot find a concrete paradigm case for an emotion term it becomes a myth. We use emotion terms and this may give us the impression that we know more about them than we really do.

Emotion terms may be seen to sometimes reduce to ethical terms which in turn reduce to descriptive statements about situations, likes, wants, etc. The openness or vagueness of emotion terms is suggested by H. Warren in his *Dictionary of Psychology and Cognate Sciences* as follows:

"In preparing our definitions we have been struck by the extreme difficulty of finding a good technical meaning for many of the terms in common psychological use. This is particularly true in the field of emotion."

D. O. Hebb stated,

"The discussion of emotion has been about as confused as that of any topic in psychology, partly because the terminology is often equivocal and partly because tradition carries great weight in this part of the field and it is hard to keep a modern point of view consistently."

Emotions are often regarded as complex descriptions or open-context. Melden wrote, "Emotion is many pronged," (231) "There is no single paradigm of anger; but cases and cases," (231) and "Anger is a cluster concept." (219) Because of this openness or vagueness emotions are seen to lack intelligibility. Melden wrote, "Traditional views concerning the nature of emotion . . . persuasive as they may appear to be . . . are incoherent." (200) A statement in Plato's *Philebus* is that pleasure is not one but many.

Such statements suggest that emotion, in itself, is a fiction. Emotions are nothing in themselves. They reduce to non-emotion terms. In this sense emotion is not qualitatively different from other activities of the human organism.

We equivocate with emotion words when we apply them to quite diverse situations. Terms applied to children ought not be used in the same way when applied to adults. To say a child is angry is not the same as saying an adult is angry. The context is too different to correctly apply the same term, anger. Again the "emotionally disturbed" patient cannot be said to be angry in the same way as is a normal person. Animals cannot be angry in the way man is angry partly because animals do not have our language. A dog cannot be angry with the government.

Emotions are characterized as having a wide range of interpretations. "Sadness" may be described as loneliness, walking in a desert, thinking of unpleasant things, depression, etc. Love and happiness have a great many possible meanings. Such meanings often conflict. One may wonder if he is happy, in love, joyous, elated, and not be clear about what he means by such terms. When the possible interpretation is found to be wide, the meaning of the emotion terms in question is seen to be questionable. Emotion terms become elliptical for many different and diverse kinds of body states, situations, etc. The methods of substitution, synecdoche, and metonymy become applicable. There is no emotion as such, but only a paradigm, e.g., depression is the experience of the impossibility of carrying out actions adequate for adaptation, or it is the feeling of being rejected, etc.

One reason for the vagueness of emotion terms is that they seem to refer to a psycho-physical relation and state of which we are ignorant. We are not sure how rational beliefs become translated into feelings or physical states. Thus emotion words must contain a vagueness. If we say, "She has a passion for him," it is not clear if she has a feeling, a thought, an assessment, etc.

The general principle used in this book is that all abstract terms, if they are to be intelligible, must be reduced to concrete terms and examples.

James Hillman wrote,

"Such terms as 'emotion,' 'energy,' 'conflict,' etc. cannot be reduced to neutral counters. They have a multitude of shadings; they are full of metaphysical and irrational overtones." (14)

John Austin wrote,

"All words for emotions . . . tend to cover a rather wide and ill-defined variety of situations: and the patterns they cover tend to be, each of them, rather complex." (153-154)

Emotion includes behavior, judgment, feeling, context, and intention. In saying one has an emotion it is not clear which aspect has most emphasis. Being very jealous may stress one's intentions but not his feelings and he may not have any negative feelings. It may be that there is a clear-cut jealous situation. If it is the case that the feeling component is stressed, then it may be that the person is in a state of fatigue such that after rest he will no longer experience the emotion in question. Emotions do not come pure. Every anger or emotion is particular involving a unique combination of factors.

Emotions in reading are different than in speaking or in behavior. Emotions of women differ from those of men and children. Emotions differ wherever goals, abilities, and feelings differ. They differ when one is alone and when one is with other people. It would be interesting to determine what emotions a person would have if he never met any other people. People often smile, even when alone, while speaking on the telephone.

People do not laugh when they try to tickle themselves — others are needed to bring this about. A number of emotions are defined so as to include a time context, e.g., apprehension, hope, patience, boredom, etc. Different ages produce different emotions. Chaucer's emotions are not ours. Depression may be due to forgetting the difficult circumstances under which a conflict occurred. If we know more about a depressed person we instead say he is confused about a certain conflict. Depression may also be due to the inability to carry out actions adequate for adaptation.

One expresses emotion "in" looking at a picture; it is in the situation that the emotion arises. Each emotion may be studied in terms of the way it arises. It includes histories as well as patterns. There is no such thing as love, envy, anger, etc. as such. There is sadness in many things, e.g., "The dog has such sad eyes." One cannot have an experience of patriotism as such, cannot be patriotic to his pet or his family. Music creates a mood. A combination of line, form, color, etc., can produce emotion. Situation ethics may stress the individual case because one cannot feel an emotion as such, but only have a feeling as part of a context. Unfortunately existentialist writing seems to regard emotion as self-justificatory. When we speak of our emotions we proceed to tell a story. Metaphor is often required to render the complexity of the context. Melden wrote,

"What in one set of circumstances counts for anger, in another way will count for malice or jealousy." (219)

"Nothing could be more foreign to the poet's account than the idea that feelings are internal entities, conceptually sundered from the circumstances, the situations of the character who is in the throes of his passion." (209)

"No account of anger is adequate unless it recognizes the pertinence of the situation." (213)

Sources:

John Austin "Other Minds" Logic and Language Second series, A. Flew, ed. Oxford: Blackwell 1961

D.O. Hebb Organization of Behavior New York: Wiley 1949

James Hillman Emotion Northwestern University Press 1961

A. I. Melden "The Conceptual Dimensions of Emotions" Human Action T. Mischel, ed. New York: Academic Press 1969

H. C. Warren Dictionary of Psychology and Cognate Sciences 1934

Emotion, Language, and Reason

INTRODUCTION

The study of emotions begins with what is usually said about emotions and a careful description of the situations and linguistic contexts in which emotion terms and behavior are observed.

"Emotion" is a very general term and a vague term. If we begin to speak about emotions in general like this we may be led into thinking that there is one explanation which can be given for all emotions, e.g., "All emotions are really just mental confusions." We are led to speak of "an" emotion as if it were a single entity, as if it were a thing. We may continue to inquire as to where the emotion is and how long it lasts. We ask "What is an emotion really?" and nothing comes.

Where does the problem of emotion arise for the average person? "I had a problem of emotion last night," is unusual. So also is "I wonder how many emotions I have." These are questions we do not usually ask. Emotion is not an entity but an abstraction. As an abstraction, emotion cannot be numbered, serve as a cause, effect, or reason. Emotion is not an entity but is elliptical for other things just as color in itself is not an entity but elliptical for specific colors. A more specific color, red as such, though more specific than color, is still an abstraction. So also jealousy, rage, etc. are abstractions. One cannot see color or red, as such, and one cannot have an emotion or jealousy, rage, etc., as such.

One cannot see the abstraction, color, or red, and one cannot have or experience the abstraction emotion or fear, jealousy, etc. They are the wrong sorts of things to experience. Red and fear

13

do, however, reduce to behavioral activity which can be observed and experienced.

In this respect emotion cannot be a cause because it is not an entity. "My emotions caused me to do it," can be misleading and unfounded if emotion is regarded as an abstraction. B. F. Skinner (1953) wrote,

"The emotions are excellent examples of the fictional causes to which we commonly attribute behavior." (p. 160)

William Hunt (1941) wrote,

"Strange as it may seem, the existence of some unique, scientific experimental content in emotion has never been demonstrated adequately." (p. 265).

Similarly John Dewey (1894) says,

"There is no such thing as *the* emotion of fear, hate, love. The unique, unduplicated character of experienced events and situations impregnates the emotion that is evoked."

In the area of psychoanalytic theory, Ostow (1959) states,

"There is no systematic treatment of affect as a category in psychoanalytic theory."

We make a distinction between technical words and models used to talk about emotions, and the more common emotion expressions and models used by most people. One usually thinks that an emotion is a certain kind of feeling he has. He usually thinks it is an innate part of his behavior, that it is like a feeling, e.g., "I just feel angry." Anger, here, is alternatively regarded as an emotion and as a feeling. One thinks that he has to express and release his anger because if he doesn't it will become "stored up" within him causing mental damage and frustration. This account treats anger as an entity, something which can be "stored up." It is the technical Freudian language made common. The picture is entirely misleading because the "entities" "stored up" have never been located. The above picture of anger can do much harm because it leads one to think he can have no control of his anger, that his anger is like a feeling he just has or is born with. The picture is a deterministic, fatalistic one. As our account of emotions will show, anger is neither a feeling one merely "has," nor is it something necessarily determinate or fixed. Anger can be controlled and eliminated. A. Ewing (1957) wrote about the similar emotion, hatred, "Hatred is never justifiable." (p. 67)

If anger is "stored up" why not also "love," "envy," "jealousy," "fear"? These are not the sorts of things which can be stored. This is because they are not things at all. They are not merely feelings.

The observer determines emotions by the circumstance or situation. An emotion word seems to be an elliptical word covering both feelings and the contexts involved. Geldard (1962) wrote,

"The role of context is beautifully illustrated by some of the early experiences in film production. The Russian directors Kuleshov and Pudovkin took a closeup of the face of the actor Mosjukhin, while in a quiet pose, which they joined in three different combinations. The same closeup was followed by a) a picture of a plate of soup, b) one of a coffin in which lay a dead woman, and c) one of a little girl playing with a funny toy bear.

'When we showed the three combinations to an audience which had not been let into the secret the result was terrific. The public raved about the acting of the artist. They pointed out the heavy pensiveness of his mood over the forgotten soup, were touched and moved by the deep sorrow with which he looked on the dead woman, and admired the light, happy smile with which he surveyed the girl at play. But we knew in all three cases the face was exactly the same.' " (46)

The emotion, then, is not merely a feeling. The ascription of emotion may imply that the man in the picture must be having the same feelings the viewer would have if the viewer were in that situation. The emotion is not just represented by the expression on one's face, or by his posture. It does not just represent inner feelings. Because emotion words often partly refer to and cover situations and contexts they are not the sorts of things that can be stored up or released. However, some intelligible paradigms might be worked out for what might go for the "storing up" or "release" of anger. It will be argued that such a paradigm has much to do with our language uses. It may be noted that phobias are often named in terms of the situation which gives rise to them, e.g., agoraphobia, claustrophobia, or in terms of specific external objects.

If one must "release" one's anger perhaps also he would have to release his love, envy, revenge, hatred, melancholy, etc., when he is "in" those states. But there are alternatives to "release" and there are various kinds of "release" possible. In the first place it would be desirable not to get oneself in the position of having certain emotions. In the second place to just "release energy" (if such is possible) does not seem effective in getting at the cause of the difficulty.

A specific example may help. One often thinks that revenge is a natural emotion to experience and one often, in one way or another, takes his revenge. A friend pours molasses on your books and furniture. You know this is more than a joke, that he has gone too far, and take your revenge. You pour molasses on his books and furniture in the traditional "tooth for a tooth" fashion. You immediately feel relieved but after a while you begin to feel as if you had yourself done a mean act. In addition it may turn out that your friend had been mistreated by his parents and friends and did the above act in his misery and confusion at a time when he needed friends most. Your revenge was the worst thing you could have done to him, it helped to drive him into a neurotic condition. When you realize this you wish you had not gotten revenge.

In any case, revenge has no purpose or point, but is an unthoughtful and merely reactive act on the part of the harmed party. Revenge does not get at the cause of the problem. If we regard one who does harm to another as not being well, or as being ignorant or unintelligent, then it would not help such a person to take out revenge on him. It does not help many criminals to merely lock them in prison for a certain number of years. They often come out worse than when they went in. What is needed is correctional action directed at that which caused the person to do the harm in the first place. Our penal system is perhaps more a system of obtaining revenge than a correctional or preventative system. Criminals often are not psychologically well enough to fear imprisonment threats, and being in jail seems not even relevant to the cause of their being there. Thus, although harmed by another, one might realize that revenge has no intelligent function. In the above example one might instead go to one's friend and ask why he poured the molasses and how things have been going for him. After acting in this way on a number of occasions one can find that it gives him a pleasant feeling of helping out other human beings, and eventually, that he no longer experiences the game of revenge. This is because emotion is assessment which guides feeling. If the rational aspect is changed the feelings change. One no longer has that emotion of revenge, or at least one immediately overcomes that emotion. No outburst or release is needed, only common sense and intelligence regarding cause and effect. It is not that emotions are ever released but only that our assessments change thereby bringing about a change in our feelings.

A similar argument, or example, may be offered for anger and hatred. They are not innate necessary forms of behavior, but may be considered as expressions of one's inability to adjust or act in a certain situation. They can be overcome when they occur and, more important, one finds that such emotions eventually can even stop occurring. Psychiatrists often say one of the greatest deterrents to successful therapy is the patient's view that he cannot change his emotions and his behavior when, in fact, he can. The psychiatrist, Albert Ellis, wrote,

"What are some of the major illogical ideas or philosophies which, when originally held and later perpetuated by men and women in our civilization lead to self-defeat and neurosis? . . . The idea that one has virtually no control over one's emotions and that one cannot help feeling certain things — instead of the idea that one has enormous control over one's emotions if one chooses to work at controlling them and to practice saying the right kinds of sentences to oneself." (Ellis 1958)

The average person holds also that emotions are, or are like, feelings and so are inevitable and cannot be changed. Rather one can change one's emotions and to a large extent determine and encourage some while eliminating others. This is an intuitive observation at this point which will gradually be given support.

In addition, in opposition to popular opinion, one can schedule one's emotions, turn them on and off, within limits. "I just cannot get in the mood," is often an excuse or psychological limitation which might be overcome, rather than a fact.

An examination of the relationship between emotion and language shows what emotions are and also suggests why and how we may control and change them. Descartes' dualism of mind and body has long been in decline. It can no longer be maintained that we merely have ideas and then express them in words. Rather the epistemological starting point is not thought, but language. To present a theory or view we must use language.

An argument mentioned by Aristotle against the skeptic is that if the skeptic is to present his theory of skepticism he must say something. If he says something he must mean something by the words he uses and must assume that he can communicate intelligibly to others. He must presuppose meaning, language and communication and to that great extent cannot be a skeptic. He is caught in what I will call the "linguo-centric predicament."

In the attempt to found an epistemological starting point other assumptions have been thought to be more basic than language. Descartes, for example, presented one of the most well-known formulations of what the first "truth" is which one must accept, all else being initially in doubt. In his *Meditations* Descartes assumes the guise of a skeptic who doubts everything and initially rejects all knowledge both rational and sensible. He suggests, even, that he is being deceived in what he thinks exists, by an evil genius. Descartes does not notice that he has already assumed meaning for all the words he has thus far used as well as language and its communicability. This is partly because his skeptical doubt is a methodological doubt not a sincere thoroughgoing doubting. He is setting up a hypothetical doubt only to bring in doctrines which he already holds such as the substance-quality doctrine, clear and distinct ideas, a doctrine of levels of being, the doctrine that there must be at least as much reality in the cause as in the effect, and a belief in God is intimately connected with these. He, in effect, is offering us scholastic slogans.

Descartes, then, instead of noticing that he is presupposing language asserts something else as one first thing which he must assume. He says that although a bad genius may be deceiving him the one thing that he cannot be deceived about is that he is being deceived. That is, what one doubts may or may not be the case but one cannot doubt that he is doubting. One may think he sees or seems to see a tree and it may or may not be one, but one cannot doubt that he thinks that he sees a tree or seems to see one. The epistemological starting point for Descartes, then, is the "I think," or "I doubt." Phenomenologists have similarly begun with this Cartesian "ego" or, as it is sometimes put, "consciousness."

Yet when one looks at Descartes' argument many sorts of assumptions are to be found. Descartes says we have to intuit the acceptance of the "I think" partly because one has to accept the language and the various assumed concepts his formulation contains. Do we have to start with "I think," "I doubt," "I seem to see," or "I seem to hear"? Descartes' argument does not lead up to "I think." He has already assumed a "me" when he says an evil genius may be deceiving "me," and he again assumes an "I" in "I think." The "I" is already given, already assumed, not argued for.

Again the seemingly convincing device Descartes uses to try to convince us that thought is the first starting point is that *what* we think about, what we think *of*, may be illusory, but our thinking is not illusory. But why isn't it? Why cannot the evil genius deceive us about this also. Can't we think we are thinking yet not be? This is especially possible since we are not quite sure exactly what thinking is. Descartes himself stirred the dust over thinking by separating mind and body as well as by accepting a problem riddled substance-quality doctrine of mind, and then integrating it all with an even more tenuous religious entity. Descartes' formulation of the first epistemological starting point makes these difficulties easy to see. A phenomenological interpretation, although similar to Descartes', places great stress on the "of" in "thinking of" something. For the phenomenologist thinking becomes "intention," "intentionality," and already Descartes' assumption of thought becomes revised and in effect replaced.

4) "I think therefore I am a thinking substance."

Descartes says about "I think," that certain concepts follow from that starting point. They may be represented by the assertions:
1) "I think therefore I am."
2) "I think therefore I have a mind."
3) "I think therefore I am a thinking thing."

In the formulations instead of "I think" one may, of course, substitute "I doubt," "I think I see," "I think I am deceived," or even "I think I do not exist therefore I exist." In the first assertion "I think therefore I am," it is circular to say that "I am" follows from "I think" because "I" is already contained in "I think," "I" is already assumed. It does not follow that because "I think" non-physically, that therefore "I am" physically. It is not clear here whether the "I" in the premise is meant to refer to the physical self or the mental self, both, or neither. Descartes sometimes says it only refers to the mental "I."

What one may conclude from "I think" is only something like "I think therefore I think," or "I think therefore thought takes place," and that is only if we accept that in fact we do think and know what we do when we do think, that is, that we know what thought is.

The second assertion "I think therefore I have a mind," jumps from "I think," to "I have a mind." That does not follow and, in fact, there are effective contemporary ordinary language arguments indicating that it does not make sense to speak of "mind" as an entity "in" which ideas somehow exist.

The third assertion, "I think therefore I am a thinking thing," assumes that because one thinks, he is a thing. Once again it would be more accurate to say, "I think, therefore thought takes place, or therefore there is thought."

The fourth assertion, "I think, therefore, I am a thinking substance," reveals more clearly Descartes' acceptance of the substance-quality or substance-accident doctrine. According to this doctrine wherever there is a quality it is assumed there is a metaphysical substance underlying that quality. Ideas, for example, must exist in a mind or mental substance. The substance-quality doctrine is, however, by no means implied by "I think," nor is it self-evident. It is rather an object of a raging argumentation.

The most effective part of Descartes' starting point is his assertion that we must begin with thought, with "I think" in this sense. But thought has no meaning apart from language. In addition you may see if you can think of an idea without using language. The very notion of thought is specified and isolated by means of language. In beginning with thought or "I think" we have already assumed language. "I think" loses its place as an epistemological starting point. In its place we may put language.

Consider a theory according to which ordinary language is regarded as distorting and inadequate. Many philosophers have asserted this sort of view. Such a theory must be presented in the very language which it condemns. The theory cannot account for its own establishment, its own presentation. What is presented is contradictory to its presentation. This is another reason why we may prefer to take language as our starting point. (See W. Shibles *Philosophical Pictures)*

In a way, it would seem that nothing is changed from the Cartesian starting point, but it has. Although the words "I think" are revived again they are not given starting point status. They are rather regarded as words deriving their meaning from their use in a language system. We do not have to assume that there is a process going on called "thinking" or "think" in order to present a theory, but we do have to speak or write in order to present it. The shift is that instead of language being an expression of thought, thought gains its meaning in language and if thought even has any very clear meaning at all it is at least secondary in epistemological status to language. We would not, then, first investigate thought and then see what implications it might have regarding language, but rather reverse the investigation.

By the linguo-centric predicament is meant that 1) there are good reasons for taking language as our epistemological starting point; 2) the "I" in "I speak" has meaning only in language, and language becomes both the object of investigation as well as the means by which we investigate it.

Even the word "thought" is a part of language. One can have language without "thought," but one cannot have thought without language. It is not clear that we would know what thought is if we had never learned a language. To assume that one just has thoughts, and then puts them in words assumes that one would know how he would think if he had never learned a language. It assumes that he would know what thinking is entirely independent of language. But we are not in such a position. We have a language already. And this language usage is or constitutes most of what we usually mean by thought.

Our intelligence tests deal almost solely with language ability. We just do not have direct access to thought pure or bare. There are not such entities as mental thoughts, ideas or meanings. We do not introspect to find discrete "ideas" or "thoughts." It was the old associationist-atomist view of mind that there are discrete ideas linked to each other by laws of association. Thinking is referred to as "stream of consciousness," "train of ideas," "association of ideas," "mental chemistry," etc. But there is no evidence for ideas as such. They are part of a fictional fairy machinery of the mind. As the Whorf-Sapir hypothesis suggests, language partly constitutes reality. This view is meant only to be suggestive. We must examine the relation between language and emotions. Whorf (1965) wrote, "Thinking is to a large extent linguistic." (p. 66)

The behaviorist, John Watson (1930), regarded thought as primarily consisting of verbal behavior, especially subvocal speech, "internal speech," or talking silently to oneself. One learns to speak aloud and then exercises that ability to speak silently to himself. He states,

" 'Thinking' is largely 'subvocal talking. ' " (268)

"The final response or adjustment, if one is reached, must be verbal (subvocal)." (267)

"The term 'thinking' should cover all word behavior of whatever kind that goes on subvocally." (243)

"Once verbalization of the manual activity begins, word organization soon becomes 'dominant' because man has to solve his problems verbally." (265)

Watson also gives a place to manual ability and visceral activity as forms of thought especially for the new-born baby. But language soon becomes so intricately involved with them that it achieves dominance:

"We, as sophisticated adults, behave as though verbal conditionings were of the primary order and the manual and visceral of the secondary order." (255)

Our thinking is a total reaction of our manual, visceral, and linguistic abilities. Memory is largely the verbal part of our habitual actions. It is "the running through or exhibition of the verbal part of a total bodily organization." (256) The so-called "unconscious" is visceral and manual experience which is not made verbal, where the verbal organization is blocked, or where there is not verbal association made. Because gesture and other body responses may be substituted for words, "thinking" may go on to some extent without words as such. Such substitution is a metaphorical activity and depends on linguistic primacy. Watson also notes that new thoughts come into being by means of the manipulation of words.

It is not clear that language and emotions are two things, two separate things. Would we ever have the concept of emotion without the word emotion or without ever having learned the language? "Emotion" has a use both in a language and in a situation or context of life, that is, it gains its meaning from what has been called a "language-game." To see what the word means we must look at its use. This study of emotions will examine many such uses. The meaning of the word "emotion" is its use in specific paradigm cases or concrete examples. Here, then, "emotion" is a language use. We may also remove the quotes from around "emotion" to yield emotion. The quotes suggest the word, and the word without quotes suggests the thought or thing. But since language partly constitutes its object and thought, the distinction between word and object, or quoted term and non-quoted term breaks down. In the philosophy of science, the notion that models partly constitute their objects and the notion that the scientist actually sees in terms of his model (seeing-as) is relevant to the view that language partly constitutes reality. There are not ideas or mental entities and so they cannot be referred to. By putting quotes around the word "emotion" we suggest many things depending on context. It may suggest that it is only to be taken in the context of a language thought of as marks and/or sounds, or it may mean that the term is unfounded or confused and so deserves no better than to be put in quotes.

We should separate all the various uses of emotion from that special use which is the descriptive use of emotion. That is, does emotion in the descriptive use refer to an entity or a function of some sort? Psychologists have usually attempted to find that internal physiological disturbance which serves as that which an emotion supposedly really is — however, without much success even by their own admissions. Skinner (1953) wrote,

"In spite of extensive research it has not been possible to show that each emotion is distinguished by a particular pattern of responses of glands and smooth muscles."

It is thought that an emotion names something that must be in us as a feeling is. This we saw can result in a naming-fallacy or hypostatizing of entities, and can be unfounded. We may think that such words as love, hate, revenge, anguish, describe or name internal states or discrete entities. They may rather be operational or refer to processes and contain within themselves reference to feelings, objects, and situations. One does not just feel jealous of no one. It is not just a feeling that comes over one in any situation. Jealousy has reference to an object and situation as well as to ourselves and our reaction. If jealousy were merely an internal feeling it might be driven away by having a pleasant dessert. Can one fall in love with no one? One does not reply to "With whom are you in love," "No one, I'm just in love."

One may consider a bachelor who thought about being married and about having a wife. He then imagined that she was unfaithful to him. Although he was still single he nevertheless became, in fact, very jealous. Here the jealousy was not just a feeling but had to do with a situation, though it was an imagined situation.

This may also be an instance of a mistaken or misguided emotion, for he mistook an imagined situation for a real situation. Emotion is mainly a rational assessment which guides feeling. But also feeling and reason may at times seem simultaneous and inseparable as in the case of the Croce-Collingwood view that art is expression, which will be presented later. Also feeling may come before rational assessment — as in the case of illness or drug-taking or bodily disorder.

Because we have emotion words we may tend to think that we must have something corresponding to them. For example we must experience rage, anger, fury, irritation, annoyance, upset, etc. Often, however, it is merely a matter of style that we choose one word rather than another. Yet the style partly determines what the emotion is. One cannot, in this sense, "blow up" without these words. One cannot be "angry" without the word "angry." One may say, "But you must be in some special state." But "in some special state" again assumes language, and one could not be "in some special state" without these words. These words may have little descriptive use anyway. Emotions may be expressed without use of so-called emotion words and here especially the style of description or presentation determines what the emotion is. By his style a novelist may create as well as describe emotion. The view that style renders emotion and that language is central epistemologically to knowledge of emotion is represented by writers such as Croce, Collingwood, and Bosanquet in terms of their view that emotion is expression. The psychiatrist, Albert Ellis, as will be seen, presents a rational account according to which emotion involves uttering sentences to oneself. Henceforth the words "thinking" and "idea" will refer to language use and some imagery. The notion of the distinction between statement and sentence covertly presupposes the mind-body, thought-word, distinction and so is unacceptable. There are not two processes: thinking, and language use. Thinking is largely speaking, although some images and other abilities are involved. Meaning is merely patterns of marks, sounds and objects. A mark is associated (non-mentally) with a sound and objects. This is all that meaning is. (W. Shibles "Meaning as Patterns of Marks")

CREATION OF NEW EMOTIONS

Emotions are usually regarded as fixed entities or part of our nature. Poets and novelists are said to render or describe the subtle aspects of these emotions. But if emotion is largely assessment or reason and if reason reduces largely to our use of language and metaphors, then poetry and novels do not just render or describe emotions but to a large extent constitute them. In poetry and novels, emotions are created not merely described.

A. I. Melden wrote,

"Unlike the vocabulary used by philosophers (limited as it is to a few simple summary names: pleasure, pain, distress, anger, etc.), that of poets and novelists is constantly in the making as they seek by means of new techniques and devices to do justice to the endlessly varied and complex nature of our feelings and emotions. They may use similes, but there are also the rhythms of speech and the images and allusions that these afford." (p. 209)

This suggests that novelists and poets create a new vocabulary for emotions and represent emotions in new ways. Anxiety is expressed by someone sitting in a garbage can. But it is perhaps rather the case that the novelist is not describing emotions already there but creating them. By presenting a certain situation, by using certain language, a view of the world is arrived at. This yields or guides specific feelings. Such feelings may differ from reader to reader, but insomuch as the reader follows the statements presented the feelings produced may be quite similar. The novelist decides about the emotion on the basis of plot, social relations, context. The meaning of the emotion often has to do with the language used and the situation. Style can determine what the emotion is. There are emotion fads, and social induction of an emotion. If one is expected to have an emotion he is often described as having it. One may be said to be grieving whether he is grieving or not. Emotion can be a fiction and fiction can be an emotion.

Upon reading a novel I may supposedly become aware of or discover certain new emotions in myself I had never noticed before. If I read one kind of literature I may find that I begin to think and feel like the characters portrayed. If one's reading concentrates on dread, alienation, or anxiety, one may find that he suddenly has these new "emotions." One can learn to be anxious, learn to play the game of anxiety. One may imitate actions and assessments of characters in film, books, poetry. By hearing a description of an emotion I can thus become aware of or discover (or create) one in myself. This may show the close tie between our beliefs and our feelings. One may create certain feelings in himself merely by thinking of certain situations or problems.

Wordsworth wrote in a letter to John Wilson (1800),

"That poetry (and art in general) is essentially the expression of feeling can, then, be taken as the first principle of Romantic aesthetics . . . " The poet "ought, to a certain degree, to rectify men's feelings, to give them new compositions of feeling, to render their feelings more sane, pure and permanent."

For Wordsworth, art was also considered to be a source of knowledge and has cognitive status.

LANGUAGE

The psychologist, G. Mandler, wrote,

"Relatively little agreement can be found across theories and among different psychologists on the definition of classes of behavior called emotional. What agreement there is appeals to an intuitive understanding of the common language, and there is of course a good deal of agreement in the way we use some of these emotional words, if for no other reason than that we learn these terms rather uniformly within our language culture." (306)

Davitz and Mattis (1964) report,

"The problem of defining the emotional meanings of relatively complex verbal statements remains to be solved." (174)

Wittgenstein stresses the role language has in constituting emotion concepts in terms of the view that words gain their meaning from the context of their use rather than from naming "internal" entities:

"How is one to define a feeling? Is it something special and indefinable? But it must be possible to teach the use of the words." (185)

In the *Blue and Brown Books* he also states,

"We think of the utterance of an emotion as though it were some artificial device to let others know that we have it." (103)

Language has epistemological primacy and to a large extent determines how we assess and deal with reality, and so also with emotions. To think is to be able to use language, make assertions, describe, argue, discuss. One may never have learned words like "remorse" or had assessments of a remorseful sort and so not had the emotion. Emotions are learned as part of a linguistic context. They are not reducible to non-verbal actions, visceral or feeling behavior alone. Certain emotion statements become "reinforced." One accepts a friend's or parent's expressions and intonations and so finds himself in this way taking on their emotions and beliefs. It is a kind of subliminal linguistic transformation or transference. In novels the meaning of an emotion has to do with the plot and the contexts the character is in, rather than with internal states. The style and context largely determine or create the emotion experienced. Metaphors and long description are involved in such linguistic renderings.

By discussing and speaking, one may begin to clarify his thinking and so also his emotions. To clarify language is to clarify emotions. Thus one says, "I feel . . . " followed by statements. The description of an emotion is in terms of how things seem to you.

Emotion is largely a verbal skill. It involves not introspection or "looking within" but rather looking at our language. "Introspection" would be more appropriate for paying attention to our feelings. "Internal" emotion is actually mainly speaking to ourselves silently (i.e. thinking) and paying attention to accompanying feelings. One may ask oneself, "Am I really angry with her, or is it jealousy, or both?" These general and elliptical names of emotions may captivate or mislead and so are broken down into finer cognitions, i.e., concrete terms. "I love my horse," is seen to be different than "I love Jane." We are not only linguistically assessing the emotion but the emotion term itself is a linguistic category. Put intuitively, linguistic expression clarifies and partly constitutes emotion. By hearing a description of an emotion I may become aware of or consequently "discover" it "in" myself.

"Désespoir" points to a different behavioral category than does "despair," *"Verzweiflung,"* or *"disperazione."* By learning different languages one may increase his behavioral potential. The fact that language is usually of a substantive-modifier type leads to naming-fallacies.

It may be better to speak of emoting rather than emotion. Emotions are language-games and we may act out "indifferent" and "bored" as we act out "triangle" and "circle." Emotion is inseparable from emotion words. Perkins wrote,

"It is the emotion as a whole that gets 'named', not the bodily feeling which enters into it. Emotions get fixed as facts as a consequence of the abiding presence in language of common names for them." (153)

To have negative emotions, e.g., to be angry, is to be possessed by language. Sadness is having read or learned about sadness. The way to a man's emotions is through his language. Anger occurs when people cannot agree on language uses. Metaphors are closer to us than fists.

Both emotion words and reason words function in language in such a way that except by artificial convention there is no absolute distinction between them. We can interchange "I feel that this is correct," and "I think that this is correct." Language-games are on the same level. Instead of "I am anxious about their coming," one could say "They shouldn't come."

PERFORMATIVE UTTERANCE

To find out what emotions are one must examine the use of emotive language, what we usually say about specific as well as general emotions. This is to some extent in keeping with the ordinary-language directive: to find out what a word means, look at its actual use in a language-game, that is, its linguistic context as well as its situational context.

John Austin (1970) presents the view that certain utterances are "performative utterances," e.g., "I do" uttered at a wedding. To say the words is partly to do what is said. "I do" is required as part of the ceremony. One must utter these words. The words "I think so, I rather like him" would not be appropriate or apt. In view of the "meaning-is-its-use" theory one may suggest that every word is in some sense a performative utterance. To utter a word is to use or perform it, to say it is to do it. What the word means is its performance or use in its context. We seem to speak of emotions in similar ways. One seriously says, "I love you," and to say this is partly to do it. It is one way of expressing love if it is uttered in the appropriate circumstances. One may say, "I love you," when he really does not, or the situation is entirely inappropriate. The expression is a statement about emotion and the emotion implies an appropriate context to qualify as an emotion. Otherwise it is a "mere statement," "false statement," or as one might say, a "false emotion," or "unjustified emotion."

Similarly the hostess of a dull party may say, "What a marvelous time we are having." The statement may help to suggest to the company that all are having a good time, but appears not to be an accurate description. To say "I love you" is not necessarily to love someone, nor is to say "What fun," necessarily to be having fun. It is a different thing to 1) say one is having a feeling or emotion and 2) have an emotion, except in the case where the expression of the emotion is a performative utterance. In saying, "I am in love," one takes on this emotive classification of love and can be captivated by it such that it serves as a performative utterance. By telling oneself one is depressed one may be and become depressed.

The above case where one can say, "I love you," but not really love or even know how to love may be conceived not as an exception to the view that it is a performative utterance but as a category-mistake. The expression was intentionally or unintentionally misused. This happens frequently with emotions because we are unclear about them and their subtle workings. Psychologists have elaborate yet conflicting theories about what emotions are and how they work. Perhaps this is one reason why novelists prefer that emotions be suggested indirectly by speech and situation rather than tersely and directly described. To say "I am angry," may be quite ineffective in comparison with showing one's anger. The point about performative utterance is that insomuch as we use emotion terms we are thereby performing or engaging in emotive behavior. One who observes the non-linguistic showing of anger insomuch as he terms it "angry behavior" is creating emotive behavior by labeling it "angry." The novelist is sometimes involved with both speaking of emotion, expressing emotion, and a narrator as well. To say "I am expressing my emotion," is to see oneself as others would see one. But even to say "I am angry," is to use a public language, to have learned from others how to use the words, "I am angry."

The notion of performative utterance, paradigm case, language-game, may be thought of as rhetorical terms or devices. They characterize emotions because they mould language and style in the rendering of emotions, or better, the rendering is the emotion. (cf. Shibles "Review of K.T. Fann *Symposium on John Austin*"; Fann's book may be consulted for a critical review of Austin's notion of performative utterance.)

RHETORIC

Rhetorical terms may be regarded as terms which name, describe, or involve emotions. Emotion now is thought to be part of psychology and philosophy but formerly it was treated as a part of rhetoric. A speaker had to persuade and influence by oratory. Character or "ethos" was important for the speaker to possess. "Bathos" is a sudden appearance of the commonplace, a let-down; "pathos" is an evoking of pity or compassion, etc. Rhetoric involves figures of pathos. This involves figures of affection and vehemence. "Ethos" consists of figures revealing courtesy, gratitude, etc. Richard Lanham (1969) gives as one type of rhetorical term, "Emotional Appeals and Exhortations." Also Warren Taylor's (1972) definitions may be consulted for a more thorough account.

amphidiorthosis: to hedge or qualify a charge made in anger.

apaetesis: a matter put aside in anger is resumed later.

apodioxis: rejecting an argument indignantly as impertinent or absurdly false.

ara: curse or imprecation.

bdelygma: expression of hate or abhorrence.

donysis: describing or reenacting strong emotion.

ecphonesis: an exclamation expressing emotion.

emphasis: stress of language in such a way as to imply more than is actually stated.

epiplexis: asking a question in order to reproach rather than for information.

eulogia: commending or blessing a person or thing.

exuscitatio: emotional utterance that moves hearers to like feelings.

indignatio: impassioned speech or loud angry speaking.

mycterismus: mockery of an opponent, accompanied by gestures.

oictros: evoking pity or forgiveness.

optatio: a wish exclaimed.

paeanismus: an exclamation of joy.

paramythia: consoling one who grieves.

pathopoeia or pathos: a general term for arousing passion or emotion.

peroration: an impassioned summary.

philophronesis: an attempt to mitigate anger by gentle speech and humble submission.

protrope: exhorting hearers to action by threats and promises.

sarcasmus: a bitter gibe or taunt.

tapinosis: undignified language that debases a person or thing. Misterming to humiliate.

thaumasmus: exclamation of wonder

threnos: lamentation of a misery suffered by the speaker.

Interjection indicates emotion, e.g. "Well!" "My!" "Oh!" They are not grammatically related to other words in a sentence.

Aristotle deals with emotion as part of rhetoric in his *Rhetoric* (Book II). Here he points out that emotions play a part in determining how one views a speaker's argument. The audience must be emotionally disposed to the speaker and his views. Also the speaker must be concerned with the nature of emotions so that he can arouse the desired emotions in the audience. Aristotle defines emotions as those states which are accompanied by pain and pleasure. Anger is defined as "an impulse attended by pain, to a revenge . . . and caused by an obvious, unjustifiable slight." Love is defined as the act of being friendly, or "wishing for a person those things which you consider to be good — wishing them for his sake, not just for your own — and tending so far as you can to effect them." A friend is "one who shares another's pleasure." Fear is defined as "a pain or disturbance arising from a mental image of impending evil of a destructive or painful sort." Shame is "a pain or disturbance regarding that class of evils, in the present, past, or future, which we think will tend to our discredit." The other emotions defined are defined mainly in terms of pleasure and pain. They are put in strict genus and species classifications. Anger is a slight, a slight is "an active display of opinion about something one takes to be worthless," and there are three species of slights: contempt, spite, and insolence. He in addition shows descriptively that and how "emotions are produced or are dissipated." He notes three aspects for each emotion: 1. what the mental state of the person is, 2. whom the emotion is directed at, 3. what usually gives one that emotion.

Rhetorical terms often report the situation, the language terms used, as well as the effect. They function exactly as do many emotion terms. One difficulty is that one could not have a term for every possible combination of such factors. Collingwood asserts that since no two expressions are the same, no two emotions can be the same. Each is unique. Thus a rhetoric of emotions could not specify each emotion. Everything we say and do involves language, feeling, context.

One way of clarifying our rhetoric is to give it more sound philosophical foundation. This may be done by carefully examining our language and its use, in line for example with techniques used in ordinary-language philosophy and philosophical psychology. Clarification and therapy would be the result. The Aristotelian basis of traditional rhetoric could be largely abandoned. It would be seen that every word and drop of grammar contains in it a whole philosophy. "Is" has been magnified into metaphysics, and quotation marks create a covert theory of meaning. One may regard each word as a rhetorical model or experience through which to see the world, just as Sartre saw it in terms of the terms anguish, anxiety, guilt, or even stickiness. Life can be regarded as sticky — a new emotion, and a new rhetorical device.

In the general presentation thus far the following points concerning emotion have been stressed:

1) Emotion and emotions often involve naming fallacies, and statements about them may be based on misleading analogies (such as that they are like sensations).

2) Language partly constitutes emotion:
    a) as a language-game.
    b) as a "form of life" or given.
    c) by means of style and rhetoric.
    d) because of its close relation to metaphor.

3) Emotion partly involves context, or a description or analysis of a situation. It is to a large extent rational and can be controlled, changed or even eliminated. Such control is often involved in therapy by means of a reexamination of our language.

Sources:

Aristotle The Rhetoric of Aristotle Lane Cooper, trans. New York: Appleton-Century-Crofts, Book II 1932

John Austin Philosophical Papers 2nd ed. J. Urmson and G. Warnock, eds, Oxford: Clarendon Press 1970

Joe Davitz and S. Mattis "The Communication of Emotional Meaning by Metaphor" The Communication of Emotional Meaning J. Davitz, ed., New York: McGraw Hill 1964

John Dewey "The Theory of Emotion" Psychological Review 1 (1894) 553-569; 2 (1894) 13-22

Albert Ellis "Rational Psychotherapy" Journal of General Psychology 59 (1958) 35-49

A. C. Ewing "Symposium: The Justification of Emotions" Proceedings of the Aristotelian Society 31 (1957) 59-74

Frank Geldard Fundamentals of Psychology New York: Wiley 1962

William Hunt "Recent Developments in the Field of Emotion" Psychological Bulletin 38 (1941) 249-276

Richard Lanham A Handlist of Rhetorical Terms Berkeley: University of California Press 1969

G. Mandler "Emotion" New Directions in Psychology R. Brown, et al, eds., New York: Holt, Rinehart and Winston 1962 pp. 267-339

A. I. Melden "The Conceptual Dimensions of Emotions" Human Action T. Mischel, ed., New York: Academic Press 1969

36

M. Ostow "*Affects in Psychoanalytic Theory. Symposium on 'Current Theories of Emotion'* " *American Psychological Association Meeting, Cincinnati 1959*

Moreland Perkins "*Emotion and Feelings*" *Philosophical Quarterly* 75 (1966) 139-60

W. Shibles "*Meaning as Patterns of Marks*" *Philosophical Pictures*

W. Shibles *Philosophical Pictures* 2nd edition, Dubuque, Iowa: Kendall Hunt 1972

W. Shibles "*Review of K. T. Fann Symposium on John Austin*" *Philosophy and Phenomenological Research* 33 (1) (1973) 443-444

B. F. Skinner *Scientific and Human Behavior* New York: Macmillan 1953

Warren Tayor *Tudor Figures of Rhetoric* Whitewater, Wisconsin: The Language Press 1972

John Watson *Behaviorism* revised edition, University of Chicago Press 1930

Benjamin Whorf *Language, Thought, and Reality* John Carroll, ed., Cambridge, Mass.: MIT Press 1965

Ludwig Wittgenstein *Philosophical Investigations* 3rd edition, G. Anscombe, trans., New York: Macmillan 1968

Character and Personality

Goethe wrote,

"If we take people as they are, we make them worse. If we treat them as if they were what they ought to be, we help them become what they are capable of becoming."

After the problem of how to stay alive, man's most central problem is to try to improve human character. In order to do this we must learn how man's emotions work, how to describe personality, and how to change emotions. Knowledge in all of these areas has been lacking. The result is that people are crippled by their emotions and are hardly able to relate deeply with even one other person (including one's spouse). The result is an experience of loneliness and a mystical hope for love. What man desires above all else is being emotionally fulfilled and emotionally satisfied. Hate, anger, depression, revenge, and other negative emotions cause great physical and psychological harm including crime and war. R. Lazarus and E. Opton wrote,

"In the context of human experience, frustration of interpersonal and intrapersonal goals are as important as threats related to bodily harm, if not more so." (259)

Insofar as the average man has negative emotions he is neurotic or has a personality disturbance. But if one is unable to find non-neurotic friends he may change the emotions of others so as to create friends.

"What is the purpose of emotion?" and "What is an emotion for?" can now be answered. Traditionally it was regarded as a mechanism of survival. It seems rather that negative emotions are forms of self-destruction. On the other hand, positive emotions can lead to physical well-being and long life. One of man's major goals is to achieve a close relation with his fellow man, and to achieve this, positive emotions and knowledge of how emotions work are essential. To a large extent, the goal of life is love and emotional well-being. One lives so that he can become a better person. One may also help others to become better people by means of possessing and imparting a knowledge of emotions. It is not, then, the case that emotions are non-purposive or merely irrational.

In this respect, a government to be adequate and relevant to humanity must set a priority on finding ways in which man's emotions can be satisfied and negative emotions changed. In spite of this, most concern in political science ignores emotions and personality, or deals with it only in the antiquated terms of pleasure and pain in a utilitarian sense.

Traditional categories for describing personality are stereotyped and no better than traditional theories of emotion. The behaviorist, Pavlov, even spoke seriously of the (medieval) categories of phlegmatic, choleric, melancholic, and sanguine temperaments. Classifications of personality are given by the American Psychiatric Association's Manual of Mental Disorders (1968) on the basis of neurotic and psychotic classifications. Such classifications are controversial. (See chapter criticizing them.) Psychological tests are usually inadequate in determining personality or emotions as an examination of the questions asked would readily show. (For a more sound test see Emotion Questionnaire in the appendix of this book.) Rorschach tests are actually tests of metaphorical ability rather than of emotions. Other classifications of personality are based on highly theoretical and controversial theories such as Freudian theory, e.g., oral, phallic, and fixation types, etc. Some personality classifications are based on body-build, and others on the basis of various unacceptable psychological theories of emotions. Such theories are unacceptable because they are based on inadequate theories of emotions.

A sound theory of personality should take into consideration, among other things, research in philosophical psychology, behaviorism, ordinary-language philosophy and a knowledge of metaphor. Solomon Asch (1955) wrote a relevant article entitled, "On the Use of Metaphor in the Description of Persons." For additional annotated sources see the indexed classification "metaphor, as descriptive of persons" and "metaphor, as descriptive of emotions" in W. Shibles *Metaphor*. People are described as swift, magnetic, neat, dull, sensitive, etc. The style of a novel determines and creates emotions and personality. In the courtroom a limited personality is constructed for legal purposes by restricted testimony. One's role often describes his personality. And it is important that each person take pride, if allowed, in his occupation regardless of its nature. People often seem to lack pride or a sense of accomplishment in what they do, thus making everyone unsatisfied and the work poor. One may have as much or more pride in being a candy-store clerk than in being a college professor. The clerk can be as much help as can a psychiatrist in communicating with people and helping them to achieve a satisfying relationship with other people.

Kant's view that each man should be regarded as an end in himself has unfortunately seldom been accepted. The emphasis seems to be on things rather than people. In industry the profit, not the good of mankind, is the goal. But one of the finest and most consequential experiences is to treat each person as important, as a person, and show aggressive immediate and individual concern toward him. To do less and to have negative emotions is to be less than human. Personality involves the knowledge of how to deal with people and to be adequate a knowledge of how emotions work is a prerequisite. Without this understanding one may happen to have an attractive personality in some respect, but not an adequate personality. For an adequate personality an ongoing critical ability and interest in inquiry is required. This inquiry then informs one's emotional behavior and development. It is often erroneously thought that emotions and assessments are separate and that personality mainly consists of emotions as feelings. A full human relationship cannot be based on feeling alone. Love primarily requires understanding and communication. (See chapter on love.) By "sensitive" person we mean an understanding person, although it is sometimes used to describe those who overreact or anger easily or are moody.

A knowledge of the creative use of metaphor allows one to be a more interesting person because metaphor allows one to create new insights and perspectives, provide alternate options for action, say things in more interesting ways, describe things otherwise impossible to describe, create humor, enliven, express emotions, etc. A person who says the same sort of thing everyone else says or who continually speaks in literal language may be said to have an inadequate personality, a stereotyped personality. This is also the case with those who rigidly follow culturally learned expressions of emotion, e.g., smiling. Such expressions often become meaningless mechanical conventions and so deny honest meaningful relationships.

In Japan, one smiles when being scolded by a superior or when the situation is sorrowful or regrettable as when one's favorite son dies. To us, wide eyes suggest surprise, to the Chinese it is a sign of anger. Surprise for the Chinese may be expressed by stretching out the tongue. We clap hands to praise or applaud, but to them it means worry or disappointment. They also faint in anger and have the view that one can die of anger. Such views may serve as self-suggestions. If one thinks life is dreary he may lead a dreary life. Certainly negative emotions are physically harmful.

Such stereotypes allow actors as well as others to fake emotions, although stage actors traditionally seem artificial as if they were acting as actors. Film actors and television actors are often more lifelike. Soap operas are especially emotional and often stress negative emotions and maladaptive models of behavior. The characters are often overdistressed, oversentimental, overupset, revengeful, hateful, irresponsible, etc. It is assumed that such emotions are a natural and necessary part of life. These soap operas fill daytime television offerings and provide one of the ways one learns emotion behavior.

One reason for encouraging positive emotions is that it presupposes encouraging communication and discussion of assessments. This is the central way to resolve conflict in society. Nevertheless, no institution directs attention to the improvement of emotions. A liberal arts college education affects assessments which may help improve emotions by improving one's understanding. But the literary studies, education courses, psychology courses, etc., do not as yet adequately clarify emotions, and they fail to improve personality. One could easily have the same negative emotions after completing his education as he had before, or he may even become emotionally worse off.

Students learn emotion habits from such unreliable sources as television, astrological charts, fiction, friends, parents, the church, the words of popular music. Often one is paid or bribed by means of gifts to have positive emotions. American courtship practices involve such bribery. This does not lead to an adequate personality or positive emotions which endure. It is not total concern with the person as an end in himself and does not adequately fulfill emotional and intellectual needs. The solution to the problem is not marriage versus commune or new permutations and combinations of couples or a new political form of government but rather an understanding of emotion. Because emotions can to a large extent be changed each man can decide what sort of person he wishes to be, what kind of personality he wishes to have.

Sources:

Solomon Asch *"On the Use of Metaphor in the Description of Persons"* On Expressive Language *H. Werner, ed. Clark University Press 1955 pp. 29-45*

Richard Lazarus and E. Opton, Jr. *"The Study of Theoretical Formulations and Experimental Findings "Anxiety and Behavior C. Spielberger, ed., New York: Academic Press 1966 pp. 225-262*

Alexander Shand *"Character and the Emotions"* Mind *5 (April 1896) 203-226*

Warren Shibles, *Metaphor: An Annotated Bibliography and History* Whitewater, Wisc.: The Language Press 1971

Aesthetic Emotion

"Art is expression," is an incomplete sentence. It is not clear what art is an expression of. If it is an expression of ideas or thought it is unfounded because ideas and thoughts are pseudo-psychological entities which do not exist as such. Similarly, "Art is expression of meaning," is inadequate because meaning is a synonym of idea and there are no ideas or meanings as such. Ideas, thoughts, and meanings are not mental entities but should be regarded as terms elliptical for uses of language, associations of objects, images and behavioral abilities.

"Art is expression," may also mean expression of emotion. Again emotion is not a mentalistic entity within us, but is rather a rational assessment which guides feelings. This definition of emotion, to be discussed more fully in subsequent chapters, may take several forms: 1. the description, belief or assessment may precede the feelings produced as when one feels angry after observing an injustice, 2. feeling and rational assessment seem to come at the same time as in the case of shock where the assessment involves great conflict or confusion. The Croce-Collingwood theory below stresses this type of emotion or synthesis of sensuous and rational assessment, 3. assessment follows feeling, feeling is the object of the assessment. When one is ill or intoxicated these feelings are reflected in or are objects of one's assessment. One may be depressed or judge poorly when he is tired. Depression, however, may be the result of one's assessment of himself and environment and in this case be of type #1 where feeling follows assessment. There is no specific aesthetic emotion in the same way there is a feeling. Stephen Pepper (1937) wrote, "There is no specifically aesthetic emotion."

43

Bosanquet (1894) says that aesthetic emotion reduces to expressiveness. The emotion is in the style, the expression, the arrangement of objects. It is not a dualism of having an emotion in us and then just expressing it. A subject, e.g., death, is itself modified by the manner of its presentation. He states,

"We cannot say, 'Here is the content and now we will add the "expression" ' . . . The content is or constitutes the expression of emotion, being simply that which is felt, because it must be felt in a certain way."

About a work of art he states,

"We enter into it as something which embodies for us the emotion that craves utterance . . . When we enjoy it fully, we seem to have made the presentation transparent or organic through and through, as the vehicle of our emotion . . . All emotion is expressed; perhaps indeed emotion may be found to consist in little more than the physical side of the movements of organic changes which in part constitute its expression. For plainly there is no distinction of principle between an inward physical effect and one which happens to be visible or audible."

He says that emotion is not merely "discharged" or "released," but rather it is expressed, prolonged, accentuated and portrayed. The expression embodies the emotion. The two are inseparable:

"The emotion simply is the whole presentation, including both its sensuous and its ideal elements." "Every emotion exists only as correlative to its expression; or that strictly speaking we do not first have an emotion and then proceed to express it; but that an emotion assumes its character, or becomes what it is, through the mode and degree of its expression."

This view, in common with Croce's and Collingwood's, derives from Kant's view that the mind contributes its form of understanding to the matter given by means of sensation in a single inseparable synthesis. There is no concept without embodiment in sensation and no sensation unformed by concepts. Emotion, then, is treated as an inseparable synthesis of ideal and sensuous elements.

Because emotion must be embodied in the concrete it must be individual. If it is abstract or general it cannot render emotion. Bosanquet states,

"None but a highly individual presentation . . . can be the expression of such an emotion . . . " (158)

Metaphor often makes the abstract concrete and the more concrete it is the more individual, the more determinate is the feeling or emotion.

"The production of the same emotion by different contents is impossible." (160)

"All that we can do by analysis to explain a nexus of this kind would seem to consist in drawing out the content which is implied in the more individual among the presented elements — say a 'springing curve,' or a certain sequence of notes — and showing how this content is related to larger ideal characters which it modifies and reinforces . . . Whether we start from emotion or from content, what we are analyzing is in the last resort the same matter, the relation of content, as expressed, to life." (158)

Arthur Berndtson presents a similar view:

"An emotion is not aesthetic until it is expressed," and "The emotion that is expressed may be one that is elicited by abstract thought and is expressed in a concrete form that pays tribute to such thought." (1969 pp. 150-154)

Emotion is regarded as a kind of linguistic experience. Because the ideal or conceptual enters into emotion this element may be regarded as involving language, as an utterance (perhaps at times an utterance even performed silently to oneself as A. Ellis and T. Sarbin maintain). Bosanquet states this as follows,

"I maintain, then, that even an enjoyable color is not a mute gratification of sense, but is felt as an utterance . . . "

Bosanquet, above, speaks of emotion as existing "correlative" to its expression. This, as he clarifies, is misleading because there is a synthesis not a correlation of the two. One finds this synthesis in W. H. Auden's question, "How can I know what I think till I see what I say?" (1948) On the other hand, Eliot's view of correlative in his "objective correlative" differs. Eliot writes,

"The only way of expressing emotion in the form of art is by finding an objective correlative; in other words, a set of objects, a situation, a chain of events which shall be the formula of that *particular* emotion; such that when the external facts, which must terminate in sensory experience, are given, the emotion is immediately evoked ... You will find that the state of mind of Lady Macbeth walking in her sleep has been communicated to you by a skillful accumulation of imagined sensory impressions ... " (1960)

Here there is an external correlative of an internal state. Emotion is thought of as being particular and internal. He implies the dogma of mind-object, mind-body dualism or separation, rather than a synthesis. He assumes that the external facts just cause the emotion. It is for this reason that Eliot's "objective correlative" is unacceptable. Objects and situations play a part in emotions but merely as "correlations." There are not just two things, one internal and the other external.

Collingwood also holds the "emotion is expression" view:

"When a man is said to express emotion, what is being said about him comes to this. At first, he is conscious of having an emotion, but not conscious of what this emotion is ... While in this state, all he can say about his emotion is: 'I feel ... I don't know what I feel.' From this helpless and oppressed condition he extricates himself by doing something which we call expressing himself. This is an activity which has something to do with the thing we call language: he expresses himself by speaking ... The emotion expressed is an emotion of whose nature the person who feels it is no longer unconscious." (1938 pp. 109-110)

Just as Auden says, "How can I know what I think till I see what I say?" Collingwood in effect says, "How can I know what I feel till I see what I say?" By expressing it we find out that we are jealous, envious, etc., or we find out what the aesthetic emotion is. To express the emotion is to identify it. We express emotions partly, then, to ourselves, make them clear to ourselves by expressing them:

"Until a man has expressed his emotion, he does not yet know what emotion is. The act of expressing it, therefore, is an exploration of his emotions. He is trying to find out what these emotions are." (1938 p. 111)

Emily Dickinson presents a similar view in the following poem (III, 1212):

"A word is dead / When it is said, / Some say. / I say it just / Begins to live / That day."

Wallace Stevens said in *The Necessary Angel* that a poet's words do not exist without the words.

The cathartic effect of this expression is that involved in finding out, and knowing at last, and creating what emotion is. However, to say what the emotion is, is not the same as expressing it. A distinction must be made between stating that one has an emotion and showing that one has it.

"Expressing an emotion is not the same thing as describing it. To say 'I am angry' is to describe one's emotion, not to express it. The words in which it is expressed need not contain any reference to anger as such at all." (1938 pp. 111-112)

In this way, Collingwood, in effect, gives support to the view that what goes for thought is mainly expression or language, and the expression of emotions is bound up with language in an individual concrete way — perhaps one might even say as a "language-game" or "form of life," to use two expressions of ordinary-language philosophy.

Collingwood states,

"The work of artistic creation is not a work performed in any exclusive or complete fashion in the mind of the person whom we call the artist." "The aesthetic activity is the activity of speaking." (1938 pp. 317, 323, 324)

This is not to say, however, that expression involves only language. Croce's view of intuition as expression came before Collingwood's theory. For Croce art is alogical because it synthesizes concepts and the sensuous (or feeling). Art for him is intuition, is expression, is feeling. It is intuitive knowledge. One might find here some support for the view that to be true, in one sense, a statement must be interesting, it must have intuitive impact and not merely conceptual or logical knowledge. It must, one may say, involve feeling. Croce wrote,

"To intuit is to express; and nothing else (nothing more but nothing less) than *to express.*" "How can we really possess an intuition of a geometrical figure, unless we possess so accurate an image of it as to be able to trace it immediately upon paper or on the blackboard? . . . Feelings or impressions, then, pass by means of words from the obscure region of the soul into the clarity of the contemplative spirit. It is impossible to distinguish intuition from expression in this cognitive process. The one appears with the other at the same instant, because they are not two, but one . . . " (1922)

Croce states that there is a "prejudice that we possess a more complete intuition of reality than we really do." He opposes the view that one has great ideas but cannot or hasn't the technical ability to express them. To have a great idea or feeling is to express it, otherwise one does not have it.

In view of the theories presented here an emotion is not an internal state separate from reason or external activity and contexts. "Emotion is expression" is another way of saying that feeling or the sensuous is bound up with reason and reason is largely use of language and other expressive behavior. The synthesis may be rendered by the metaphor or antithesis, "Emotion is reason."

Sources:

W. H. Auden "Squares and Oblongs" *Poets at Work* Charles Abbott, ed., New York: Harcourt, Brace and World 1948 pp. 171-181

Arthur Berndtson *Art Expression and Beauty* New York: Holt, Rinehart and Winston 1969

Bernard Bosanquet "On the Nature of Aesthetic Emotion" *Mind* 3 (April 1894) 153-166

R. G. Collingwood *Principles of Art* Oxford: Clarendon Press 1938

Benedetto Croce *Aesthetic* New York: Farrar, Straus and Giroux 1922

T. S. Eliot *Selected Essays* New York: Harcourt, Brace and World 1960 (1950)

Stephen Pepper *Aesthetic Quality* New York: Scribners 1937

Emotion, Knowledge, and Understanding

Hume grounded ethics on the passions, A. Ayer on emotive statements, C. Stevenson on attitudes, and Hare on evaluative terms and sentences. Work in ethics suggests a shift from thinking of emotions as a state to treating emotions in terms of language. "Attitude" suggests an emotion as well as an ethical term. This trend is expanded by the logicians in their talk of "propositional attitudes." These are statements of belief, doubt, etc. "I believe . . . " is regarded as an attitude or as emotive because it seems to involve psychological factors such that one cannot say whether the belief is true or false. Ethical statements were found by Positivists to be emotive because such statements could not be found to be either true or false. "X is good" is neither true nor false and so it was thought to be emotive. The same applies to belief statements. In "I believe X," it is not clear whether one wishes to assert "X is true," or "X is sometimes true." Thus belief statements, or propositional attitudes, were thought of in this emotive way. Belief is a certain kind of emotion. This might also suggest that every mental state whatsoever is an emotion or feeling state. We say "I feel that that is true," and mean the same thing as "I think that that is true." "Feel" and "think" are used interchangeably here. Perhaps, however, when a statement is irrational, deviates from the normal, or is highly exaggerated, we then notice it and call it an emotion. In this case, because it cannot be reduced to the categories of truth or falsity it is held to be an attitude.

If emotion is on a continuum with thought it may be regarded as one kind of reason. The word "persuasion" suggests that reason and emotion come together. To persuade someone is to alter his emotions and reason in a certain favorable way. Truth is truth for man, and man is both rational and emotional. Nietzsche stated that every truth is a bloody truth. This means that truth must be meaningful and adequate to the full nature of man. For one to say something is true but not interesting is, in a sense, to say it is not true to him. In this sense to be true is to be interesting. In more traditional terms, education must involve the emotions, it must motivate. Put a different way, one meaning of "X is true," is "I enjoy X." It reduces to an emotion.

One may suggest or criticize. If what is in fact only a suggestion is taken as an emotive-value statement it may be thought of as criticism. By criticism, here, is meant that someone disapproves of one's action. This often does but need not, involve emotion. One can learn to take criticism objectively without emotion, even if the criticism is unjust, as it often is. Negative feeling or emotion seems to serve little or no purpose and perhaps ought always to be avoided. "He criticized me. He doesn't like me." This is not crucial. He merely made a suggestion.

It has been mentioned that emotion is often thought of as feeling, something internal. This seems to justify an emotion, that is, one does not on this view ask, "Is your emotion (or feeling) true or false, good or bad?" A feeling or emotion, it is thought, cannot be true or false. One merely has it. An emotion, however, is not just a feeling, an internal state. Insomuch as this is the case, then, the emotion depends on intellectual assessments, reason, the ways in which we are able to view the situation, the possible choices which are open to us. Emotion depends on our knowledge and understanding. It depends on our knowledge of emotive, ethical concepts, and on our knowledge of cause and effect relations. To have a successful emotional life one needs intellectual inquiry. To be ignorant of such things is to involve oneself and others in needless and undesirable emotions. We must know how emotions work, what emotion words refer to, what each other's thresholds are, etc. The current stress on the ultimacy of emotion by existentialists and others is misguided to the extent that the nature of emotions is not clarified or inquired into adequately and to the extent that emotions are regarded as having a self-righteous dignity. One is frequently told to do whatever he feels. The lack here is that the person may be ignorant and confused, thus resulting in confused emotions and feelings. Emotions are formulated by understanding, appraisal and our interpretations of situations. If our understanding is faulty our emotion is also. One may think an act is acceptable if it satisfies his present cognitive-emotion but later realize this act was mistaken. An instance is that by believing that a spouse should not be "possessive" of his or her mate he or she may therefore engage in extra-marital relations. It may be seen that "possession" may be misguided here. The spouse was not possessed but rather regarded with "concern." What was thought of as "being possessed" may be rather interpreted as "being regarded with concern and affection."

Or one may regard jealousy as a defect in the spouse's character and so engage in extra-marital relations because he feels he should not be blamed or responsible for the defect which is the other person's jealous behavior. The assessment however may later be seen to be unrealistic, because people usually do become jealous and have other limitations as well. To assume one need not become jealous is to assume an ideal rather than a real world. There is no total freedom or totally ideal relationship. One must learn to respect another's emotions. However, he may discuss or try to revise another's emotions, or he may wish to terminate his association with him. One ought to resolve the nature of jealousy so as to make it unnecessary. Nevertheless to merely ignore it in another can be unjustifiably cruel. One who ignores the jealousy of an intimate friend often prefers his own emotions as being absolute.

We often use the term understand in regard to emotional as well as intellectual matters. "I understand how you feel," often means "I understand your emotional shortcomings." One usually thinks he knows much more about his own and other's emotions than he really does. Our knowledge of the nature of emotions in the history of thought has been found wanting. To the Socratic view that one only does wrong out of ignorance one may add that one only has bad or harmful emotions out of ignorance. De La Chambre wrote,

"If a man but knew the injury that vice and ignorance bring, he would fear them more than the greatest perils that could menace his life or fortune." (Gardiner p. 145)

Emotions are in many ways regarded as involving reason, or are thought to be unnecessary or undesirable. Passions were often thought to be erroneous judgments (e.g., by Chrysippus). Cicero thought emotions were hasty opinions. According to Augustine, Gods and angels do not have passions or emotions. The Bible treats as sins such emotions as jealousy, anger, envy. Gardiner wrote that passions "not only disastrously affect judgment, they take their rise, according to the Stoics, in judgment, and . . . are described as kinds of judgment or opinion." It is not that emotions are entirely denied. Apathy often referred only to a denial of negative emotions to allow for an increase of positive ones. Hillman (1961) also presents this aspect in his statement that Hartmann stresses Epicurean ideals of refinement, enrichment and education of feeling-life to heighten capacity of enjoyment more conducive to self-mastery. The skeptic advocation of complete indifference to all things can be modified to become a view of intelligent enjoyment of all things. *Ataraxia* is a state free from worry which allows one better to enjoy life. It is not a goal in itself, but a state allowing one to have better emotions. The Stoic, Zeno (335-265), advocated mastery over emotions as the only way of being happy. There is a special, unchanging, transcendent, and sublime sort of experience obtained by overcoming negative emotions. Hobbes stated that when one enters into a social contract he turns from a brute beast into a civilized man and notices a great elevating change coming over him. He becomes a better, more elevated person.

C. D. Broad (1954) states that all emotions are cognitions. George Pitcher wrote, "A change in knowledge can, by itself, result in the restraint or the removal of an emotion." R. Peters (1958) and Bedford (1964) treat emotions as forms of judgment.

Melden (1969) provides one of the clearest statements regarding the rational nature of emotion:

"Whatever else anger may be, it cannot be an internal feeling or state conceptually unrelated to the functions of intelligence in the social circumstances in which it occurs . . . Nothing less than our status as rational and social beings in situations of enormously varying degrees of complexity — as the whole human beings that we are — must be involved in order to provide any reasonably adequate account of the role of emotions in our lives." (216, 221)

"I feel jealous." This would seem to report an emotion. But it is largely a judgment. Our emotion does not flow out pure but depends upon our judgment of it, our description. The description and judgment partly constitute the emotion. "I feel jealous," is like "I feel that or I think that I am jealous." There is an appraisal of a situation here and the appraisal becomes part of the situation. Emotion depends on knowledge because one must *know* what to desire or hate, etc. It makes no sense to say "He was unhappy all of his life, but didn't know it." If one can have an emotion without knowing it, it is not clear that it can be an emotion or a certain kind of emotion. It could, of course, be an emotion of not knowing. It may be something like anxiety. But we must learn "anxiety," learn the language-game of anxiety, before we can play that game. There are no inward states involved here or in the following statements: "I am disgusted with your behavior," "I fear that . . . " "I am sorry to say that . . . " "I'm ashamed to admit that . . . " "I'm embarrassed to report that . . . " One can therefore see every action as emotional because he can see it that way. Thus one may find writers who assert that there is no such thing as non-emotional behavior. Emotion depends on one's opinion. One can be miserable if he thinks he is. The expression "Change your attitude," similarly suggests that emotion depends on judgment.

"He is emotional" need not express a special state one is in, but merely means that he is irrational. "Emotional" here may merely be used as a term of condemnation. It is to say, "I do not like the sort of things he is doing," or "I cannot understand his behavior." "He is emotive," can mean merely "He is ignorant." Emotion seems to be a violation of a social law. When one does not act normal or as expected he may be said to be emotional. This does not mean that he is in an emotional state or that he has emotions.

"Emotion interferes with thought." This may suggest that there are two separate things here. If emotion is largely thought, especially confused or conflicting thought then it by definition "interferes with thought." The statement is circular: "Confused thought and negative feelings interfere with thought." Extreme feelings, e.g., great pain, may prevent one from reasoning carefully. But a category-mistake is committed when one identifies emotion with feeling and then asserts that emotion interferes with thought. To a large extent emotion is thought. One harmful consequence of negative emotion is put as follows by the National Safety Council *Defensive Driving Course* (1971):

"Emotional strain is a poison to the mind and can be particularly serious to a driver. Don't drive if you're upset about something. Avoid quarrels in the car." (20)

"Love" may involve a certain amount of physical attraction. Even physical attraction is a result of one's beliefs. Not every man sees every woman as physically attractive though every such woman is indeed physical. Husbands and wives must have intellectual interests and beliefs in common and be able to communicate with one another for a satisfactory relationship to be maintained.

Knowledge precedes emotion or feeling in many ways. To fear an object implies that we know about it and assess it in a certain way. We do not fear a snake if we do not know that it is harmful or nearby. Children often do not at first have fear of snakes. Judgments of good and bad often precede and instigate emotions. Thus emotion is sometimes regarded as avoidance. Nothing is an emotion but only thinking makes it so. We become frightened by our very thought. Emotions may fade out or be brought to a sudden end by an abrupt change of ideational and affective content. They are to this extent volitional. Our emotions depend on our knowledge and our ignorance. Intelligence can lead to positive emotions, and ignorance to conflict, confusion and negative emotions. An ignorant person may, however, be happy if he has the assessments allowing him to do so.

Any human action is capable of more than one description. An action may be enjoyed under one description but not under another. An illicit affair may be enjoyed until one thinks of it as irresponsible or unfair to others. Emotion may be regarded as a seeing-as. One's emotional reaction *is* how he sees a situation. Shades of emotion change with each way one views the situation. The description of the situation is crucial. The emotion may quickly change due to a change in assessment as in the case of one who hates a house when it is owned by another, but when owned by himself regards it with favor.

If one is ignorant about emotions he becomes a slave of his ignorance. He cannot have new positive emotions successfully if he is ignorant about them. They become limits on his freedom and obstructions to fulfillment of desires. Emotions may be observed and corrected so as rather to be sources of self-discovery. One can find out how he reacts and then alter his assessments to in turn alter his reactions.

The violence caused by administrators or those in power is often due to their lack of understanding of their own emotions, the emotions of others, and what an emotion is in general. Their beliefs determine their emotions and they then think that their negative emotions are justified by their beliefs. But there is little justification for negative emotions. To display or induce negative emotions is to be less than human. In this sense anger is wrong.

Some emotions arise and are partly constituted by confusions. Love is sometimes merely a splendid confusion. We sometimes do feel more things or have interesting emotions when we are confused about something. We may let the background music be confused with, rather than separate from, the motion-picture. We may speak with people or be in a situation acceptingly and uncritically. By letting things happen to one, certain emotions are produced.

"He is a sensitive person." Does this refer to one's feelings and emotions? We may mean he is sensitive about social problems. In this case sensitive refers to his ability to carefully assess a situation. It is erroneously thought that one must suffer certain feelings or emotions in order to accurately assess a situation. It may, however, mean that the person can understand what feelings others are experiencing.

In another sense, "He is sensitive," refers to a disturbed person. Being sensitive is being easily bothered by events around one. Such a person has an exaggerated assessment of danger. Even here "sensitive" need not refer to feelings or emotions. We may have the picture of or false analogy to a sensitive wound. "Sensitive" in this case does refer to a feeling. "Sensitive person" refers to thought rather than to feeling or emotion.

To just have feelings and emotions without thought (language) would be ineffable. We would never know feelings or emotions as such. To know is largely to be able to say something about something.

We speak of feelings in terms of objects or places. "The pain is in my leg," "It is a *sharp* pain," etc. Talk of feelings and emotions is metaphorical. We do not have clear and distinct sense ideas or clear access to feelings and emotions. We do not just have emotions and feelings in themselves. Even hunger and thirst have cognitive content. This raises the question of the difference between reason and emotion.

There is no black and white distinction between emotion, thought, and feeling. In one respect, reason and emotion are too abstract to yield a clear-cut distinction between them. Their paradigms do differ. The difference between reason and emotion has to do with context and so is a rational sort of thing. The novelist decides whether a person is angry, in rage, or furious, not on the basis of internal states but rather in terms of plot, social relations, and situations. Both emotion words and reason words function in language in such a way that, except by artificial convention, there is no absolute distinction between them. Are "tree," "like," "good," "true," emotion or reason words? As words in language, both emotion words and reason words are equally comprehensible. Instead of "I am *anxious* about their coming," one could have said "Let them stay where they are," or "They shouldn't come." For nearly every emotion word or sentence, an equivalent non-emotion word or sentence could be substituted.

Is "I believe elves exist?" a rational or emotive statement? To say it is emotive is only to say one holds a belief for which there is no ordinary evidence. The emotive statement is, then, only a form of reason. Perhaps the statement means that the speaker is emotive, not just the belief. But everyone is emotive in the sense that everyone can be said to have feelings. Is belief emotive? Belief is usually distinguished from reason only because it is a statement for which little evidence can be produced. No emotion or feeling need be involved in belief. This is all that need be meant when referring to an "attitude" toward a proposition or, more traditionally, "propositional attitudes."

Emotion and feeling may, then, be regarded as forms of consciousness rather than separate from it. It was stated that one cannot *feel* envy or jealousy without thinking or knowing he is envious or jealous. Emotion may be a kind of belief. For example, remorse may be the belief that one did wrong plus the feelings or experiences which go with that belief. One may not have such a belief, not have learned words such as "remorse" and so not know what remorse is. To the extent that beliefs are not inherited, we do not inherit anger, though it is often said that we do. We may not like someone because of our beliefs about him but be wrong both about why we dislike him and about our belief. A critical analysis of such beliefs may result in a change in our likes.

If emotion is regarded as largely belief or rational assessment, our knowledge of other's emotions (the problem of the knowledge of other minds) is a problem largely of our access to his knowlege and beliefs, not a problem of access to private entities. To know how another person thinks is to know a great deal about his emotional life. Feelings, however, are to some extent private and known by analogy to our own case and reasoning. Certain feelings accompany our own reasoning and we expect that they will do so in the case of another person. However, each person's beliefs and knowledge are so diverse that we can often only generalize as to what another person is feeling. Such factors as his report and his actions can offer us additional specifications of such feelings.

"Did you enjoy concluding from the premises?" This suggests that even logic can be regarded as emotional. One can enjoy reading and reasoning. Is this for one to be emotional about rationality? Compare this with, "I feel that the conclusion follows from the premises." Logic is not the main paradigm for reason nor are feeling and emotion excluded from reason. Insomuch as logic contains a great number of false assumptions and confused concepts, as it does, it may itself be regarded as an emotional activity. B. Croce (1917) wrote, "As the science of thought, logistic is a laughable thing." (147) (See also W. Shibles "Pictures of Reason")

The fact that we command others to have emotion suggests that it is a rational controlled activity, e.g., "Love your neighbor." Pep talks are given to provide the proper "frame of mind" or persuasion, thus constituting emotions. To wine and dine is to provide a framework for emotions, a persuasion.

Emotion and reason come together by means of the distinction sometimes made between mental pleasure and physical pleasure. The utilitarian, J. Bentham, spoke of physical pleasure, and John S. Mill spoke of mental pleasure. But mental pleasure appears to be a disguised oxymoron. If mental refers to reason and pleasure is an emotion, "mental pleasure" means "rational emotion." But this is in keeping with the general view presented here that emotion is largely rational activity, emotion is a form of reason.

Sources:

C. D. Broad "Emotion and Sentiment" Journal of Aesthetics and Art Criticism 13 (Dec. 1954) 203-214

B. Croce Logic as the Science of the Pure Concept D. Ainslie, trans. London: Macmillan 1917

H. Gardiner, R. Metcalf, and J. Beebe-Center Feeling and Emotion New York: American Book Co. 1937

J. Hillman Emotion, a comprehensive phenomenology of theories and their meanings for therapy Northwestern University Press 1961 (Based on his PhD Dissertation)

Richard Peters The Concept of Motivation London: Kegan Paul 1958

George Pitcher "Emotion" Mind 74 (July 1965) 326-346

W. Shibles "Pictures of Reason" Philosophical Pictures 2nd edition, Dubuque, Iowa: Kendall-Hunt 1972

Ethics

In regard to the relation between ethics and emotion or feeling, Melden wrote,

"The whole subject of feeling has been very badly mismanaged in philosophy. And it is scandalous that those who write in moral philosophy and in the philosophy of taste take little or no pain to get clear about what for them is a matter of fundamental importance." (pp. 209-210)

Ethical terms may be characterized as being essentially open-context terms with a limited range of substitution instances. (W. Shibles, "Ethics as Open-Context Terms" PP, 1972) For example, "good" could mean a great many things. Emotion terms are open-context but have different substitution instances. Perhaps one reason why ethical terms may be regarded as emotive is that they are so vague and open. They in themselves say nothing yet covertly imply one or several of many possible things or statements. Because they are vague, such statements do not seem to say anything and so seem to be emotive. The paradigm case for emotive here is that ethical words are vague, non-descriptive and irrational, and what is irrational is thought to be emotive. It is thought, whether erroneously or not, that emotion is the opposite of reason. Another paradigm is that ethical terms just express feelings. To say "This is good," is merely to express an emotion or feeling.

Now it is seen that ethical and emotion terms are alike in being open-context, and that ethical terms are sometimes themselves regarded as being emotive. In addition, on this view, emotion terms insofar as they are open-context may be regarded as being emotive. Thus to say "He is in love," is for the speaker to be emotional. His statement merely expresses his own emotion. To say, "I

59

am in love," is to be emotive about one's own emotion. This may be taken as one gloss for the expression "The only thing to fear is fear itself." This would be because "fear" is a descriptively confused and open-context term. "Anxiety" may even refer in one instance to a lack of ability to cope with emotion terms and ethical terms because they are open-context terms.

Next it is seen that what we sometimes mean by "x is good," is "I like x," or "I envy x." That is, we replace an ethical term with an emotion term. The reverse may be true also. By "I love x," we may mean "x is good," or "x is valuable." But to speak of ethical terms in terms of emotive terms is to gain little clarity, as both are open-context terms. Both types of terms really or ultimately imply or reduce to descriptive and empirical statements often having to do with concrete cause and effect situations.

There is no value, morality or ethical realm in itself. An ethical term gains its meaning from, implies, is elliptical for, and is parasitic on descriptive and empirical statements. "X is good," may mean only "X is in accordance with the law," or "X is what my friends do." The case is similar in regard to emotions. There are no emotions as such. Emotion words are elliptical for certain descriptive and empirical statements. "X is loved" may mean only such things as, "X is given much companionship," or "X is spoken to kindly."

There are special substitution instances for statements of emotions which occur in historical description. We read such statements as "The king was remorseful," "Napoleon felt . . . " "The president was envious." Here the substitution instances are special ones which the historian himself has dug up by putting together documents, a knowledge of the situation, etc. It may well have been that the person in question actually had no such emotion, had a different emotion, or had no special feelings relevant to the situation historically reconstructed. The admission by an historical figure, "I felt remorse," is not incorrigible. He may have been confused about his emotions. Someone else may be a better judge of them than the person himself.

There are subtle relations involved in ethics and emotional behavior. There can be subtle transferences of the following sort. One's friend or a member of one's family tends to say things in a certain way. He becomes emotional about certain things. He may not say "X is good," or "X is bad," but his intonation and expressions covertly suggest a value judgment. One may find he disagrees with his friend or parent yet nevertheless finds that he has taken on their expressions and covertly their values (empirical statements) as well as their expressions of emotions. There is, here, a covert transference whereby one takes on values and attitudes or emotions he may not consciously wish to accept. In this respect, one's friends as well as one's enemies can adversely affect one.

We often think that if we believe that something is morally wrong we therefore must become emotional about it as well. We are often expected to cry or feel emotionally upset at a funeral, or to be anxious and depressed because the environment is being polluted. But just because something is seen as bad is no reason why one must feel bad. These two need not become confused. One may face the difficult situation cheerfully and try to do something about it, or if this is not possible at least adjust to it. Emotional depression may cause more harm than its supposed cause. One can always find some external cause as an excuse for being depressed.

There is another close connection between emotion and ethical terms. The word "pleasure" seems to be an emotion. It is also regarded as central to ethical and moral theory. Utilitarianism asserts that we should promote the greatest pleasure for the greatest number. Here it is not clear what pleasure is or how to set up a hedonistic calculus to quantify pleasure. One finds emotion and ethics come together in the phrase "I feel good." And one gloss for "pleasure," is "good feeling," or "good emotion." There is a circularity in saying that good reduces to pleasure and pleasure reduces to a good feeling. One may still ask, "What is a good feeling?" But one has or does not have a feeling. It is in itself neither good nor bad. A good feeling or emotion could be a feeling one wants. Pleasure would mean feelings or emotions one wants. Ethics may reduce in some cases to an emotion, a desire, need or want. Envy in some cases is a desire to have what someone else has. Desires, needs, wants, emotions have and involve objects. One begins with one's desires, one's emotions, and attempts to organize them in satisfactory ways. This is the descriptive, empirical task of ethics. To become clear about ethics is to become clear about emotions such as pleasure, desire, envy, remorse, revenge, jealousy, etc. (See chapters on pleasure and jealousy.) Emotion terms reduce to non-emotion terms.

E. Bedford (1964) relates emotions and ethics in still another way. His main view is that emotion words do not mainly report internal states but rather are appraisals. They presuppose social relations, and moral, aesthetic, and legal judgments. An emotion is not just a feeling and cannot be a cause. To think of an emotion as an entity is a naming fallacy. He states, "An emotion is not any sort of experience or process." (p. 77) We do not just introspect emotions. There are, however, said to be individual feeling differences associated with each emotion. Being angry does not necessarily imply any feelings: "One cannot understand what it is to feel angry without first understanding what it is to be angry." (p. 79) We do not observe another's feelings but just see that a person is angry and we normally say just that.

Moreland Perkins (SH 1966) says that we normally justifiably say we "see" that a person is emotional, e.g., angry. It is no good to say "I can't be jealous, I don't feel jealous." To report an emotion is not just to report a feeling. It is to report the context of our behavior. If we know our own emotions better than those of others it is not just because we know our feelings better but because we know the context of our behavior better. The same behavior may be regarded differently in different circumstances. The difference between shame and embarrassment is a difference between context rather than a difference of behavior. This is also why an emotion is not merely a disposition to act or a piece of behavior. Bedford says, "If an emotion were a feeling no sense could be made of them at all," (p. 91) and "Statements about emotions cannot be said to describe behavior; they interpret it." (p. 83) His view is that "Emotion words form part of the vocabulary of appraisal and criticism." (p. 89) Ashamed and shame apply only if the act is subject to criticism. Vain, envious, resentful are terms of appraisal or censure. We usually say one is not to blame for having a feeling and cannot be commanded to have one. Because emotions are not feelings we can condemn and justify them, e.g., "You ought not to be envious." Emotions are value or evaluative terms. In "I envy Schnabel's technique," "envy" may serve not to describe a feeling but rather as a term of praise. In addition, he states that emotions are moral terms of character: "There is an overlap between the lists of emotions, and the lists of virtues and vices that are given by philosophers." (p. 90)

Moreland Perkins (EF 1966) agrees with Bedford's view and states that *"What* we feel when we feel angry is not to be explained simply or even mainly by telling what we feel in our body when we feel angry." But Perkins stresses the fact that emotion terms often do involve some reference to bodily feelings. This makes sense of the statement by Diogenes of Apollonia (460 B.C.) that the tongue is very sensitive to emotions. All feelings or senses relate to emotions.

The Russian psychologist Pavel Simonov (1970) states a view somewhat similar to that of Bedford. For Simonov emotions are not necessary and may be dissipated by understanding the situation involved. He states, "If a man or animal is fully aware of what he should do to meet his needs, then emotions are unnecessary." (p. 52) He gives a rough formula to show that the degree of the emotion is determined by the amount of difference between the information needed to achieve a need (In) and the information available or acquired (Ia), i.e., $E = -N (In - Ia)$. He gives the examples of fear and rage:

> "We experience fear when there is a need to protect ourselves and we do not have sufficient information to do so. Rage is the result when we have a strong desire to crush the enemy (great N) and lack the means to do so." (p. 53)

The theory is suggestive but rests on questionable notions of classical conditioning, and on the inadequate view that emotions may be measured by physiological criteria such as blood pressure. He also speaks of "neural noise," which seems to be an obscure concept.

Ethics and emotions come together in ethical theories such as those of the emotivists, Epicureans, Stoics, etc. For the Epicureans the pleasures of the mind are stressed over the sensuous feelings and emotions. One's feeling or emotional life should be enriched and refined to allow one to enjoy life more fully. The emotions are to be mastered. Such mastery serves as a goal of life; and negative emotions are regarded as being undesirable. For the Stoic, the highest good is to attain happiness through knowledge. One must master his emotions by means of reason. These views place emphasis on the role of reason in regulating the emotions but also set such regulation as a goal or duty which man must seek. For the Stoics, emotions, especially negative ones, are diseases of the mind.

In the determination of what kind of government one should have, it is no longer acceptable to say that it must be one which is in accord with the nature of man. Rather the consideration must also be what kind of "nature" or person ought man to be, what kind of emotions should he develop. In this respect, government and political systems should rest on the problem of emotion and personality. Also, lack of understanding and control of emotion leads to racial prejudice, violence, war, super-nationalism, etc. In "Distrust of Merits" Marianne Moore said that we will not have conquered war until we conquer that in ourselves which causes war. Thus the question is not just what is good or bad in terms of our nature, but what kind of "nature" should we have.

Regulation of emotions may be a goal, but also goals affect one's emotions. If one's goals are realistic and adequate one's emotions may tend to be positive ones. The rational assessments involved will guide positive feelings. Confused goals or lack of a conscious or realistic goal leads to negative emotions. Pleasantness may then be regarded as being successful. If one experiences negative emotions one may look for the presence of ill defined goals, lack of or conflict of goals.

If "interest" is regarded as an emotion and "true" as a rational assessment, it may be that to be true is to be interesting. This is because "interesting" is a rational assessment guiding positive feelings. Something may be interesting because it clarifies something.

"Interesting" may suggest a value term such as good. One does not say "I do not like interesting things." To be interesting is to be good or to like something. If "good" means "like," here, then one tends to like something because of the rational assessments involved in liking. That is, one has certain positive feelings because of his guiding assessments and so says of something that it is interesting. On the other hand "hate" seems to imply that something is bad. Hate is not usually thought to be good. Hate may here be reduced to an ethical term which is in turn reduced to a like which is in turn based on certain beliefs and assessments. What is wrong with hate? It may in some situations be preferred and be in some rare situations an intelligent type of reaction. In any case, "like," and "hate," may involve ethical terms.

Anger is not always seen to be wrong or bad. In the court room it is often determined that a person's violent act is justified if he becomes as angry as a normal person might be in such circumstances. But this allowance assumes that anger is acceptable. If emotions are not feelings and are largely rational, then they can be controlled and changed. We are not, then, justified in becoming angry and so causing uncontrollable violence. There is good reason to outlaw poor emotions and make it illegal to be angry. Negative emotions almost always cause actual mental and physical damage to oneself as well as others. Anger is in this sense wrong.

It may be observed that we have good emotions when we do what we think is good, and bad emotions when we do what is bad. But this is not necessary. One may enjoy doing what is wrong — and its being wrong may be what makes it especially enjoyable. But such enjoyment is often a learned activity which is self-defeating. One seeks things which are especially likely to fail. One assesses the situation in such a way that his choice of hurting himself is thought to be the best course of action and the best way of adjusting to a situation. A detailed analysis of one's situation and beliefs can clarify such self-defeating actions. The reason we have good emotions or feelings when we do what we assess is good, is because emotions are themselves partly assessments. Moral indignation and shame are examples of ethical emotions whereby the feeling is guided by the assessment.

Emotions are often thought to be self-justificatory. Norman Mailer wrote in "The White Negro,"

"What fitted the need of the adventurer even more precisely was Hemingway's categorical imperative that what made him feel good became therefore The Good," and "It is impossible to live such an [existential] life unless one's emotions provide their profound conviction."

Camus in *The Stranger* appears to present the existentialist view that emotions justify themselves, that one should do what he "feels" like doing and if he feels like killing he should do so. It is as if there is a dignity of even negative emotions. Robert Cunningham (1970) states,

"Sartre believes that . . . where values are too uncertain and abstract to determine the right choice, 'nothing remains but to trust in our instincts.' But if one is to trust one's instincts or feelings, how does one estimate the strength of a feeling? Is the student's feeling of love for his mother stronger than his love for his country? . . . Sartre concludes: 'No rule of general morality can show you what you ought to do: no signs are vouchsafed in this world.' (8) . . . Sartre fails to give any concrete moral advice. He directs: Be authentic! but provides no criteria of authenticity." (10)

An emotion may be thought to develop its own justification. This would not, however, be the case if one had uncritical, false, or limited assessments which inform such emotions. It might, on the other hand, be understandable how one came to have the emotions and feelings he does have. Therapy may involve such reconstruction. We ask for the reasons for being angry or for having certain emotions and then see whether they are justifiable reasons, e.g., "Why are you so jealous?" "Why do you love her?" In religion there was condemnation of the seven mortal sins (or emotions): pride, lust, anger, envy, sloth, gluttony, avarice. One speaks of "true" happiness. We can be mistaken about our emotions, e.g., think we are angry when we are instead jealous. We can be mistaken in a way similar to the way our descriptions and knowledge of cause and effect can be mistaken. Certain emotions may be found to be self-defeating or harmful and so unjustifiable.

One may not like another person because of beliefs held about him. If the beliefs are seen to be false then the dislike may be seen to be unwarranted. It is possible, as Plato asserts in the *Philebus,* to have false pleasure. In a similar way our other likes and dislikes may be found to be false or unjustifiable. Even likes which are primarily sensations such as tastes may be changed by revised assessments. There is good wine and bad wine, good music and bad music, etc.

Emotion may be misplaced as when one loves money more than people, a superstition more than man, or one responds with positive emotion after killing the enemy in battle. Feelings may be inappropriately dissociated from cognition in a number of ways such as laughing when one usually cries, not responding at all, or mood swings. A. I. Melden wrote:

"Emotions, no less than beliefs, actions, and desires, are subject to appraisal as reasonable or unreasonable, justified or unjustified. And, as Aristotle put it, to feel them 'at the right times, with reference to the right objects, towards the right people, with the right motive, and in the right way' is no easy matter." (216)

One can ask what an emotion is for or what the purpose is of having a certain emotion, but not "What did you have that feeling for?" or "What is the purpose of having that feeling?" Assessments alter feeling but only under special circumstances such as when greatly distracted. Only to a very limited extent can sensation, feelings, and perception be said to be true or false. By thinking of emotion as a feeling or merely physical event no criteria of or reasons for emotion can be given. They could not be seen to be misplaced, irrational, rational, genuine, etc.

"Anger is wrong," seems like an oxymoron, conceit, or combination of opposites. It, rather, reveals insight. Because emotions are not feelings but are within our control to change, all negative emotions such as rage, anger, hatred, disgust, revenge, etc. may be said to be unjustifiable in the sense that they are self-defeating, harmful to oneself and others and unwanted by the person who displays them. One's anger does not justify him for screaming at someone. The philosopher A. C. Ewing (1957) states this same view concisely, "Hatred is never justifiable."

Emotions are sometimes thought to be irrational but it is the assessment portion of the emotion which is rational or irrational not the complex emotion. The feeling portion can be neither rational nor irrational.

Feelings and their behavioral counterparts may be thought to be irrational because they seem non-purposive and not goal directed. They are, then, irrational only in terms of a purpose. On this logic, rational thinking may be irrational from the point of view of behavior at a party. One may seem to be cheerful for no reason at all, but on consideration it may be especially important to be cheerful when there seems to be no reason to be.

In the sense that one uncritically learns the emotions of the group he associates with, the emotions may not be justifiable. Fads of behavior are prevalent and group pressure to accept such behavior is strong. Also one tends to imitate or fake the feelings of others, such as in sympathy, even when the feelings are due to faulty reasoning. Pity, revenge, and over-sentimentality result and such feelings lead to actions performed out of self-righteousness. One criterion for justifying emotion is its ability to be shared. If two or more report the same feeling or emotion this would seem to make it a valid experience. One of the difficulties with psychiatric patients is that they are not able to share feelings or emotions in the usual way.

Emotion may often be justifiable or considered best if a realistic and adequate goal is served. This may sometimes make the difference between a shallow emotion and an adequate one, a poor work of art and an aesthetic work of art. This may suggest a meaning for the expression "true happiness." Adequate emotions may unify and give insight into diverse areas of experience. To some extent, for a statement to be true, it must be interesting and so relevant. And that which is interesting often yields insight and truth.

Emotions are also appropriate in respect to degree. Excessive anger may be condemned. Love often involves excess and once was thought to be a disease. But love may in some sense be a disease because it often is an irrational way of coping with erotic and other desires so as to induce erratic behavior. One kills or dies out of love. (cf. "Love-pact" suicides)

It was said that if emotions are partly judgments we can have true and false emotions. Thus it is no longer possible to exempt emotions from rational consideration as in expressions such as "I can understand and accept it rationally but not emotionally." To assert this is to be self-righteous or prejudiced. If the statement only means that one's habits, perceptions and feelings are hard to change, that is another matter. Self-righteous emotion is like "prejudice" in the sense that both involve preceding judgments which are assumed uncritically independent of the circumstance in question.

Certain emotions by definition imply ethical terms and thus justification, value, and ethical theories are applicable. "Guilt" implies "My action was wrong or bad." "Shame" suggests wrong-doing, etc. Love and hate may involve value assessments. Such emotions involve value assessment and can be no more clear than the value terms implied. Such terms as good and bad are often thought to be meaningful in themselves such that "I am bad," is accepted as an objective statement and so leads to unfounded assessment of inferiority. "Bad," here, if reduced to specific actions and situations, allows one to see what the problem is and solve it. If his acts are harmful he can make up for them and change them. If we are unclear about how ethical terms work we will be unclear about emotion terms as well. Irrational phrases such as "I'm no good," lead to neurosis and psychosis.

Besides emotions based on open-context ethical terms there are emotions which have no name. These are complexes of assessments with their accompanying or consequent feelings. It may be thought that an emotion cannot be justified or not justified if it has no name. The assessment can be justified whether or not the complex is regarded as an emotion. (cf. chapter on Fletcher's situational ethics.)

The view that "passion" is self-justificatory is unacceptable. It will not do to say one did an irresponsible act "out of passion."

Emotion was once called passion. "Passion" derives from the Latin *passio* meaning "suffering, affection, being affected."

"Pathos" derives from the Greek word meaning, "suffering, passion, misfortune." "Affection" derives from the Latin *affectus* meaning "to do something to," and from *affectionem* "a permanent state of feeling." This commits the fallacy of thinking that emotion is passive like a feeling. Spinoza in *Ethics* treats emotion as passion, something which merely happens to one, but then goes on to assert that it is more like confused thinking and thus has a cognitive element:

> "The more an emotion becomes known to us, the more it is within our power and the less the mind is passive to it."

> "An emotion, which is suffering (confused, frustrating, painful) ceases to be a passion as soon as we form a clear and distinct idea of it."

One usually thinks emotions just happen to him and that he cannot control them, rather than that people actively determine and create emotions. One may wish to think his emotions are passive so as to give up responsibility for them and so that his actions will not be criticized or questioned. It also serves as a rationalization for not changing one's emotions. If emotions are merely feelings one has, then he can do nothing about them and so does not have to change his negative emotions. But emotions, being largely cognitive, can be changed. It is no excuse to say "Its my nature to be angry," or "I'm not in the mood."

Feelings are more passively experienced than are emotions. Assessments may alter feelings but they largely constitute emotions. Because emotions have a feeling component one may be erroneously led to think they are passive, non-cognitive, and unchangeable. Certainly suffering is relatively more passive than aggressive hatred, though both involve agitation and negative feelings. But we still speak of being "in" a rage, "in" love, etc. as if all emotions were passive. We learn and imitate emotional behavior, and with repetition develop emotional patterns of behavior or habits. Such habits become familiar and so seem necessary and natural forms of behavior. They are neither necessary nor natural. Also, emotion often involves imagery of wished-for things and because it is merely imagined imagery rather than active seeking, emotions may seem passive. Imagery, however, can actively help to clarify and set goals and ways of attaining goals. Emotion may sometimes be wishful thinking without a grasp of means and ends. Both feeling and seeing are not entirely passive for both involve assessment.

Ataraxia derives from the Greek word meaning "calmness, impassiveness, imperturbable." The Epicureans preferred this particular emotion or state over negative emotional agitation. "Apathy" derives from the Greek word meaning "freedom from suffering." This suggests that apathy is not simply passive inactivity but merely freedom from negative emotions. By means of apathy one may arrive at a positive emotional state. The sense of beauty is sometimes referred to as a calm emotion.

Sources:

Errol Bedford "Emotions" *Essays in Philosophical Psychology* Donald Gustafson, ed. New York: Doubleday 1964

Robert Cunningham, ed. *Situationism and the New Morality* New York: Appleton-Century-Crofts 1970

A. C. Ewing "Symposium: The Justification of Emotion" *Proceedings of the Aristotelian Society* Suppl. vol. 31 (1957) (Reply to Warnock)

A. I. Melden "The Conceptual Dimensions of Emotions" *Human Action* Theodore Mischel, ed., New York: Academic Press 1969

Moreland Perkins "Emotion and Feelings" *Philosophical Quarterly* 75 (1966) 139-60.

Moreland Perkins "Seeing and Hearing Emotions" *Analysis* 26 (6) (1966) 193-97

Warren Shibles "Ethics as Open-Context Terms" *Philosophical Pictures* 2nd edition, Dubuque, Iowa: Kendall-Hunt 1972

Pavel Simonov "Emotions and Creativity" *Psychology Today* 4 (3) (Aug. 1970) 51-55, 57

A Critique and Defense
of Ellis on Emotions

One of the most sound and useful theories of emotions is that presented by Albert Ellis in his major work on the subject, *Reason and Emotion.* The theory will be critically presented, conceptually clarified, and given some philosophical support which has hitherto been lacking. (See also his *Humanistic Psychotherapy* 1973)

Ellis' view is, for example, in keeping with ordinary-language philosophy to the extent that he stresses actual concrete language usage in specific situations, and to the extent that he rejects metaphysical explanation and mentalistic (e.g., Freudian) pseudo-psychological entities. He does not, for example, accept the traditional distinction between reason and emotion. They are obscure terms needing clarification. Emotion is not the opposite of thinking. Rather it is partially comprised of thinking or reason.

"A good deal of what we call emotion would seem to be a kind of appraisal or thinking . . . " (48)

"Human thinking and emotion are *not* two disparate or different processes, but . . . they significantly overlap and are in some respects, for all practical purposes, essentially the same thing." (38)

Emotions are not merely internal feelings. They are of a number of components not just one. Such factors are sensory, motor, feeling, cognition (or reason). Thus he states,

"None of the four fundamental life operations — sensing, moving, emoting, and thinking — is experienced in isolation." (39)

73

It would not be strictly accurate to say someone thinks about a problem or feels emotional about it but rather,

> "Smith senses-moves-feels-*thinks* about this problem." (39)

> "Emotion does not exist in its own right, as a special and almost mystical sort of entity; it is rather, an essential part of an entire sensing-moving-thinking-emoting complex." (47)

Emotion then, is seen to involve cognition or reason, motor activity, perception and sensation, feeling. By feeling he means relatively pure sensory states and sensory appraisals. Emotions differ from feelings in involving more cognition. His definitions here may be made more clear by regarding feelings as bodily sensations and then noting that even bodily sensations involve some kinds of assessment, e.g., one may not feel certain bodily sensations if distracted or psychologically disturbed. Emotion, thus, as Ellis states, would be composed of bodily feeling, perception, and cognition. On my view, because "feeling" refers primarily or as much as possible, to sensations, it is a category mistake to say, "I feel x," where "x" is an emotion. It is misleading, for example, to say "I feel jealous." Jealousy is largely a cognition and so not merely a feeling. One could instead say, "I think jealousy." Ellis seems to recognize this distinction, also, by noting that "feel" has several ambiguous senses:

> "Unfortunately, we use the same term, *feelings,* to cover the pleasures and displeasures of a) pure sensations, such as pain or warmth, b) sensory appraisals, such as pleasure at feeling warm, and c) cognitive sensory evaluations which may or may not be connected with relatively pure sensory states." (52)

On the other hand, he sometimes talks of "feelings of anger" as being "immediate and non-reflective." (45)

Ellis realizes that even bodily sensation is not entirely pure or free of cognitive association. On this analysis, the claim that, for example, sex is pure sensation only, is mistaken. Rather it has complex cognitive and associational factors. There is no such thing as pure sexual feeling.

If emotion is largely rational, a clarification of reason is required. It is here that Ellis takes a clear and significant step beyond other theorists. He does not merely rest his analysis on such vague and mentalistic terms as thought, idea, reason, cognition, judgment, etc., but rather reduces them to a clear model. By thinking or reason he means language use, statements we utter to ourselves or aloud:

"Since man is a uniquely sign-, symbol-, and language-creating animal, both thinking and emoting tend to take the form of self-talk or internalized sentences; and that, for all practical purposes, the sentences that human beings keep telling themselves *are* or *become* their thoughts and emotions." (Ellis in Sahakian 559)

"Humans seem almost invariably to think in words, phrases and sentences. And it is these sentences which really are, which constitute . . . neurosis." (28)

"Much of our emoting takes the form of self-talk or internalized sentences." (5)

"For all practical purposes, his internalized sentences *are* his thinking." (50)

In fact, without cognition or self-talk there would be few emotions. Emotion implies reason. In this sense, if there is no reason there is no emotion.

"Without an adult human being's employing, on some conscious or unconscious level, such thoughts and sentences, much of his emoting would simply not exist." (S 559)

Because human emotion involves thinking and thinking involves human language animals cannot be said to have emotions in the same sense that man does. To confuse the two cases commits a category-mistake as well as the pathetic fallacy of attributing human emotions to animals. Ellis wrote,

"Human beings, I began to see, are not the same as Pavlovian dogs or other lower animals; and their emotional disturbances are quite different from the experimental neuroses and other emotional upsets which we produce in the laboratory in rats, guinea pigs, dogs, sheep, and other animals. For human beings have one attribute which none of the other living beings that we know have in any well-developed form: language and the symbol-producing facility that goes with language." (14)

"Human neuroses are qualitatively different from animal neuroses." (18)

For Ellis, then, by reason is primarily meant use of language. He arrived at this view, he says, in his psychiatric observation and practice. After having been educated in a Freudian mentalistic tradition such immediate observation may be regarded as a difficult accomplishment and breakthrough. Instead of speaking of an id, ego, superego, unconscious mind, psychic energy, life and death instinct, etc., Ellis was able to describe the actual situation. It was a shift from the *a priori* or theoretical method to the descriptive, empirical, observational method. The method is to deal with what people actually say and do.

"What both the Freudians and the behaviorist-conditioning psychologists are misleadingly doing, I clearly began to see, is to leave out a great deal of the *telling* or *language* aspect of human neuroses." (18-19)

His stress on language may be expanded and given philosophical support by contemporary research in philosophical psychology. According to Ludwig Wittgenstein and Gilbert Ryle we have no evidence for "mind," "idea," "emotion," "thoughts," "meanings," as mentalistic states or entities inside of us. Such words insomuch as they purport to describe or name internal entities, are naming-fallacies. Freud's analysis of mind is based on such fallacies. Thus in order to find a more satisfactory account of "thought," a non-mentalistic analysis must be given. It may then be seen that by thought we mainly mean what people say aloud, in writing, or to themselves. Examinations in school and human communication are primarily verbal. We do not know how we would think or what thinking would be if we had never learned a language. Language has epistemological primacy. (See W. Shibles "Linguo-Centric Predicament" and articles on meaning in *Philosophical Pictures*) It is not the case that we have ideas and then put them into words. If there are no words there are no "ideas." There may be images or abilities, however. By thinking or reasoning, then, is meant mainly use of language, but also some imagery, and physical abilities such as building a house. Written or spoken sentences are concrete behavioral criteria for thought. Internal sentences we have evidence for just as we have evidence for imagery. They need not be thought of as mentalistic entities but rather as events which can be easily produced. One can have an "image" of a rooster or say to oneself "I think I will go to Europe." Theodore Sarbin (1972) gives an analysis of imagery and "mute speech" such that mentalism is avoided. We first learn to speak aloud and then learn to have the experience of speaking without saying anything aloud. Sarbin states that imagining or having an image is not having a "picture-in-the mind." Seeing an image is not like seeing an object. There are no inner eyes. On Sarbin's theory imagery and self-talk are skills of performing as-if behavior, role-taking fictions, pretend or hypothetical activities. Self-talk is muted speech learned partly by talking to others, then to oneself, then playing speaking or muting speech. Self-talk is a kind of imagery but not literally talking to oneself any more than having a visual image is seeing a picture in one's head. Sarbin notes that,

"Persons who are efficient imitators and convincing role-players are also skilled at imagery tasks." (344)

Self-talk may be largely what we usually mean by thinking, and it is a means of adaptation and **problem-solving.** Thus Ellis' view that by reason or thinking we mean mainly self-talk or statements we utter aloud or to ourselves, has support in terms of some of the work being done in contemporary philosophy and psychology. It will be seen that this view also arises out of some more historical philosophical writings, e.g., Marcus Aurelius' philosophy.

At one point Ellis even describes what I have called the "assessment theory of emotions."

"What actually seems to happen is that he [the patient] first tells himself these sentences; then feels physical sensations in his gut; and then by a feedback mechanism perceives his own physical sensations, which he finally interprets as his 'emotion.' " (50-51)

By "assessment" I mean to include descriptive as well as value statements. One judges or assesses what the situation is and may also pass value judgment on the described situation. The philosopher Errol Bedford (1955) presents the view that the thinking or statements involved in emotion are primarily value statements.

Ellis often holds a similar view. For Ellis the statements which guide negative feeling are irrational, illogical or negative value assessments; and rational statements or positive value assessments guide positive feelings:

"It would appear, then, that positive human emotions, such as feelings of love or elation, are often associated with or result from thoughts, or internalized sentences, stated in some form or variation of the phrase 'This is good,' and that negative emotions . . . stated in some form of . . . 'This is bad.' " (S 559)

"Much of what we call emotions is nothing more nor less than a certain kind — a biased, prejudiced, or strongly evaluative kind — of thought." (41)

"What we usually label as emoting, is a relatively uncalm, passionate, and strong evaluating of some person or object." (47)

A case could possibly be made out whereby some rational negative assessments can guide positive feelings. Negative emotion often involves value assessments such as "That is terrible," "I am bad," "I am inferior," etc. Ellis is again correct in his analysis, and a philosophical clarification of ethical terms may give his theory more clarity as well as support. (See W. Shibles "Ethics as Open-Context Terms.")

Ethical terms such as "good," "bad," "right," "wrong," "ought," "ought not," are open-context terms with a loosely limited range of substitution instances. In themselves such terms are meaningless. To become meaningful a specific empirical and descriptive meaning must be substituted and a specific context provided. Thus it is a misuse of language and a failure to understand how ethical or value terms work, to say, "I am bad." This statement in itself says nothing. Similarly, "Premarital love is bad," is unintelligible until a specific substitution for, or meaning, is given to "bad." But people do often think that such value terms are meaningful in themselves and so think that in themselves they are "bad" people or that their actions are "horrible." Such confused assessments lead to negative feelings, depression, neurosis, inferiority complexes. Thus one of the consequences of being confused about or unclear about how ethical terms work, is neurosis or negative emotion. Although what Ellis says about negative value judgments resulting in negative emotions is reasonable, it may, in view of philosophical clarification of ethical terms given above, also be seen what mechanisms are involved. If a person sees that "I am bad," is an open-context or incomplete statement he would not take it seriously but reduce it to concrete descriptive and empirical statements. There is no separate non-empirical, metaphysical or mystical realm of value. One may say he is a bad person without even knowing what he means by "bad" or why he is "bad." Reduction of the term to concrete instances often dissolves the thought that one is "bad." What is being condemned may turn out to be trivial or inconsequential, e.g., "I burned the toast, therefore I am a bad person." Also because one can only do what it is within one's power to do, such self-blame is unrealistic. Ellis wrote,

"Blame, hostility, and anger are almost certainly the most essential and serious causes of most human disturbances." (68)

On the open-context theory of value terms, nothing is in itself good or bad but rather some things are needed or desired in terms of consequences. Ethics reduces to empirical descriptions and situations, and knowledge of cause and effect. Ellis partially seems to support this view when he quotes Shakespeare's Hamlet:

"There's nothing either good or bad but thinking makes it so." (54)

Negative emotions are caused by irrational descriptive statements or irrational value statements. This leads to what Ellis calls his ABC Theory:

"It is rarely the stimulus, A, which gives rise to a human emotional reaction, C. Rather, it is almost always B – the individual's beliefs regarding, attitudes toward, or interpretations of A – which actually lead to his reaction, C." (215)

What causes negative emotion is irrational statements or self-talk at B. Some relevant statements and examples are:

"The angry individual fails to see that he invariably has a pronounced thought just prior to his anger . . . e.g., 'I can't *stand* his behaving in that *wrong* manner.' " (409)

"Self-verbalizations have been and still are the prime source of their emotional disturbances." (S 560)

"All sustained negative emotions that people feel stem from their *own* internalized sentences, rather than from outside events." (282)

Because it is our irrational interpretations and self-talk which cause negative emotion it may be seen that it is we, not others or the environment, who cause our own emotional problems. One way of putting this is that the only thing to fear is fear itself, the only emotional problems are those we ourselves create. We anger ourselves, bore ourselves, irritate ourselves, make ourselves jealous, make ourselves feel inferior, etc. Ellis shows agreement with this view:

"I am creating my own hostility; it is *not* being created by external people or things." (418)

"Unhappiness largely comes from within and is created by the unhappy person himself." (73)

"Human beings fear imagined stimuli." (17)

"Man often becomes fearful of *purely* verbal or other signalling processes." (18)

"Humans fear their *own* self-signallings and self-talk." (18)

Another way his view might be put to allow insight into it is to say that our metaphors determine our emotions. We live and feel our metaphors. Metaphors may make us sad or sublime. Then, further clarification may be given to assessments by bringing to bear on them recent knowledge of the types and functions of metaphor. (See W. Shibles *Metaphor)*

The ABC Theory is an excellent account and seems to be a restatement of the philosophy of Marcus Aurelius and the stoics. The stoics stressed reason and realistic assessment. It is instructive to add Marcus Aurelius' own statements from *The Meditations:*

"If you are pained by an external thing it is not this thing that disturbs you — but your judgment about it." (93)

"Say nothing more to yourself than what the first appearances report. Suppose that it has been reported to you that a certain person speaks ill of you. This has been reported; but that you have been injured, that has not been reported." (93)

"It is our own opinions which disturb us." (128)

"A cucumber is bitter — throw it away. — There are briars in the road — turn aside from them. — This is enough. Do not add, And why were such things made in the world?" (94)

On Ellis' Theory the irrational assessments are often other's ideas or definitions which are then taken on as one's own. They are statements taken on from one's culture, parents, church, associates. These purely verbal fears he calls "definitional." An example he gives of what definitional means is:

"You start with an axiom or hypothesis, such as 'Unless I do perfectly well in life, I am worthless' " (26)

The next step in Ellis' theory is to point out that negative emotion and neuroticism is maintained only by repeating irrational statements to oneself. This may be referred to as fixed "ideas," or better, "fixed statements." It is to be captivated by a model or metaphor. It is a kind of self-hypnotism or autosuggestion. Ellis wrote,

"It appears to be almost impossible to sustain an emotion-outburst without bolstering it by repeated ideas." (49)

"Sustained emotion . . . is the direct result of sustained thinking." (49)

On the basis of his theory that emotions are largely statements, Ellis attacks behaviorists and Freudian psychoanalysts:

"Classical psychoanalysts and the conditionists also stress the supposedly nonverbal or subcortical early influences on the child and often seem to think that these 'nonverbal' influences are even more important in creating emotional disturbance than are language indoctrinations. In this, I am quite convinced, they are wrong." (19)

The major accusation seems to be that behaviorists have failed to give an adequate account of human behavior because they failed to deal with self-talk or language assessments. They dealt with animal "emotions" as if such behavior was the same in humans. Also Ellis accuses behaviorists of dealing only with symptoms of emotions rather than with the cause. (327) Such modifications of behavior if they do not deal with the irrational thinking causing the disturbance, will not be successful in eliminating psychological problems. The behaviorist in effect says, "I don't know why the patient is depressed but by conditioning I can change some of his behavior." This is a metaphysical approach to behavior. It treats man as a mystery and deals only with a small part of his behavior. Ellis agrees with the behaviorist's view of learning to the extent that we may be conditioned to behave in self-defeating ways. It would then seem that behaviorism would be acceptable if it dealt with language and faulty assessments and thus gave an adequate account of human behavior. One must deal not just with outward behavior, but also with one's language and assessment. The human "can also be rewarded or punished by his *own* thinking." (16) The behaviorist view, then, seems to regard emotions as inaccessible, mystical entities which cannot be dealt with. Ellis regards them as concrete statements we utter to ourselves with resulting feelings.

The psychiatric accounts and Rogerian accounts are opposed because they too passively or inadequately deal with one's assessments thus precluding success. The Freudian account of an "unconscious" is rejected. Ellis proposes instead an active therapy designed to actively change the patient's irrational thinking.

One objection to Ellis' view may be that it is too rational and that one may change his assessments but still not be able to change his emotions. Ellis has an adequate reply to this objection because he, in fact, does include factors other than cognition. It was mentioned that sensory, motor, feeling, and cognition are involved and so to change emotions all or some of these factors must be altered. For example, one's perceptions may have to be changed. But still it is important to see that perception itself, to some extent, involves assessment.

"Their difficulties largely result from distorted perception and illogical thinking." (36)

"An individual *evaluates* (attitudinizes, becomes biased) when he perceives something as being 'good,' or 'bad,' . . . Evaluating always seems to involve both perceiving and responding." (44)

"Emoting usually, probably always involves some kind of bodily sensations . . . " (44)

Emotion is seen to involve behavior, perception, sensation, dreams, imagery, motor behavior, in addition to cognition. And Rational Therapy takes all of these factors into account. Rational Therapy is, to a certain extent, eclectic and may draw insights from various schools of psychology and therapy. Because emotions involve judgments, emotions can be changed by changing one's judgments. This revolutionizes all previous and popular views according to which emotions are internal states, feelings, or are passive such that one cannot help having them. Ellis, however, does not think all emotions can be completely changed, but rather significantly changed.

Rational Therapy may also be called "Philosophical Therapy" now because it is seen that conceptual clarification is needed for one to avoid negative emotions and to induce positive emotions. The goal of contemporary ordinary-language philosophy is to clarify confused concepts in our language and so it serves as therapy. Ludwig Wittgenstein wrote,

"The results of philosophy are the uncovering of one or another piece of plain nonsense and of bumps that the understanding has got by running its head up against the limits of language." (PI 119)

"What is your aim in philosophy? To show the fly the way out of the fly-bottle." (PI 309)

Ellis comes very close to ordinary-language philosophy when he stresses what he calls,

"Philosophic causation — what to un*say* and un*think*. I had been neglecting (along with virtually all other therapists of the day) the precise, simple declarative and exclamatory sentences which the patients once told themselves in creating their disturbances . . . " (21-24)

He states that we must "depropagandize" ourselves. (286) The philosopher stresses striking and critical formulations and juxtapositions. Ellis speaks of the necessity for the therapist to have a "circuit-breaking" attitude. (298) The therapy involves not just changing immediate irrational ideas, but giving conceptual clarifications which will help prevent negative emotions and future neuroses and psychoses.

The question as to whether philosophical or rational therapy can deal with all types of patients is answered by Ellis as follows:

"Rational therapy is *more* effective than *most* other kinds of therapy with *most* patients." (38)

"The more emotional and less persuasive methods of psychotherapy are relatively ineffectual and wasteful." (37)

The method is said to work for personality disorders and neurotics, but also for psychotics who do not have primarily organic disorders. In many of these cases, no method works well but Ellis thinks Rational Therapy is usually the most effective method. The psychiatrist, Aaron Beck, in his book, *Depression,* presents a similar view. (cf. Chapter on Beck)

Although clarification of concepts is essential for therapy Ellis realizes that it is a difficult task. He states,

"I am fairly well convinced [of] the inherent biological limitations of a human organism to think straight, and especially to think clearly and logically about his own behavior, for any consistent length of time." (238)

"Concerted and consistent focusing on *any* life problem is itself difficult for the average human being." (399)

In his experience as therapist, Ellis found that females, especially, tend to become depressed, panicked, hostile or emotionally disturbed. (412) In a marital relationship it may be healthful if the husband be aware of this possible tendency so as to be able to accept and adjust to it.

Ellis presents what he has found in his practice, ten of the most common irrational ideas or "philosophies" which tend to lead to negative emotion, self-defeat, and neurosis:

1) "The idea that one has virtually no control over one's emotions and that one cannot help feeling certain things — instead of the idea that one has enormous control over one's emotions if one chooses to work at controlling them and to practice saying the right kinds of sentences to oneself."

As was indicated, because emotions are seen to be assessments, emotions can be changed by changing the assessments. Perhaps the greatest block to therapy and mental health is the view that emotions cannot be changed or can be changed only slightly. The prevalent notion that emotions are fixed in us by nature is a mistaken justification for retaining one's anger and other negative emotions. Ellis' view thus revolutionizes popular views of emotion, and opposes Freudian and non-cognitive theories which stress 'releasing emotions," as if the latter were fluids dammed up, rather than being mainly irrational statements leading to negative feelings. His view is that when one becomes angry or engages in physical therapy it is not a release of emotion which is being accomplished, but, rather, if the therapy succeeds in getting at the cause, it is because the patient is reassessing his irrational thinking.

2) "The idea that it is a dire necessity for an adult to be loved or approved by everyone for everything he does — instead of his concentrating on his own self-respect, on winning approval for necessary purposes (such as job advancement), and on loving rather than being loved."

The basis for this and many of the following statements may be found in stoic philosophy according to which a) we can only do and be responsible for that which is within our power and so should not try or expect to do more or blame ourselves for not doing more, b) we should be realistic in regard to our abilities and expectations, c) we should avoid negative emotions for they serve no useful purpose and are self-defeating.

In this case, it is not within one's power to make everyone or many like him. Also it is unrealistic to believe that everyone or many will or could like him. It is, however, within one's power to love others. This ability to love, incidentally, will depend upon how rational one is and how clear one is about how emotions work.

3) "The idea that certain acts are wrong, or wicked, or villainous, and that people who perform such acts should be severely punished — instead of the idea that certain acts are inappropriate or antisocial, and that people who perform such acts are invariably stupid, ignorant or emotionally disturbed."

This was presented earlier in terms of the philosophical clarification of ethical and value terms. One of the consequences of the failure to inquire into and clarify ethical terms is negative emotion and neurosis. These irrational ideas are also ways of becoming captivated by a model or metaphor. Metaphor captivation is an expansion of Ellis' view that they are "definitional." (See chapter on metaphorical method of therapy.)

What Ellis calls irrational ideas may be referred to, in terms of contemporary ordinary-language philosophy, as language-games, category-mistakes or naming-fallacies. Ellis mentions a few of such devices but there is an endless number. There are defense-mechanisms, logical fallacies, misleading analogies, metaphors, and uses of language. (See chapters on these devices.) Ethical terms are frequently misuses of language. Ellis seems to appropriately reduce ethical terms, in the above example, to empirical considerations of consequences. This is in agreement with the theory that ethical terms are elliptical open-context terms not a separate realm of metaphysical value. Thus it makes no sense to say something is bad in itself (to blame or criticize). The following ideas are also irrational because of the reasons given earlier.

4) "The idea that it is terrible, horrible, and catastrophic when things are not the way one would like them to be."

5) "The idea that much human happiness is externally caused and is forced on one by outside people and events — instead of the idea that virtually all human unhappiness is caused or sustained by the view one takes of things rather than the things themselves."

Many Liberationists often commit this fallacy by blaming their upbringing, men, or the environment for their unhappiness, whereas by their negative emotions they are degrading mankind. This is not to say that both men and women have not been unfairly discriminated against. It is to say that negative emotion is self-defeating, not a way to solve problems, and is something that is caused by man rather than mainly by his environment.

6) "The idea that if something is or may be dangerous or fearsome one should be terribly concerned about it — [rather] one should frankly face it and try to render it non-dangerous . . . and stop telling oneself what a terrible situation one is or may be in."

7) "The idea that it is easier to avoid them than to face life difficulties and self-responsibilities instead of the idea that the so-called easy way is invariably the much harder way in the long run and that the only way to solve difficult problems is to face them squarely."

8) "The idea that one needs something other or stronger or greater than oneself on which to rely — instead of the idea that it is usually far better to stand on one's own feet and gain faith in oneself and one's ability to meet difficult circumstances of living."

Relevant to this, the following is presented by Albert Ellis in his article, "The Case Against Religion." Religion is seen to be a faith not founded on fact, a belief in a superhuman power to be worshipped, etc. He finds religion to be "pernicious . . . for virtually all the commonly accepted goals of emotional health are antithetical to a truly religious viewpoint." He finds that the religious person is masochistic and denies himself, is unable to be independent and self-sufficient, is intolerant due to his absolute beliefs, is usually blindly obedient, is unable to truly accept himself insomuch as he believes that one is guilty from birth and a sinner and so deserving of severe punishment, dehumanizes himself by belief in an inhuman absolute law, by damning himself and others creates emotional disorder, dishonestly imagines absolutes and perfection instead of facing the risk of imperfection and chance which daily confront us, does not allow for intellectually and emotionally necessary flexibility, lacks inquiry and openness because of a belief in absolute truth, is thus "bigoted." The religious person by accepting an absolute moral code based on "authority" is prevented from using this intelligence to decide what in fact is right or wrong, harmful or beneficial. The religious person is unscientific. Science and religion are in significant conflict. Ellis states,

"Religious commitment tends to be a) obsessive-compulsive, motivated by anxiety and dire need rather than joy-giving desire; b) opposed to other beneficial commitments, such as to sex-love relations, to science or to art; c) guilt-ridden or hostile; d) based on falsehoods and illusions (e.g., rewards in heaven and punishments in hell) and therefore easily shatterable and prone to cause severe disillusionment; and e) fanatical and over-compensatory, masking the individual's underlying feelings of extreme inadequacy."

"True believers in just about *any* kind of orthodoxy — whether it be religious, political, social, or even artistic orthodoxy — tend to be distinctly disturbed, since they are obviously rigid, fanatic, and dependent individuals . . . Religiosity, in my estimation, is another name for narrow-mindedness, emotional disturbance, or neurosis. Or, in some extreme cases, psychosis."

Ellis here takes a humanistic view of religion but stresses some of the effects he has found of religious beliefs. There are of course, many who would argue with him.

9) "The idea that one should be thoroughly competent, adequate, intelligent, and achieving in all possible respects — instead of the idea that one should *do* rather than always try to do *well* and that one should accept oneself as a quite imperfect creature, who has general human limitations and specific fallibilities."

The idea that one must be perfect seems often to lead to suicide and depression due to failure to reach the unrealistic goal of perfection.

10) "The idea that because something once strongly affected one's life, it should indefinitely affect it — instead of the idea that one should learn from one's past experiences but not be overly-attached to or prejudiced by them."

The American pragmatist, John Dewey, emphasized that one's beliefs (values) must be constantly reexamined so as to be relevant and appropriate to changing circumstances. To retain a belief because it is what one learned in childhood from one's parents, because it is familiar or because it is traditional is to commit the informal fallacy of argument from tradition or argument from authority. One may similarly commit the fallacy of argument based merely on what the majority of people think. One must, as Nietzsche said, constantly, carefully and honestly inquire and by so doing one goes beyond tradition and the majority views, one transcends good and evil.

Sources:

Marcus Aurelius *The Meditations* G. Long, trans., New York: Doubleday (No date given)

Aaron Beck *Depression* University of Pennsylvania Press 1967

Errol Bedford "Emotions" *Proceedings of the Aristotelian Society* 56 (1955-6)

Albert Ellis *Humanistic Psychotherapy: the rational-emotive approach* New York: Julian Press 1973

Albert Ellis "Rational Psychotherapy" *Psychopathology Today*, W. Sahakian, ed., Illinois: Peacock Publishers 1970

Albert Ellis *Reason and Emotion in Psychotherapy* New York: Lyle Stuart 1962

Albert Ellis "The Case Against Religion" *Mensa Journal* no. 138, Sept. 1970

Theodore Sarbin "Imaging as Muted Role-Taking: A Historical-Linguistic Analysis" *The Function and Nature of Imagery* P. Sheehan, ed. New York: Academic Press 1972

Warren Shibles "Linguo-Centric Predicament," "Ethics as Open-Context Terms" *Philosophical Pictures* Dubuque, Iowa: Kendall-Hunt 1971

Warren Shibles *Metaphor: An Annotated Bibliography and History* Whitewater, Wisconsin: The Language Press 1971

Ludwig Wittgenstein *Philosophical Investigations* 3rd edition, G. Anscombe, trans., New York: Macmillan 1958 (1968)

A. I. Melden's Contextual Theory of Emotion

The need for the clarification of the nature of emotion is seen to be as critical in philosophy as in other areas:

"The whole subject of feeling has been very badly mismanaged in philosophy. And it is scandalous that those who write in moral philosophy and in the philosophy of taste take little or no pain to get clear about what for them is a matter of fundamental importance." (209-210)

According to the ordinary-language philosopher, A. I. Melden (1969), emotion is not a single entity, an internal state or feeling. He gives a superb account of emotions.

"We do not speak of *having* an anger as we do of having a pain . . . It is in fact at least a very queer way of speaking to say that one has a feeling of anger . . . Unlike the case in which, when one feels pain, the pain is the feeling that one has when one feels it, there is no simple or single feeling one has such that feeling anger consists in having it and nothing else." (205)

When we are angry we need not know that we have certain bodily feelings, and such feelings are not necessary or sufficient to determine the emotion. Melden even points out that one may even enjoy anger. Also anger shades into other emotions. The point he is making is that emotions are not just feelings but rather also include circumstances or contexts the person is in. In this sense, feelings are often rather irrelevant to emotions. He agrees with E. Bedford that emotions are not just internal states but opposes his view that feelings need not at all be involved.

91

"No account of feeling does justice to the facts except by reference not only to bodily states but also to the ways in which, in thought and in action, those who feel emotions deal with the matters that confront them." (210)

"No account of anger is adequate unless it recognizes the pertinence of the situation." (213)

"Any general account that ignores the details of circumstances and situation may mislead." (219)

One of the reasons why Melden stresses context is that what we ordinarily mean by an emotion includes the context, people, and situation involved. If emotions are regarded merely as physical states or internal feeling, we would not be able to understand what is usually meant by them:

"The trouble . . . lies . . . in the attempt to find the essence of anger — the necessary and sufficient conditions for its presence — in some internal factor, in total abstraction from the situation in which the emotion occurs." (213)

"And it is because of this background understanding we do have of human beings that learning that a person is angry sometimes does enable us to interpret his actions — to see more clearly the patterns of anger in what might otherwise appear to be altogether innocent or puzzling conduct." (218)

This last statement may, if expanded, suggest that one can tell a great deal about a person's *thought* by means of his emotions. If a person is angry we know something about how he cannot cope with his emotions, and that things are not going well for his mental life and perhaps also for his environmental situation.

Because context is part of the meaning of an emotion, the emotion cannot be reduced to a single factor or context.

"There is no single paradigm, but typical cases, varying from circumstances to circumstances and from situation to situation." (220)

Melden states this in a different way also, by regarding emotion terms as "cluster concepts." This is to say that emotion terms reduce to concrete paradigms but also to say that abstract terms must, for intelligibility, be reduced to concrete operations and objects. What is regarded as anger in one situation may in another circumstance be interpreted as love.

"What in one set of circumstances counts for anger, in another way will count for malice or jealousy." (219)

"Here nothing less than our status as rational and social beings in situations of enormously varying degrees of complexity — as the whole human beings that we are — must be invoked in order to provide any reasonably adequate account of the role of emotions in our lives." (221)

Because of the diversity of contexts and situations and the few terms we have for emotions, metaphor and symbol are often used. One characteristic of metaphor is that it can serve to unite a number of diverse contexts, and does so. Metaphor can allow one to say things which can be said in no other way. A situation can often be described best by means of metaphor. Poets mean to include more in their metaphors than merely internal feelings.

Most of our terms for emotion involve metaphors. We speak of it in terms of water, such as, the "gush of emotion," the "flow of emotion," and "release emotion," as if it were water in a dam. Metaphors may also be used to express emotions. Internal states and subjective experience are often rendered by metaphors because of the inaccessibility to the senses of such states. The danger here is of taking our metaphors literally and creating entities where there are none, such as in the case of thinking we have a mind, id, ego, superego, imagination or other entitative faculties. On the other hand, metaphor can give insight to emotions by combining words, and contexts which do not usually go together. This juxtaposition suggests new connotations of the emotion situation not usually noticed.

"To apply 'a heavy heart' to someone is thus to intimate far more than a characterization of bodily movement; it is rather to intimate something of the special character of his feelings and experiences as he goes about affairs in which, normally, these feelings do not occur at all." (209)

"Our vocabulary of feeling words is quite poor; hence the use of similies." (209)

"To be told what such feelings are like . . . is to be told something of the way in which one views and responds with horror to a situation in one's life, and in a life of a certain kind at that." (209)

We are not sure what is going on inside us when we have an emotion so we may think that it is only bodily feeling. Melden states that there is more going on than that but that we don't know what more, thus his previous stress on metaphor, though he does not mention metaphor or have a theory of metaphor. But one candidate for what might be going on is that when we have an emotion there is thinking-plus-feeling, and by "thinking" is meant largely using language such as talking silently to oneself. Images and bodily actions and habits may also form a part of the emotion but the verbal assessment is often central. The assessment is usually that which brings about the emotion (feeling) in the first place. On Melden's view, however, it is not that the assessment is first, but that it is part of what we mean by emotion.

"He remains calm and quiet and gives no inkling of the anger he feels; yet he *is* angry, so there must be something going on. And what on earth can this be? Here we are likely to have recourse to bodily events . . . but just what events these are that are present whenever and *only* whenever one is angry, no one knows."

Melden sometimes does seem to suggest that language may be a significant aspect of emotions:

"There are emotion terms that require for their intelligible application . . . their use in sentences in order to impute responsibility, to praise or blame, or to assess the moral quality of an agent or his conduct." (216)

An emotion is not a single atomistic event taking place in a brief duration of time.

"It would make no sense to suppose that his love or his grief or his playing chess are complete and entire in a relatively brief moment in the way in which this is true of his pain or even of his fear or his anger." (215)

One reason why one can only apply emotion terms to humans and not animals is that distinctively human contexts are implied by such terms. Emotion terms presuppose human memory, human understanding, or in other words, human language.

"The emotional life of animals is limited in both character and range." (214)

"Not even joy or sorrow could be significantly ascribed to an animal, whose life is limited to its responses to what is given to it immediately and directly." (215)

"The terms 'shame,' 'guilt,' and 'remorse' do not apply to the offending pet caught in the act." (215)

"A dog . . . does not feel guilt or shame." (215)

Melden notes that one of the factors in emotion is value judgment, e.g., praise or blame. But it may be added that one reason why researchers have been slow to clarify the concept of emotion is that they have not had a clear idea of how ethical terms work. Emotion terms such as blame may be reduced to "X is bad," where "bad" is a value term. But "bad" is an open-context term only elliptical for some possible, but as yet to be specified substitution instances. "Bad" has no meaning in itself. The substitution instances are ultimately descriptive empirical statements involving wishes, likes, consequences in terms of beliefs, etc. Thus emotion terms are vague. Both ethical and emotion terms may be clarified by seeing that ethical terms are open-context terms with a loosely limited range of substitution instances.

Melden states that emotions often only make sense in the context of justification, approval, or appraisal. One cannot, for example, experience shame unless the shameful act involves censure. Also we often say that one should not or has no reason to be angry, jealous, guilty, etc., which suggests that emotions themselves can be judged and, what is more important, that they can be avoided.

"Emotions, no less than beliefs, actions and desires, are subject to appraisal as reasonable or unreasonable, justified or unjustified . . . It is essential to our concept of anger, the concept *we* employ with respect to human beings, that it be appraisable in these ways just as it is to our concept of belief and action. Whatever else anger may be, it cannot be an internal feeling or state conceptually unrelated to the functions of intelligence in the social circumstances in which it occurs." (216)

Because of the above analysis of emotions Melden opposes much of the work being done by psychologists. Emotions cannot be reduced to a) a few basic reactions as Watson suggests, b) internal physiological states, c) an atomistic cause-effect relation, d) dispositions to action (in opposition to the view of G. Ryle, 1949), e) drives, etc. Psychologists in their analyses usually presuppose emotions and emotion terms rather than clarify them.

"Psychologists who purport to discover the roots of anger in certain factors (whether the readiness to strike, aggression, hostility, or certain allegedly basic needs or drives), of whatever sorts these may be, cannot, without logical incoherence, identify the emotion with such factors. Indeed, both the formulation of their theories and the adducing of empirical evidence in support of them presuppose not only that the concept of anger cannot be elucidated in terms of these factors but also that this concept, in its everyday employment, is sufficiently clear and coherent to serve as a basis for empirical investigation." (213)

"Various attempts to formulate explanations in terms of drives or tendencies of one sort or another do not appear to me to be auspicious steps in the search for fundamental laws." (221)

Melden's view of emotions can be made more clear if related to his theory of human action. Emotions have been regarded as involving total situations, cluster concepts:

"Here nothing less than our status as rational and social beings in situations of enormously varying degrees of complexity — as the whole human beings that we are — must be invoked in order to provide any reasonably adequate account of the role of emotions in our lives." (221)

In his book, *Free Action* (1964), Melden maintains that "action" is a term which covers both cause and effect, and describes generally a total configuration of events. It is not acceptable to say a certain mental event causes us to act. We never discover such an event. Descriptions such as "The feeling I have when raising my arm, causes me to raise my arm," are circular because they presuppose the action, and the feeling is only knowable and describable in terms of the action. An action is not just a single event. Thus intention, desire, wish, willing, motive are not single events, especially of a mental sort, but are more like actions or activities. An intention, for example, includes the entire history of an event. (cf. W.

Shibles "Intention") The basic units in speaking of human actions may be summarized by the following list of terms. Melden, in an attempt to give an account of so-called "mental events" and human action, defends the view that the terms in the right column are more appropriate to humans than those in the left column:

Physical events	Human Action
happening	doing
event	action
cause	reason
thing	person
mental-occurence	circumstance
technical language	ordinary language
law-like	categorical

An action is said to be a configuration of events which includes both cause and effect describing people acting for certain reasons in ordinary circumstances. How one performs the action of raising his arm has to do with language and reasons, etc., not just a mental event causing a thing to happen. The answer to "How do I raise my arm," is not simply, "My sensations advised me to do it," or "A mental act caused it to happen." "Action" includes all the factors in the situation and seems to act as a "cluster concept." Melden gives the following example:

"In order that one might predict that the person will raise his arm in order to give the signal, one needs not only a knowledge of the central nervous system and of the appropriate stimulation of the end-organs, but also of the circumstances in which the agent − not the bodily mechanism − is placed and of what, in these circumstances, he will do. We need to know, in short, that we have an agent, a motorist, who is driving and whose action of raising the arm is to be understood in terms of the appropriate rule of the road as a cause of signalling a turn as the crossroad comes into view." (*Free Action* 209, 210)

Melden's theory of emotion coheres with his theory of human action. Both appear to be cluster concepts not atomistically analyzable into traditional cause and effect relations. Thus while other cognitive theorists, such as A. Beck (1967), speak of assessment causing feeling, Melden speaks of emotion as a configuration of diverse experiential factors.

Although Melden's attack on mentalistic states is well-founded, it seems to be argued at the expense of the method of cause and effect. Certainly some descriptions of actions are circular, but this does not mean that there is no way to specify a number of causes for a certain action. (See W. Shibles "Free Will," and "Are All Statements Circular.") Melden seems to agree to the extent that he accepts reasons as causes. It would, however, seem possible in the future to give all of the causes for one's performing an action. But Melden is certainly correct in seeing that an action, as we usually understand it, is not always a single, atomistic event and so cannot be regarded in simple cause and effect terms. There does, however, seem to be no reason why an action or emotion cannot be regarded as elliptical for a number of specific linguistic and other events which may be treated in terms of cause-effect, or stimulus-response. Cause and effect do not exist in reality but it is we who see reality in terms of the concepts of cause and effect. It is up to us if we wish to view events in terms of cause and effect. We can merely do so. In opposition to Melden's view, we can apply cause and effect to human actions. Thus behaviorism, if adequate, that is, if it includes linguistic, imagistic, motor and other factors, could possibly analyze action as well as emotion. This would be in line with the view that all abstract terms should be reduced to concrete operations, objects, or events.

Are emotions causes? If they are not singular or internal entities they are not causal entities. Insofar as emotion is a fiction it is not a cause. They may however be causes in a general or metaphorical sense, as is "depression," in "The economic depression brought on an uprising."

"He boasts because he is vain," erroneously ascribes a cause. Also the statement is circular. "He did it because of fear," seems to make fear a cause, first the fear then the action. A clearer way of putting this is that we first assess and then act. The feeling involved does not make one do anything but may be a factor in the assessment. "He did it out of fear," may be a reason rather than a cause.

In some cases an emotion may be a cause in the sense that a habit is a cause. This is a dispositional, if-then, sort of cause. "He stole the money because he is a thief," is only to say he habitually steals and so could be expected to steal. He could, however, change his habit and it is not contradictory to say, "He is a thief but did not steal the money." Similarly one may say, "He laughed because he is a jovial person."

William James suggests that behavior causes emotions whereas, on the assessment theory, assessment causes feelings resulting in a complex pattern called emotion. Beliefs determine emotions. In some cases feelings themselves are assessed and so may be thought of as the object of assessment rather than as the cause. Feelings in themselves are neutral until assessed. Assessment involves deciding what to do and then doing it. One cannot "feel" pride in doing a task unless he has assessed and taken part in the task.

Emotion is not a cause of one's emotional problems and so the advice to let the emotions have an outlet is misconceived. Faulty assessments or lack of coordination between feeling and assessment cause problems. Emotions are not outlets of problems but "causes" of new problems.

Primarily it is we ourselves who cause emotions. It is not the case that an angry man makes us angry, but rather that we allow ourselves to be made angry. We make ourselves angry. "I became sad," is rather "I created my own sadness."

There is, however, a partially contingent relation between the causal assessment and the feeling induced. One can lose a battle and laugh. We can look for the symptoms and causes of anger and cure ourselves of anger.

Sources:

Aaron Beck *Depression* University of Pennsylvania Press 1967

A. I. Melden "The Conceptual Dimensions of Emotions" *Human Action* T. Mischel, ed. New York: Academic Press 1969

A. I. Melden *Free Action* New York: Humanities Press 1964

Gilbert Ryle *Concept of Mind* New York: Barnes & Noble 1949

Warren Shibles "Free Will," "Are All Statements Circular" *Philosophical Pictures* 2nd edition, Dubuque, Iowa: Kendall-Hunt 1971

Warren Shibles "Intention" *Wittgenstein, Language and Philosophy* Dubuque, Iowa: Kendall-Hunt 1970

Classification of Emotions

INTRODUCTION

There is no agreed upon classification of emotions. This is partly due to the fact that there is no agreed upon theory of emotions. Recent statements about classification are indicated in the following statements.

"The words 'emotion' and 'sensation' do not stand for clear-cut classifications, nor is there a clear-cut concept of object which enables us to establish the lines between them." (Gosling 1965)

"Individual philosophers and psychologists have differed widely over the contents of their lists of emotions." (White p. 124)

The 1950 Mooseheart Symposium published in *Feelings and Emotions* was devoted entirely to a study of emotions. One reviewer concluded about it:

"The total impression of the book is that we are still far from a solution; — we do not even have a consensual definition of feelings and emotions." (Zinkin p. 91)

One of the most recent psychological dictionaries states:

"Emotion is virtually impossible to define . . . except in terms of conflicting theories." (English 1958)

Edward Titchener wrote,

"The words which denote emotions are neither sufficiently numerous nor sufficiently delicate for psychological purposes: they are rough, general names, carrying different side-meanings to different minds. Hence it is not likely that any two psychologists would make up series . . . in precisely the same terms." (p. 232)

R. Plutchik states that the three main types of theory of emotion deal with 1) introspection, b) behavior or overt expression, c) physiology or neurology. (p. 24) But another way of conceiving of theories is in terms of models. The models usually given only apply to some of the factors involved in metaphor as if they include all the factors. Such models may be regarded as metaphors or hypotheses of a heuristic sort rather than as adequate descriptions.

The following definitions are from *Webster's Seventh New Collegiate Dictionary* (Etymology from Kline's *Comprehensive Etymological Dictionary*):

affect (L. to do) "The conscious subjective aspect of an emotion considered apart from bodily changes." This statement stresses the assessment aspect of emotion.

affection "A moderate feeling or emotion; tender attachment; the feeling aspect of consciousness." By "gender attachment" is meant a positive assessment or regard. It is suggested that feeling may accompany all statements (i.e., consciousness). When descriptive of feeling the term affection points to its moderateness. Thus the term applies to feelings or emotions but not in the same way.

temper (L. to mix in due proportion) "A characteristic case of mind or state of feeling, calmness of mind, state of feeling or frame of mind at a particular time, heat of mind or emotion, proneness to anger." The terms used here are vague and mentalistic. They stress a temporary or permanent feeling, or pattern of behavior.

temperament "The peculiar or distinguishing mental or physical character determined by the relative proportions of the humors according to medieval physiology, characteristic or habitual inclination or mode of emotional response, extremely high sensibility, esp. excessive sensitiveness or irritability." The stress here is on habitual action and behavior, ease of arousal, and irritability.

temperamental "Excessive sensitivity and impulsive changes of mood."

sentiment (L. to perceive by the senses, to feel) "An attitude, thought, or judgment prompted by feeling; refined feeling, delicate sensibility, emotional idealism, a romantic or nostalgic feeling verging on sentimentality, an idea colored by emotion, the emotional significance of a passage or expression as distinguished from its verbal context." This would be an instance of feeling preceding assessment, but the emotion term includes reference to both.

mood (ME. mode, mood, OE. mind, intellect, heart, courage) "A conscious state of mind or predominant emotion, a prevailing attitude, pervasive and compelling quality of the emotion." This definition stresses cognition. "Attitude" is defined as "a feeling or emotion toward a fact or state." This commits the fallacy of thinking a feeling can be toward or about something. Rather a feeling is just had or experienced. The definition may merely be using feeling metaphorically and, if so, it is still misleading because it is not clear that it is intended to be so used. It sounds odd to speak of "emotion toward a fact or state." The feeling part of emotion is not toward anything, though the assessment can concern itself with facts and states. Mood seems to be primarily a relatively fixed way of viewing facts and states, which guides assessment which in turn guides feelings.

desire (L. to feel the want of, long for) "To long or hope for, desire emphasizes strength of feeling and often implies strong intention."

grief "An emotional suffering caused by or as if by bereavement [loss]." This calls attention to the value assessment regarding the loss of someone or something and the resulting negative or painful feelings.

envy "Painful or resentful awareness of an advantage enjoyed by another joined with a desire to possess the same advantage, an object of envious notice of feeling." This describes an assessment of a situation, involves a desire and may involve feelings.

What is seen about the above definitions is that they are often circular, e.g., affection is defined as an emotion and emotion as an affection. The definitions confuse feeling with emotion and presuppose mentalism and unfounded theories of mind.

Emotion terms are in part explanatory, descriptive and elliptical. The terms refer to various combinations of sensation (feeling), action, situation or context, and greatly diverse sorts of assessment. Emotion terms alone do not adequately represent emotions. Rather sentences and phrases are required. It would be more appropriate to speak of emotional life (a "form of life") than emotion terms.

Each emotion term occurs in various grammatical forms. We speak of love, a loving person, loving, lovely, lovable, loved, etc. Emotion involves an experience. A distinction must be made between a first person report or experience of an emotion and a second or third person report of an emotion. The evidence for "I love," is not the same as the evidence for "He loves." This involves the problem of "other minds," or more appropriately, "other emotions." Words like "charm" designate or describe the process of arousing emotion, whereas "charmed" names the experience. One may urge another or feel urged. Many terms not usually classified as emotions nevertheless involve emotion. "Argue" usually connotes emotion whereas "discuss" does not. "Conflict" also suggests emotion. "Want," "like," "strive," "try," also suggest emotions. These are examples of assessments which guide feelings. *Webster's New Collegiate* states that desire "emphasizes strength of feeling" whereas a want is a "felt need or lack." This talk of "feeling a need" opens up a whole range of possible emotions.

If it is possible to say "I feel X," then perhaps X may be regarded as an emotion or as associated with an emotion if X is not a feeling or sensation. Feelings, of course, would be involved unless feeling is used metaphorically. Although "I feel X," where X is an emotion, is a category-mistake because it suggests that X is a feeling, the formula nevertheless serves as a guide to locate emotion or emotion related terms. The following are a few examples:

"I feel lonely."
"I feel secure."
"I feel dressed-up."
"I feel independent."
"I feel left-out."
"I feel that is correct."

These appear to be assessments which guide feelings. That is, there are feelings associated with the beliefs and descriptions. It would be more accurate to say "I experience X," than to say "I feel X," when X is an emotion. "I feel X," or "I sense X," may be reserved for feelings and sensations.

Descriptions, and expressions of emotion often involve metaphor in everyday discourse as well as in philosophical and literary creation of emotions. The following are some examples:

It makes my blood boil, it rubs me the wrong way, sore, unfeeling, warm person, cold person, darling, steel nerves, cold feet, to be undone, sheepish, jumpy, yellow, fall for, lose one's heart to, treasured, blow one's top, etc. Often, or even usually, the only way to describe feelings, emotion, and character is by use of metaphor. Metaphor describes internal states which cannot be seen or touched and because language is intersubjective we use terms usually used for observable objects, e.g., sharp pain, dull pain. Metaphor also lets a concrete term represent a large number of diverse factors thus unifying them, e.g., she is a warm person, he is an ace. It also can serve as a hypothetical model by means of which one may gain insight into an emotion or person, e.g., one may complete the sentence "X is Y," by substituting an emotion or person for X and a metaphorical term for Y. An example is, "Love is hate, when one has one of these there is trembling in the other." One often says, "I feel like such and such," e.g., "I feel like a slave," "I feel like my leg is filled with soda-water," "I feel like I'm on a cloud." A description of a situation may be enough to suggest that emotions or feelings are present. That is, there are emotion producing situations.

The following four aspects are involved in emotion: Sensation (or feeling), action, situation, assessment. Emotions are here classified according to which factor is stressed. All emotions fall into all or most of the following categories.

SENSATION OR FEELING

"Feel" and "sense" are used here as properly or literally referring to sensations. Other uses are regarded as metaphorical. "Feels" in "He feels pain," means something different than "I feel pain," because the descriptive constituents and criteria differ. It was mentioned that metaphor is often used to describe "internal" (itself a metaphor) states and sensations. We have no clear description of inner private states because our language itself is intersubjective and because the states themselves are difficult to distinguish. "Private" is applied metaphorically to inner states. What is private in this case cannot be made public as other private matters can. Sensation suggests specific sense organs whereas feeling refers most properly to touch or internal or general states. We do not literally say, "I feel a ringing." Visual perception is not a feeling but is a sensation. We do not say "I feel brown," or ask, "What does seeing feel like?" "Outer" sensations may be those referring to sensations derived from objects outside of the body, e.g., tactile, auditory, visual sensations. If these sensations are imagined they become images or internal sensations. Sensations associated with the body of a general or specific sort are internal sensations, e.g., aches, pain, tranquility, feelings, general joyous feelings, feelings of well-being, calmness, nervousness, tension, warmth, pang, itch, twinge. Some of these terms, such as pain, can be internal or external, specific, or general. Because they can also be metaphorical there are a number of quite different uses of the same term. As can be seen, sensations rarely ever come neat or alone. They involve associations of all sorts including assessments, e.g., the terms: savor, erotic, uneasy, tense, giddy, cheerful, excitement, delight, joy, thrill, passionate, amorous, distaste, tickle. Many emotion terms, such as these, stress the feeling or sensation aspect. Often the feeling of a sensation term is derived from the description of the object or activity involved with it, e.g., "The sensation of moving my arm," is described in terms of moving my arm.

Specific sensations have quality, amount, and duration. Generalized feelings may be less distinct, e.g., a specific pain is more "sharp" or distinct than a feeling of well-being. One of the reasons is that such terms include a great number of feelings as well as assessments. Thus a feeling of well-being or happiness does not end at 2:01 on Saturday, though it may well gradually come to an end. (See other sections on feeling, imagery, perception.)

ACTION

Emotion terms are often assessments which include descriptions of action or imagined action, e.g., jealousy, rage. The action may be one's own or that of another. Descriptions of others' emotions are usually based on actions performed. This includes behavioral and even physiological and physical concomitants of emotions. But emotions cannot be reduced solely to such physiological or physical aspects. Besides including descriptions or references to actions, emotion terms may refer to assessments which guide or lead to actions. These terms are classified under assessment (IV). The following classification of emotions is only of descriptions of actions of others or oneself. The terms could be used in the first person case, however, as in "I feel cheerful," as opposed to "I am cheerful." Some of the following actions are only distantly associated with emotion:

1) behavioral traits, manners, or disposition. (cheerful, aloof, blushing, rage, withdrawn, strut, nervous, startled, sulk, kindness, sigh, huff, pose, affected, mean, loving, flighty, crying)

2) facial "expressions." (grimace, smile, scowl, frown, shamefaced, laugh, giggle, chuckle, sneer)

3) linquistic "expression." (intonations, acerbity, outburst, "growl," "snap")

4) passivity. (stupor, dispassionateness, apathy, hesitation, shyness)

5) caused actions. (annoy, excite, ridicule, frustrate, shy, loved, irritated, aroused, moved)

6) approach or retreat. (aversion, repression, hostile, temper tantrum, withdrawn, love, hate, repulsion, set, preparedness)

7) degree of action. (May also include degree of feeling.) (rage, fury, passionate, apathetic, terror, panic, emotional, sensitive, greed, bitter, acerbity, incensed, hot-headed, vitriolic, stirred, chagrin. Characteristics of neurosis and psychosis may be added)

108

SITUATION OR CONTEXT

Emotion terms often imply objects or events such that the emotion makes no sense without reference to them. Assessments of situations are included under assessments, e.g., to love is to love someone or something, to feel patriotic involves one's country, to be courageous involves some deed. Jealousy involves fear or anger regarding an event or object. A situation or object may be regarded as emotion-producing but assessment is needed for them to actually produce emotion. The situation must be perceived, understood, or regarded in a certain way. A child may not naturally fear snakes but may learn to fear them later in life.

1) emotions involving objects or events. (phobias, patriotism, envy, lamentation, grief, *Weltschmerz*, avarice, greed, zest for life, or joy of life)

2) emotions not involving objects or events. (moods, dispositional emotion terms, class concepts of emotions, anxiety, happiness, depression, sadness)

3) emotions involving people. (grief, pity, gratitude, appreciation, sympathy, contempt, embarrassment)

4) temporal factors.
   a) duration. (patience, worry, anguish)
   b) change. (moody, sensitive, ruth)
   c) past. (remorse, regret, revenge, reminiscence, resentment)
   d) present or sudden. (alarm, fright, shock, surprise, impetuosity, asperity or quick temper)
   e) future. (anticipate, hope, desire, long for, anxious)

ASSESSMENTS

By "assessments" is meant statements we make aloud or silently to ourselves. All emotions involve assessments. This definition reduces the vague terms "thought," "idea," "belief," "intention," "cognition," etc. to concrete elements accessible to observational and scientific analysis. The evidence for speech is public. The evidence for speaking to oneself is subjective but has indirect evidence and intersubjective agreement. One can say to himself silently, "I love her," or "I am a bad person." Emotion is intricately bound up with such language. Feelings and sensations become associated with such statements. For example, conflicting statements often lead to undesirable feelings. Emotions may be descriptions which are accompanied by, or cause feelings.

1) perceptual or sensation judgments. (All feelings and sensations involve assessment of the feeling or perception of an object or situation. To some extent, assessments may also alter the sensation feeling. The degree of alteration is marked by certain types of diagnosis or classification given in psychiatry, e.g., psychosomatic, psychic blindness, anesthesias, frigidity, etc. Where one could ordinarily feel sensation it is no longer experienced. This is often due to confused and conflicting beliefs.)

2) value judgments.

    a) good. (pleasure, delight, joy, beauty, love, predilection, superiority ("better"), like, patriotism, pride, admiration, gratitude, appreciation enthusiasm)

    b) bad. (depression, contempt, inferiority (worse), hate, guilt, intolerance, shame, humiliation, despise)

    c) obligation. (loyalty, devotion)

    d) justification. (right or wrong) (guilt, shame, righteousness, indignant)

3) Order of assessment and feeling.

    a) assessment precedes feeling. (most emotions and attitudes)

    b) feeling coexists with assessment. (shock, sympathy, pity, compassion)

    c) assessment follows feeling. (sentiment, hangover, "feel bad," misery, agony, torment) Often the feeling involved is itself assessed.

4) emotions about emotions. An emotion may be assessed resulting in a new emotion. One may become angry because he often becomes embarrassed, or hate himself for his jealousy. These are assessments of emotions which guide feelings, e.g., fearing fear, fearing embarrassment, fearing love. One may fall in love with love itself. Feeling repressed may involve negative feelings resulting from one's assessment of his inability to express or clarify his thoughts

which are causing tension. Another word for this is emotional frustration. This is one form of mixed emotion.

Is consciousness of emotion on a different level than having an emotion? "I am conscious of my emotions." But suppose someone were to say, "We have all the human emotions but don't know it, and may never be conscious of many of them." If this were the case it would not make any difference. Statements such as "I am angry," "I am aware of being angry," "Anger is an emotion," are all on the same level in the sense that they are all language-games. To be self-conscious implies, at times, wondering what another person thinks of him. No one language-game is the same as the other. It is not acceptable to say that for emotion to be emotion one must be conscious of it. This is because not all language-games need involve the single language-game of consciousness. This does not mean we are unconscious of emotions either, for "unconscious" is an obscure term. "I am angry," need not presuppose or involve the different statements "I am conscious that I am angry," or "I am not conscious that I am angry." Similarly, descriptions and explanations of emotions are on the same level as reports or expressions of emotion. That is to say, emotions cannot be reduced to explanations of emotions, although there are explanations of emotions. *Instead of speaking of "levels" of emotions one may speak of different language-games.* Consciousness may be thought of as taking a new metaphor or perspective, or seeing a situation in terms of a wide or long-range context.

"I have a hidden desire." This is not on a separate level than "I have a desire to go to Europe," but the two desires are different. "I have a hidden desire" might be like, "I do not know what I want." This does not mean there are "unconscious" wants.

"I wonder if I am jealous." This is a statement about wonder as well as about jealousy. But shouldn't one know if he is jealous? Quite often we do not know, yet we are said to be jealous. It depends on who is doing the describing. I may be jealous only as others see me, or only as I see myself. "I am jealous," is not on a different level, then, and does not reduce to, "I know I am jealous."

"Do I really love her?" Some say that if he asks the question he doesn't. But this is not a higher level statement about loving. It is a question. "I love you," is an assertion, although it is often used in diverse or obscure ways. "I love you," is not "I'm not sure I love you." Talk about emotions is not on a higher level but a different use of emotion terms. And feeling is not a low level emotion, or emotion a high level feeling. The case is similar with emotions about emotions. It is not higher level to hate pleasure, to enjoy hate, to love to love, or hate to hate.

5) epistemic or knowledge factors.

    a) degree of certainty. (stubbornness, doubting, trust, anxious, persuasive)

    b) possibility. (hope, suspicion)

    c) confusion, irrational thinking, or conflict. (wonder, awe, curiosity, interest, shock, irritation, anger, astonish, surprise, appalling, alarmed, fright, amaze, confused, befuddled, dazed, perplexed, stunned, flustered, agitated)

    d) understanding. (sympathy, pity, sensitivity, love as a form of new seeing or knowledge, compassion, attitudes, statements beginning with "I feel that .. ," patience, stubbornness) Philosophy derives from the Greek word for "love of truth and wisdom," or "desire for knowledge." Reason is desire for knowledge and may be thought of as an emotion.

6) intention, goals. (wants, needs, libido, motivation, desires, likes, hunger, thirst, lust, crave, envy, love, "feel like having or doing something," appetite (cf. "Will" or appetitive tendency.), revenge, ambition, avarice, relief, succeed, interest, confidence, eagerness, pretend, emotions of an actor, acting-out of a neurotic, urge, inclination, impulse, frustration.) Although "tendency," "appetite," were used to describe action without judgment, they do involve assessments of intentions. "Appetite" is usually more specific than "desire." Desire may involve more cognition than appetite. (See W. Shibles "Intention" *Wittgenstein, Language and Philosophy*)

7) language. The language categories, grammar, diction, metaphors, forms of words, etc., partly serve to limit what and how emotions are experienced and described. (See section on metaphor and emotion.) For example, we think and feel in terms of polar concepts such as love-hate, gratitude-ingratitude, affectionate-unaffectionate.

As a result of the previous discussion of emotion as the term is used in everyday language and life, and in accordance with the way emotions have been seen to be classified, a definition of emotion may now be given. It was just seen that emotion terms refer to sensations or feelings, actions, situations, and assessments. Some emotion terms stress some of these factors more than others. Emotions may be defined as rational assessments which guide feelings. This theory will be referred to as an assessment or cognitive theory of emotions. These terms need to be defined.

a. By "rational" or reason, is meant language use or saying things aloud or silently to oneself, or writing. Reason, thought, and ideas are synonyms. We have no evidence that there are thoughts or ideas as such. We do not catch an idea or see one. That we have ideas is based on the substance-quality doctrine, or mind-quality doctrine according to which we have a mind and we think with it, and that we have ideas in our minds. But there is no more evidence for a mental substance called "mind" than there is for ideas. "Ideas" were derived from atomism in the form of the principle of the association of ideas. It was thought that just as atoms are associated so also ideas are associated. This was called "mental chemistry." But again there was no evidence for these mental idea atoms. William James even spoke of a "stream of consciousness" instead of atomistic ideas. Reason, thought, ideas as mental entities are pseudo-psychological entities.

"Reason," "idea," "thought," have a great many uses in language and not merely the use of attempting to describe an internal entity of some sort. In examining the use of such terms it is seen that what we mainly mean by "He thinks well," "He reasons well," "He has a good mind," is not that he has mental processes and entities but rather that he speaks or writes well or has abilities such as being able to swim. Reason or thinking largely refers to language ability. We do not know what it would be like to have a wordless idea. All of this is to say that language, not thought or reason, has epistemological primacy. (See W. Shibles *Philosophical Pictures* for further support of this.) Thus to say that emotion is a rational assessment which guides feeling, is really to say that emotion is or reduces to linguistic formulations which guide feelings. This is exactly what the psychiatrist Albert Ellis (*J. of General Psychology* 1958) states when he says the emotional disorders are caused by repeating unintelligent things to oneself and that one should "practice saying the right kinds of sentences to oneself." The actual language used is extremely important in understanding and correcting "emotional disturbance." This is why communication is especially important in grief therapy and treatment of the dying patient.

b. By "assessment," is meant a description of the context and situation. Jealousy, for example, is not an internal feeling but largely a description of a situation. If someone says he is jealous we do not ask him how it feels, but about the situation. We say, "Tell me about it," "What happened?" or "Who got involved with whom?" That is, we ask about the context and the situation. "Jealousy" is a word which partly describes an assessment of a situation. It may or may not involve a feeling also. If feelings are involved they may be different every time one "feels" jealous. But because emotion is partly a description of a context or situation it is not just a feeling. It is thus a category-mistake to say "I feel x," where x is an emotion. One cannot feel jealous. One cannot feel grief. Emotions are not feelings. In opposition to the traditional view, emotion is not irrational but rather is largely constituted by reason. Emotion is reason. The statements one utters or writes may be true or false. Both true and false beliefs may induce negative feelings. Thus the rational or descriptive statements which go to make up an emotion may be true or false.

c. By "feeling" is meant such experiences as we refer to as "bodily feelings." They involve such concrete experiences as pain, warmth, tickles, nervousness, "butterflies" in one's stomach, the feeling of blood rushing to our cheeks, tenseness, etc. If one sees an unjust act he assesses the act as unjust and this may induce negative feelings in him such as that which accompanies increased blood pressure.

Although emotions are usually regarded here as assessments preceding feelings, two other cases were also mentioned. The feeling may come at the same time as the assessment. This may especially be the case with shock. If one has not thought in advance about the death of someone close to him he may experience surprise, confusion and negative bodily feelings at the same time and so experience shock. The third case is where the feeling comes before the assessment. This happens especially when the feeling itself is being assessed as in the case of illness, drunkenness, hangovers, tiredness, or reports of drug reactions.

Perhaps some of the above points may be expressed by the following "tale."

The King and the Cat: A Tale of the Passions

Consider the following statements made by the king:
1) "I fear the bear." (in the presence of a bear)
2) "I fear a possible revolution."
3) "I fear that I am mistaken."

In statement #1 the fear may be referred to as occurrent. It is an immediate response to danger. This expression may be replaced by the fear behavior of running away. Both king and cat may perform the same act. Instead of "I fear the bear," the king may utter "Watch out," and the cat a concerned "meow."

In statement #2 the king may be concerned with future events, possibilities, hopes. He may have emotions regarding governments, and entities cats can know nothing of. It would seem that cats cannot fear revolutions nor can they fear possible or future revolutions, for what is future time or any time to a cat? And without our language it cannot have the sorts of fears we have. It cannot hope, and perhaps cannot experience despair as can man. Not even church mice can have religious awe. We may refer to type #2 statements as dispositions or conceptual assessments.

To say "I fear a possible revolution," is not necessarily to report an internal state or feeling. One may instead have said, "I think there will be a revolution." One can fear a revolution without feeling anything. Or, stated differently, the king is here using the word "fear" metaphorically. It would be equally metaphorical (a "pathetic fallacy") to speak of the cat smiling as, for instance, Lewis Carroll's Cheshire cat. That the smile of his cat was all that was left after the cat disappeared may suggest how stereotyped, abstract and unfeeling a smile can be.

The king can assess in a way the cat cannot and so can have fears the cat cannot have. This is the price he must pay for being a king. It is the price one pays for consciousness especially if one misconceives or is ignorant of how to control one's emotions.

The cat cannot fear future death as we conceive of it, and this is a great price we pay for our consciousness. Wittgenstein asks (*Zettel* 518), "Why can a dog feel fear but not remorse? Would it be right to say 'Because he can't talk'?"

Schopenhauer pointed out that man is worse off than animals because with man's greater cognitive power goes greater susceptibility to pain. But knowledge of the future can be revised. It may be argued that time in itself is nothing. By time we mean only change of real objects such as the hands of a clock, or sand in an hourglass. In one respect such emotions as hope, or fear of the future are in reality fears of a real configuration of events (in the "present"). In this respect we may ask not only what is time to a cat, but what is time to a person, even if he is a king? Fear of future reduces to fear of present configuration of events, not fear of something "which has not yet happened." There is no time for it to happen in. The cat and the king, in this respect, may both live in a timeless though different world. In "I fear a possible revolution," "fear" may function as an evaluative term. The king suggests by it that it would be a bad thing if a revolution took place.

The third statement, "I fear that I am mistaken," again seems not to regard fear as an emotion word at all. He could have instead said, "I think that I am mistaken." "Fear" here may be used merely as a stylistic device suggesting much the same idea as does the word "mistaken." No one wishes to make a mistake. But no "fear" as such need be experienced. In this the king and the cat could agree if the cat could talk. Although, of course, a cat cannot be mistaken.

Plutarch (46-120 A.D.) regarded lust, anger, fear, etc. as perverse opinions and false judgments. This resulted in the view that animals have no passion. It was thought that because passion is a disorder or disregard of reason and since animals, including cats, do not have reason, they have no passions. But that was a long time ago.

The above analysis may be partially summarized by the words of C. D. Broad:

"This is just one more instance of the extreme complexity of human life and experience as compared with anything that occurs or could occur in animals. I take leave to doubt, for this reason among others, whether even an exhaustive study of the emotions of rats in mazes furnishes a very adequate or a very secure foundation for conclusions about the emotions and sentiments even of the quite ordinary human beings who pursue that study. To introspect carefully, to note sympathetically the talk and behavior of one's fellow-men in their intercourse with each other and with oneself; to read autobiographies and the novels of great novelists; and to study and to watch performances of the plays of great playwrights; these are the only effective ways of learning about emotion and sentiment in their specifically human forms."

Sources:

C.D. Broad "Emotion and Sentiment" Journal of Aesthetics and Art Criticism 13 (1954) 203-214

Physiology and Internal States

Early psychologists such as Wundt and Titchener assumed that one could introspect emotions. Contemporary phenomenologists and existentialists make the same assumption. But introspection assumes that there are internal states, in the mind-body tradition of Descartes. Such a view is unacceptable to both contemporary behaviorists and to the major writers on philosophical psychology such as Ryle and Wittgenstein. The approach used here will be that of regarding language rather than thought, emotion, or internal states as an epistemological starting point.

Perhaps one of the reasons why behavior is said not to be reducible to physiology and responses is that the behavior of language is inadequately taken into account. Buytendijk, for example, states,

"Behavior can never be reduced to physiological processes and explained as a result of the integration of reflexes."

Physiological psychologists may best present the status of their own research on emotions. Morgan in *Physiological Psychology* recently wrote,

"Relatively little is known about its [emotion] sensory or experience aspect because this has been difficult to study and to quantify," and "Because of all the patterns and shades of emotional *experience*, it has been very difficult to work with it scientifically or, more specifically, to understand its physiological basis."

One difficulty is that in order to correlate an emotion with a physiological event one must know what an emotion is. But since emotion is not just a physical response but involves a description of a situation one cannot find a correlate for the belief or description. Melden, Bedford and others have recognized this. Moreland Perkins states,

"It is the emotion as a whole that gets 'named,' not the bodily feeling which enters into it. Emotions get fixed as facts as a consequence of the abiding presence in language of common names for them."

A physiological correlate for an emotion would have to involve physiological correlates for our language and assessments as well. Emotions are not just fixed responses or internal states in a certain part of the body as in the case of visceral agitations. R. Drake (1954) wrote,

"There are no definite physiological patterns which serve to differentiate one emotion from another." (61)

Although psychologists do not seem to recognize the significant role language plays in behavior they are aware of their failure to find physiological correlates. B. F. Skinner (1953) wrote,

"In spite of extensive research it has not been possible to show that each emotion is distinguished by a particular pattern of responses of glands and smooth muscles," and "It has not been possible to specify given sets of expressive responses as characteristic of particular emotions, and in any case such responses are not said to *be* the emotion." He concludes, "As long as we conceive of the problem of emotion as one of inner states, we are not likely to advance a practical technology."

Psychologists instead of clarifying the concept of emotions or an emotion have tended to simply presuppose that there are emotions and then try to find an objective scientific physiological correlate for them. The procedure is question begging as well as inadequate. In a survey of psychological theories of emotion William Hunt states,

"As yet no psychologist can write an exact equation for the visceral responses in emotion, but every psychologist knows he will ruin his dinner if he loses his temper beforehand," and "Psychology seems willing to accept and discuss the subjective aspects of emotion but unwilling to attempt a scientific treatment of them." (pp. 253, 264) He continues, "The amusing result is that psychologist, physiologist, and neurologist alike show preference for the objective approach through a study of behavior, neurohumor, or thalamic lesion; yet no sooner do they find some unique aspect of their material than they proudly offer it as the possible basis for the experience of emotion, an experience whose existence, uniqueness, and characteristics are still largely a matter of supposition." (p. 264)

Much of the work on emotions in psychology assumes there are innate responses which once had survival value. Darwin maintained this view and Watson attempted to develop a fixed number of innate emotions from which all of the others derive. About this enterprise Hunt concludes,

"The concept of emotion has proved to be a vague one. It designates a rough field which has been held together by the idea of 'innate responses' in 'emergency' situations. Any of the current definitions may be, and have been, challenged." (p. 271)

In general it is found that little analysis is given to the full context of the emotion. Emotion is a word for a context, feeling, linguistic assessment, etc. To experience an emotion is to experience or involve all of these. Emotion is not merely an internal feeling. Emotion is not just felt but is partly a knowing, understanding and perceiving. These points are suggested by the following statements of David Rapaport:

"The significance of the physiological processes present in emotional states is obscured by the fog which conceals all psychosomatic interrelations. The experimental accumulation of physiological facts, valuable though it is, has not explained how 'emotional experience' occurs."

"On the basis of the material surveyed, nothing can be definitely stated as to the relation to 'emotion felt' of physiological processes concomitant with emotions. Proof has not been offered to show that the unusually described physiological processes are *always* present when emotion is felt. Nothing is known about the physiological processes *underlying* emotional experience. However, sufficient proof has been adduced that neither the James-Lange theory nor the hypothalamic theory explains the origin of 'emotion felt.'" (21)

120

Sources:

F. J. Buytendijk "The Phenomenological Approach to the Problem of Feelings and Emotions" Feelings and Emotions Reymert, ed. 1950

R. Drake Abnormal Psychology New Jersey: Littlefield, Adams 1954

William Hunt "Recent Developments in the Field of Emotion" Psychological Bulletin 38 (5) (May 1941) 249-276

Clifford Morgan "Emotion" Physiological Psychology 3rd ed., New York: McGraw-Hill 1965 306-338

Moreland Perkins "Emotion and Feeling" Philosophical Review 75 (2) April 1966) 139-160

David Rapaport Emotions and Memory New York: International Universities Press 1959

B. F. Skinner Science and Human Behavior New York: Collier-Macmillan 1953 esp. pp. 161, 167

William James: Emotion as Feeling

James attempts to redefine emotion because past attempts to do so have been unsatisfactory:

"The merely descriptive literature of emotions is one of the most tedious parts of psychology . . . As far as 'scientific psychology' of the emotions goes . . . I should as lief read verbal descriptions of the shapes of the rocks on a New Hampshire farm as toil through them again." (99)

James presents a sound theory of classifying emotions on the basis of purpose. The kind and method of classification only depends on and has meaning in terms of our purposes.

"Any classification of the emotions is seen to be as true and as 'natural' as any other, if it only serves some purpose; and such a question as 'What is the "real" or "typical" expression of anger, or fear?' is seen to have no objective meaning at all." (105)

One could then say that James' own theory and classification is determined only by his purposes. One of his purposes is to attempt to find an observable scientific way of dealing with emotions without having recourse to unobservable spiritualistic or mental entities. Several ways of doing this are to treat emotions in terms of a) physiological states b) physical reflex reactions c) objects. It will be seen that his attempt to do this fails. By reducing emotions to feelings he covertly implies a cognitive theory of emotions. In his analysis of "subtler" or derived emotions he explicitly presents a cognitive theory of emotions. Also he at times presents a mentalistic account.

121

James presents two types of emotions 1) Four "coarse" or fundamental emotions: a) grief, b) fear, c) rage, d) love. 2) "Subtler" emotions which derive from these. The basic emotions are regarded as feelings and as having physical causes:

"The emotion here is *nothing but* the feeling of a bodily state, and it has a purely bodily cause." (110)

James even attempts to bypass feelings or regard feelings as if they were the same as bodily states.

"The immediate cause of emotion is a physiological effect on the nerves." (109)

"The general causes of the emotions are indubitably physiological." (100)

By regarding emotion as a feeling, James has covertly assumed cognition and subjective states. This is because feelings are not just physical events but rather are subjective reports, and their nature is often modified by means of cognition and our linguistic assessments. The following is perhaps the best-known formulation of his position:

"Our natural way of thinking about these coarser emotions is that the mental perception of some fact excites the mental affection called the emotion, and that this latter state of mind gives rise to the bodily expression. My theory, on the contrary, is that *the bodily changes follow directly the perception of the exciting fact, and that our feeling of the same changes as they occur* is *the emotion.* Common-sense says, we lose our fortune, are sorry and weep; we meet a bear, are frightened and run . . . This order of sequence is incorrect . . . the more rational statement is that we feel sorry because we cry, angry because we strike, afraid because we tremble." (100, 101)

The assertions here are:

1) It is not the case that mental perception first excites mental affection and then produces bodily changes.

2) Rather, bodily changes follow the perception of the object.

3) Emotion is just the feeling of such bodily changes.

4) We do not run because we fear, but fear because we run.

In assertion number one, James avoids assuming there is cognition between the object simulus and the bodily response. But this stimulus-response theory is in terms of the following sequence: object to perception of object to bodily state to feeling of body state. Both the perception of the object and the awareness of the feeling involve cognitive states and assessments. Perception is never direct but always interpreted in terms of our prior learning, beliefs, language, assessments. Even sensation may be modified by cognition. The theory does not just present a behavioral stimulus and a behavioral response. Thus James' theory is a covert cognitive theory of emotions.

In assertion two, to say that bodily changes follow the perception of the object is like saying feelings follow cognition. The picture cannot be that of a body change responding to an object in terms of seeing the bear. Perhaps if one touches a hot stove the body state would respond more directly to the stimulus object. But in this case it would seem that responding to a hot stove is a reflex not an emotion. By regarding feelings as involuntary reactions (113) he fails to see that prior learning and cognition affect feeling.

"The elements are all organic changes, and each of them is the reflex effect of the exciting object." (104)

He presents the case of a boy fainting upon seeing a horse bled. The analysis of the example fails to note that blood has cognitive associations leading to conflicts and dysfunction of the body. If there were no such conflicts the boy could have objectively witnessed the scene:

"The blood was in a bucket, with a stick in it . . . He stirred it round and saw it drip from the stick with no feeling . . . Suddenly the world grew black before his eyes." (108)

In statements three and four, emotion is erroneously regarded by James, as a feeling. When we speak of emotions such as grief or love we mean much more than to report a feeling within us, although there may be feelings also. In addition, feelings may involve cognitions. We evaluate our feelings. James' theory seems to reduce emotions to only one factor in emotion, and to deal with only one type of basic emotion. That is the type where, as indicated in statements two and four, the cognition is only about the sensation itself. His example of fearing because we run would be more appropriate to cases in which one feels ill or has a hangover, which feelings are then assessed resulting in an emotion of depression or "feeling low." It does not account for cases in which feelings follow or come at the same time as cognitions.

At times, James modifies his theory thereby seeming to suggest that emotion is not just the same as the feeling of body sensation, but rather the consequence of bodily action:

"Emotion follows upon the bodily expression in the coarser emotions at least." (100)

By saying that emotions are physiological he contradicts himself when he states in various places that a thought or imagination of an object can produce emotion:

"The mere memory or imagination of the object may suffice to liberate the excitement." (93)

"The thought of 'yearning' will produce the 'yearning.'" (109)

This is a clear statement of a cognitive theory except that it deals with only one type of cognition, the object. Rather, cognitions of all sorts may lead to feelings and so result in emotions.

One method James uses in arriving at his theory is to abstract from emotions their essential elements. He finds that feelings, not cognitions, are the necessary elements of emotions. As was mentioned, he mistakenly thought that if all cognitions were omitted from emotions the latter would still be emotions. Rather if there were no consciousness one could not have feelings or emotions, and certainly not as we usually know them. He states, "A purely disembodied human emotion is a nonentity." (103) One could also state that a purely noncognitive emotion is a nonentity. In addition, the way we ordinarily use emotion words suggests that feelings often form a minor and obscure part of what is meant by emotion. "He is a happy person," may refer to one's behavior rather than his feelings. "He loves to write," may refer to intellectual satisfaction rather than just a certain kind of feeling. Also, we often use emotion terms metaphorically as when we say that we "love" our job, our country, or ice-cream. Actually James' theory might apply better to sense experiences such as liking ice-cream than to emotions such as loving another person. The consequence of his view is that emotions are no longer emotions, but only feelings. And he does conclude that emotions are feelings. The purpose of his view is to avoid assuming a mentalism of the "O" in S-O-R (stimulus-organism (thought)-response):

> "The vital point of my whole theory is this: If we fancy some strong emotion, and then try to abstract from our consciousness of it all the feelings of its bodily symptoms, we find we have nothing left behind, no 'mind stuff' out of which the emotion can be constituted, and that a cold and neural state of intellectual perception is all that remains." (102)

This view also illegitimately assumes a difference between emotion and cognition, as if they can be separated, as if cognition need not involve any feelings or emotions at all, a "feelingless cognition." Yet James himself seems to object to treating emotions atomistically. He states,

> "The trouble with the emotions in psychology is that they are regarded too much as absolutely individual things." (100)

His attempt to avoid mentalism is secured at the expense of adequacy. In place of mental or cognitive factors he could have substituted language use (abilities and imagery) and by so doing given a concrete scientifically accessible object for scientific analysis. Instead of the mental he could have stressed language. If he had, he would not have presented this inadequate view that emotions are only made up of bodily changes. He wrote, in this regard,

> "Moods, affections, and passions I have are in very truth constituted by, and made up of . . . bodily changes." (103)

James, himself, often uses mental terms and believes in mentalism. He wrote, for instance, "The bodily condition takes the lead, and . . . the *mental* emotion follows." (112) He speaks of "acute *mental* pain." (95) It is not clear what he could mean by "mental" pain.

A case is presented in which pleasure is obtained by the pain of crying.

"There is an excitement during the crying fit which is not without a certain pungent pleasure of its own." (95)

But if the emotion of pleasure were a feeling then one could not have a feeling of pleasure and a feeling of pain at the same time, although these states could alternate. In any case, pleasure is not just a feeling. On a cognitive theory one could assess a painful feeling in such a way that it becomes pleasurable. A physical pain may be cognitively pleasurable and so explain the paradox of how one can have pain and pleasure at the same time. This same explanation would apply to Freud's view that one may ambivalently love and hate the same person.

In attempting to make his theory more adequate, James attributes the individual differences of emotions to differences of feelings. Thus the same physical object may produce different physical responses. However, on a cognitive theory the individual differences would be due to both feeling differences as well as to contextual and cognitive differences.

He argues that the fact that pathological cases have emotions without objects or reason for them, supports his view. It does not. Aaron Beck and A. Ellis have shown that people become neurotic and psychotic largely because of their confused assessments and irrational ideas.

Because emotions are thought by James to be sensations and bodily states, therapy would involve only the manipulation of such physical states. This is both an inadequate and harmful method. To control emotions one is asked only to breathe deep, stand erect, and this will supposedly make anxiety vanish (110):

"Count to ten before venting your anger, and its occasion seems ridiculous. Whistling to keep up courage is no mere figure of speech." (113)

"To conquer undesirable emotional tendencies . . . we must . . . go through the *outward movements* of those contrary dispositions which we prefer . . ." (113)

"Smooth the brow, brighten the eye . . ." (114)

It is not clear how one can brighten his eye, but physical therapy of the sort he recommends can help to distract the patient and to break undesirable motor habits which he may have. Unfortunately it does not get at the cause of the emotion and so cannot serve as a cure. Both physical and chemical methods of therapy are nearly always, if not always, accompanied by cognitive therapy. If a person is emotional because his friend has died, he is jealous, or he has just been drafted, no amount of walking and whistling will overcome the emotion permanently. What is needed is cognitive reassessment. It is often the thinking one does while doing physical activities, rather than the physical activity itself, which helps one to cope with his emotions. In certain cases where motor abilities are impaired, physical therapy can be of greater value.

By thinking of emotions as electric feelings and internal bodily states, James creates a fictive model of the mind consisting of charged entities dammed up within it. The entities must supposedly be released because if they are not they will come out anyway: James committed the metaphor-to-myth fallacy by being captivated by his metaphors.

"But if tears or anger are simply suppressed, whilst the object of grief or rage remains unchanged before the mind, the current which would have invaded the normal channels turns into others, for it must find some outlet of escape." (116)

This view is harmful because it encourages the patient to express negative behavior and so leads to violence. It also suggests that emotions cannot be changed but only released. On the cognitive theory, the emotion of anger, etc., can be prevented by reevaluating one's assessments. Negative emotions may be prevented and largely eliminated. Anger need not be "expressed" or "released" but rather understood and reassessed, because cognition is part of emotion.

This account, so far, has dealt with the basic or "coarse" emotions. The "subtler" emotions are those of pathos, courage,

magnanimity, beauty; "moral, intellectual and aesthetic feelings."
(118) The moral and intellectual emotions especially, are accompanied by cognitions. Thus this is partly a cognitive theory of emotions.

A repeated "subtle" emotion supposedly loses its feeling component and may become an "intellectual emotion . . . pure and undefiled." (121) Besides this separation of reason and emotion, James seems to be offering a paradoxical and new contradictory creation: "intellectual emotion." I had thought that on his view something could be intellectual or emotional, but not both.

The view that emotions must weaken if they are repeated seems false.

"Emotions blunt themselves by repetition more rapidly than any other sort of feeling." (125)

"What they gain for practice . . . they lose for feeling." (126)

"The oftener we meet an object, the more definitely we think and behave about it; and the less is the organic perturbation to which it gives rise." (126)

One reason this may be so is because the assessments concerning the emotion are poor or the feelings involved satiated. But people do become motivated by their interests and hobbies, and repetition only reinforces their interests and assessments. The assessments one has while engaged in a task, largely determine what sort of emotion will result. And, in fact, variety is often more feared than familiar experiences. With the proper assessments one may enjoy more things more than he otherwise thought possible. It is one of the main tasks of aesthetics. One need not give up love-making, aesthetic enjoyment, or one's favorite hobbies out of fear of repetition.

Sources:

Aaron Beck *Depression* University of Pennsylvania Press 1967
Albert Ellis *Reason and Emotion* New York: Lyle Stuart 1962
William James "The Emotions" *The Emotions* C. Lange, W. James, New York: Hafner 1967, pp. 93-135

Schachter's Arousal-Label Theory

Stanley Schachter (1954) presents a view of emotions which combines a traditional physiological arousal theory with a cognitive theory of emotion. In an experiment, students were injected with adrenaline and asked to report their experiences. Seventy-one percent reported having certain physical sensations, the rest described "as-if" emotions, for example, "I feel as if I were afraid." In the first case, then, there is physical arousal. But if Schachter is attempting to determine what an emotion is and what causes emotion, it is unsatisfactory to inject subjects with adrenaline and then claim that is or causes emotion. The procedure is circular. It would be more adequate and significant to try to determine how emotions arise in the first place, rather than merely injecting adrenaline and assuming, or then claiming, a physiological arousal theory or activation theory of emotion.

In an article coauthored by Jerome Singer (1962) emotions do seem to be partially equated with a physiological state:

"Emotional states may be considered a function of a state of physiological arousal and of a cognition appropriate to this state of arousal." (398)

Schachter's assumption is that "a general pattern of sympathetic (nerve) discharge is characteristic of emotional states." However, the injection of adrenaline could not result in an adequate reproduction of the physical changes involved in all or any particular emotion. We may, however, assume that this was not their task but that they were rather concerned with the relation between certain artificially induced states of physical arousal and cognition. With these limitations the theory is interesting.

It is found that what determines which emotion is experienced, is the cognition one has and the kind of linguistic labelling one does. There is supposedly a general state of arousal and the cognitive assessment, perception of the situation, and activity involved determine what specific emotion is felt. Subjects who were aware that the cause of their arousal was adrenaline reported no emotions. The conclusion is reached that "cognitive factors may be major determinants of emotional states." (139) Schachter represents the case as follows:

"Given such a state of arousal it is suggested that one labels, interprets, and identifies this state in terms of the characteristics of the precipitating situation and one's apperceptive mass ... An emotion state may be considered a function of a state of physiological arousal and a cognition appropriate to this state of arousal. The cognition, in a sense, exerts a steering function. Cognitions arising from the immediate situation as interpreted by past experience provide the framework within which one understands and labels one's feelings. It is the cognition that determines whether the state of physiological arousal will be labeled 'anger,' 'joy,' or whatever." (139)

On this view, a physiological state or visceral activity alone cannot induce an emotion. Cognition is also necessary. This is not, in one sense, unlike the James-Lange theory of emotion according to which emotion is the perception of our bodily state. James played down cognitive function and stressed physiological arousal. Schachter regards his view as a modified James-Lange view. (160)

On Schachter's view a perception of a situation can cause a physiological arousal. What arousal it is, is determined by the way the situation is seen and assessed. Cognition does not cause but only correlates to physiological arousal. Cognition only "steers" arousal.

One of the difficulties with this view as with the James-Lange Theory is that it is not seen that the "perception" of a situation is rather the cognition of a situation. Emotion and physiological states, then, follow cognition. R. Lazarus offers the following criticism:

"This injection procedure limits the conclusions that can be drawn about emotion in the normal life situation . . . The individual perceives and appraises a situation relevant to his welfare, and this appraisal is a crucial antecedent to the emotional reaction . . . The activation follows, it does not [usually] precede, the cognition about the situation." (260)

Nevertheless Schachter offers the important insight that emotions are partly linguistically determined by means of labelling and assessment. Emotion, then, is partly a description of context and situation, and includes resulting feelings. Emotion does not merely name an internal physiological state.

Schachter and Singer (1962) state,

"Given a state of physiological arousal for which an individual has no immediate explanation, he will label this state and describe his feelings in terms of the cognitions available to him." (398)

This theory, although it does not adequately account for emotions in which cognition precedes feeling, may nevertheless account for cases such as fatigue, hangover, etc., in which feeling does in fact precede cognition. Such states may, however, be perceptions of sensations rather than emotions. Also, one reason why arousal may be thought to be needed is that often it is only in such a state that one can overcome taboo or guilt to permit sexual feelings. Publilius Syrus wrote, "You must anger a lover if you wish him to love."

Elaine Walster (1971) uses Schachter's theory to explain romantic love. Such love supposedly requires physiological arousal and requires that the arousal be labelled in a certain way. Romantic love is often based on frustration and obstacles, to make it work. The lovers are separated by distance, opposed by their families, etc. The love is not based on simple reinforcement. On Walster's view, the negative frustrations produce the arousal needed, and the positive assessment or label attached to the arousal determines it as being love. If the label "hate" were attached to the arousal one would experience hate. Objections to this view of love are the same as those against Schachter's view above. Walster herself offers the qualification,

132

"Unfortunately, experimental evidence does not yet exist to support the contention that almost any form of high arousal, if properly labeled, will deepen passion." (85-99)

Sources:

R. Lazarus *"Emotion as Coping Process" The Nature of Emotion* M. Arnold, ed. *Baltimore: Penguin 1968*

Stanley Schachter *"The Interaction of Cognitive and Physiological Determinants of Emotional Behavior" Psychobiological Approaches to Social Behavior* P. Leiderman and D. Shapiro, eds. *Stanford University Press 1964 pp. 138-173*

Stanley Schachter and J. Singer *"Cognitive, Social, and Physiological Determinants of Emotional State" Psychological Review* 69 *(1962) 379-99*

Elaine Walster *"Passionate Love" Theories of Attraction and Love* B. Murstein, ed., *New York: Springer 1971 pp. 85-99*

Ryle and White on Classifying Emotion

Gilbert Ryle

In the *Concept of Mind*, Ryle states that emotion refers to inclinations (or motives), moods, agitations (or commotions), and feelings. The terms overlap because they may be used to refer to several different types of emotion.

1) Inclinations (or motives) are not feelings or occurrences and so are not causes, but are rather dispositions or law-like statements. They are not violent or mild, public or private, not acts or states, but are intentions and propensities, or explanations of actions and thoughts. Examples given are: vain, considerate, avaricious, philanthropic, patriotic, indolent. Interest and vanity can be neither private feelings nor causes. "The vain man never feels vain." (87)

2) Moods are elliptical terms for a complex situation involving thoughts, situations and feelings. They are short-term or temporary tendencies to get in a certain "frame of mind." Moods are not themselves feelings but they name classes of feelings. Examples of mood are: tranquil, jovial, happy, energetic, worried, embarrassed, sulky, depressed. "I feel energetic," is not like "I feel a tingle." Moods are seen to involve a complex context: "To be in a particular mood is to be in the mood, among other things, to feel certain sorts of feelings in certain sorts of situations." Ryle seems to allow assessment as saying things aloud or to oneself. Mood seems partly to be a language-game. A person may find out he is bored "by finding that among other things he glumly says to others and to himself 'I feel bored' and 'How bored I feel.' " (103)

3) Agitations (or commotions), unlike inclinations, are mild or violent, have feelings connected with them, and are not propensities to act rationally. In fact, agitations are feelings experienced because we are not able to act purposively. Agitations are even said to require conflicts of inclinations, habits, or facts. For example, grief is affection opposed by death; suspense is hope opposed by fear. Agitation is an intention which is inhibited thus causing conflict or confusion. Love, want, desire, pride, eagerness, may be inclinations or agitations resulting from interference with inclinations. Some examples of agitations are: anxious, startled, shocked, excited, irritated, harrassed, thrilled, surprised, relief, homesick, in suspense.

The view presented above of grief and suspense is oversimplified and overtheoretical. It defines one emotion in terms of another when the definition of emotion is still in question and seen to be vague. Grief involves many more and perhaps entirely different assessments than that of affection opposed by death. Ryle presents an assessment view of emotions when he says,

"We can induce in ourselves genuine and acute feelings by merely imagining ourselves in agitating circumstances." (107)

4) Feelings are occurrences, for example, thrills, twinges, pangs, throbs, wrenches, itches, etc. Feelings are often distinguished from body sensations, e.g., "feel a throb," versus "a throb"; "pricking of conscience," versus "pricking of a finger," "glow of pride," versus "glow of warmth." Ryle uses 'feeling" here in a metaphorical way.

"We talk of feelings very much as we talk of bodily sensations, though it is possible that there is a tinge of metaphor in our talk of the former which is absent from our talk of the latter." (84)

"In one sense, then, of emotion the feelings are emotions." (84) That is to say that feelings are not emotions.

In his article, "Feelings" (1951), Ryle speaks of several uses of the word "feel" which should not be confused, e.g., feel how hot the water is, feel for matches in your pocket, feel the rope around your neck (as-if experience), feel a tickle, feel sleepy (a general condition), feel that something is the case, feel like doing something. To use all senses of "feel" in the sense of "feel a tickle" would be mistaken.

Ryle's definitions seem not to be adequate to the full range of assessments involved in emotions. The notion of disposition is interesting, however, for attempting to avoid thinking of emotions as feelings or causes when they are not the sorts of entitative things which could be causes.

On the other hand, disposition is too narrow a model to adequately render the emotions included in such categories. For example, patriotic is not just a disposition or explanation, but rather assessments which guide feeling. "Patriotic" refers to descriptions of situations also. The patriotic man may not have patriotic feeling, but he may have feelings which partly constitute what we mean by patriotic. Ryle comes close to saying this at times. Also, dividing emotions into the four classifications of inclinations (or motives), moods, agitations (or commotions), feelings, is not adequate nor are the four categories distinguished clearly enough.

Alan White

Alan White gives the following classification of emotion and feeling. His views are based largely on those of Ryle.

1) Intellectual Feeling

This is to feel *that* such and such is not the case. White's category, perhaps, accounts for merely one metaphorical use of the term "feel" and could be a category-mistake if used literally.

2) Perceptual Feeling

This refers to a perceptual object felt. One may "feel for" an object with his hand, feel an object in his pocket, or note that the radiator feels hot or smooth.

3) Feeling a Sensation

White states, "There is no criterion for the existence or nature of a sensation other than its being felt . . ." This appears to be circular because sensation seems to be a synonym of feeling, thus resulting in the statement "I only know feeling by feeling." White treats feeling, seeing and hearing as forms of consciousness rather than objects of or means to consciousness. To ask where a pain is, is only to ask where the cause of the pain is, but the pain itself is a form of consciousness. On this view, both sensation and feeling are raised to the level of consciousness, and the statement about feeling a sensation is still circular. It would be non-circular, however, if there were a consciousness of bodily sensation, but this is not the case. Feeling and sensation are regarded as given, immediate, experiences; because they are given, evidence for them could only be derivative from the experiences themselves, and so White states that the having or not having of evidence does not apply to knowing one's sensations.

White, like Ryle, notes the metaphorical and contextual uses of sensation terms. He wrote,

"What makes either the sensation or the sensation-like feeling an expression of some condition is not its own peculiar characteristics, which may be the same when it indicates quite a different condition, but its relations, causal and otherwise, to other factors, the composition of which is that condition." (114)

4) Feeling as an Inclination

To feel inclined involves knowing what one feels inclined to do. White puts this as a kind of feeling whereas it would seem to be merely another metaphorical use of the word feel as it applies to "inclined." He gives the examples: hope, fear, anxiety, indignation, tenderness, pity, curiosity, interest, laughter, joy. This classification seems inadequate because one may have an inclination without having a feeling or an emotion. One may simply have a reason to go or an assessment. Furthermore, hope, fear, etc. cannot merely be reduced to the language-game of "inclination." White stresses inclination as an impulse to action, but anxiety need involve no inclination to action. Anxiety, hope, etc. would be better thought of as assessments guiding feeling, some of which assessments involve desires to act or decisions to act.

5) Feelings of General Condition

These are lasting general conditions which others may observe, as well as ourselves, and which one may be quite mistaken about.

"There is no reason why a person in one of these conditions should know—much less, know better than others —what he feels." (117)

"Some people who feel angry or envious not only do not realize that this is so, but quite sincerely and even strongly feel that they are really unperturbed or full of admiration." (118)

"One may feel envy or jealousy without feeling—or thinking, much less knowing—that one is envious or jealous." (120)

White first states that general conditions are feelings, then goes on to point out that they really aren't. For example, anger is not felt as a coin is felt. On the assessment view these general conditions would be called emotions. Also to speak of general condition fails to include the assessment, and situational aspects of emotion. Jealousy, for example, involves the assessment of someone doing something to someone else. He gives the following types of feelings of general condition:

a) bodily feelings, e.g., feeling hungry or sleepy. Although he regards these as bodily feelings they involve linguistic description (sleepy, hungry) and are rather assessments of feelings. They are to be distinguished from feelings of sensation (No. 3) because they are supposedly general. But feeling hungry is not general, because it is not a collection of instances of particular feelings. Feeling sleepy and hungry involve different kinds of things such as assessments and sensations.

b) moods. This is what Ryle called inclinations. But inclination has already been classified above (No. 4). White classifies anxiety under inclination and depression under mood. Neither term is defined and it is not clear why they should be classified separately. Supposedly, moods have duration, are pervasive, and inclinations to behave in certain ways. Types of moods given are: depressed, irritable, melancholic, joyful, jovial, out of sorts. By saying they "pervade one's thought and action" he is implicitly offering an assessment theory of emotion. But on an assessment view all of his classifications except feeling or bodily sensations may be regarded as types of emotion.

c) emotions. On White's view, emotions are feelings one can be full of, or stirred by. They vary in intensity and duration and have objects. Although he erroneously regards emotion as a feeling, he observes that the identification of an object is part of the meaning of emotion, that we have no organs of emotion, that in fact we cannot even feel or get better at feeling an emotion, that emotions have patterns and histories, that emotions involve inclinations and that emotions involve assessments such as "feeling" that one has done wrong. It would then seem that White does not regard emotion as a feeling at all but rather as a word which refers to situation, context, and some feelings. Thus he is in fact holding an assessment theory of emotion.

"It is not its intrinsic characteristics that make the emotion what it is, but its relationship to its object and to its situation." (126)

Examples given of emotions are: pity, fear, pride, admiration, anger, indignation, shame, love, hate, hope, remorse. He then states that some of these are states one can be in, e.g., fear. Thus he does not see that emotions partly include or describe situations and objects. Emotion is not a feeling, as he has admitted, and so should not be regarded as a state one can be in.

d) agitations. White quotes a dictionary definition according to which emotion is "agitation of mind, an excited mental state." This is an unacceptable and misleading mentalistic definition. What is being agitated? A mind? An idea? Because it does make sense to speak of the agitation of an atom, does not mean that it makes sense to speak of the agitation of an idea. Agitations are supposedly passive states which relate to specific objects. Examples given are: startled, shocked, excited, amazed, horrified, grief-stricken, convulsed, thrilled.

On the assessment theory, this category would involve emotions in which feelings and assessments come at the same time, e.g., one is confused and so suffers shock. Such agitations are based upon prior assessments and beliefs but, on White's view, little insight is given as to how agitations arise or what they consist of. It is not helpful to say they are "agitations of the mind," "felt inclinations," or that they "relate to specific items." Shock need not be a felt inclination, but rather an immobility. Also, startle or any reflex action may be better thought of as a motor reflex and feeling, rather than as an emotion.

e) completions. Completeness feelings consist in the lack of an opposite. One may feel well, tranquil, confident, content, satisfied, bored, indifferent, fed up, full, empty, etc. Such states are supposedly grouped on the basis their being felt partly or completely, rather than intensely or vaguely. But it is not clear why, for example, boredom cannot be intense as in "He is very bored." Certainly it sounds strange, as White suggests, to speak of "perfect doubt," or "absolute worry." "Worry" already implies an ongoing or incessant activity. "Absolute worry" sounds strange because what is in process is not also completed. One can be doubting but not tranquilling. D. Browning (1970) refers to doubting as an "epistemic emotion." Completions, then, seem not to involve processes, but rather are completed states.

Sources:

Douglas Browning "The Privacy of Feelings" *Persons, Privacy, and Feeling* D. Van de Vate, ed., Memphis State University Press 1970

Gilbert Ryle "Emotions" *The Concept of Mind* New York: Barnes and Noble 1949 pp. 83-115

Gilbert Ryle "Feelings" *Philosophical Quarterly* 1(3) (1951) 193-205

Alan White "Feeling" The Philosophy of Mind New York: Random House 1967 Chapt. 5, pp. 104-130

Feeling and Emotion

"There is no simple or single feeling one has such that feeling anger consists in having it and nothing else." (Melden 205)

Feelings may be a part of what we mean by emotion. They may precede, coexist with or follow cognition. By feeling is largely meant sensation or bodily state. Cognition can usually affect or alter feeling only slightly. Feeling may depend on interest and attention. One may attend to the back of his neck or how his foot feels. In psychiatric cases great aberration may be found, including anesthesias and psychic inability to sense. Sensation words, like others, were learned in the intersubjective context of language and are to this extent bound up with language. It is not clear whether or not a man without language would "know" he senses or how he would conceive of feelings. To guess would be like guessing how birds and insects "think."

Feeling words have many uses. They should not be confused. Compare the following:

I feel as if we are out of gas.
I feel depressed.
I feel pain.
I feel like a glass of water.
I feel out of it.
I feel in.

1) Evidence for "I sense" differs from evidence for "He senses." But even "I sense" was learned in an intersubjective language-game and so is not a completely private experience. Also assessment affects sensation and perception.

2) Although we feel or sense with certain organs we do not have emotions with certain organs. We do not ask, "What organ do you feel happy with?"

3) Feeling and emotion words do not necessarily refer to feelings and emotions, e.g., "I feel that that is correct," "I am not anxious about the exam."

4) Descriptions of sensations are often circular, e.g., "I feel my arm moving," where the feeling presupposes the description, or "I see red," where red presupposes seeing, and seeing presupposes such things as red.

5) In one sense, to define feeling is merely to add additional statements to feeling statements without replacing them. That is, to define is not to define.

6) Intellectual feelings must be separated from bodily sensations. Feeling applies only metaphorically to cognition. "I feel a pain," is not like "I feel *that* the leader should decide." "Mental" pleasure is not physical pleasure. Being pleased with the government is not like being pleased with the taste of food. Being angry is not like having mumps. "What is your anger (mumps) about?"

7) In one respect, sensations are value-neutral. In itself, a sensation is merely experienced, neither good nor bad.

8) What kind of feelings do we have when we are angry? Anger feelings? The feelings had, vary from individual to individual and may be learned or unlearned. Our terms for feelings are metaphorical and vague and so difficult to specify. Thus complex emotion terms are often used metaphorically to refer to feelings, e.g., "feeling of anger." Non-emotion terms are also used, e.g., "I feel blue."

9) We ask for reasons for emotions but not for feelings. It was indicated that it does make sense to ask for reasons for feelings when interest and cognition influence feelings. One can improve his ability to sense, e.g., look carefully, listen attentively. "Why don't you listen?" We are not attentive to sensations we experience, and it is a joke to say to someone, "Sit down, if you think you would enjoy that."

10) Wordsworth speaks of poetry as a "spontaneous overflow of powerful feelings." If this were so, poetry would never be written. Poetry is a use of language, and especially of metaphor. More accurate would be the statement that poetry is an expression (not an "overflow") of emotions.

11) Is the absence of feeling a feeling? Sadness is "not feeling glad." But negation is a positive configuration of events. All negations and terms such as "nothing" refer to actual, real events. There is no absolute nothing. "Nothing" always refers to concrete empirical events.

12) Feelings have relatively more fixed durations than do emotions. "The pain lasted ten minutes," but not "I loved her for ten minutes."

13) Being angry does not involve feeling angry, although feelings may be involved. Anger is not determined merely by having certain feelings.

14) A feeling is more specifically located in the body, an emotion is not. Emotion does not make one itch.

15) Because emotions involve cognitions they can be shared, whereas, feelings cannot be shared. Sympathy involves having similar feelings or understanding another's feelings.

16) Feelings do not have objects as emotions do. "I enjoy golf," and "I enjoy a feeling," but "pain" in "I feel pain," is not an object of the feeling but the feeling itself. One can enjoy a feeling but it is a category-mistake to say he feels an enjoyment.

17) "Say it with feeling," suggests that feeling can be controlled and changed. The statement suggests that one should speak in a certain way, not that one should have the actual feeling. It is a form of pretending or imitation. No special feeling need be involved.

18) If emotion were a feeling then it would seem that physical irritations and pains would have to be regarded as emotions. They are not.

Source:

*A. I. Melden "The Conceptual Dimensions of Emotions" Human Action
T. Mischel, ed., New York: Academic Press 1969*

Wittgenstein's Language-Game Theory of Sensations and Emotions

Wittgenstein argues that sensations and emotions have been misconceived as being things or entities within us. This is one result of our being misled by our language. According to the traditional theory of meaning, words stand for or refer to objects, meanings or ideas. For Wittgenstein meanings and ideas are pseudo-psychological notions for which we have no evidence. He stresses language usage in place of thought or meaning. I have argued earlier that language, not thought, has epistemological primacy. Wittgenstein may be seen to hold a cognitive theory of emotions. By cognition or thought he means language-game.

LANGUAGE-GAMES

For Wittgenstein, meanings are not mentalistic entities as is usually thought. Rather, meaning is the use of a word in a language-game. That is, what a word means is its use or relations in the context of a language and in a certain situation (game) just as the meaning of a pawn in chess is its use in playing the game of chess. To ask, "What is a pawn really?" is to ask about a use, to ask about the rules of the game. In itself, "pawn" has no meaning. It does not correspond to an "idea" nor does it necessarily name an object.

"You learned the *concept* 'pain' when you learned language." (PI 384)

" 'How is one to define a feeling? It is something special and indefinable.' But it must be possible to teach the use of the words!" (PI p. 185)

"A concept is in its element within the language-game." (Z 391)

The meaning of sensation words, like other concepts, is derived from an intersubjective learning situation, in the context of a language, and in the context of a situation. (For further discussion see W. Shibles *Wittgenstein, Language and Philosophy)*

"But 'knowing' it [how your finger moves] only means: being able to describe it." (PI p. 185)

"Why can a dog feel fear but not remorse? Would it be right to say 'Because he can't talk'?" (Z 518)

"Knowing" does not refer to thinking or mentalistic functions but to the use of language in a language-game. "To know" mainly means to be able to describe or say something.

"How do words *refer* to sensations? . . . Words are connected with the primitive, the natural, expressions of the sensation and used in their place. A child has hurt himself and he cries; and then adults talk to him and teach him exclamations and, later, sentences. They teach the child new pain-behavior." (PI 244)

" 'So you are saying that the word 'pain' really means crying?' —On the contrary: the verbal expression of pain replaces crying and does not describe it." (PI 244)

"The words 'I am afraid' may approximate more, or less, to being a cry. They may come quite close to this and also be *far* removed from it." (PI p. 189)

Sensation and emotion are analyzed in terms of the language-games we ordinarily play. Language is inextricably bound up with thought and objects. It partly determines and constitutes reality. For this reason, one cannot have an emotion or sensation as such.

However, this does not mean that the words "I am afraid," are the same as a cry, or take the place of a cry, or that a cry becomes the words. A "cry" has its own linguistic problems and uses. "I am afraid," is a use, not a description.

"Imagine that the people of a tribe were brought up from early youth to give no expression of feeling *of any kind.*" (Z 383)

"I want to say: an education quite different from ours might also be the foundation for quite different concepts." (Z 387)

What sensation and emotion terms mean depend on the language used. "Love" in one language would have different meanings than it would in another language. "Love" cannot be precisely translated.

"Sensations . . . got their significance only from the surroundings: through the reading of this poem, from my familiarity with its language, with its metre and with innumerable associations." (Z 170)

It should be stressed that Wittgenstein may seem to contradict himself if one fails to note that the meaning of what Wittgenstein himself says is its use, and that what is true in one language-game may be false in another. Thus, while discussing one language-game of emotion, it may seem that a general theory of emotions is being presented. This is not the case. To confuse different language-games and contexts would be to create category-mistakes. Each language-game has its own criteria of truth and its intelligibility in its complex concreteness.

FORMS OF LIFE

" 'I am in pain' . . . To use a word without a justification does not mean to use it without right." (PI 289)

"Being sure that someone is in pain, doubting whether he is, and so on, are so many natural, instinctive, kinds of behavior towards other human beings, and our language is merely an auxiliary to, and further extension of, this relation. Our language-game is an extension of primitive behavior. (For our language-game is behavior.) (Instinct)." (Z 545)

" 'Grief' describes a pattern which recurs, with different variations, in the weave of our life." (PI p. 174)

A "form of life" is a given. It is to say that our language as we learned it is a primitive, primary experience and cannot be explained by another kind of experience. An explanation is only one kind of use and cannot be a substitute for the words explained. "Form of life" refers to the notion that we live our language, or that language is a basic form of life. "Form of life" means "language of life," as well as the "life of language." Because language has epistemological primacy it must be regarded as a given. It does not rest on prior notions of thought, objects, or behavior. Language is not just a form of behavior but, rather, behavior is one form of language-game, that of using and speaking about the word "behavior." There is a givenness of language beyond which it makes no sense to go. Nor could we go there.

"Can only those hope who can talk? Only those who have mastered the use of a language. This is to say, the phenomena of hope are modes of this complicated form of life." (PI p. 174)

That sensation terms refer to inner or mental entities may be doubted. But the use of sensation terms as given language-games may not be doubted. "It means nothing to doubt whether I am in pain." (PI 288) This is because we learned how to speak the language. The difficulty only arises if we must think that we have things in us that are sensations or emotions. We do not literally "have" sensations and emotions, though we do have them. They are not descriptions of entities.

SENSATIONS AND EMOTIONS AS NAMING-FALLACIES

" 'But mustn't I know what it would be like if I were in pain?' —We fail to get away from the idea that using a sentence involves imagining something for every word." (PI 449)

"One thinks that learning language consists in giving names to objects." (PI 26)

" 'Joy' designates nothing at all. Neither any inward nor any outward thing." (Z 487)

Words may sometimes refer to or name entities, but to think they always do is to commit a naming-fallacy. As was mentioned, words have many uses other than that of naming. A subject (substantive)—modifier (quality) language such as English, leads us to think that all nouns are substances. Thus it is erroneously thought that pain, joy, mind, etc. name entities:

"Suppose everyone had a box with something in it: we call it a 'beetle.' No one can look into anyone else's box, and everyone says he knows what a beetle is only by looking at *his* beetle. —Here it would be quite possible for everyone to have something different in his box. One might even imagine such a thing constantly changing. —But suppose the word 'beetle' had a use in these people's language? —If so it would not be used as the name of a thing. The thing in the box has no place in the language-game at all; not even as a *something*: for the box might even be empty. —No, one can 'divide through' by the thing in the box; it cancels out, whatever it is. That is to say: if we construe the grammar of the expression of sensation on the model of 'object and designation' the object drops out of consideration as irrelevant." (PI 293)

It is not the case that because sensation words do not just name objects, that there are no such things as sensations. The point is that we do not have direct evidence of private, internal states of sensation or emotion. Something may be going on in us, but "it" is not something we can adequately express in terms other than those of a language-game experience:

" 'And yet you again and again reach the conclusion that the sensation itself is a *nothing*.' —Not at all. It is not a *something*, but not a *nothing* either! The conclusion was only that a nothing would serve just as well as a something about which nothing could be said. We have only rejected the grammar which tries to force itself on us here." (PI 304)

If sensation words were to name entities it is not clear what they would name. Pain and warmth are not like tables and chairs within us. That is, something or other may be going on within us but it is not clear what.

"Are the words 'I am afraid' a description of a state of mind?" (PI p. 187)

"Describing my state of mind (of fear, say) is something I do in a particular context." (PI p. 188)

Words may be used in games of describing, greeting, explaining, etc. However, some words such as mind, sensation, soul, angel, emotion, idea are used as descriptions of entities but, upon examination, no evidence is found for such entities. The words do, however, have other uses, e.g., "*Mind* the store," I *feel* that the statement is true."

SENSATIONS AND EMOTIONS ARE NOT THE SAME

"Sensations are not the emotions." (Z 488)

"Fear is not a sensation." (Z 492)

"Suppose it were said: Gladness is a feeling, and sadness consists in *not* being glad. —Is the absence of a feeling a feeling?" (Z 512)

Usually emotions are regarded as sensations by psychologists and others. In everyday English one says "I *feel* sad," or "I *feel* glad." These uses commit the category-mistake of confusing bodily sensations with emotions which include much more than bodily sensations. One of the consequences of this mistake is to give an inadequate analysis of emotions and sensations, another is that if emotion is thought of as a sensation then one would erroneously tend to think that one cannot change the emotion. *"Feel* emotion" is always a category-mistake.

"Love is not a feeling. Love is put to the test, pain not. One does not say: 'That was not true pain [cf. true love], or it would not have gone off so quickly.' " (Z 504)

"A thought rouses emotions in me (fear, sorrow, etc.) not bodily pain." (Z 494)

Wittgenstein expresses here a cognitive theory of emotion. Thought (language-games) leads to emotion and partly constitutes what is meant by emotion. In our ordinary use of emotion terms, more is meant than feeling. Actually, if thought leads to emotion and emotion involves feeling, then thought may lead to feeling or bodily pain.

PICTURING SENSATIONS AND EMOTIONS

"We talk, we utter words, and only *later* get a picture of their life." (PI p. 209)

That is, the linguistic usage comes before the picture and is not based on the picture.

" 'I know . . . only from my *own* case' —what kind of proposition is this meant to be at all? An experimental one? No. —A grammatical one? . . . It is a picture, and why should we not want to call up such a picture? Imagine an allegorical painting taking the place of those words. When we look into ourselves as we do philosophy, we often get to see such a picture. A full-blown pictorial representation of our grammar. Not facts; but as it were illustrated turns of speech." (PI 295)

When we say we know our own sensations it seems as if we have pictured something, but it is not clear what. What we are doing is imagining rather than looking to see what we are in fact doing when we refer to our own sensations. If there are no things for sensation words to refer to, we tend to imagine some. The sensations and emotions then end up being described in terms of emotions, e.g., "sharp" pain, "flow" of emotions.

"The image of pain certainly enters into the language game in a sense; only not as a picture." (PI 300)

Part of the use of sensation terms may involve images, but pain does not refer to only the image or the object of the image. Pain is not literally picturable.

"If water boils in a pot, steam comes out of the pot and also pictured steam comes out of the pictured pot. But what if one insisted on saying that there must also be something boiling in the picture of the pot?" (PI 297)

Here is how it is. This is how one may become captivated by a picture and a false analogy. Saying we "express" sensations or emotions, is like assuming there is something boiling in a pictured pot. Because we want words to refer to entities we try to picture sensations within us. There is less to sensations than meets the eye of imagination.

"The *content* of an emotion—here one imagines something like a *picture*, or something of which a picture can be made. (The darkness of depression which descends on a man, the flames of anger.) The human face too might be called such a picture and its alterations might represent the *course* of a passion." (Z 489, 490)

To think of emotions in terms of "contents" is to picture, to employ an analogy to a box and its contents. But "contents" does not apply, or applies only metaphorically. We *could* take the human face as the way we picture emotion, but to do so is to be captivated by a picture or metaphor. (A recent example of this is Carroll Izard's *The Face of Emotion* 1971.)

"When we tell a doctor that we have been having pains—in what cases is it useful for him to imagine pain? —And doesn't this happen in a variety of ways?" (Wittgenstein Z 544)

There is not a single image which goes with the concept of pain but many possible images as they relate to contexts and purposes. "Pain" means different things in different contexts. Images, like sensations, may be analyzed further into language-games. (See chapter on perception)

EMOTIONS AND SENSATIONS ARE NOT PRIVATE STATES

"If anyone says: 'For the word "pain" to have a meaning it is necessary that pain should be recognized as such when it occurs' —one can reply: 'It is not more necessary than that the absence of pain should be recognized.'" (PI 448)

Pain is not recognized as an entity even in one's own case. It will not do to say, "Well, I know I have a pain, because I am the one who has it." This just runs the same words around. The question is, "What evidence does one have for private states?" The answer given here is that sensation terms, because they were learned in an intersubjective language, are not private but public. Pain no more has to name an entity than does the absence of pain.

" 'If I suppose that someone has a pain, then I am simply supposing that he has just the same as I have so often had.' —That gets us no further. It is as if I were to say: 'You surely know what "It is 5 o'clock here" means; so you also know what "It's 5 o'clock on the sun" means . . .' " (PI 350)

The analogy of our own state to that of others, that is, the assumption that others feel what we feel, is unwarranted. This is partly because it obliterates the linguistic distinction between the first person case and the second and third person case. When speaking of another person we do not use the word "I." The feelings and emotions of others are already vouchsafed and, in fact, we first learn of others' feelings and emotions before our own in the sense that we learn intersubjective words for feeling and emotions.

What has been done here? Our talk of feelings and emotions is much the same as always except that now one would not get a false picture of feelings and emotions as entities or private states.

" 'Putting the cart before the horse' may be said of an explanation like the following: we tend someone else because by analogy with our own case we believe that he is experiencing pain too. —Instead of saying: Get to know a new aspect from this special chapter of human behavior— from this use of language." (Z 542)

THE LOCATION OF SENSATIONS AND EMOTIONS

"I should almost like to say: One no more feels sorrow in one's body than one feels seeing in one's eyes." (Z 495)

" 'Where do you feel grief?' . . . Yet we *do* point to our body, as if the grief were in it." (Z 497)

"The place of bodily pain is not the body." (Z 511)

One reason for these assertions is that emotions are not just feelings. Because, as was seen, sensation terms do not refer to objects or entities, and because their meaning is in their contextual use, it makes no sense to ask where they are. One may ask, "Where is grief?" or "Where is love?" but to do so is to commit a category-mistake. "Where" does not apply when used in this descriptive sense. It could apply if it refers to a contextual configuration of events. But suppose someone were to say "I feel fear in my fingers." Well, then, he perhaps has a paradigm. But fear is not in his fingers.

It does make sense to say "I have a pain in my leg." It makes sense as a use but not as the language-game of describing an entity as being in a place. Is this subtle?

Elsewhere Wittgenstein says,

"Pain-behavior can point to a painful place—but the subject of pain is the person who gives it expression." (PI 302)

CAUSES AND OBJECTS OF EMOTIONS

"Does it follow that the sadness is a *sensation* produced by this [glandular] secretion?" (Z 509)

"(The horribleness of fear is not in the sensations of fear.) ... 'I am sick with fear' does not assign a *cause* of fear." (Z 496)

The cause of sadness is not sensation. Emotion is not a single thing or physical occurrence and so not strictly caused or the cause of something else. Only loosely and metaphorically can it be said to be a cause or effect.

"If anyone asks whether pleasure is a sensation, he probably does not distinguish between reason and cause, for otherwise it would occur to him that one takes pleasure *in something*, which does not mean that this something produces a sensation in us." (Z 507)

To take pleasure in something implies cognition and assessment, the two elements which are relatively lacking in sensation. Instead of speaking about the physical cause of emotion it may be more relevant to speak of the reason for emotion.

"We should distinguish between object of fear and the cause of fear. Thus a face which inspires fear or delight (the object of fear or delight), is not on that account its cause, but—one might say—its target." (PI 476)

"The language-game 'I am afraid' already contains the object." (Z 489)

It is misleading to say the bear causes one to be afraid. One could see a bear and not be afraid. The bear is only the subject or "target" of the fear. Emotions as language-games include the subject within them. The cause of emotions is not merely an object. "A bear is coming toward me," is a description. "A bear is coming toward me and that is bad," is an interpretation of a description, one which leads to emotion.

EXPRESSION AND EXHIBITION

"I do not infer my emotion from my expression of emotion . . ." (Z 576)

"Instead of 'I can't exhibit my sensation' —[say] 'in the use of the word "sensation," there is no such thing as exhibiting what one has got.' " (Z 134)

"I can exhibit pain, as I exhibit red, and as I exhibit straight and crooked and trees and stones. —*That* is what we *call* 'exhibiting.' " (PI 313)

"Expressing" and "exhibiting" are language-games, uses. They need not describe entities. "Express" means to "press out," but in the case of emotions nothing is pressed out. Nor are emotions literally "repressed," as Freudians suggest (though there are non-literal paradigms for repression). The word, "express," may mislead in another way. If one assumes that something is an expression, it leads us to look for that which is being expressed. But the assumption that it is an expression may be false—or the assumption that it is an expression of an inner mentalistic or pseudo-psychological state may be false. If there is an expression, then something is expressed, but there may be no expression, only a language-game. Similarly, if one calls something an effect, then, of course, one assumes a cause. "Who created the world?" is such a multi-question, question-begging fallacy.

CONTEXT

"Only surrounded by certain normal manifestations of life, is there such a thing as an expression of pain. Only surrounded by an even more far-reaching particular manifestation of life, such a thing as the expression of sorrow or affection." (Z 534)

"The concept of pain is characterized by its particular function in our life." (Z 532)

"Pain has *this* position in our life; has *these* connections." (Z 533)

Emotion is seen to be more general and context-bound than sensation, though both are language-games constituted by contextual situations and objects. Although physical events may be dealt with to a large extent in terms of scientific laws, emotions and feelings require an adequate linguistic and human context for their explication.

Sources

Warren Shibles *Wittgenstein, Language and Philosophy* Dubuque, Iowa: Kendall-Hunt 1970

Ludwig Wittgenstein *Philosophical Investigations* G. Anscombe, trans., 3rd edition. New York: Macmillan 1958

Ludwig Wittgenstein *Zettel* G. Anscombe, trans., London: Blackwell 1966

Emotion and Circularity

Several definitions given of circularity are as follows: 1) the premise is assumed true without warrant, 2) what is to be proved is implicitly taken for granted, 3) a word is defined in terms of a synonym yielding "S is true because S is true," 4) a word is defined in terms of another word which covertly contains or is indirectly synonymous with the word to be defined, e.g., S is true because A is true, and A is true because B is true and B is true because S is true.

As such definitions are complex and abstract, specific instances need to be examined in regard to their alleged circularity. Examples may be seen to be a) circular, b) not circular, c) partly circular, d) neither circular nor not circular.

The important thing about noticing circularity is not just to reject a statement because it is circular but to a) note that if it is circular it gives no insight though it may seem to do so, and b) avoid confusing the circular sense of a statement with its non-circular sense. A statement may seem true because it is covertly circular and so one may erroneously take the non-circular aspect of the statement as true also. "One ought to do his duty" seems true because it is circular. Duty means "That which one ought to do." But it is not true in the sense that one ought to do any kind of duty or follow any kind of command.

In psychology, emotions are often assumed and merely correlated with an internal physiological event. If the attempt is to find out what an emotion is, this procedure is circular. Emotion cannot be correlated with a physical occurrence until it is determined what an emotion is. This circular situation is presented by the psychologist, G. Mandler, as follows: "At the present time there is no classification of emotional stimuli independent of an organism's response." (308)

We describe emotions in terms of activities and then wish to regard the emotion as separate from them. One cannot have the enjoyment of fishing without fishing. The pleasure of eating candy is not the pleasure of swimming. It thus seems odd to say that the pleasure is one thing, e.g., a sensation or internal state, and the activity is another, or that the activity causes the pleasure. The activity is here part of what is meant by the pleasure. Pains do not arrive already distressing. They are put into a context already known and described in terms of that context. Phobias, for example, hydrophobia, are named after a circumstance. In "He is annoyed that the tickets are gone," the annoyance is described in terms of the object. It is circular to assume there is an emotion separate from an object and then only be able to describe the emotion in terms of the object.

By emotion we may have meant to include a description of the object in the first place. Emotion terms often partly describe feelings, objects, as well as the general context. We often learn an emotion term, e.g., jealousy, in a certain situation and only later apply this term to our feelings. We say, "I feel jealous" or "I am jealous" rather than that it is a jealous situation. Although we may blame someone for being jealous it may not be his fault. Rather he may be in a jealous situation and forced to be jealous. Suicide is coming to be thought of less as a "mental disease" or "emotional disorder" and more as a situational configuration of events. In addition, completions of feeling sentences specify the feeling in terms of the object, e.g., I feel fit, tranquil, confident, content, satisfied, bored, fed-up, full.

In "I have an emotion of fear," the object of emotion is not fear. Fear is merely included in the class, emotion. Fear also partly makes up the class emotion and so "emotion of fear" is largely circular or tautological. In "I experience fear," fear is the same thing as experience. One could have said "I fear," instead. It is not intelligible to say, "I fear but have no experience." In "I have a sensation of red," red cannot be known apart from the sensation and sensation cannot be known apart from red. It is circular. It yields, "I have a sensation of red-sensation, or red-sensation of red." "He boasted out of vanity" may add nothing to "He boasted" or "He is vain." It seems, however, to ascribe a cause or reason, as if vanity refers to a feeling which causes the boasting. But to be vain is not to feel vain, though some feelings may be involved. In "He jumped from fear," fear may only report that he is habitually fearful, not that he *then* felt fear.

We may regard a situation as emotional because it depends on emotions being present. But emotions are often partly defined by the situation and our regarding it as an emotional situation. This procedure may involve circularity. "I like it because it is beautiful," may involve a circularity. To be beautiful something must be liked and, in one sense, all that is meant by beautiful is that it is liked. Thus the object is not in itself beautiful but rather to say it is is only to say one likes it. What one person likes another may dislike and so what one person regards as beautiful another may regard as ugly. One doesn't say "I don't like beauty," or ask "Do you like beauty," for the above reasons. It is also odd to say, "It is beautiful whether you know it or not." This could, however, mean that one could come to like it once one saw it in a certain way or knew enough about it.

"Disposition" or words for dispositions such as "thief" and "character" are also used in a circular manner. "He has a disposition to get angry" suggests that one "has" something. A disposition, however, only means that which one usually does. To say one has a disposition to do x only means he usually does x. Thus in this respect it makes little sense to say, "He stole the money because he is a thief," "He did it because of his character," "He did it because he has a disposition to do it," where thief and character refer to dispositions. "I did it because I have a disposition to do it" reduces to "I did it because I often do it," or even "I did it because I did it."

"I am annoyed at her dishonesty but I do not really think she is dishonest." This is strange. This may show that we do not just have an emotion, e.g., annoyance, separate from the object or assessment, e.g., her being dishonest. This is because the object of emotion here is a belief. It is not annoyance at a person. One cannot be annoyed with a thing in itself, e.g., "I am annoyed at the sky." The annoyance is at one's assessment of the thing and one's beliefs about what the object means or does. "I hate him" involves equivocation and category mistakes insomuch as we hate some act the person does, not his body, face, eyes, or even all of his actions. When the person corrects the act or acts he was hated for, he is often not hated any longer. There seems no reason why one should hate a person as a person or hate a person in every way when one actually only hates one or two acts a person does. An alternative is "I love you as a person but I condemn these of your acts." This salvages humanity. In "I am annoyed at her dishonesty but I do not think she is dishonest," one is annoyed at a specific belief not with a person and it is contradictory then to be annoyed at a specific belief about a person yet not have that belief. The emotion is only meaningful in terms of the belief and the belief defines the kind of emotion had. It may or may not involve feelings.

Astrologers are often thought to be able to determine one's emotional make-up and personality by means of their study of what the configurations of the stars or planets are at the time of one's birth. One of the reasons why such descriptions seem true is because they are very detailed and put in everyday rather than technical language. Little is known by contemporary scientists and scholars on the subject of personality or emotion and so this allows the astrologer an area of expression where it is not easy to produce against him well-founded support or contradiction. There is a certain vagueness about personality description. The astrologer's descriptions and predictions may seem true due to this very vagueness and lack of correct theory. Also his predictions may appear correct because of their great generality. One may seem to be told something very specific when told that if born under Mars one will be bellicose and have a scar on his face. But most people are somewhat bellicose, and facial scars are extremely common. The same applies to predictions of back or knee injury or an impending good or an impending evil. The astrologer's view that our emotions and personality are determined at birth is a deterministic, if not fatalistic, view and ignores the fact that emotions are not just internal states or entities. The result may be disastrous for therapy. Also astrology is partly based on outdated theories of humors, metaphysics and mythology.

One circularity is to observe a person's expressions and behavior and then to say that the person must be experiencing an emotion. The equivocation here is that when we see someone smiling we want to know also what he is feeling or even what he is thinking. But it is not legitimate to say that the outward emotion is really the inward emotion or that the emotion is the feeling. The behavioral evidence for emotion is behavior in itself and, to some extent, that is what is meant by the emotion. In asking what an emotion is, one begins with external behavioral criteria and this is often our everyday criteria for having an emotion. But especially what one says to oneself or aloud is what will determine the difference between having an emotion and pretending to have one. An actor will say, for example, "I hope I can do this crying right," and he may have feelings usually associated with trying to succeed.

A circularity arises in asserting that emotion is contrary to reason. Reason may be defined as that which is not emotional. But more important, and subtly, emotion may be regarded as that which is not usual and ordinary, and reason as that which is. Emotion is an excess of some sort and not natural. If emotion is so regarded it cannot by definition be rational or natural and so would have to be contrary to reason. Thus if emotion is regarded as an excess it would by definition be contrary to reason. The question is whether it is an excess, or unnatural, or unusual. Emotion may, instead, be found to be one kind of rational assessment and not opposed to reason if reason is defined differently.

Sources:

G. Mandler "Emotion" New Directions in Psychology I R. Brown, et al. eds., New York: Holt, Rinehart and Winston 1962 pp. 267-339

Irving Thalberg "Emotion and Thought" American Philosophical Quarterly (Jan. 1964) 455

Two Cognitive Theories:
M. Arnold and R. Lazarus

Magda Arnold

Magda Arnold draws heavily on the work of the Catholic theologian, St. Thomas Aquinas, for her assessment theory of emotion. She states (1969):

> "An emotion is a strong appetitive tendency toward or away from something appraised as good or bad for the person here and now that urges to appropriate action and is accompanied (but not initiated) by physiological changes." (172)

The appetitive tendency involves movement and action. Emotion consists of the following:

> "Perception (preliminary appraisal, recall, appraisal of object, imagination of action and possible consequences, appraisal for action), appetitive tendency, and action: This sequence represents not only a logical analysis but a causal sequence . . ." (185)

Arnold claims that there are neural and physiological support and correlates for each factor in her analysis of emotion. Stress on appraisal and cognition allows her to take needed cognizance of the cerebral or association cortex. This evidence is presented in her two volume work, *Emotion and Personality*. On this analysis, perception is not mere sensation but already includes past and present cognition. Seeing a bear involves recognition and knowledge. There is a first "intuitive appraisal" which is defined as a feeling of like or dislike, or feeling that something is good or bad.

Then a "second appraisal" or deliberate, conscious appraisal determines what kind of action is to be taken. The intuitive appraisal as good or bad provides the stimulus or urge to act, and the deliberative appraisal assesses the best way of acting on the urge, of avoiding or approaching the object in question. Arnold speaks of the event as follows:

"The thing-appraised-as-good-for-a-particular-action, that produces the desire to do something in particular, that arouses a specific appetitive tendency." (171)

The general theory is interesting because of its stress on assessment, but the terms used need clarification. In the first cases, because "good" and "bad" are open-context terms, to say one assesses in terms of them is unclear. (See Shibles "Ethics as Open-Context Terms") Such assessment would reduce rather to assessments of likes, wants, beliefs, consequences. She does come close to this view by speaking sometimes of likes rather than of good and bad. Also she regards intuitive assessment as feelings or feeling assessments. Feelings are empirical data. On the other hand, "feeling assessments" seems contradictory. Bodily sensation is not cognition. But sensation and perception are never pure. They always involve a complex network of associations and cognitions. This may be what is meant by speaking of these initial or intuitive assessments as urges.

On Arnold's view, all emotion tends toward or away from something, it leads to action of some sort. This may be based on traditional views which speak of emotion only in terms of pleasure and pain, going toward an object or going away from an object. But it would seem that many more sorts of assessments are made than those of good or bad or assessments for action. Many emotions seem not to be directed to action, e.g., depression, anxiety, boredom, etc. What is rather needed is an analysis and clarification of all those specific assessments which people in fact make which lead to emotions. She does not provide this clarification.

Arnold does point out some factors others overlook, e.g., motor memory, motor imagination. (See W. Shibles "Memory and

Remembering.") Assessments involve anticipating pleasures on the basis of past pleasures. She even speaks of improving one's abilities by means of the use of imagery:

"Jacobson has found that motor imagination activates muscles actually used in the imagined action . . ." (176)

This view might be extended to serve as an analysis of how one speaks out loud, and then learns to speak silently to oneself. Self-talk would be a kind of imaginative activity. On this expanded view, appraisal could be largely thought of as self-talk or saying statements to oneself. This would, then, provide a concrete meaning for reason, judgment, cognition, thinking, idea, assessment. Such terms would refer mainly to self-talk or written and spoken language. This is one reason why animals do not have the emotions man has. They are not able to verbally assess as man does. Arnold suggests this when she states that animals may have primary appraisals but not secondary appraisals.

Although not explicitly stated, the view that visual images are involved in thinking so as to improve one's motor and perceptual ability may be helpful in therapy. Patients who have phobias, for example, may imagine themselves not having such fears, and imagine themselves in the situations they fear without being afraid, acting rationally and normally. Imagery also has a motivating function in terms of developing goals. A person may see himself as what he wishes to be, e.g., a pilot, executive, teacher, etc. In addition to reassessing cognitions, emotion therapy involves changing imagery, perception, and motor behavior.

Because emotions involve cognition they can be changed, although she underplays the extent to which they can be changed. Negative emotions supposedly may be somewhat prevented. Also she proposes keeping positive emotions in check so as not to distract from reason:

"Negative emotions, like fear, sorrow, hopelessness, and dejection, interfere with physical well-being." (185)

"Negative emotions may make one less than human." (190)

Arnold opposes self-righteous, and existentialistic "do-your-own-thing" views of emotions. Emotions involve reason and so are not self-justificatory:

"Emotions, whether mob violence or passive live-ins, seem to have been chosen by many young people as the sole guide of their actions." (192)

It is an especially useful insight to note that the sort of specific assessment one has determines the kind of emotion which results. Thus, instead of characterizing an emotion with the general terms, anger, jealousy, etc. one may give them specific individualized renderings by specifying the assessments held in the specific case. There are many different types of angers, loves, etc.

"Emotions are chameleonlike and change with every new aspect that is evaluated." (184)

The following summary of Aquinas' theory shows that Arnold follows it quite closely. St. Thomas Aquinas presents a view of mind involving faculty psychology, mentalism and spiritual entities. Nevertheless, his view that reason is involved in emotion is interesting. Each of the following is regarded as a distinct "power" for a distinct type of behavior: sensation, estimation, memory, and imagination. There is supposedly a vegetative soul (for nutrition, growth, generation), a sensitive soul, and a rational soul. The sensitive soul consists of apprehension by the five senses (and common sense). The sensitive soul also consists of imagination and estimative power. Estimative power, which animals also have, is in man called *vis cogitativa* or cognitive power, and involves the process of comparison. Perception contains both sense, and reason or assessment. The estimative power was sometimes referred to as "sensible reason," and sometimes as the faculty of sensitive apprehension of intentions which do not come through the senses. Sensitive appetites involve natural attractions or repulsions between things. Volition or will is a rational appetite. "Concupiscible power" is movement to assess how to avoid what is harmful. This is the basis of the passions: love-hate, desire-aversion, joy-sadness. "Irascible power" serves to resist hindrances of concupiscible power and yields: hope-desire, fear-daring, anger. The passions sometimes are thought to refer to acts of the sensitive appetites. The body is thereby aroused and reason affected. For Aquinas all thinking is in terms of imagery and symbol. The passions are aroused by imagery. Love is said to be the main source of the passions but also the result of clear and adequate knowledge. The rational faculty knows only what comes through the senses. This brief summary indicates that M. Arnold follows Aquinas in basic outline with special stress on the estimative power and on the various faculties involved such as sensation, estimation, appetite, memory, imagination, reason.

Sources:

Magda Arnold *Emotion and Personality* 2 vols. *New York: Columbia University Press 1960*

Magda Arnold *"Human Emotion and Action"* *Human Action* *T. Mischel, ed. New York: Academic Press 1969 pp. 167-197*

Magda Arnold, ed., *The Nature of Emotion* *Baltimore: Penguin 1968*

Warren Shibles *"Ethics as Open-Context Terms"* *Philosophical Pictures* *2nd edition, Dubuque, Iowa: Kendall-Hunt 1972*

Warren Shibles *"Memory and Remembering"* *Wittgenstein, Language and Philosophy* *Dubuque, Iowa: Kendall-Hunt 1970*

R. Lazarus

R. Lazarus (1968) presents a theory of emotion according to which an assessment is prior to feeling or emotion.

"Threat is the product of appraisal, and the action tendencies aroused by threat may be regarded as coping processes .... We employ the terms 'primary' for threat-producing appraisal and 'secondary' for additional appraisals related to the coping process. The final shaping of the reaction thus involves processes and conditions not germane to the production of threat itself, such as anticipations about the probable reaction of the environment to any behavioral response ...." (249)

His argument involves the following factors:

1. The stimulus-response theory alone is inadequate in analyzing all of the factors involved in coping behavior. It does not indicate sufficiently the conditions under which such behavior occurs. (249) One must include appraisals. His purpose is not to reject behaviorism but to clarify it and make it more adequate. (257)

"We think that an explicitly cognitively oriented, phenomenological frame of reference such as ours ... [is] better ... than the more simple stimulus-response frameworks." (257)

2. Appraisals help determine how much, if any, danger there is and the course of action to take.

3. "Emotions like fear are the result, not the cause of cognitive activity." (253)

4. The appraisal need not be true, or rational, or conscious. The appraisal may be immediate rather than an involved deciding. It may take place automatically.

5. One must recognize threat before one can react emotionally to it.

6. Because negative emotion almost always accompanies threat it may have led psychologists to erroneously think it is the emotion which is the cause.

7. When people say that a reaction is emotional they often mean merely that it is an irrational reaction. Being irrational it is an assessment not a feeling.

8. In order to correct or change an emotion the assessment must be changed:

> "To blame emotion for [an emotion producing] decision is to focus on the wrong factor, since the emotion and the unwise decision can best be changed by altering the belief system on which the appraisal is made." (256)

9. "Emotion" is only a hypothetical construct which consists partly of assessments. Thus an emotion is not literally a cause and also, then, is not a cause of the coping process. "Emotion does not cause these reactions, but is part of the reactions themselves . . ." (257)

10. By thinking of emotion in terms of assessment the variation of emotional reaction can be explained.

11. The assessments involved in emotion were often those learned prior to any particular emotional experience.

Sources:

J. Averill, E. Opton, and R. Lazarus "Cross Cultural Studies of Psychophysiological Responses During Stress and Emotion" Journal of Psychology 4(1969) 83-102

R. Lazarus "Emotion as Coping Process" The Nature of Emotion M. Arnold, ed. Baltimore: Penguin 1968

R. Lazarus Psychological Stress and the Coping Process New York: McGraw-Hill 1966

Aaron Beck's Cognitive Theory
of Emotion and Depression

Aaron Beck in his excellent book, *Depression* (1967), surveyed the previous scientific and psychiatric studies on depression. Because of a general lack of clarity about this concept, classificatory systems such as that of the American Psychiatric Association, are found to be inadequate as is therapy based on such classifications. Personality inventories, such as the Minnesota Multiphasic Personality Inventory fail to adequately detect depression. Yet depression is perhaps the most fundamental concept in psychotherapy. John Donne had once regarded it as a disease. According to Beck,

> "There is sharp disagreement among clinicians and investigators who have written about depression. There is considerable controversy regarding the classification of depression and a few writers see no justification for using this nosological category at all." (4)

Beck offers a clarification of the concept of depression but, although he does not say so, his analysis could apply equally well as a theory of emotions. What his theory of depression indicates is that the assessment theory of emotions applies to the area of psychiatry as well as to normal behavior.

Beck holds a cognitive theory of emotion in accordance with which the cognition or thought precedes the emotion.

> "The affective state can be regarded as the consequence of the way the individual views himself or his environment .... There is a predictable relationship between an antecedent event and the affective response." (261)

"In my clinical studies I noted that changes in the intensity of the depressed feeling followed changes in the patient's cognition." (262)

"The mood disorder is secondary to the cognitive disorder." (261)

This relationship between cognition and affect or emotion is largely based on prior learning and association. One's irrationality leads to emotional problems. Beck's terms here are abstract. He speaks of "ideas," "thoughts," "cognition," "affect," "emotion," and "feeling," but he does not adequately distinguish them. He states,

"The term cognition refers to a specific thought such as an interpretation, a self-command, or a self-criticism. The term is also applied to wishes (such as suicidal desires) that have a verbal content." (230)

It is not clear what he means by thought. He seems to think that there are ideas as such. A correction to this would be to suggest that because "idea" and "thought" are pseudo-psychological categories, we may think of these terms as mainly referring to public language use and self-talk. Beck does refer to Ellis' notion of "self-talk" (282) and states, "A cognition refers to any mental activity which has a verbal content . . ." (283) Beck, when referring to the cognitions which cause emotional disturbance, gives statements the patient utters to himself as well as to others. He calls Ellis' "self-talk," "automatic thoughts." This term is less descriptive and less helpful than "self-talk" or "self-verbalization." Thus, although Beck is vague about thought, his practice as well as his theory is sound. He also treats imagery and behavior as if that is also what is meant by thought. Thus "thought" and "idea" only refer to language use, imagery, perception and behavior. They do not refer to private mentalistic entities. That he opposes mentalistic entities comes out especially in his criticism of Freud's theories:

"In attempting to account for paradoxical aspects of depression, some writers have presented formulations that are so elaborate or abstract that they cannot be correlated with clinical material. Freud's conceptualization of depression in terms of the attack of the sadistic part of the ego on the incorporated loved-object within the ego is so remote from any observables in clinical data that it defies systematic validation." (253)

Also Beck notes that an emotion is not just one thing but is elliptical for a complex pattern:

"There is considerable doubt that depression should be conceived of simply as a mood disorder rather than as a complex disorder involving affective, cognitive, motivational, and behavioral components." (187)

The following statements may be compared in analyzing his view of emotion as it relates to feeling, mood, attitude and cognition:

a) "The change in his feeling may be explained as being consonant with a change in his conceptualizations." (260)
b) "The way an individual structures his experiences determines his mood." (261)
c) "The affective response is determined by the way an individual structures his experience." (287)
d) "The term *emotional manifestations* refers to the changes in the patient's feelings or the changes in his overt behavior *directly* attributable to his feeling states." (16)
e) "... attitudes such as 'I am capable'..." (276)

He divides symptoms into emotional, cognitive, motivational, and physical. The relation between these terms is not made clear. It would seem that emotion is confused with feeling. Individual emotions are mentioned as if they were merely feelings. Cognitions are treated as if they cause or interact with individual emotions. This confusion may be clarified by the adoption of the view that emotions refer to and consist of both assessments and feelings, and that therefore an emotion is not a feeling. It would then be a category-mistake to say, as Beck does, that joy, anxiety, depression, etc., are "felt." One could as well have said that such emotions are "thought"—or better yet felt-thought. Feelings may be reserved to refer to body sensations only. His use of "attitude" seems to be a belief or include both cognition and feeling. Beck's general theory is excellent and such distinctions as given here are meant to offer supportive clarifications rather than basic criticisms.

Beck notes that a number of other researchers emphasize the cognitive approach: G. Kelley (1955); O. Harvey, D. Hunt, and H. Schroder (1961); A. Ellis (1962); S. Arieti (1963). To this may be added Magda Arnold (1961); R. Lazarus (1966); the philosophers A. I. Melden (1969), E. Bedford (1964), and others. Insomuch as the psychiatrist or psychologist attempts to determine what the patient thought or is thinking, there is at least some kind of presupposition involved regarding cognition.

Beck notes that S. Kraines' biological explanation of depression in terms of hormonal changes and hereditary susceptibility is not yet supportable. Such abnormal hormone functions have not been found. It may be noted that on Kraines' view the process involves a stimulus from the cerebral cortex exciting the hypothalamus, then somato-visceral, reticular system, thalamus and limbic system and back to the cerebral cortex. As this process stresses the cerebral cortex, the assessment or cognitive view would seem to be given some support. Beck also finds insufficient evidence as yet for a biochemical theory of depression though there is hope that such causes will be found. It may be noted that even if chemicals were found, that need not disqualify Beck's theory because the very act of thinking is also chemical. Thinking in one way would produce different chemical reactions and bodily sensations than would thinking in another way. Cognition would still be the cause of a number of feelings.

Depression appears to be the major cause of mental suffering in and outside of mental hospitals.

"Depression is second only to schizophrenia in first and second admissions to mental hospitals in the United States, and it has been estimated that the prevalence of depression outside hospitals is five times greater than that of schizophrenia." (4)

"As yet no completely satisfactory explanation of its puzzling and paradoxical features has been found." (3)

Beck points out that the term ordinarily covers a number of different phenomena: normal mood, change in mood, loneliness, transient sadness; abnormal condition of depression; a subjective state; a complex of feeling, thought and action; a definite psychiatric disorder; result of organic disease; a classificatory term; etc. Thus the sense in which the term "depression" is used should be specified. To support and expand his view it may be added that the term should in each instance of its use be reduced to its concrete usage in a specific context. Each use has a different paradigm. The meaning of the word is its use in a context or language-game. To see this is to avoid ambiguity. This is in accordance with Wittgenstein's avoidance of naming-fallacy by means of his theory that a word be regarded as a use rather than as a name of an entity, and his theory of meaning in accordance with which meaning is only the association of one word with another in a language, and with a situation or context (i.e., a language-game).

For Beck, depression (and I would add, any emotion) develops out of the concepts one develops throughout his life:

> "Once a particular attitude or concept has been formed, it can influence subsequent judgments and become more firmly set. For instance, a child who gets the notion that he is inept, as a result of either a failure or of being called inept by somebody else, may interpret subsequent experiences according to this notion . . . . Once a concept is structuralized, it remains permanently with the individual even though it may be dormant; it becomes a cognitive structure, or *schema*." (275, 276)

If certain negative concepts are part of one's schema he may be especially apt to develop a neurosis or psychosis. The schema is developed on the basis of stimulus-response learning. Eventually a single association may call up an entire negative experience or response. "Schema" is certainly a Kantian notion: we sense the world in terms of our categories. There is no sensation without cognition, and no cognition without sensation. Thus one might also say there is no emotion without cognition and sensation, because emotion on the assessment view consists of both. Beck's cognition theory comes close to this view. Experience consists of both cognition and feeling, that is, it consists of emotion.

We see the world in terms of our schemas. Schemas refer to patterns of cognitions, and central to cognition is language. Thus Beck's view may be made specific by thinking of schemas more in terms of language or statements, and behavior than in terms of "ideas." Thus schemas may be thought of largely as statements we make to ourselves and to others. His talk of "free associations" dangerously borders on the now rejected theory of the atomistic "association of ideas," which was once called "mental chemistry." He wrote for example:

"The notion of schemas is utilized to account for the repetitive themes in free associations, daydreams, ruminations, and dreams, as well as in the immediate reactions to environmental events." (283)

"Associations" and "ruminations" need only refer to statements we utter to ourselves or others. They are associations of words, images, and perceptions, not of ideas or mental entities. (See W. Shibles "Meaning as Patterns of Marks") Beck sometimes does give emphasis to language when he states,

"The particular schema utilized may be a simple linguistic category." (283)

Thus schema may mean linguistic formula, habit, or image. These schemas may be clarified and expanded by relating them to some notions in contemporary philosophy as well as to everyday thinking. He states,

"There has been a notable lag in applying the structural concepts generated by studies of normal thinking to the thinking disorder associated with various psychiatric syndromes." (281)

Linguistic schemas may refer to rhetoric or, as was mentioned above, language-games, This is an expansion and extension of Beck's view of schema. The defense-mechanisms common in psychiatry are rhetorical devices or language-games. So also are the informal fallacies of logic. (See chapter dealing with these devices and metaphor.) The schemas may be rational or irrational statements.

Another term for schema or rhetorical device is metaphor or model. Metaphor is the central device of rhetoric. Many have asserted that all thinking is metaphorical and, if so, then here is a device which can relate everyday thinking with psychiatric thinking. Similar processes are involved. (See W. Shibles *Metaphor*) It has been argued that each philosophy or theory in science is based on one or more basic models, schemas, or metaphors and then expanded. An hypothesis is one form of metaphor. (See W. Shibles *Models of Ancient Greek Philosophy*). What it is important to see is that metaphors should not be taken literally, fixated, or treated as an exclusive perspective. To do so commits the metaphor-to-myth fallacy. Both the sane as well as the insane may be fixated on a single metaphor, a single perspective.

By seeing schemas as metaphor we may relate schemas to all of the different kinds of metaphor and rhetorical devices. For example, it was said that schema refers to linguistic formulae, habits and images. Simile, substitution, symbol, synecdoche, parataxis, etc. are a few of the hundreds of linguistic metaphorical categories. Habits may be thought of in terms of metaphorical behavior such as gesture, mimicry, play-acting, etc. Schemas as images lend themselves to metaphorical analysis, and metaphor is often called imagery. The imagist poets attempted to explore imagery metaphorically. In the philosophy of science, imagery takes the form of seeing-as. Norwood Hanson spoke of scientific method as involving the process of seeing-as. That is, we see the world in terms of our theories and our theories (statements) partly constitute reality, as well as color our perception. We begin to literally see the world in terms of our theories just as the psychotic may see a revolving door as a large machine trying to grind him up.

It may be noted that Freud's emphasis on early childhood erotic, anal, and oral experiences as determining subsequent experience may, instead of the analysis he gives, be due to the fact that as children we learn schemas, metaphors, or models which are formative of much of our experiences of later life.

The schema determines a certain kind of feeling. Beck thinks that for each thought there is a specific affect.

"It is postulated that the schema determines the specific type of affective response. If the schema is concerned with self-depreciation, a feeling of sadness will be associated with it . . . . An analogous relationship between the content of the schema and the corresponding feeling holds for other affects, such as anger and elation." (288)

A distinction should be made here. If Beck is saying that for any specific cognition a certain feeling must be evoked, the theory is questionable. If he only means that in our past we learned to relate certain cognitions with certain feelings, then the theory may have better support. One need not naturally or from birth, be fearful of snakes. Beck is not here discussing whether some emotions are natural or more basic than others. On the other hand certain cognitions do seem to bring on negative feelings. Some cognitions are contradictory, false, irrational, self-defeating, suicidal, etc. The particular schemas which tend to lead to depression, Beck discusses at length. (A. Ellis in *Reason and Emotion* presents ten to twelve irrational ideas which lead to negative emotions.) Cognitions may also bring on positive feelings:

"Among the positive (or self-enhancing) self-concepts are such attitudes as 'I am capable,' 'I am attractive,' 'I can get what I want,' 'I can understand problems and solve them.' Examples of negative (or self-diminishing) self-concepts are 'I am weak,' 'I am inferior,' 'I am unlovable,' and 'I can't do anything right.' " (276)

Not only does Beck seem to have a view similar to that of Ellis concerning the emotional effect of holding rational or irrational "ideas," but he presents these "ideas," as Ellis does, as statements uttered to oneself or aloud, e.g., "I am inferior."

The consequence of holding the schema "I am bad," or "I am inferior," is neuroticism and psychosis. These expressions are based on a confusion about value terms. Such terms as "good," "bad," "right," "wrong," "should," "should not," are open-context terms which are in themselves meaningless. To say "x is good," is unintelligible. Nothing is good or bad in itself. To make sense of "good," "bad," etc. one must substitute a descriptive or empirical term. "X is good," may mean "I like x," "x is legal," "x produces desirable consequences," "x coheres with my other beliefs," etc.

Ethical or value terms may be basically characterized as being open-context terms with a loosely limited range of substitution instances. That is all they are. Each substitution instance reduces to an empirical statement concerning a like, desire, wish, cause, consequence, description. To be ethical, then, would mean that one must know about himself and his environment so that he would know about the consequences of his actions for himself and others. To be rational he must not be captivated by misleading language such as category-mistakes or naming-fallacies, and he must understand how ethical terms work so as not to be misled by them. (See W. Shibles "Ethics as Open-Context Terms.")

When we say "x is good," we imply one or more of the possible meanings of "good," but it is not stated which meaning or substitution instance is intended. Worse, we may not know what we ourselves mean by "good," or "bad." This may be the case when we say "x is just bad, that's all," or "I am bad." One may have learned to say and believe he is "bad" but not understand that "bad" is an open-context term such that if what is meant by bad were discovered the person would not feel bad at all. There is no reason why one should ever feel bad or blamed. To feel bad implies a standard when there are no absolute standards. It is irrational to feel bad. To have negative feelings which "I feel bad" induces, does not solve problems. Instead of having bad (disliked) feelings, one should think and act rationally to correct and solve the problem at hand.

Beck seems to suggest some of the ideas in the above account according to which our confusion about ethical or value terms can bring on negative feelings, neurosis, or psychosis:

"Concepts such as good and bad are 'superordinate constructs' (Kelly 1955). A specific attribute may not be regarded initially as either good or bad but may, as the result of social learning, be organized under such a superordinate construct . . . . When an individual perceives himself as bad or undesirable he is likely to experience an unpleasant feeling such as sadness." (276)

The Kelly-Beck notion of ethical terms as "superordinate constructs" may be clarified and expanded in terms of the above view that ethical or value terms are open-context concepts. The ideas, whether rational or irrational, are associated with negative feelings by means of learning and conditioning.

"The process may be likened to conditioning in which a particular response is linked to a specific stimulus; once the chain has been formed, stimuli similar to the original stimulus may evoke the conditioned response." (278)

Although Beck does not mention it, it would seem that a perfectly rational idea could, by means of conditioning and learning, be associated with negative feelings. One may condition his negative feelings so that they are associated with various statements. "Bad" is a word used to evoke negative feelings. Negative feelings are then used consciously and by outside influence as a kind of power weapon to manipulate oneself or one's environment. What is questionable about this is whether or not such negative feelings are in fact necessary. Negative feelings seem to serve as defense mechanisms. But because such feelings are undesirable and can lead to physical and mental disorder, it would seem that they are diseases more than defenses. It may be argued that negative feelings are never desirable and should be prevented and avoided. Instead of having to react to an unjust situation by means of anger or depression it would be better to react by means of intelligence without negative feelings. Often people merely feel bad instead of acting or thinking. It is as if by feeling bad one can change the world or oneself by magic. What rather happens is that one changes the world only by the magic of insanity.

That negative emotions should be "released" shows a failure to understand the logic of emotions. Because emotions are largely cognitive, they need not be released but expressed. We do not express feelings, we express thoughts. We show or sense feelings. Thus when it is said that we should not repress emotions what is really being said is that we must express our thoughts and clarify them. Certainly this is helpful. We may clarify our thoughts silently by reading or by speaking in discussion, but unless we are unable to communicate we need not show negative feelings such as those involved in anger, rage, etc.

Conflict and frustration may also be a source of negative feelings:

"Another type of situation that may precipitate a depression is one involving a thwarting of important goals or posing an insoluble dilemma." (279)

If Beck's previous notion that negative feelings are conditioned is sound, then perhaps it would be possible for a mature person to have a conflict yet not let it induce negative feelings. That one has a conflict of ideas, does not mean he must have negative feelings. When contradictory statements are confronted one may simply, for the time being, claim ignorance. We need not say, "I do not know, and that is bad." That we do not know is objectively given; that it is bad is not given but added by us. The addition is harmful and unnecessary.

The depressed person is one who does not see that negative feelings are unnecessary and harmful, or he has restricted his schemas and intelligence so that he does not understand what options of viewing and interpreting reality are open to him. To be ethical and sane is to be intelligent, to know about oneself and one's environment, so that one knows about cause and effect as they relate to his own and others' feelings and cognitions.

"The depressed patient shows certain patterns of illogical thought. The systematic errors, leading to distortions of reality, include arbitrary interpretation, selective abstraction, overgeneralization, exaggeration, and incorrect labelling." (285)

But it may be that one can have illogical thought without negative feelings. This may later lead to further cognitive and motor disorder. It may be suggested that mental disorder is not a disorder of logical thinking but rather a disorder of the conditioning and control of our feelings. We may learn to attach negative feelings to any thought. The psychotic often does have "inappropriate" emotions. One may argue that anger, depression, and other negative emotions are almost never "appropriate." Put colloquially, one may say, "Negative emotions bake no bread."

If one is captivated by his model, schema, or metaphor and so takes it literally he becomes fixated and dogmatic. This leads to conflict with reality. Such captivation is similar to hypnosis or self-suggestion. Such suggestion may be limiting and harmful if negative and unrealistic. Positive suggestion, however, such as "I can do it," may be helpful. Beck wrote,

"The depression-prone person experiences a *constriction of his cognitive field* and he is bombarded by negative self-judgments and negative ideas about the future." (279)

One objection to Beck's theory that cognition precedes feeling or emotion, is that it does not account for shock, or hangover depression due to physical causes. This criticism is handled by means of his "circular feedback model." He states,

"The direction has been from cognition to emotion. But it is conceivable that there is an interaction between these, and that feelings may also influence thought content . . . . This interaction, thus, consists of schemas [reciprocally inter-acting with] affective structures. This model could explain the downward spiral in depression: The more negatively the patient thinks, the worse he feels; the worse he feels, the more negatively he thinks." (289)

Becks's view does not entirely handle the objection. Perhaps the cognition and feeling come at the same time. The possibilities may rather be as follows:

1. Cognition and perception precede feeling.
2. Cognition, perception and feeling occur at the same time as in the case of shock.
3. Cognition follows feeling as in the case of illness or a hangover. The feeling is reported or assessed by means of a cognition.

One always has assessments gathered from prior experience. In this sense cognition is nearly always prior to feeling. And feelings are largely rendered in terms of cognitive language, e.g., "I am depressed," "I feel bad." But certain specific cognitions may follow feelings. There are, then, assessments of many kinds some of which precede, some come at the same time, and some come after feelings. All of these may be part of a particular emotion.

Up to now I have supported and expanded Beck's excellent account. There is, however, one slip. It involves the concept of "energy." He wrote:

"It is possible to travel into still more speculative areas by incorporating the concept of energy into this formulation. Let us assume that initially the schema is energized as the result of some psychological trauma. The activation of this cognitive structure leads to the stimulation of the affective structure. The activation of the affective structure produces a burst of energy, which is experienced subjectively as a painful emotion. The energy then flows back to the cognitive structure and increases the quantity of energy attached to it. This then produces further innervation of the affective structure." (289)

In a footnote he states,

"In discussing structure and process it is difficult to avoid the introduction of energy concepts. Such concepts are often vague and elusive and their utility and validity in personality theory have been strongly challenged .... On the other hand, the concept of energy is employed by many disparate schools of psychoanalytic theory." (289)

Beck correctly suspects his own analysis of energy. "Energy" is a vague abstraction and leads to a naming-fallacy. There is no "energy" as such. It is elliptical for a concrete process or configuration of events. Abstract terms if they are to be intelligible should always be reduced to concrete operations, objects, or situations. In Beck's usage it is not clear what energy means. It seems to cover a kind of mentalism held by other psychoanalysts. But that many psychoanalysts use the term is no argument for it. Physicists also use the term, but they commit the same error. What is meant, for example, by saying there is energy in a magnet is simply such things as that iron filings move toward the magnet. On the chemical level, "energy" should be similarly defined in terms of concrete observable events or operations. There is no "energy" as such. To think there is is to commit a naming-fallacy. Beck could legitimately hold an "energy" model if he realized, as I think he really does, that it is only a metaphor, and if he expanded the model to make it intelligible — which he does not do.

As a result of his cognitive theory of depression he proposes a "cognitive (insight) therapy" to deal with depression. He gives support to what I have called long term and short term assessment:

"Cognitive psychotherapy may be used symptomatically during depressions to help the patient gain objectivity toward his automatic reactions and counteract them. During non-depressed periods, the therapy is designed to modify the idiosyncratic cognitive patterns to reduce the patient's vulnerability to future depressions." (318)

The patient's individual cognitions or irrational ideas must be corrected as well as his view of cause and effect and knowledge of reality generally. Beck calls the former the "microscopic" technique, and the latter the "macroscopic technique." Both techniques would seem to involve the sort of critical inquiry and clarification which philosophers traditionally do. It is for this reason that A. Ellis calls his own technique "philosophical or rational psychotherapy."

Beck suggests an examination of one's misconceptions, superstitions, syllogisms, etc. His suggestion may be made more concrete. Because thought is largely language use, to examine one's thinking is mainly to examine one's language. An adequate analysis would also involve imagery, habits, behavior, and perceptions. One's language may, then, be reduced to concrete examples in concrete contexts or situations. Each word and movement should be examined. This approach would oppose abstraction, mental constructs such as id, ego, superego. But also it would oppose formal logic. Symbolic and Aristotelian logic have very little to do with the way humans think. Benedetto Croce wrote, "As the science of thought, logistic is a laughable thing." (*Logic* 1917) The symbolic logician, A. N. Whitehead, wrote, "Logic, conceived as an adequate analysis of the advance of thought is a fake." Thus Beck need not have stressed the syllogism as if we think syllogistically. Language is more complex than that. What does have to do with thought is ordinary language and the way it is specifically used in concrete situations. But this is only to say that ordinary-language philosophy is at the same time psychotherapy. Ludwig Wittgenstein wrote,

"The philosopher's treatment of a question is like the treatment of an illness." (PI 255)

"A main cause of philosophical disease—a one-sided diet: one nourishes one's thinking with only one kind of example." (PI 593)

"When philosophers use a word—'knowledge,' 'being,' 'object,' 'I,' 'proposition,' 'name'—and try to grasp the *essence* of the thing, one must always ask oneself: is the word ever actually used in this way in the language-game which is its original home? —What *we* do is to bring words back from their metaphysical to their everyday use." (PI 116)

"The results of philosophy are the uncovering of one or another piece of plain nonsense and of bumps that the understanding has got by running its head up against the limits of language." (PI 119)

Thus, one way of providing concrete therapeutic techniques is to use some of the methods proposed by Wittgenstein and ordinary-language philosophers. This book is one such account. One method is to understand how metaphor, language-games, and ethical terms work and to avoid the informal fallacies of logic. (Informal fallacies are really types of rhetorical devices of ordinary language, whereas formal logic is patterned after numbers and mathematics and has little to do with language.) Some such examples of concrete verbalizations are contained throughout Beck's book,

"When she started to prepare a roast, she had the thought, 'I won't be able to do it.' She reasoned the problem through and verbalized to herself, 'I've done this many times before. I may be a little slower than usual because I'm depressed but I know what to do and if I think it out step-by-step there's no reason why I can't do it.' She felt heartened after this and finished preparing the meal." (325)

Beck has given a beautiful analysis here and its profundity is mainly due to its simplicity. He was able to report the sorts of things which by close examination in fact take place. To describe what is immediately before one can be quite difficult. One might, then, suggest that one way to treat neurotic and psychotic patients is by having one therapist deal with one patient continuously or for long periods of time so that each statement and action of the patient is deliberately corrected. A pilot project of this sort should be tried in "mental" hospitals. Both therapist and patient should benefit.

Albert Ellis, following the views of philosophers such as Marcus Aurelius, states that it is not the event that is psychologically damaging but our interpretation of the event. Ellis refers to this as his A-B-C theory. Beck seems to hold a similar view when he states,

"At the beginning of therapy the patient is generally aware only of the following sequence: event or stimulus [to] affect. He must be trained to fill in the link between the stimulus and the affect: stimulus [to] cognition [to] affect." (322)

Imagery was earlier found to be one kind of captivating schema. It therefore also has importance for therapy:

"When he contemplates an event in the near or distant future, the patient has a pictorial image of a negative outcome." (329)

"I have found . . . that it has been possible to alleviate pessimism by inducing the patient to have more realistic fantasies about anticipated events. Another technique of combating the sense of inadequacy or deprivation is to suggest that the patient recall in pictorial form certain past successes or gratifications." (330)

"In an attempt to help her deal with the expectation of frustration and humiliation, I asked her to imagine the scene in the supermarket again. This time she felt less humiliation."

The last mentioned technique is that of having the patient imagine that which he fears, but imagine it with the proper assessment and understanding. If properly done the irrational fear often vanishes. One of the techniques involved in teaching sailing is to have the student purposely tip the boat over so he will learn what to do and not be afraid as he might otherwise. One may be captivated by a picture or image just as one may be captivated by an irrational schema or metaphor. Often both verbalization and imagery are intertwined as they are in metaphor.

Beck found that the dream imagery of depressed patients shows a consistent pattern involving the following categories (209):

1. Deprived, disappointed, or mistreated.
2. Thwarted.
3. Excluded, superseded, or displaced.
4. Rejected or deserted.
5. Blamed, criticized, or ridiculed.
6. Legal punishment.
7. Physical discomfort or injury.
8. Distorted appearance.
9. Being lost.
10. Losing something of value.

On the basis of his theory and experimental results, Beck clarifies and characterizes depression as follows. It involves: sadness, pessimism, failure, dissatisfaction, guilt, punishment, self-dislike, self-accusations, suicidal wishes, crying, irritability, withdrawal, indecision, poor self-image, work inhibition, insomnia, fatigue, anorexia (loss of appetite), hypochondria, libido loss. (200) He divides these into four groups: affective (sad, lonely, etc.), motivational (wishes for help, etc.), cognitive (e.g., pessimism), physical and vegetative symptoms (e.g., loss of appetite).

One of the difficulties with this analysis is that one emotion, depression, is defined in terms of other emotions, e.g., guilt and sadness. But guilt and sadness reduce to further cognitions which guide feelings. It would be better to mention the specific cognitions and feelings, and avoid obscure emotion terms. Beck does mention, in great detail, specific cognitions and specific statements made.

The cognitive disturbances in depression are presented in the form of a triad. These lead to negative affects, motivations, and physical states. There is a negative view of the 1) world, 2) self, and 3) future. Thinking is illogical. The depressed patient has fixed ideas, overgeneralizes, focuses on negative aspects, exaggerates, labels improperly, magnifies, minimizes, is unable to accurately criticize or inquire. The triad is expanded as follows: 1) Negative view of the world: The depressed person views his situation negatively in spite of the facts. He exaggerates defeat, thwarting, deprivation, depreciation, 2) Negative View of self: He devalues and blames himself, 3) Negative view of the future: His schema, or fixed metaphor, through which he views the future is pessimism.

The affect changes with the cognition. Motivation change involves paralysis of the will, escapism tendencies, suicidal wishes, dependency wishes. Beck specifies at great length the specific cognitions which constitute depression. Cognitions of inadequacy, being deserted, or being sinful lead to affects of sadness, loneliness, or guilt, respectively. (230) For example, the depressive often utters self-coercive cognitions involving nagging, prodding, "shoulds" and "musts." It may be noted that "should" and "must" are open-context ethical terms which need to be questioned. Why "should" one do x? The answer often reduces to an if-then proposition such as "If you want x you must do y, and I assume you want x." The patient may then see that he may not want x. To say "X is a duty in itself," or "One should do x for its own sake," is not intelligible but irrational, and these are obscure ideas leading to neurosis, compulsive or obsessive behavior, etc.

Sources:

Aaron Beck <u>Depression</u> University of Pennsylvania Press 1967

Albert Ellis <u>Reason and Emotion</u> New York: Lyle Stuart 1962

Norwood Hanson <u>Patterns of Discovery</u> Cambridge University Press 1961

G. Kelly <u>The Psychology of Personal Constructs</u> New York: Norton 1955, Vol. I

S. Kraines "Manic-Depressive Syndrome" APA Meeting, New York, May 6, 1965

Warren Shibles "Ethics as Open-Context Terms," "Meaning as Patterns of Marks" <u>Philosophical Pictures</u> 2nd edition, Dubuque, Iowa: Kendall-Hunt 1972

Warren Shibles <u>Metaphor: An Annotated Bibliography and History</u> Whitewater, Wisconsin: The Language Press 1971

Warren Shibles <u>Models of Ancient Greek Philosophy</u> London: Vision Press 1971

Ludwig Wittgenstein <u>Philosophical Investigations</u> 3rd edition, New York: Macmillan 1969

Carroll Izard's Differential
Theory of Emotions

Izard's most recent book on emotions, *Patterns of Emotions* (1972), presents a theory of emotions which contrasts with the cognitive or assessment theory of emotions. The following is a defense of cognitive theory against his views and objections. His position is stated, followed by support of or objections to his views.

1. According to Izard there are nine fundamental emotions upon which all other emotions are based. These basic emotions are: interest, joy, surprise, distress, anger, disgust, contempt, shame (shyness, guilt), and fear. (2, 52, 84)

This view simply defines one emotion in terms of other emotions. The procedure is circular if one wishes to know what an emotion is. The basic emotions chosen are, in fact, not basic because each may be reduced to a number of cognitive and contextual factors. On the assessment theory an emotion is assessments which interpret and describe contexts and these assessments guide feelings. Such assessments and contexts are too diverse to be rendered by such abstract terms as interest, joy, shame, etc. What Izard could have rather done would have been to find the basic feelings (not emotions) one has and then relate these to assessments and behaviors. Feelings are relatively more basic than emotions and are, for the most part, given or basic experiences. Thus, instead of starting with basic emotions, he could have started with basic bodily feelings such as pain, warmth, etc. Emotions are pseudo-concepts which only have meaning if reduced to their specific non-emotion components. (cf. B. Skinner, etc.)

189

190

2. "A fundamental emotion will be felt." (57)

This commits the fallacy of identifying an emotion with a feeling. Because emotion consists largely of cognitive assessments, and partly describes a situation or context, we can no more properly say that we "feel" emotion than that we "feel" a statement or that we "feel" a context. Objective descriptions are not felt. (cf. E. Bedford, A. I. Melden, etc.)

3. Each basic emotion serves an adaptive purpose and helps one to survive. (2, 69)

This Darwinian theory lacks support. Emotions such as anxiety and depression cause psychosomatic disorder, neurosis, and psychosis. They are non-adaptive and destructive. They do not help one to survive. We often become angry or are in shock because we fail to adapt or cope. Anger is the result of confused and irrational thinking and may be regarded as a sign that there is a breakdown in our understanding. We may then correct our misjudgment, but the anger itself does not cope with the problem encountered. One may be startled at a noise and this may be thought to produce the same reaction certain animals and insects have when they play dead (thanatomimesis). The startle may not be defensive at all but rather detrimental when a tiger is about to leap on the startled person. However, some insects and animals cannot see certain objects unless they are moving. Anger and such emotions often cause one to be less able to use cognitive functions, thereby impairing sound judgment. (The activation of certain nerve systems associated with emotion inhibits cortical function.) Also, for these reasons, it cannot be clearly made out that all the emotions once had a survival function. Depressed people tend to be highly suicidal, and an angry person would be disliked and be more likely to be attacked than one who is not angry. Negative emotions would seem to be neither adaptive nor survival mechanisms. Magda Arnold states:

"Not only is excessive emotion harmful because it prevents effective action, but emotion often interferes when it is not at all excessive . . . .It could almost be said that there is *always* danger that emotions will lead us astray." (187)

4. Each basic emotion is comprised uniquely of all three of the following components: a.) neurophysical (innate), b.) behavioral-expressive, c.) experiential (including cognition). (2, 52)

This analysis fails to include the fact that what we mean by emotion usually includes a description of a context or situation as well as assessments of various sorts. Jealousy, for example, partly describes a situation in which one person did something in regard to someone else. Also it is the assessment of the situation which is basic, not the feelings or physical response. That each basic emotion has a definite neurophysiological basis has not been clearly made out. Knowledge of the neural mechanisms involved is far from adequate. In addition, such mechanisms are involved in cognition also. To speak about neurophysiology is to speak on a certain level. What we usually mean by emotion has nothing to do with neurology or chemistry. It has to do with descriptions of people, situations, and feelings. It is a category-mistake to say "I feel chemical," or "I feel (literally) nervous."

By suggesting that the basic emotions such as anger and disgust are innate, Izard is suggesting that they are part of one's nature and so perhaps cannot be changed. This is a destructive view for therapy. On the assessment theory, because emotions are largely cognitions, one can learn to dissipate anger and disgust by changing one's assessments, perceptions, and habits based on such assessments. Even feelings can be greatly modified, for example, psychogenic pain.

5. Neither one of the above three components alone constitutes emotion. For example, emotion is not just an autonomic-visceral process as some psychologists believe. (2)

The assessment theory is in agreement with this.

6. "Emotion tends to involve the whole organism rather than to remain a process confined to a single system." (3)

Assessment theory is in agreement.

7. Emotions rarely occur pure or alone, but rather in combination. This is the basis of what Izard terms his "differential emotion theory." For example, we seldom have

fear alone but rather fear and interest, or fear and guilt. This theory seems to be basically a theory of mixed emotions. (Preface)

Rather than clarify emotions this theory compounds them. Izard believes that we could not understand emotions in the past because there were several emotions present at the same time. On the assessment theory we could not understand emotion because emotion terms are abstract pseudo-concepts. What is needed is to reduce such terms to concrete paradigms, operations and objects such as feelings, statements, specific contexts, etc. Izard's view is atomistic and he seems to be engaged in a kind of "mental chemistry" according to which atoms make up various molecules. But his notion of atom is not adequate or is more stipulative than descriptive.

8. The reason scientists have not found physiological correlates of emotion is due to the fact that emotions rarely exist pure or alone. (9)

On the cognitive view one of the reasons involved is that the neural and chemical correlates of language use are not yet known and have been left out of the analyses. Any adequate analysis of emotion must include and account for cognitive assessments which man makes. Another reason is that emotion is not a single entity but an elliptical term standing for a number of factors. The failure is not due to the circumstances of there being several basic emotions to deal with at once.

9. Because non-basic emotions are complexes of emotions they are not just simple causes or responses. They are not unitary concepts. (45, 46) (cf. number 25)

The assessment theory is in agreement except that the definition of emotion differs greatly.

10. Emotions are usually too complex to regard simply as polar opposites. (53)

This is an interesting point and may help correct the view that love is the opposite of hate. The assessment theory is in agreement except for the definition of emotion.

11. "The emotion process can begin with memory or imagination in the ideation centers of the brain or with perception of, or excitation of receptors by, an external emotion-effective object or event." (55)

This statement seems to give support to the assessment theory or cognitive theory of emotion. When a process "begins" may be difficult to determine, but because of the importance of assessment and language one could say the latter "determine" or "guide" subsequent processes. The cognition can determine whether there will be a feeling response as well as what kind of response it will be. On the assessment theory, cognition may also follow and occur at the same time as feelings and perceptions. But is it mainly our interpretations of a stimulus which determine whether or not we will become emotional about it. A reflex action such as touching a hot stove is not regarded as a full emotion. It could be regarded as one if assessments become prominent. Such experiences are usually said to be reactions rather than emotions. That they involve bodily feelings makes them seem somewhat like emotions. Assessment may occur contemporaneous with feeling as in the case of shock, or after feeling, as in the case of assessing a stomachache. The latter case may be regarded as a bodily feeling rather than as an emotion. Shock contains elements of conflicting prior assessments, confused cognitions, and inability to assess.

12. The cortex is regarded as the ultimate integrating mechanism of emotion. (25)

This seems to offer support to the cognitive theory.

13. Therapy regarding emotion involves analyzing complex emotions into their basic emotions. (58)

This technique would be inadequate for reasons previously given and because what therapy mainly needs to deal with is the assessments an individual has. (cf. A. Beck, A. Ellis, A.I. Melden, R. Lazarus, M. Arnold, et al.)

14. Cognition follows or interacts with emotion. Emotions guide and select sensory data leading to cognition. Cognition is a by-product of emotion. (68, 69, 79, 81)

"Life experiences are typically characterized by a pattern of emotions and feelings that direct or influence cognition and action." (282)

The relation between cognition and feeling is discussed above (no. 11). One of the reasons Izard holds that emotions precede cognition is that he has not clearly distinguished between emotion and feeling. On the assessment view, cognition is part of emotion and so, in this sense, one could say emotion comes before assessment. But to do so is only to say that cognition plus feeling comes before further cognition. To speak of emotion and feelings as directing or selecting may seem to refer to perception, to discrimination. But perception is never direct. It is highly dependent on cognition and past assessments. The very experience of 3-D and depth depends upon assessments. When the assessments are mistaken illusion results. We tend to see things in terms of our needs and beliefs. We see both more and less than meets the eye. (cf. chapter on perception.) Feelings do not select, although we can only feel what it is possible to feel with the limited sense organs we possess. Feelings are never pure. If they were, we wouldn't experience them. This is because feelings are always related to other experiences. The test of this would be to try to have a feeling independent of present and prior cognitions and unrelated to anything else. But such purity would be like invisible white.

If Izard were right about cognition following emotion, it would mean that emotions would be difficult or impossible to control and that cognitive therapy would be of little use. However, all or most psychotherapy relies on cognitive methods of treatment.

15. Babies experience emotions, e.g., distress, even at the age of six months. (68)

To say that babies experience "distress" as adults do is to use the term metaphorically. Izard appears to think that the term applies literally to babies. Compare "The student was distressed with his friends," with "The baby was distressed with his friends," or "The dog was distressed with his friends." Babies would not seem to have this kind of distress. They would need to understand our language to be able to experience distress as an adult might experience it.

16. We do not learn how to have an emotion but only what to be emotional about. (69)

This erroneously treats cognition and emotion as entirely separate, though interacting, things. On the assessment view, emotion is partly rational. In addition, one *can* learn to have an emotion and also how to dissipate or prevent having emotions. It is necessary for therapy that we be able to do this. By changing our assessments we can change our emotions.

17. Cognition is not the autonomous cause of emotion. Innateness is a factor as well as prior emotions. (67, 68)

It is agreed that cognition is not the only condition or factor in an emotion. On the other hand, without cognition the emotion might never be experienced. In Kantian terms, there is no cognition without sensation and no sensation without cognition.

As was mentioned earlier, it is dangerous to believe that emotions are innate because it suggests that they cannot then be changed. As Albert Ellis stated, one of the irrational ideas most harmful to therapy is the prevalent view that emotions cannot be changed because they are part of one's nature or because they are innate.

"Innate" indicates that there are genetic determinants of emotions. But such determinants are yet to be found. "Innate" may merely mean that man has certain frequently repeated patterns of behavior. Even if both the genetic pattern and notion of frequency is intended, neither account precludes the possibility that the emotion can be changed.

18. Emotions may even operate without cognition. (70)

It has been pointed out that cognition is essentially involved in both perception, sensation, and emotion. On the assessment view, emotion cannot operate without cognition because emotion partly consists of cognition. Also, because we do not know how we would think or what thinking would be independent of language, language, and thus cognition, has epistemological primacy. (See W. Shibles "Linguo-Centric Predicament.")

There is an ambiguity in the statement that emotions may even operate without cognition. Does this mean there is no present cognition or no past cognition? Certainly there are at least past cognitions. Cognitions and emotions may become habitual. If a cognition becomes automatic it does not lose its status as a cognition.

19. Emotion should not be regarded as a "disease" or "syndrome." Emotion is a natural and normal subsystem of the person or organism." (71, 72, 80)

Lazarus and Averill are mentioned as having regarded emotions as diseases. It may be added that Engel in "Is Grief a Disease" (1961) argues that it is a disease. He showed that grief has a definite syndrome and predictable symptomatology and course. Grief is like a disease and should be treated therefore as something one can treat and cure. Erich Lindemann (1944) also regards grief as a disease. He shows that it has a definite immediate or delayed syndrome and results in psychiatric and bodily disorder. (See chapter on emotion and therapy.)

On the assessment view, negative emotions can be prevented and, if present, eliminated. To say negative emotions are "natural" and "normal" is like saying that disease is natural and normal. To suggest that anger, hatred, rage, etc. are normal can be very harmful. Rather both negative emotions and disease can to a large extent be eliminated.

20. The cognitive theory cannot deal with objectless fear or free-floating anxiety. (73) Undirected arousal is really several emotions together. (77) Indecisiveness is conflict between emotions. (231)

On the assessment theory, emotions involve cognition and so a conflict of emotions is partly a conflict of assessments. If "emotion" only meant "feeling" it would not be clear what it would be like for feelings to conflict. Statements conflict, not sensations. The assessment theory can handle anxiety better than can Izard's theory because anxiety (barring special chemical causes) is due to confused or absent goals, confused ideas, or conflicts of ideas (statements). It is odd to say that my emotions or my feelings are indecisive.

21. Izard opposes over-inclusive theories of emotions which include contextual situations and purposive actions. "Cognitive theory fails to distinguish the emotion process from processes that are antecedent, concomitant, or consequent to the emotion process." (80, 81)

He holds this view because he seems to regard emotions as if they were feelings. Feelings may be regarded as relatively independent of the context and situation, but not emotions. But to understand the meaning of "love" of one's neighbor, involves one's neighbor. Part of what is meant by "shame" is that someone is, was, or may be critical of us. We can only understand emotions if we know something about the context in which they occur. What in one context is hate is, in another context, an act of love. What we usually mean by emotion words includes contexts, goals, cognitions, purposes. Even the feelings we have are described in terms of situations and external events, e.g., "sharp" pain, feel "blue," etc.

22. Arousal and activation are distinct from emotion. (75)

S. Schachter has presented a theory of emotion in accordance with which cognition determines what form bodily activation will take. (cf. chapter on Schachter) Cognition determines whether the activation is to result in love or anger. In this sense arousal is not distinct from emotion. On the other hand, the assessment theory is in agreement with Izard's view in the sense that emotion is not the same thing as arousal or activation. Even excitement and nervousness involve cognition.

23. Izard accuses cognitive theorists of holding that cognition produces a single enduring emotion whereas on his theory several emotions are involved at the same time. (77)

On the assessment theory, emotion changes each time there is a new cognition and there are constantly new cognitions. Thus emotion is not a fixed atomistic or molecular entity as it is on Izard's view, but is rather a constantly changing experience. No two emotions are exactly alike and the same cognition may later produce a different feeling (emotion). However, in the case of perseveration or "fixed idea" there is a more or less static experience. By examining one's cognitions the subtle, dynamic aspects of emotions may be explicated. Novelists and poets as well as psychiatrists, philosophers and social scientists often explore such aspects.

24. For each fundamental emotion there is a corresponding facial expression. (85)

This is often the case because we partly mean by emotion the particular facial expression. "Fear" and "surprise" often include reference to one's facial expression. It is, then, not the case that the emotion *corresponds* to facial expression but that emotion includes the facial expression as part of its meaning.

But there are great cultural and individual differences between people which preclude judging emotion by facial expression. An actor uses facial expression as a means of pretending to have a certain emotion. Smiling may be a poor guide to one's emotions because in our culture we are expected to smile. In Japan, one smiles in situations which we would regard as entirely inappropriate here. The psychotic also has inappropriate facial expressions. It would be simplistic to conclude that the normal person, neurotic, or psychotic has a certain emotion because he displays certain facial expressions. Facial expression would seem to be a "superficial" aspect of emotion.

A brief account follows of Izard's *The Face of Emotion*. It is first pointed out that research on emotions has been inadequate.

"Psychological science lags far behind common sense." (14)

"In spite of their importance, science has generally neglected the emotions and contributed relatively little to our ability to understand, control, or utilize them." (V)

Izard's main point in this book is that facial expression is not merely a result of subjective experience but partly constitutes it. Facial expression is not merely a response. In regard to emotions, he stresses action and the neuromuscular over reason or judgment. Thus, the patient must restructure his behavior, imagery, muscular activity, esp., facial patterns. His view is:

"Emotion has a motor or striate muscle component and this component can provide the most efficient and effective means of controlling and regulating emotion." (421)

"Emotion demands motor action, be it imaging, vocalization, or a subsequent organismic function or instrumental motor act." (422)

"The face is the major vehicle for the expression of emotion." (81)

25. Each emotion is a special internal state. "Each discrete emotion is thought to constitute a special state or process in the organism and to have particular motivational and experiential properties." (Izard and Bartlett 130) (cf. no. 9)

This view suggests mentalism, the existence of internal and private states. The argument against mentalism need not be elaborated here. It is adequately presented by G. Ryle, L. Wittgenstein, A. I. Melden, E. Bedford, et al.

26. Anxiety is a derived emotion consisting of two or more of the fundamental emotions of fear, distress, shame, anger, interest. (40, 41) Grief consists of anger, disgust, contempt, guilt. (177)

As was mentioned earlier, this merely defines one emotion in terms of others and treats emotions as entities or atoms to be combined. It ignores the basic cognitive constituents of emotions. The definition may, however, serve as a very general or rough guide to some but not all of the behavioral patterns which occur when someone is said to be anxious.

27. "We often say of Freud's analysis of a clinical problem that very little can be added that is really new and different." (196)

Izard's support of Freud here may be contrasted with the former's statements of the views of S. Kraines and A. Beck:

"Kraines prefaces his position with a rather severe criticism of Freud and the psychoanalytic theory of depression. He characterized the psychoanalytic view as imaginative, metaphorical fantasy. Some of his criticism is well taken, as is his criticism of the seeming circularity of some psychoanalytic thinking." (216)

He summarizes Beck's view as follows:

"Beck made two quite telling criticisms of the psychoanalytic formulations of depression. First some of the conceptualizations are so remote from observable behavior that they defy validation . . . Beck also indicated that psychoanalytic theories often account for only some aspects of the complex picture of depression and correctly pointed out that any adequate theory would have to account for a wide variety of psychopathological phenomena." (224)

28. S. Kraines is a cognitive theorist and presents objections against psychoanalytic theory. Izard thinks that these objections would also apply against cognitive theory. The following are replies to such objections. (216, 217)

a) "Many persons become depressed without any discernible precipitating factor." (Kraines)

Depression is usually caused by disorganized, unrealistic, or confused assessments. But sometimes by taking a certain drug one may become depressed. But in the latter cases it would result in a different kind of depression and would involve different factors. We may wish to say a person is physically depressed rather than psychologically depressed, although psychological depression may follow physical feelings of pain, etc. One could be physically ill yet learn not to be depressed. Psychosis, which is conceived of as an emotional and cognitive disorder, is usually defined as a disorder for which there is no known physical cause. The disorders are often controlled by means of drugs but in perhaps every case cognitive therapy is used. The drugs alone do not cure the disorder. Even in cases where the disorder may be due to a physical cause, cognitive therapy may be used in overcoming it. For example, one may learn how to live with a painful illness. It would seem that depression is not the sort of thing that can have a physical cause because by depression we partly mean cognition. If depression has solely a physical cause it may be more like a feeling such as pain, not depression.

b) "Even some psychogenic factors considered to be precipitating factors may have occurred on numerous previous occasions in the person's life without bringing on a depression."

Cognition is part of what is meant by depression. Although certain irrational or confused cognitions tend to be followed by certain negative feelings it may be contingent that certain specific feelings follow certain cognitions. We may learn to avoid negative feelings — for example, by accepting ourselves, or our situation. Thus, in opposition to Kraines' objection, it is not necessary on the cognitive view that *certain* psychogenic factors bring on depression.

    c) There are often several decades between a child-hood trauma and the onset of a depression."

On the assessment or cognitive theory, this just means it is not the trauma itself that causes depression but confused and repeated cognitions which eventually result in negative feelings. The trauma itself is due to confused, conflicting and inadequate cognition. Both trauma and depression may be avoided by developing long-range, critical, and adequate assessments regarding oneself and one's environment.

    d) "Many people suffer a 'serious ego trauma' without developing a serious depression."

Perhaps this is the case, if one says so. But what is meant by "serious ego trauma" or "ego"? What exactly is being suffered from? If one has a traumatic experience it need not result in depression. The manic and hysteric need not be depressed. Of course, one could *stipulate* that whenever someone deviates from the normal it is because he is basically or covertly depressed. But to stipulate is not to accurately describe. Rather, the sorts of cognitions (language used) a person has would give a clear notion of what is meant by "ego" here and also determine, on the basis of learning, what sorts of emotions will result.

    e) "Age, sex, and climatic change have been shown to be related to depression."

That this is sometimes the case does not mean that it needs to be the case. Also physical feelings may change or be different due to age, sex, climate. This would only mean that the feeling part of emotion would be different. Men and women may have different feelings in different cultures, roles, and climates. It is not a denial of the cognitive theory.

"Involutional melancholia" is an official classification listed by the American Psychiatric Association. By "involutional" is meant that there is a physical cause, menopause or climacteric, of the depression. This disorder occurs more in women than men. But of this classification the psychiatrist, A. Beck, writes,

"There is no specific psychosis of the climacterium," (103) but rather there is "strong evidence against the notion of a specific, involutional syndrome distinguishable from other depressions on the basis of the symptomatology." (105) "A survey of the systematic studies of involutional depression raises strong doubt regarding the usefulness of this nosological category." (107)

f) "Psychodynamic factors are idiosyncratic and highly varied, yet depression tends strongly toward a patterned process of onset, course, and termination."

A. Beck has pointed out in his book, *Depression*, that there is a very consistent pattern of cognition which leads to depression. Albert Ellis has similarly shown that it is basically a certain number and type of irrational ideas which lead to depression. Beck has even suggested that mental disorders be reclassified on the basis of cognitions and he has himself offered some such reclassifications. Nevertheless, as was stated in #b above, the connection between certain cognitions and feelings may be contingent and just learned.

g) "Depression is typically time-limited and often cyclic."

This objection seems to apply especially to the manic-depressive category. A. Beck points out that although sometimes the swing from elation to depression is absolutely regular, the swing between cycles is seldom regular. (Beck 115) But even if there were regularity it may be seen to be a regularity of how one feels, whereas emotion involves cognition as well as feeling. That one has a time sense at all may be partly due to prior cognitive sets such as saying to oneself, "I must wake up at seven tomorrow morning." The assessment may then tend to guide feelings and motor activities. Similarly saying to oneself, "I must be careful," guides certain motions and activities. After repeated experience and practice one could learn to develop careful work habits or to wake up at a certain time. It is likely that one could change the regularity of the manic's time cycle of mood swing by changing the patient's assessments.

> h) "Radical therapies such as electric shock often prove therapeutic."

Izard himself gives evidence which may be used against this statement. He quotes J. Davis: "The antidepressants are clinically neither specific nor highly effective." Electroshock therapy may have some effect on depression but increases anxiety. R. Drake in *Abnormal Psychology* states about shock therapy:

> "Best results are obtained if psychotherapy accompanies the shock treatments." (123)

> "After 15 or more daily [insulin shock] treatments the patient is expected to show more lucidity . . . The psychiatrist or clinical psychologist uses these periods of improved contact with reality to change fixed ideas and attitudes which may have caused the maladjustment." (123)

> "Generally, no great improvement results [from the use of sodium amytal] unless accompanied by psychotherapy." (124)

> "The shock is not a cure and does little more than to put the patient into contact with his immediate environment so he may be reached by psychotherapy." (124)

> "Physiotherapy and physical methods should not be expected to cure a patient who has a mental conflict. They may only alleviate discomfort and put the patient into a more tractable condition for removing the real cause of his maladjustment." (126)

It may also be observed that drug and shock treatment may have the cognitive effect of acting as placebos, or cause self-suggestions.

204

Sources:

Magda Arnold "Human Emotion and Action" Human Action T. Mischel, ed.
    New York: Academic Press 1969
Aaron Beck, Depression Univ. of Pennsylvania Press 1967
Errol Bedford "Emotions" Essays in Philosophical Psychology D. Gustafson,
    ed. New York: Doubleday 1964
Charles Darwin Expression of the Emotions in Man and Animals London:
    Murray 1904
J. Davis "Theories of Biological Etiology of Affective Disorders" International
    Review of Neurobiology 12 (1970) 145-175
Raleigh Drake Abnormal Psychology New Jersey: Littlefield, Adams 1954
Albert Ellis Reason and Emotion New York: Lyle Stuart 1962
G. Engel "Is Grief a Disease?" Psychosomatic Medicine 23 (1961) 18-22
Carroll Izard The Face of Emotion New York: Appleton-Century-Crofts 1971
    Patterns of Emotions New York: Academic Press 1972
R. Lazarus Psychological Stress and the Coping Process New York: McGraw-
    Hill 1966
Erich Lindemann "Symptomatology and Management of Acute Grief" Ameri-
    can Journal of Psychiatry 101 (1944) 141-148
A. I. Melden "The Conceptual Dimensions of Emotions" Human Action T.
    Mischel, ed, New York: Academic Press 1969
Gilbert Ryle Concept of Mind New York: Barnes & Noble 1949
S. Schachter "The Interaction of Cognitive and Physiological Determinants of
    Emotional States" Psychobiological Approaches to Social Behavior
    P. Leiderman, D. Shapiro, eds. Stanford Univ. Press 1964
Warren Shibles "Linguo-Centric Predicament" Philosophical Pictures 2nd edi-
    tion, Dubuque, Iowa: Kendall-Hunt 1972
B. F. Skinner Science and Human Behavior New York: Macmillan 1953
Ludwig Wittgenstein Philosophical Investigations G. Anscombe, trans. New
    York: Macmillan 1958

Emotions and Objects

General Considerations

"Object" derives from the Latin "objectus," meaning "to throw or put before or against." "Object" refers to cognitive elements, situations, or things. It is an elliptical and abstract term standing for our observations and assessments. What kind of objects do emotions have and can an emotion itself be an object? Emotion is not a thing or entity but rather a configuration of events involving cognition, feeling, and situations as factors. Thus fear of fear may involve fear of one's assessment of fear, rather than fear of the complex configuration which fear is. We often concentrate on the object involved in the emotion rather than on our experience, our feeling, and thought (language). Sensitivity training can change our emotional awareness in this respect. The object of emotion is not a thing. Man's love for woman may spread out over everything he sees, thinks, and feels. In the Croce-Collingwood Theory the content or object of emotion is the expression. The "object" of emotion is "thinking" or "thought" itself.

The feeling aspect of emotion is often described metaphorically in terms of objects, e.g., sharp (knife-like) pain, dull (object-like) pain, etc. In addition, the object involved with an emotion, may be a feeling, as in the case where an assessment of a feeling leads to depression.

"Feeling" emotion is not like feeling an object. It is a category-mistake to think "feeling" anger is like feeling a coin. This is because anger is a contextual configuration not a thing, but also because it is a category-mistake to speak of an emotion as being "felt" at all. Emotions involve feeling, but are not felt as such. One cannot feel angry, though one can be angry. "I felt an ache," is not like "I felt a fear."

205

Psychologists have generally regarded emotions as objects or entities. They have treated them on an analogy with a color chart. Just as there are primary colors which can be mixed and which have complements and opposites, so also there are said to be basic emotions from which all other emotions are derived. These emotions also supposedly mix, have complements and opposites. The analogy is atomistic and unfounded partly because it treats emotions as objects or entities. We speak of "our emotions" as if we have a portfolio of them. This view more or less treats emotions as feelings. It excludes cognitive aspects such as are involved in rhetoric, language-games, assessments, intentions regarding objects, etc. If emotion is merely a feeling it cannot account for the fact that objects and events are intended and assessed. To enjoy a picture we must attend to and assess the picture, not our feelings of the picture, although feelings may be experienced.

We often say an emotion is experienced about, at, over, with, on account of something. But the reasons for and objects of emotion are not physical objects. They are rather objects of thought. People respond differently to the same object and it would not be correct to say the object causes the emotion.

The object involved in emotion may be an imagined object or an object in the past or future. The grammar may mislead as to the object, and our language is based on subject-object categories. One says "enjoy yourself," as though oneself is the object of enjoyment. Of course, an egotistical person may do just that.

Emotion terms are used in sentences as if they were things. Compare:

He was filled with gratitude
He was filled with hamburgers.

He was overcome with hatred.
He was overcome with a virus infection.

He forgot his fear.
He forgot his pencil.

He created a lot of anxiety.
He created a lot of noise.

He was full of hate.
He was full of beer.

Some emotions seem to involve no objects. Anxiety is sometimes regarded or defined as an objectless emotion. It may involve "fear of the unknown." The object of fear is sometimes found to be non-existent. One may fear silence. The statements, "I am extremely happy," and "I enjoyed not swimming," seem not to involve objects.

There are objects involved here but not single physical objects. Negations are positive configurations of events. We may merely imagine an object of fear. Enjoying not swimming does involve a positive, objective pattern of events; being unhappy involves assessments and feelings as does anxiety. In any case, concepts of objects, not objects, cause emotion. In the case of perceiving an object certain emotions may result and, in this case, the sensing of the object, not the object, is the ground of the emotion. It is often better to speak of the "grounds" of an emotion rather than the "cause" of an emotion.

The specific problem in the case of dread, fear, or anxiety regarding death is that if it is not clear what death is, then one's assessments will be confused and result in negative emotions. It is not so much that the emotion is objectless as that conception is confused. The same is the case with "fear of the unknown." Sometimes this state is referred to as "free-floating anxiety," but this is a misleading description because it treats anxiety as an entity or as if there is no object of the emotion. In the case of not knowing what will happen in the future, one may also have anxiety or apprehension. This does not mean that anxiety is a special state or internal emotion, but merely that certain sorts of assessment may lead to negative feelings. One can then feel anger and emotion at nothing, at no object at all.

There are some emotion terms which do involve objects in their definition in some respect. To be grateful implies being grateful for something. But we do not have a toothache for something. Feelings do not have objects in the way emotions do. Compare:

I feel the chair.
I fear the chair.

I am grateful for it.
I have a toothache for it.

I hate him.
I feel pain.
What you touch is the cause of feeling.
What you fear is the cause of fear.

One may say "I feel warm" without feeling anything, but the thing felt here is the description of the feeling, namely, warmth. That is to say that "warm" is not the object of the feeling, but a quality and description of feeling. In the case of "I love him," "him" does not describe the love but is an object involved in the love. It would make no sense to say one just loves, but does not love anything in particular. Such a love may be created as a love-anxiety whereby the lover is not sure which of several people or objects he loves. But what would it be to just love without loving anyone or anything at all? This would be to love love perhaps, to be in love with love itself. This would not make sense unless some object is involved somewhere along the line. This is to say that love is not just a feeling. One cannot have interest, scorn, pity, in itself without any sort of object, in the way one can have a sensation of pain without an object. "I am very interested." "In what?" "Nothing." To be interested without an object is not to be interested. To be interested is to be interested in something, even interested "in" finding something out. One cannot enjoy eating without eating, or just enjoy as such. To enjoy is to enjoy something. The object of an emotion may be an emotion, e.g., "I am ashamed about being ashamed," "I experience guilt about my guilt."

Kenny and Wilson on Emotion

Kenny presents the view that emotions cannot be reduced merely to physiological or private states, but rather must involve objects. Traditional psychological theories regarding emotions as physiological states, are inadequate because they fail to deal with the intentional aspect of emotion. He states, for example,

"The psychogalvanic reflex was found to occur with varying intensity in any sort of excitement, from startle to sexual pleasure. Were we to identify the emotions with bodily phenomena of this kind, we should have to say that shame differed from rage in degree and not in kind, and that a feeling of apprehension, if it grew stronger, would turn into passionate love." (39)

"Bodily states cannot be identified with emotions." (48)

Emotion is said to have causes and objects. The distinction between cause and object is that the object must be known but the cause may not be known:

"Faced with any sentence describing the occurrence of an emotion, of the form 'Aϕd because p,' we must ask whether it is a necessary condition of tne truth of this sentence that A should know or believe that p. If so, then the sentence contains an allusion to the object of the emotion; if not, to its cause. Thus . . . I cannot be angry because of the way a man speaks, if I do not notice the way he speaks; but I may well be angry because I am hungry without realizing that I am hungry." (75)

This view appears to rest on Wittgenstein's statement which Kenny quotes:

"We should distinguish between the object of fear and the cause of fear. Thus a face which inspires fear or delight (the object of fear or delight) is not on that account its cause, but — one might say — its target." (PI 476, Kenny 71)

What seems to be meant by "object" is mainly an assessment of an object. What more than physiological change for an emotion to involve are context and assessment? This seems to be what Kenny means by speaking of the necessity for emotion to have an object. He elsewhere stresses context:

"The occasion on which an emotion is elicited is part of the criterion for the nature of the emotion." (49)

"There must be something in the environment to serve as a target for the animal's fear: say, some physical object which he avoids . . ." (50)

The difference between feeling and emotion is supposedly that feeling refers to internal bodily states whereas emotion involves feeling "that" or feeling something about an external object. (55)

Kenny's theory could easily be appropriated to the assessment theory by noting that by "object" he means context, and that context is a known or assessed situation. The stress on situation allows for an adequate analysis and also provides behavioral criteria, rather than private introspective reports, for emotion. Kenny even indicates the importance of language for emotion:

"Only beings who are capable of manifesting a particular emotion are capable of experiencing it. In particular, those emotions which can be manifested only by the use of language (e.g., remorse for a crime committed long ago, or fear about the distant future) can be experienced only by language-using beings." (62-63)

"Bodily states are identified as states of a particular emotion partly by their connection with motivated behavior and (in man) with the verbal expressions of emotion." (48)

Kenny follows Wittgenstein's theory that so-called private states such as emotion cannot be private to the extent that they are terms learned in an intersubjective language:

"The reason why it is not possible that all emotions should be concealed emotions is that if they were, the meaning of emotion-words could never be learnt." (65)

Such emotion terms were learned as part of concrete situations and contexts, not merely as names of internal, private, or physiological states. Kenny further analyzes the emotion of fear into four factors: a) fearful circumstances, b) symptoms of fear, c) action taken to avoid what is feared, d) the speaker's use of connected and similar concepts. (63, 71) Not all of these elements need be present for a given emotion. He gives the example, "The man-eating lion advances roaring; the defenseless planter screams, pales, and takes to his heels." (67)

Whereas Kenny says, "Emotions unlike sensations, are essentially directed to objects," (60) and "Emotions are specified by their objects," (73) it may be more clear to speak of assessments and contexts than of objects. Emotions partly refer to and are constituted by assessments and contexts. It is not primarily objects which characterize emotions, but assessments. This distinction between cause and object may break down when it is seen that assessments cause feelings and so bring about and partly constitute emotion. To speak of feelings as causes of emotions would account for only a few kinds of emotions, e.g., hangover, sensual pleasures, etc. However, the latter may not be emotions but rather assessments of body sensations. Kenny seems mistaken when he states that emotions "do not give us information about the external world." (56) The reverse is the case. Emotions are partly comprised of assessments which are about the external world.

J. Wilson (1972) in *Emotion and Object* presents at length and criticizes Kenny's theory. Kenny is said to hold the following:

1) What essentially distinguishes emotions, e.g., from sensations, is that they are necessarily connected with or directed to objects. Sensations supposedly do not have objects but rather causes. Because emotions are necessarily connected with objects the relation is not causal.

2) Traditional causal laws do not apply to human emotions, only reasons do. Thus a separate realm of human action is created which differs from causal physical law. One reason for this is that mental events are said not to be singular or entities of the sort which can serve as causes. The relationship between emotion and object is not simply one of cause and effect. If it is said that an art object causes an emotion, this is too simple. Rather reasons and justifications are needed.

3) Emotions are specified by their objects. The emotion cannot be identified without identifying the object. To know someone is angry is to know what he is angry about.

Wilson, on the other hand, argues that there is no special mystical realm of reason which is exempt from empirical causal law. Causation does apply to the relationship between object and emotion, though it is of a particular "mental" kind, that is, the causal link goes through thought or perception. For Wilson the report of an emotion is the report of a state of consciousness:

"Emotion is a complex state whose principle of unity is causal." (89)

Emotion is caused by observing or learning of the objective event:

"A's emotion is caused by perceiving B or by thinking about B or by in some way having his attention drawn to B." (89)

People relate emotionally to external objects. Also there are action tendencies toward or away from the object. Wilson gives the example, "Pity for someone is caused by the perception of him as unfortunate, and includes the impulse to help him." It is not a necessary but a contingent fact that one feels pity. Wilson notes also that "most emotions involve beliefs and desires which can only be had by a user of language." (92) This stress on language is more specific than his general claim that, "emotion is *caused* by a mental state, namely, attention to the object." (102)

Wilson's theory seems to reduce to an assessment theory of emotion and, in fact, his objection to Kenny's view is that the latter mainly speaks of objects as characterizing emotion. Wilson says that rather,

"An emotion is caused by a thought about the object . . . Emotions typically arise from the apprehension of certain characteristics in the object, and involve certain tendencies or impulses to behave in regard to the object." (178)

He notes that not all emotions have objects though all have intention, even if the intention is based on mistaken beliefs. Wilson opposes Kenny's definition of cause as being too general to be useful, and states that Kenny fails to adequately distinguish between sensation and emotion.

Wilson is certainly correct in asserting that Kenny's theory is none too clear, and this may be one reason why Kenny might not hold some of the views attributed to him. Wilson's interpretation may be compared with the quotations given earlier. If Kenny's view is to be appropriated to that of A.I. Melden then there are some good reasons why emotion is essentially linked to its object. The object is part of what is meant by the emotion and so cannot be the cause of the emotion. If what is meant by envy is envy of someone, then that someone is a part of what is meant by envy. One cannot be envious in itself, or envious of nothing. The object is, then, necessarily and logically contained in the emotion concept.

Melden, in *Free Action*, states that an intention or a volition are pseudo-psychological terms and not internal states. Thus they cannot serve as causes. Human behavior is described in such a way that it includes both cause and effect in it. Action includes the context and circumstances involved, and is not just a report of a single "mental" event being caused by an object or relating to an object. We describe our sensation of moving our arm in terms of the result or description, "moving our arm."

Emotions seem to involve intentions. Bertrand Russell wrote, "Nothing is less 'intelligible' . . . than the connection between an act of will and its fulfillment." Wittgenstein asked, "What kind of super-strong connection exists between the act of intending and the thing intended." An intention does not seem to name one thing, especially a mental state. Intentions are often circularly defined, they are not known apart from the description of their objects. (See W. Shibles "Intention.") Thus there is a necessary relationship between intentions and their objects. This may parallel Kenny's statement about a necessary relation between an emotion and its object.

For example, in attempting to characterize the notion of intention it seems that we do not have access to an intention as such. We say "I intend to be at the meeting," but here the intention can only be indicated by a description of what is intended, namely, "to be at the meeting." On this view an intention cannot be described independent of the description of the consequence alleged for it. It is not as if there are two things here, an intention and a description of what is intended. T. Daveney calls the link between intentions which are supposedly logically, but not casually, connected with actions, "identical descriptions."

On this view, it is not that intentions and emotions are exempt from causal law but only that some concepts are general enough to include both cause and effect within them. Emotion is such a complex term. It includes within it descriptions of context, assessments and feelings.

214

Sources:

T.F. Daveney *"Intensions and Causes"* <u>Analysis</u> 27 (1) (Oct. 1966) 23-28
Anthony Kenny <u>Action, Emotion and Will</u> New York: Humanities 1963
A. I. Melden <u>Free Action</u> New York: Humanities Press 1964
Warren Shibles *"Intention"* <u>Wittgenstein, Language and Philosophy</u> Dubuque, Iowa: Kendall-Hunt 1970
J. Wilson <u>Emotion and Object</u> Cambridge University Press 1972
Ludwig Wittgenstein <u>Philosophical Investigations</u> 3rd edition, G. Anscombe, trans. New York: Macmillan 1958 (1968)

Emotion and Therapy

The following statements suggest a need for clarification of the nature of emotions as they relate to therapy.

Zangwill (1948) states,

"Neither [Freud] nor any of his followers has devoted any systematic attention to the problem of emotion in general."

Landis (1932) wrote,

"In general, it may be concluded that analytical investigations of the personality traits of emotionality or psychopathy are unsatisfactory and fail to bring out decisive evidence." (p. 267)

Freud himself wrote,

"What psychology has to say about affects — the James-Lange theory, for instance ' — is utterly incomprehensible to us psychoanalysts and impossible for us to discuss." (Plutchik p. 267)

In examining the relation between language and emotion we found that language is one of the most important tools in psychotherapy for achieving a cure. Harold Vetter says that most psychotherapy relies on language as a means of effecting a cure. (1969, 1968) The close relation between metaphor, emotion, defensemechanisms, informal fallacies, and therapy will be discussed separately.

Kant, Francis Bacon, Janet, Freud, the Stoics, the Epicureans, and even the Christians regarded emotion as abnormal or as a disease. In the general philosophical tradition the stress was on reason. It was this emphasis that often separated philosophy from other disciplines. The attempt to clarify the concept of emotion

215

and show its close relation to reason leads to philosophical therapy. The use of "reason" here largely refers to our use of language. Thus to show where language misleads us is to engage in therapy. If one is clear about one's language or knowledge, one's emotions tend to be positive and in control. This is partly the point of the Stoic and the Epicurean view. It is also what is behind the philosopher's stress on the importance of realistic adjustment to one's circumstances. One must first have a clear, realistic knowledge and assessment of oneself and his circumstance before adjustment can be successful. George Pitcher wrote in this regard,

"A change in knowledge can, by itself, result in the restraint or the removal of an emotion . . ." (346)

Regarding so-called "mental disease," then, the stress is on what the patient understands, and what he says to himself and to others. His understanding depends largely on the language he has learned. Psychoanalysis may be seen to be largely the patient's taking and learning to share the rational assessments and diagnosis of the analyst, rather than an introspection of one's internal or mental state. It may, however, be to understand better one's own actions, beliefs and confused concepts. But therapy may work, for a while at least, even in the absence of clear concepts. That is, if a patient is confused he may accept Freudian terminology and explanations, or Christian or other religious dogma and, if he believes it, it may provide a unity to his thought regardless of how unfounded such beliefs are. A unifying metaphor may yield unified emotions. But such a unity and therapy must be partial and inadequate. It is an inadequate adjustment to reality and is easily toppled leading to still further confusion. Again, there is no substitute for a realistic rational assessment of one's self and world which is grounded in critical philosophical analysis. If one believes in the Freudian or Christian analyses they may organize one's life, but only at the expense of possible future disappointment as the criticism of such unrealistic or superstitious beliefs becomes known. Psychiatrists often give us metaphors they take literally thus committing the metaphor-to-myth fallacy. That is, they sometimes give us trumped-up language games of emotions. The cure involves only learning the language-game. Such language-games need conceptual philosophical clarification as well as assessment as to adequacy. Are such games necessary and sufficient for therapy? One may accept the role of a patient and the role of accepting a psychoanalytic interpretation of his behavior. But we often condemn roles as being inadequate, imposed patterns of behavior which fail to meet the needs of one's own case. Roles are seen as types of pretenses or pretending. One may play the learned games of "worry" and "boredom."

We are told we must release our emotions or tell what we really feel inside us. The picture of "release" and of emotions as things "inside us," is damaging and unhelpful. It creates the view that we are irrational and that there are evil forces within us at work which we can do little about except to let these "forces" be released now and again as water is released from a dam. The picture is rendered by the expression "blowing off steam." But if emotions such as anger must be "released" why not also vice, hatred, violence, etc.? But we have no evidence that such emotions are internal fluids of this sort calling for release. A patient who cannot understand his problems may be asked to release his emotions but this is not literally a release nor does it provide a permanent cure. Rather the patient by beginning to express himself by outbursts or in any way is making a first step at rationally understanding his problems. He could not face them, conceptualize them, or talk about them. By crying or becoming angry he may begin to do so. Hopefully, he will not always have to cry or become angry but can move to the next step of clarifying what is bothering him. Thus in client-centered therapy the patient is requested to *speak* about himself. By so doing he is beginning to understand himself. This is also what is behind the psychiatrist's expression of "working out" or "working through" a difficulty. But it is primarily the speaking and understanding which gets at the cause and brings about a more permanent cure. Therapy involved the substitution of sour sentences for sweet sentences.

This view, then, opposes that of those who say simply "emotions must be released." To "release" emotions is not to effect a cure, but in fact is to create a harmful pattern of behavior. One may find himself constantly "releasing" his emotions, thereby often becoming angry and violent.

The therapist who encourages the patient, "Look at your emotions," "Tell what you really feel," or "Be honest about your emotions," is misleading the patient. It has been established that in nearly every relevant field of inquiry it is not clear what an emotion is. Thus to tell a patient to look at them or be honest about them is to confuse the patient. He does not know how to look at them and so can neither be honest nor dishonest about them. The therapist is asking the patient to introspect a vague abstraction.

Instead, it would be more sound to ask the patient not about his emotions but what he thinks, what he has said to himself and to others, what his beliefs are about himself and others, what images recur, and what he has done. To express emotion is often merely to report past feelings rather than actually "express" present feelings. In the interview, the therapist can pay careful attention to the patient's statements and actions and note especially his language and metaphors. He thus inquires into the world as the patient saw it and sees it now. He is in this way finding out what is now the problem and how it may have arisen. Melden wrote,

> "And it is because of this background and understanding we do have of human beings, that learning that a person is angry sometimes does enable us to interpret his actions – to see clearly the patterns of anger in what might otherwise appear to be altogether innocent or puzzling conduct." (p. 218)

Emotion terms reduce to non-emotion terms and so therapy involves dealing with something other than emotion. Emotion rests on, for example, one's goals, what one reads, how he sees the world. Anxiety and identity problems are problems of one's goals and the problem of the self. They are assessment problems. A one-sided diet is to read existentialistic, liberation, and radical literature, and so by this means create "alienation," "anxiety," and "dread," in oneself. That is, one takes on a conceptual scheme. Thus, because novels and poetry revise one's conceptual scheme they may be effectively used in therapy.

The consequences of one's beliefs may be associated with psychosomatic or physical illnesses. One's attitude, e.g., worry, may lead to ulcers, insecurity may lead to colds or eczema. The phenomena of predilection to death of patients about to be operated on, and the fact that grief and bereavement can lead to one's death, are suggestive here.

An excellent study on grief is Dr. George Engel's "Is Grief a Disease?" (1961) Engel shows that grief has a definite syndrome and predictable symptomatology and course. Lindemann (1944), also presented grief as having a definite syndrome. Grief is like a disease and should be considered therefore as something one can treat and cure. Grief generally is characterized by the following pattern: a) initial shock, disbelief, attempt to deny loss; b) awareness of loss and experiences negative emotions of shame, sadness, guilt, helplessness, crying, anorexia, sleep disturbance, somatic symptoms, loss of social interest in one's work; c) recovery stage and resumption of mental health. Engel argues as follows against the common prejudices which view grief not as a disease but as normal or necessary:

1. Grief is no more a natural reaction to a life experience than a wound or burn is a natural response to physical trauma. Rather, grief is a pathological state.

2. To support grief because it is familiar or commonly experienced is no argument but merely shows man's failure to cope adequately with his experience. "One may escape both measles and grief."

3. In opposition to the view that grief is a self-limiting process requiring no medical attention, it is argued that medicine has not yet properly recognized grief as an abnormality or disease just as epilepsy, alcoholism, and mental diseases were not at one time regarded as diseases. The physician treats grief as outside of his domain, and patients fail to think grief is a disease and so do not complain of it. They complain rather of some physical ailment. Grief may be a disease whether it requires medical attention or not.

4. Grief is a deviation from the state of well-being and so should be regarded as a disease.

5. To the view that grief is a purely subjective psychological experience, he asserts that we may find out that there are bodily changes occurring during grief. (Other studies, e.g., Lindemann;

Shoor and Speed show there are definite physical and mental abnormalities resulting from grief.) Hyperparathyroidism was thought to be a subjective experience at first.

6. To the argument that nobody ever dies of grief he replies, a) it may nevertheless be a disease, and b) we do have evidence that grief may lead to death. (See following section on psychosomatic events.) There is often death of the spouse shortly after the funeral of his or her mate. Grief can lead to fatal shock. Grief has been recognized as a cause of disease from the time of Hippocrates on. Literature frequently reports the phenomenon of dying of grief.

7. To suggest that some grief is pathological while some is normal is false and misleading. All grief is negative and an abnormal detriment to health. Often grief is absent, delayed, disguised, apparently normal, but nevertheless can be found later to lead to organic or mental disease. ["Mental disease" is, of course, a misnomer. There is no mind to be diseased.]

8. To the view that grief is necessary or a healthy adaptation, he states that this would be like saying that a wound is a healthy adaptation. We may or may not survive the wound or the grief.

9. Is not grief a natural response of a healthy person to loss? He responds that we may be misled that because a person is healthy in other ways he is healthy in all ways. Grief, however, is unhealthful.

He thus recommends that medical research and practice study and treat grief as a disease. Negative emotions are unnecessary, and may be dissipated by means of an inquiry into the nature of emotions. Negative emotions, although common, are seen to be a result of confusions in reasoning. Such confusions lead to other kinds of physical and psychological disorders.

In addition to the view that a clarification of emotions will show that grief is unnecessary it may be the case that grief behavior, and other negative emotive behavior, is simply culturally imposed and learned. It can be a learned kind of role behavior. Such behavior is not necessary or inherent. Cultural differences show that what one person grieves about, another is joyful over. In one culture it is thought to be harmful for children to attend funerals, in another the child plays games at funerals and enjoys it with no harmful after effects. As we learn to act bored, revengeful, angry, we may learn to grieve. There is strong evidence that grief is an arbitrary act, not a necessary one. It is not intelligent behavior.

Funeral songs and poetry are also traditional ways of attempting to represent or express grief and emotion. As representations they are cultural, ritualistic devices. As expressions, the question arises as to whether poetry and song express emotions. The aesthetic theory that art expresses emotions is unsatisfactory because it assumes an unexamined theory of emotions. Poetry is largely based on metaphor. It is a use of language. We have no direct evidence for psychological entities such as internal atomistic "ideas" or "emotions" as such. The poem itself is the expression or emotion. Benedetto Croce and R. Collingwood said that the intuition or emotion is the expression. The expression does not just represent emotions or express internal separate emotions. In short, intuition and emotion are the metaphorical language or poem. In this respect poetry may help one to clarify his ideas about death as well as to adjust to it. Such was the case with Emily Dickinson, Dylan Thomas, John Donne, and many others including novelists. It is important for the bereaved or the patient to communicate his views about dying and death or to communicate to a sympathetic careful listener. Communication is perhaps the most important form of therapy both for the normal as well as the abnormal. (See W. Shibles *Death: An Interdisciplinary Analysis*)

Psychosomatic Events: Sudden Deaths from Unknown Causes

The term "psychosomatic" is widely used. It is however a misnomer. It derives from the Greek word which means life, breath, soul, and especially mind. But contemporary philosophical psychology has shown (G. Ryle, et al.) that there is no evidence for mind. The container theory of mind, though held by the majority of people, has not a bit of evidence to support it. "Psychosomatic" is "mind-body," and as there is no mind so psycho-somatic is a naming fallacy. If we let "psycho" stand for thought, we are still in difficulty, for what evidence do we have for an "idea" or a "thought"? These are pseudo-psychological entities. Thought reduces to ability to do things and for the most part to our ability with language. Thought is not an epistemological starting-point, but language is. We need not "think" in order to present a theory but we must write or speak. Thus "psycho-somatic" should, for accuracy and clarity be changed to "linguo-somatic." To study a patient's thought we study what he says. His other behavior should not be excluded. Schizophrenia, as well as other abnormal and normal behavior, is being studied mainly by the kind of language one uses, and the statements one says to oneself and becomes captivated by. "Emotion" may be said to refer to the psycho-physical relation and state of which we are ignorant. Emotion is this vague and so refers vaguely.

Lindemann (SM 1944) found that 33 of 41 patients with ulcerative colitis developed their disease soon after the loss of a person important to them. Unresolved negative emotions are seen to bring about bodily disturbances.

In an interesting article by Weisman and Hackett (PD 1961) concerning predilection to death, the following suggestive cases are presented:

1. Patients who are extremely anxious about their impending surgery, are firmly convinced of their dying during the operation, and who even look forward to dying, are often not operated on because such an attitude is found to bring about their death.

2. People who are told by a fortune teller (or perhaps astrologer), or even a friend, that they will die at a certain time, are found to fulfill the prophecy.

One may relate this to the biblical prophecy that "The wages of sin is death." It is found to bring on shock reaction which may cause death.

3. "Psychic" death is reported whereby patients correctly predict their own deaths, and yet no organic cause of death is found.

4. Some await God's punishment by being killed, or feel they live at the expense of other's lives, or believe in *Liebestod*, i.e., that lovers reunite after death.

5. Predilection patients commonly had, in effect, "died" socially. They had no remaining interest in human relationships. It is theorized that they welcome death by fantasied survival after death.

6. Those patients who are suddenly isolated or disowned, or rejected by family or friends, may as a result of this "social death" bring about their physical death. One man died after he found out none of his six children would give blood to help him, though no organic cause of death was found.

All of the cases Weisman and Hackett present are similar to the cases of "voodoo" death prevalent among tribal cultures. The result, in all such cases of voodoo, appears to be social rejection bringing about self-destructive behavior by starving oneself, withdrawal, etc., leading to conditions even more suitable for shock to occur. Shock is largely responsible for such deaths, as Cannon (1942) observes in his study of "voodoo" death. To mention one of the many possible causes, the *Journal of the American Medical Association* states (Oct. 4, 1971): "Emotional turmoil may indeed precipitate or aggravate congestive heart failure." Because shock is the cause, post mortem organic causes may not be as easy to find. This theory still leaves more to be explained as to the psychosomatic mechanisms involved.

Weisman and Hackett suggest some possible mechanisms. They state, " 'Death' is personified as is 'life' — It thus lends itself to many metaphors, mystic abstractions, etc." The authors are alert to the importance of metaphor in regard to understanding the nature of death and our adjustment to it. They point out that and how we adjust to death by means of fantasy. We view life in terms of various concepts and our notions of death are seen in relation to them. Our language and metaphors construct a complex world for ourselves and so cannot be adequately rendered by a single sentence or metaphor. They state, "Life as it is lived has more parameters than there are laboratory methods available to use them; death encompasses the human personality as much as life does."

They point out that our view of death depends upon our view of ourselves [our metaphors for ourself]. In fearing death we are often fearing loss of what we conceive to be our self. Fear of death may come with a new situation which forces a new view of the self upon us. [We must prepare ourselves for new metaphors of ourselves and of possible situations in which we might find ourselves. Metaphor may in this way be used as a way of coping with death]. They give an example of some fixed or stereotyped metaphors used to "explain" all things: "After a certain age every vague complaint, in the absence of surgically localized disorders, is attributed to either 'menopause' or the 'infirmities' of old age." It has been shown that such explanations are faulty.

It is pointed out that "I," "after death," and "when I am dead" are not acceptable uses. They assert that one cannot imagine his own death even metaphorically: "A phantasy of absolute subjective death is impossible to imagine."

It is also indicated how fear of death or dying is regarded. It is often "seen-as": seen as an it, pain, oncoming insanity, one's self dying, disintegration of body, accumulation of regrets, fear of others, fear of rejection, fear of one's past misbehavior. Fear of death may be confused with fear of dying. One may die in one perspective rather than in another or confuse perspectives. A pregnant coed may commit suicide not thinking she will die but only that she will be getting rid of her problems. Also, abandonment is represented metaphorically by drawn shades, hushed voices, different ways of speaking, etc.

Weisman and Hackett then assert that in order to understand the dying patient we must find out something about him, how he views life, himself, his environment, and others. To state their view in terms other than those they use, we must find out the metaphors and models the patient lives by; every phrase one uses tells a great deal. Once this is known, the authors point out, we will know what would constitute an appropriate death for a patient. They state that the criteria for the therapy to bring about an appropriate death are 1) conflict reduction, 2) the patient must be properly understood in terms of the image he has of himself,

3) important social relationships must be restored, 4) his wishes must be satisfied as much as possible. Dr. Alex Comfort, a biologist, presents a similar view when he states,

"Continuance of active work, retention of interests, of the respect of our fellows, and of a sense of significance in the common life of the species, apparently makes us live longer – loss of these things makes us die young." (1956 p. 193)

Elie Metchnikoff in 1908 stressed the fact that old people should be kept mentally alert, learn how to avoid stress and worry. This and other psychosomatic arguments presented in this chapter are strong arguments for the view that the most important goal in life must be active inquiry into oneself, one's environment, and basic critical philosophical inquiry, e.g., into the nature of emotions, death, etc. To fail to engage in such inquiry is seen to lead to one's death.

What was said above in regard to second (you), or third person (him), therapy may perhaps also apply to the first person case. That is, the more clear one is about his emotions, his life, his conceptual fantasies, his models and metaphors, the more clear will be the kind of death desired and adjusted to. Along these lines we find the authors stressing the necessity of open discussion with patients. This helps them to come to a clearer understanding of themselves.

Although the authors present their goal as getting the patient to die with dignity or, as they put it "The purpose of living is to create a world in which we would be willing to die," this can rather only be the goal of the psychiatrist. To die quietly seems to be a very limited goal. The philosopher, on the other hand, wishes always to find out more about death and dying, and it will not do to simply hold such views that will lead us to "want to die," or "die without making a disturbance."

In regard to psychosomatic phenomena, Le Shan found that poor social experiences are highly correlated with development of cancer. 42 out of 45 cancer therapy cases, but only one out of 30 control therapy cases, had a background of childhood feelings of isolation, rejection, loss of a central relationship, and sense of great despair. (Vernon 1970, pp. 100-101)

In Shneidman's survey of the 30,000 readers of *Psychology Today* 52% were found to firmly believe, and 36% tend to believe, that psychological factors can influence (or even cause) death. 43% thought that most deaths have strong components of conscious or unconscious participation by the persons who die.

Barber in his article, "Death by Suggestion," rejects the view that voodoo death is in fact caused by voodoo, sorcery, witchcraft, magic or suggestion. He found that, in most cases, poisoning could have been the cause, that often the victim does not eat or drink enough for survival, and that organic disorder may have been the cause in some cases. He fails, however, to mention shock as the main cause. Barber rejects as premature, explanations of such deaths as being based on over-stimulation of the sympathicoadrenal system (Cannon's view) or over-stimulation of the parasympathetic system.

Ashley Montagu (1956) in discussing the nature of psychosomatic medicine points out that feelings were regarded by F. Dunbar as related to bodily functions, that Selye's work on stress and endocrinology also suggests psychosomatic relationships, as does the phenomenon of "voodoo" death. It is suggested that we observe anthropological phenomena for additional clues and instances, e.g., adolescent sterility varies from culture to culture and may be due to cultural beliefs and factors rather than physiological factors alone. The main point is that "psychosomatic" involves a number of integrated factors such as somatic, psychic (which was criticized earlier in this chapter), social, cultural.

Kalish (CS 1966) asserts that social death may cause or enhance physical death. He calls this "psychosomatic death."

Walter Cannon of Harvard Medical School, in his article, "Voodoo Death," concluded that voodoo death is not magical death but death by shock. The test of such shock is rapid pulse, cool and moist skin, high red blood cell count, low blood pressure, increased blood sugar. Great fear produces physical changes. Fear serves to prepare the body, and if no action follows the body is harmed. Cannon's view here contains the Darwinian teleological assumption that all our experience has the purpose of survival. Lack of food and water cause excitement of the sympathico-adrenal system.

Soldiers who were in shock due to war wounds died from the shock rather than from the wound. It may be pointed out that the existentialist's stress on the necessity to experience "dread" from "anxiety" can be similarly detrimental, possibly leading to shock or suicide and so bring about one's death. Cannon cited a number of scientifically reported instances of so-called "voodoo death" throughout the world. It would be interesting to investigate whether one by hypnosis or self-suggestion can be caused to go into fatal shock. Some instances involve self-conviction, e.g., that demons determine them to die. Statements in the Bible are similar: "The wages of sin is death."

When one finds out the thing he did was taboo, even long after the act, he can go into shock and die within 24 hours of finding out. Often a bone is pointed at the victim and the victim thinks that he is thereby due to die. Such spells are negated only if the victim is told it was a mistake or the bone pointer undoes the spell. Such spells lead to abstinence of food and water and social rejection by the community. That is, one starves oneself making shock more likely, and also experiences social death. The condemned person is regarded as if dead. Cannon asserts that voodoo death applies to very ignorant people, but, in view of other findings in this chapter, it affects people thought to be intelligent, e.g., death caused by death of someone close. It may be noted that, according to Strehler (1957), the widowed and divorced have higher mortality rates than the single or married.

Albert Cain and Irene Fast found that a seven year old girl developed her first asthmatic attack a day after her asthmatic sister died of such an attack. The attacks recurred each anniversary of her sister's death. The researchers attribute these attacks to family encouraged identification with the deceased, e.g., the child may have been made to worry lest she die as her sister had. (*Science News* Dec. 18, 1971 p. 409)

Francis Bacon (1561-1616) was aware of psychosomatic relations. He noted that men die from great and sudden grief, fear, or even from joy.

In the Ibo tribe of Nigeria one may die as a result of a false oath. In legal dispuses a "black oath," is taken, e.g., "If my assertion is wrong let this oath take away my life." If the person is living after a year, he is freed of all guilt. In a number of cases the man, perhaps from feelings of guilt, hangs himself or kills himself by carelessness within the year. (Noon 1942) It is not satisfactory to merely assert that death may be caused by self-suggestion or hypnosis, without an analysis of the nature of suggestion and hypnosis. Such analyses show that we are clear about neither process although we can "induce" (a word derivative from magnetism) hypnosis. (Gordon 1967)

William Godwin (1756-1836) once thought that one could prolong life by gaining voluntary control over the emotions, and over bodily functions. For him, clear thinking and proper emotions can increase life. Bad news may cause disease or death. Cheerfulness leads to a longer life. His view is that reason can help create a more happy person and so increase length of life. His stress on reason is similar to that of the contemporary view of Albert Ellis in *Reason and Emotion* (1962). Ellis calls his view "rational psychotherapy." Godwin concludes that we become diseased and die partly because we consent to and because we think we will. (Gruman 1966)

In summary, it may be seen that what is important in therapy is rational, linguistic communication and clarification. Emotional disturbance is mainly conceptual disturbance (if one excludes brain damage or physical causes). The emotionally disturbed is one whose difficulty is largely language difficulty, in other words whose "thinking" is confused. The special difficulty here is that emotions are often regarded as being by definition that which we cannot have access to by means of language in the normal rational way. The inaccessibility of emotion is only due to the patient's very confusion. But to affect a cure, the patient must eventually be talked out of it or talk himself out of it. Even children eventually learn to develop realistic and rational ways of behaving. In the case of the normal person, because emotion is largely rational knowledge, the problem of emotion becomes the problem of character refinement. This in turn rests on analysis and inquiry.

Sources:

T. Barber "Death by Suggestion" Psychosomatic Medicine 23 (1961) 153-155

W. Cannon "Voodoo Death" American Anthropologist 44 (1942) 169-181

A. Christi "Attitudes toward death among a group of acute geriatric psychiatric patients." Journal of Gerontology 16 (1) (Jan. 1961) 56-59

A. Comfort The Biology of Senescence London: Routledge and Kegan Paul 1956

A. Ellis "Rational Psychotherapy" Psychopathology Today William Sahakian, ed., Illinois: Peacock Publishers 1970

A. Ellis Reason and Emotion in Psychotherapy New York: Lyle Stuart 1962

G. Engel "Is Grief a Disease?" Psychosomatic Medicine 23 (1961) 18-22

J. Gordon Handbook of Clinical and Experimental Hypnosis New York: Macmillan 1967

G. Gruman A History of Ideas About the Prolongation of Life: The Evolution of Prolongevity Hypothesis to 1800 Philadelphia: American Philosophical Society 1966

R. Kalish "A Continuum of Subjectively Perceived Death" Gerontologist 6 (1966) 73-76

C. Landis "An Attempt to Measure Emotional Traits in Juvenile Delinquency" Studies in the Dynamics of Behavior K. Lashley, ed., Chicago: University of Chicago Press 1932

E. Lindemann "Symptomatology and Management of Acute Grief" American Journal of Psychiatry 101 (1944) 141-148

E. Metchnikoff The Prolongation of Life New York: Putnam 1908

A. Montagu "Contributions of Anthropology to Psychosomatic Medicine" American Journal of Psychiatry 112 (1956) 977ff

J. Noon "A Preliminary Examination of the Death Concepts of the Ibo" American Anthropologist 44 (1942) 638-654

G. Pitcher "Emotion" Mind 74 (July 1965) 326-346

R. Plutchik The Emotions New York: Random House 1962

W. Shibles Death: An Interdisciplinary Analysis Whitewater, Wisc.: The Language Press 1974

E. Shneidman "You and Death" Psychology Today 5 (1) (1971) 43-45, 74-80

M. Shoor and M. Speed "Death, Delinquency and the Mourning Process" Psychiatric Quarterly 37 (1963) 540-558

B. Strehler, ed. The Biology of Aging Symposium, Tennessee 1957, Washington D.C.: American Institute of Biological Science. Publication 6, 1960

230

G. Vernon *Sociology of Death* New York: Ronald Press 1970

H. Vetter *Language, Behavior and Psychotherapy* Chicago: Rand-McNally 1969, esp. pp. 141-164. See also his *Language, Behavior and Schizophrenia* Springfield, Illinois: C. Thomas 1968, esp. pp. 58-74, 153-181

A. Weisman and T. Hackett "Predilection to Death" *Psychosomatic Medicine* 23 (1961) 232-256

O. Zangwill "The Theory of Emotion: A Correspondence Between J.I. MacCurdy and Morton Prince" *British Journal of Psychology* 39 (1948) 1-11

The Metaphorical Method of Therapy

The metaphorical method is based on the view that all thinking is basically metaphorical. Metaphor includes nearly all other tropes or rhetorical devices, and rhetoric is a description of our patterns of speech and thought. Each philosophy, psychiatric theory, or scientific hypothesis is based upon one or more metaphors. Robert Frost wrote, "All thinking is metaphorical." (See W. Shibles *Metaphor* 1971) If this is the case, then therapy should concern itself with the rhetorical devices and language-games people play. These devices will be described and illustrated for the purpose of indicating how the metaphorical method may be found useful in therapy.

In examining the relation between language and "emotional disorder" we find that language is one of the most important tools in psycho-therapy for achieving a cure. Harold Vetter (1969) says that in fact *most* psychotherapy relies on language as a means of effecting a cure. The psychiatrist, David Forrest (1965) wrote,

"If the study of schizophrenic communication is the principal means by which the disease may be understood, its course known, and perhaps also its causes discovered, then precise description of schizophrenic language is valuable."

Albert Ellis' "Rational psychotherapy," as was discussed earlier, shows the close relation between language and "emotional disturbance." He rejects the idea that thinking or reason is separate from emotion and feeling. "Jones thinks about this puzzle" should be rendered "Jones perceives-moves-feels-thinks about this puzzle." He goes on to say,

*Original shorter version published in Nuovo 75: metodologia, scienza 9, 1973; 10, 1974. See also *Journal of Aesthetic Education* 8 (April 1974) 25-36.

> "Both thinking and emoting tend to take the form of self-talk or internalized sentences; and that for all practical purposes the sentences that human beings keep telling themselves *are* or *become* their thoughts and emotions." (Sahakian 558)

What we mainly mean by thought is language use. Imagery and other perceptual abilities are involved, but thinking is largely saying (or writing) something aloud or to onself. To know involves mainly the ability to say something. The epistemological starting point is not ideas or thought, both of which are pseudo-psychological "entities," but rather language. That we must assume language, e.g., in order to present any kind of theory, even a theory of language itself, may be called our peculiar "linguo-centric predicament." (W. Shibles "Linguo-Centric Predicament," and "Language as Paradox")

Thought, both normal and abnormal, involves mainly language, and language may be specified by rhetorical or metaphorical devices and techniques. An account of the various types of metaphor is given here. It includes an analysis of images as well as an account of perceptual and behavioral metaphor. The devices used apply to normal and poetic, as well as to neurotic and psychotic, behavior.

We have spoken of neurotic, and psychotic "emotional disorders." These terms require description and definition. Neurotic and psychotic may be defined in terms of language, image, and behavioral rhetorical deviations. For example, the neurotic often does self-defeating, and contradictory things. He is caught with opposing yet firmly held beliefs. The psychotic can change his abnormal behavior less than can the neurotic. "Emotional disturbance" has been used in a vague way, for it was not clear what emotion is. As a result of recent work on emotion, emotion may no longer be regarded as a feeling but may be seen to be largely statements or assessments. We may, then, be able to radically change our emotions merely by changing our assessments and the behavioral and perceptual habits based on them.

Metaphor derives from the Greek, *metapherein*, (*meta*, beyond; *pherein*, to bring) means "transfer." One term is transferred from its normal usage to a new usage, e.g., "Point to your jealousy," "What shade of blue do you feel?" Metaphor is itself defined metaphorically in terms of "transfer" and "figure." It is also spoken of as a filter, stereoscope, tension, energy, or as dead. This is because all definitions are metaphorical. All definitions are metaphorical including the definition of metaphor because we think of one thing in terms of another, in terms of familiar models, and there is no one literal, universal model or definition which will apply to all situations and contexts at all times for all people. To define a term is only to take a model or metaphor, one perspective, one way of looking at the terms. One's definition determines the way in which he sees reality. There is no single definition or aspect of metaphor (or any term). Models, pictures, illusions, delusions, hallucinations, diagrams, maps, definitions, descriptions, hypotheses, fictions, formulas, are types of metaphors.

To take a single metaphor or definition literally or as the only way of looking at a situation is to be captivated by a metaphor or to commit the metaphor-to-myth fallacy. It may also be to create a category-mistake. "Time passes" is an example of a metaphor erroneously taken literally. It is therapy to find out how rhetorical devices and language captivate us. Such devices lead to self-defeating and irrational behavior. The obsessive patient is partly held captive by certain statements he continually says to himself. Scientists, psychologists, religious people, etc., as well as psychotics and neurotics, may by self-suggestion or self-hypnosis become convinced that a certain model or statement is almost exclusively true. One may be captivated by Freudianism, stimulus-response theory, religion, as well as by the view that the planets control one's life or that a great machine somewhere controls one's life. Free-association or metaphor may allow us to free ourselves from such captivating statements. One may dislike a particular food simply because he keeps telling himself that it is no good. In schizophrenia words are often taken too literally and are even taken to be the things themselves. "Emotional disorder" may be seen to be largely the adoption of certain patterns of behavior, i.e., certain rhetorical devices or language-games. We learn and create our own hostilities and emotions as we learn and create our own metaphors and rhetorical devices. We may then be as deliberate in analyzing each piece of behavior, each statement uttered, as we are with each move made in a game of chess. Every unknowingly self-defeating sentence or movement can hold us captive. Every fit of anger can be seen to be a mistake. It is a symptom suggesting that our language-games and assessments need revision.

The rhetorical devices here relate to the cause of emotional disorder. False beliefs, conflicting statements may lead to physical disorder just as when one assesses that an injustice has been done, negative bodily feelings are experienced. One may, then, erroneously think that the adverse physical state caused the emotion and that the cause is physical defeat. "Psychological disorder" usually refers to those who do not have known physical disorders or physical reasons for acting as they do. The methods proposed here are not for those disorders which are of a non-psychological, medical, or stricly physical nature such as brain damage, nutrition disorder, or disorders which can be adequately or completely cured by means of drugs or other medicine.

One may think of the human organism as an adjustive mechanism. When one cannot solve his problems, resolve his conflicts, the response may be anger or negative emotion, speech deviation, utilization of defense-mechanisms, or perceptual and bodily defense-mechanisms such as developing ulcers, nervous tics, psychological blindness, speechlessness, psychological loss of hearing, memory loss, etc. Such "defense-mechanisms" "defend" usually only at the expense of the well-being and proper functioning of the organism itself. They seem to "defend" only by removing the source of pain from consciousness. Such mechanisms form a pattern, and some of the major patterns are presented in the following analysis of metaphor as rhetorical mechanisms or language-games. These categories may be used to classify so-called "mental" or "emotional disorders." The types of metaphor mentioned here are based on traditional and contemporary views of metaphor as well as on logic, contemporary philosophical psychology, and studies and theories of abnormal psychology. Most generally, metaphor is a deviation:

1) Deviation from usual diction. Any word may be used in a new way. Any word can be used as a metaphor even the word "metaphor." Schizophrenia is largely a deviation or disturbance in association. The schizophrenic's language-games are illogical and confused. He may have "semantic aphasia" whereby he is unable to recognize the meaning of words or use abstract words. Like the poet, he produces "clang associations" relating words merely by means of sound rather than meaning. He may choose stilted language and dead metaphors in speaking or letter writing. One patient wrote, "A hearty and cheerful, and a real magnanimous good morning to you on this first Wednesday of our glorious New Year." Neologisms are also used. These are coined words or condensations of several into one as if to disguise what one is saying. Speech deviation is also found in the language of lovers, which is highly metaphorical.

2) Deviation from usual context or situational use of words. Words usually belonging to one context or universe of discourse are used in another or very different one either consciously or by mistake, e.g., "Feeling is chemical." The use of the wrong word for a context is sometimes called "catachresis." The schizophrenic often speaks a "word salad," that is, using only neologisms and unintelligible words.

3) Deviation from normal behavior. Gestures and actions may deviate from the usual accepted practices thus creating metaphorical behavior, e.g., a boy who walks upside down. He, as well as his vision of the world, describes a metaphorical perspective. Play acting, pretending, imitating, pantomime, role playing, and children's games, e.g., "You be the king and I'll be the knight," all are behavioral metaphors. The behavioral deviations of the schizophrenic have been roughly classified and are well-known. Certain behavioral gestures of the catatonic seem to be an attempt on his part to control the world as if by magic. Parapraxis refers to dissociated action which serves no useful purpose, such as twitches, tics, spasms, continual winking, ear tugging, grimacing, or special arbitrary self-induced exercises. The schizophrenic usually has inappropriate behavior. Behavior may metaphorically involve "sticking up one's nose" to shun people as if they smell bad. Behavior may be

236

purposely deviated from in order to better understand oneself and others. For example, one may blacken one's skin to see what it is like to be a black person in our society and how people react to him, or paint one's face in strange ways to see how people will respond to it and whether one can handle the inevitable comments and criticism.

One use of metaphor therapy is to play games, such as poker, with neurotic or psychotic patients. The patient may be carefully watched under such controlled conditions. Even the so-called normal person is often unable to play cards without revealing great emotional shortcomings.

4) Deviation from established categories, e.g., "a grief ago." Old categories are broken down such as subject-object, fact-fiction cause-effect, mind-body, sensuous and non-sensuous, true-false, emotion-reason, life-death. The animate may be regarded as the inanimate.

5) Deviation from culture, custom, habit, tabu, the expected, what is considered proper, the practical, the logical, the self-evident the everyday, the literal, the real (yielding the as-if or imaginary), the normal, or cause and effect order of events. Such deviations, because they are new and unfamiliar, make metaphors seem to be the language of the insane or of the poet. The poet often writes metaphors like those of the schizophrenic. Poets, lovers, philosophers are often thought mad, e.g., by Plato. Chesterton (As I was Saying 1936) even speaks of metaphors as being "mad."

The poet, William Wordsworth, speaks of poetry as an excess or overflow of the emotions. The artist is often thought to have to be in some special state in order to create works of art. The poet does not talk as we usually talk. His expressions are odd. One doesn't usually talk poetry. We call that which is out of the ordinary, "emotion." An emotional statement is one which disregards usual criteria of truth, e.g., "We are all part of one great mind." But poetry and insanity are often defined as being deviations in the first place. It is not necessarily a state the poet or madman is in but the fact that both talk differently than we usually do, that characterizes them as being either mad or artists. Both emotions and metaphors are deviations from the norm. They may be an excess or a lack. We speak in metaphors. We paint metaphorically. Poets and philosophers show how emotions relate and conflict. It is the metaphors they have direct access to, not their "emotions." One need not be "mad" to create metaphors. Thus, a person is insane or is a poet because of his metaphors. It is not that one is an artist or poet because he has a faculty of imagination, has a creative mind, or is a genius. Rather to be a poet or artist is mainly to deviate by means of metaphor. No internal mentalism such as "emotion," "mind," or "imagination," need be assumed. Such "entities" are today regarded by many psychologists and philosophers as fictions. Mental states are artificial metaphorical constructs. One is creative because he uses metaphors, he does not use metaphors because he is creative. This is in conformity with the method of looking to see what we in fact do, rather than impose a theory or pseudo-psychology on what we do.

The new seems strange or surprising. By observing different customs, cultures, and languages one sees the world and one's emotions in a new or metaphorical way. Objects and people are associated with different words, sounds, and practices. We are often intolerant of what is new or strange to us. Seeing it as metaphor may help to make it more acceptable. One may purposely make the familiar seem strange to give insight into it, e.g., ask questions we usually think we know the answers to such as, "What is love?" "What is an idea?" "What is the number one?"

Cicero says that emotion is a sudden, fresh, hasty opinion. Metaphor is like that also. Deviation from what is expected often results in humor.

6) Deviation from usual perception. A poor person may actually see a quarter as larger than does a rich person. This is sometimes referred to as "seeing-as." This leads to imagery, ecstatic visions, or hallucinations. Seeing in terms of our needs and purposes may be called "perceptual defense." We, for example, tend to recognize words related to our interest quicker than other words.

A simile is a comparison usually involving the term "like" or "as," e.g., "The brain is like a computer." Metaphor is said to be a condensed simile, a simile without the use of "like," or "as," e.g., "The brain is a computer." A metaphor may not involve the word "is" but may be a single word such as saying "goodby" when greeting someone. But to say metaphor is just a condensed simile is misleading. It is only one definition, model, or way of looking at metaphor and can only account for a very limited range of metaphors. To say "A is B" is to say something more or different than "A is like B." "The brain is like a computer," is an "open simile" because the specific sense of the likeness is unspecified. If it is specified it becomes a "closed simile," e.g., "The brain is like a computer in processing bits of information." A metaphor is even more open than an open simile. It is multi-meaning and can be given a great many interpretations. Because metaphor is not adequately reduced to the literal it is thought to be emotive. Democritus asserted that the world is atomic, and throughout history this metaphor has been given various interpretations. One expansion of this metaphor was to regard ideas as atoms, and one spoke of the "association of ideas" as he spoke of the "association of atoms" or as it was sometimes called, "mental chemistry." Thus a metaphor cannot be reduced to one literal interpretation without loss of meaning. Metaphors are perspectival and multi-meaning.

Humor is one type of emotion. Many types of humor or wit, are, in fact, types of metaphor: 1) any breach of the usual order of events, 2) importing into one situation what belongs to another, 3) anything masquerading as something it is not, 4) word play, puns, double meaning, 5) nonsense, 6) forbidden breach, 7) novelty, freshness, unexpectedness, escape, 8) irony, mimicry and imitation. (See "Metaphor: as humor" *Metaphor Bibliography*) The conceit is a farfetched or extravagant metaphor involving wit and cleverness but nevertheless may also give profound insight. "Man is a machine," now a familiar or "dead" metaphor, was once thought to be a conceit or a joke. Today it is one of our most captivating metaphors and is frequently, though often erroneously, taken literally. Metaphor has gradations of belief. It may be variously taken as serious, literal, hypothesis, fiction, false, play, a joke, etc.

One type, though not every type, of metaphor is based on analogy which is somewhat like simile. In four term analogy A: B::C: D, e.g., sound: air:: light: "ether." Because sound travels through air it was thought that light might travel through a medium, ether. This analogy is, then, an hypothesis. Analogy and metaphor are often used to create new discoveries, give insight or new knowledge and they do this partly by deviating from old categories. Such hypotheses, however, may be found to lack confirmation, to be misleading analogies. This was the case with ether. Such a medium lacks confirmation. Also we only know about other people's feelings and thoughts by an analogical inference from our own case. We know of our own case partly by means of an intersubjective language. It is found that the schizophrenic often has overinclusive thinking and so does not pass the association likeness test.

A category-mistake, sort-crossing, or type-crossing involves using a word or sentence in a new context or category without realizing it. Views of ourselves often come from others' views of ourselves. We may thus confuse their views with our own, and for example, hate ourselves because others hate us or blame ourselves because our parents blamed us. It is a category-mistake to equate being alone with being lonely. Some erroneously apply practices and terms from childhood situations to their present adult situation; they cling to beliefs no longer applicable. A probable situation is taken for a certain situation. Some other category-mistakes are to talk of mental "process" in the same way we talk of physical process; to speak of the experience of seeing as if it is chemical; to take the "gush," "flow," "damming up," or "release," of emotions literally as if "emotive water" is flowing within us; to take "time flies" or "time passes" literally. Category-mistake thus often reduces to the metaphor-to-myth fallacy. Most or all of the terms used to describe mental phenomena and "internal states" are metaphorical and should not be taken literally, e.g., "stream-of consciousness." Metaphor allows us to in some way try to represent the so-called "inner emotion" by means of the "outer," or external phenomena, e.g., sharp pain, agitated, depressed, disturbed, distracted, upset. Such outer representations tend to dissolve the idea that emotions are inner states. We know of emotions and individual feelings by means of marks (words) and objects. Some misleading analogies are: "twinge of remorse" is not like "twinge of rheumatism," "pricking of conscience" is not like "pricking of a finger," "glow of pride" is not like "glow of warmth." The "inner" is appropriated especially to seen "outer" objects. We might have learned to think of pains as round or square rather than sharp and dull.

SOME MAIN TYPES OF METAPHOR

1. *synecdoche* The substitution of part for whole, "my wheels" for "my car," "pickpocket" for "thief," "The earth is round," for "The earth is spherical"; whole for part, "Go to the university" for "Go to class," yawning for boredom; species for genus; genus for species; the name of the material for the thing made, e.g., "pigskin" for "football"; cause for effect or effect for cause.

One type of substitution of part for whole is "cognitive closure," whereby one jumps to a conclusion to "close" an ambiguous situation. In informal logic it may be called "hasty generalization." It may be an attempt to reach a solution in order to quickly reduce the tension of ambiguous situations. Gestalt psychology stresses this sort of closure, e.g., indicating that we see an almost closed circle as a circle, that we tend to complete incomplete or unresolved situations, that we tend to see unfamiliar parts in terms of familiar wholes. A paranoid individual may hastily conclude that because his orange juice tastes strange, his wife must be trying to kill him.

It's synecdoche to think that because something is true in some situations, it must be true in all situations, e.g., that rules we learned in our youth must still apply now. We often tend to cling to old solutions to problems without questioning such methods.

One may take probable statements for absolute statements, e.g., substitute "It's impossible for me to change," for "It's hard for me to change." This also involves the fallacy of the use of "all," e.g., people often say "No one can change."

A very prevalent type of synecdoche is the belief that if one does a single bad act he is a bad person generally. This determines much of the sensitivity people have to criticism. The accusation, "I see you burned the toast," may be enough to make a person feel generally inferior or inadequate for days. One reason for this substitution is that "bad" is an open-context or obscure term and in itself has no meaning. To be meaningful one must substitute a concrete context and descriptive statement such as, "I made a mistake on this letter, but that only means extra time and effort is needed to correct the mistake." To make a mistake is not "bad" as such, nor is anything in itself good or bad. (See W. Shibles "Ethics as Open Context Terms")

It is often asserted that one is not a man unless he does such and such an act. This is a substitution of part for whole, as is the view that the sexual difference between man and woman is a necessary and sufficient condition of distinguishing them. One's sexuality is not the whole person. Also, one substitutes part for whole by generalizing in the following way: Because one's wife or mother has a poor personality he may think all women are like that, thus becoming a "woman-hater."

Juxtaposition or substitution may give some clarity to issues. For example, if pregnancy were caused by touching one's face or by a wind, one may have less objection to abortion. The same may be the case if men become pregnant as well as or instead of women.

Synecdoche is the underlying basis of the psychologists' notion of "stimulus generalization." Qualities merely or even remotely associated with the stimulus become capable of setting off the same response as the original stimulus. If one learns to fear reaching for a rabbit he may, by part-whole substitution or stimulus generalization, learn to fear reaching for a white fur coat. The schizophrenic often cannot abstract, cannot substitute part for whole in an acceptable normal way. He has a difficult time with elliptical words, parables, as-if abilities, and he tends to take things literally. His thinking is rigid. It's convenient to speak elliptically and abstractly. On the other hand, abstract terms are often a source of confusion and error. The schizophrenic, in effect, has a mechanism of avoiding errors of abstraction.

The schizophrenic often relates things on the basis of only a single quality held in common, thus creating a false identity. One patient because she was a virgin claimed to be the Virgin Mary. Astrologers do this as well as the average man. For instance, if your sign is the moon you are supposed to have a round face, if you are under the ram sign, your eyebrows are supposed to meet so as to be in the shape of the horns of a ram; if born under Mars, the war-like god, you will be expected to have a scar on your face.

2. *metonymy* Metonymy is the substitution of an attribute or association of a thing for the thing, or cause for effect, e.g., "hot" for "angry." Other examples are: "Irritation is a buzzing fly," "Sadness is walking down a long, grey tunnel," "Ice cream is associated with extreme joy," "He sees red," "swollen with pride," "Anger is a bull charging," "heat of passion," "burning with love," "bitter tears." Emotions have subjective associations, e.g., brightness and animation go with joy. One may dislike cripples because he is afraid he will be one. The psychiatric expression, "flight of ideas," involves metonymy. The *post hoc* fallacy or false-cause fallacy is an association such that because one thing occurs before another it is erroneously thought to be its cause.

3. a. *allegory* An expanded metaphor which has meaning on several different levels. It may expose a subject or character, e.g., the story of an unintelligent giant may be implicitly a story about the inefficiency of the government.

b. *parable* An expanded metaphor, a story often illustrating a moral principle.

c. *fairy tale* Metaphorical, made-up story usually meant for amusement.

d. *fable* An expanded metaphor, a story illustrating a truth. It often personifies animals.

e. *anagogical* Refers to a going beyond the literal to the spiritual or mystical. It appears, however, to be the aesthetic experience of a metaphor rather than any kind of transcendence.

Similarly, the "sublime" is merely a loftly feeling one has upon reading, seeing, or hearing a metaphor. "Anagogical is defined by *Webster's Collegiate Dictionary* as, "interpretation of a word, passage, or text (as of scripture or poetry) that finds beyond the literal, allegorical, and moral senses a fourth and ultimate spiritual or mystical sense." Poets often appear to express the magical transcendent nature of metaphor. It is thought that metaphor is among man's highest achievements, that it can render his most sublime emotions.

Max Eastman (1932) even asserts that metaphor is a state one can be in. It is a state of "heightened consciousness." Perhaps one might call this "metaphor emotion." This view is also presented by literary critics of India (De 1963). For them "rasa" means "delectation" which is a state of mind of rising to the occasion, a generalized emotion susceptible to enjoyment of metaphor.

Metaphor can relate the lower to the higher and elevate the higher to the sublime. To romanticize is to elevate lower ideas or objects to higher ones. If the higher is related to the lower it is called "sinking," e.g., "The King is ticklish."

f. *archetype* This is metaphor repeated so often that it seems to be a universal idea or truth. Carl Jung erroneously spoke of archetypes as basic forms of experience, as personalized images of the unconscious by means of which the psyche communicates with us. We supposedly must interpret these images. In fact, however, one can by means of metaphorical interpretation always create an archetype. By metaphor, especially farfetched metaphor, one can find a womb in anything. One cannot fail. Neither Freud nor Jung seemed to be sufficiently conscious of the extravagance of their metaphors.

g. *irony* and *parody* involve saying or implying the opposite of what one means, and comical imitation, respectively. The "double bind" language-game involves irony. It is discussed more fully under the topic "oxymoron" or "antithesis." Briefly, it involves a contradiction such as teaching politeness rudely. Irony is used also as an escape or emotion release mechanism. It is ironical that people often are disturbed because they blame themselves and then blame themselves because they are disturbed. Having a great need for love or sex is often the very thing which may make one unappealing and so unable to obtain either one. This involves the game of playing "hard to get."

Echopraxia is a kind of parody involving a pathological repetitive imitation of the behavior of another person. He assumes the gestures of his nurse, doctor, etc.

4. *substitution* This includes substitution of all kinds, e.g., speaking is a substitution of a sound for a thing; "He vents his spleen," for "He is angry." A "kenning" in skaldic writing involves substitution. For "Sleep fell on the king," the kenning might be "The death of each day's life fell on the dispenser of rings." Similarly, Shakespeare renders sleep as "the death of each day's life, sore labor's bath, balm of hurt minds, great nature's second course, chief nourisher in life's feast." (*Macbeth* II, ii, 37) Sublimation, placebo, synecdoche, transference, symbolization, introjection, projection, identification, conversion and nearly all of the defense-mechanisms are types of substitution. Fetishism involves substitution. In our society, euphemisms are used frequently regarding taboo topics such as death and sex.

Displacement or transference is the substitution of one object for another such that, for example, instead of fearing a certain object one fears the symbol of that object. Emotionally charged words in our language are words which are avoided because of what they stand for. Some people fear not only God, but the word "God", and so will not utter the word. "I love or hate my flag," is this kind of displacement. We often learn to find substitutions for the things we desire or learn to talk ourselves out of those things we cannot obtain. Sometimes the substitution is unfitting as in *"la belle indifference,"* which is an emotion inappropriate for the situation. In conversion hysteria the symptom seems inappropriate to the cause and it nevertheless completely replaces the anxiety so that the patient no longer feels anxious. Any vicarious activity relates to substituting or as-if behavior.

The anosognosic brain damaged patient often shows a language disorder called paraphasia. This is the use of word substitutes.

The use of neologisms and substitution words allows the denial of the illness. He may, for instance, refer to a thermometer as a "gradient," "wheelchair" as a "chaise," "emergency hospitalization" as a "vacation." The euphemisms for death which the average person uses are ways of denying death. Also, he often uses the third person instead of "I."

Some patients split the world into good and bad. They, then, for example, substitute by imagining two sons for one: one son is good, one bad and they even give each "son" a different name.

5. *juxtaposition* Two objects or words which are not usually associated with each other are put together. Art (Ars) involves this process and derives from the Aryan root "Ar" meaning "join, put together." Montage in film collage, the Chinese ideogram, and much of modern art involve juxtaposition (often for its own sake). A. I. Melden (1969) wrote,

"I shall examine cases and views (actual or possible), bringing them into juxtaposition with each other, and in so doing provide reminders and conceptual features and complexities — the dimensions of emotions." (199, 200)

We pin down emotions by comparing them with other experiences. This allows us to be more attentive to the world of feeling. Juxtaposition allows us to vary feelings and emotions with various objects, situations, and other emotions. Perhaps jealousy can be accompanied by delight. One may learn to enjoy war, or laugh at danger.

6. *parataxis* A juxtaposition or placing side by side without comma or separation.

7. *conceit* A farfetched, exaggerated, or bold metaphor. A hyperbole. It may, however, be well-founded in some ways and give great insight. Hyperbole and conceit may express exaggeration of emotion. The lover says, "You are the only one in the world for me." Adults as well as children exaggerate illness to obtain love. One may hallucinate or exaggerate normal imagery and perception to obtain desired objects or goals. Egomania, grandiosity, paranoia,

megalomania (delusion of great power), hypochondria, overcautiousness, excessive fear, mood swings, magnification of one's faults, are all exaggerations or hyperboles. Conceits may name and create new emotions, e.g., "My love is like a jolly cow who gambols in the meadow," "Love is two people both putting a finger in the same puddle," "Passion is chocolate and olives." Emotion may be thought to be an extreme feeling or extreme behavior. Reporting the cause of an event is often merely a report of an unusual or extreme factor involved in the situation. We say the oily rags caused the fire. The presence of oily rags is only an unusual or dangerous factor. The fire was also caused by the presence of oxygen, other combustible material, etc. Our everyday experience involves incongruous juxtaposition. We see a work of art, pigeon tracks, a dog, then a piece of gum, etc. While in love we smell the typewriter ribbon. Farfetched metaphors are like the dissociated thinking and remote associations of the schizophrenic. There is over-suggestibility, hasty generalization, probability is taken for certainty, etc. "Redintegration" refers to the total experiencing of a past event on the basis of being confronted with a single association.

8. *reciprocal metaphor* This may also be called an interaction metaphor. It is a way of regarding the elements of a metaphor. "Man is a fox" may say something new about man but also something new about a fox.

9. *dead metaphor* A dead metaphor is one which has become so familiar that it is taken as literal. One may be captivated or misled in this way. "Dead" metaphors may be rejuvenated as in "Time passes." One may ask what or how it "passes." Fixed cliches, jargon, dialects, slang, literal language, all involve "dead" metaphor. "Jargon aphasia" refers to the stereotyped speech of psychiatric patients.

10. *mixed metaphor* A combination of several different metaphors. Poets as well as scientists often build one metaphor on another. Mixed metaphor need not be avoided but it should be used carefully. Mixed metaphors also relate to mixed emotions.

11. *repetition and omitting metaphor* It is a metaphor to repeat or omit things not usually repeated or omitted, e.g., one poem consists of the word "cricket" repeated seventy times; "The sky is the sky"; "A is A" (in logic). Poetry often omits things, e.g., a part of speech: "A gentle rain" (verb omitted). A number of psychiatric terms involve repetition phenomena: "Perseveration" is fixed persisting thoughts or words, e.g., every object shown one is identified as an orange. "Stereotypy" — constantly repeated speech or action, e.g., person may constantly put out his thumb as if hitchhiking. Ideas or tunes often recur constantly, or the first reaction one has is inappropriately used in all subsequent situations. "Verbigeration" is a meaningless repetition of words which lasts for hours and days. Ritual, compulsion and obsessions are repetitions. "Echolalia" refers to abnormally repeating in one's answer the same word the questioner used. It is like a leading question but such repeating recurs very often. Repetition is partially the basis of developing habits and learning. "Echopraxia" is the abnormal repetition by imitation of another's actions and relates to the metaphorical device of parody or mocking.

12. *root* or *fundamental metaphor* Each theory in science, philosophy, etc., is based on one or more metaphors or models, e.g., Leucippus' "The world is atomic," Thales' "The world is water," or "Man is a machine." Because metaphor is the basis of the humanities and sciences it is able to unite them more than they could be united in any other way. Metaphor may serve as a basic hypothesis in both areas, e.g., poetry, novels, atomic models in chemistry, etc. Such metaphors do not merely illustrate "reality," but to a large extent constitute it. Metaphors may be expanded into a world view, philosophy or theory. A poem or novel may be thought of as one or more expanded metaphors. One may see the world through the emotion of joy, happiness, fear, depression. An emotion may serve as a fundamental metaphor through which one sees the world and himself. A person's love for another can spread out over all other things.

13. *unifying metaphor* Metaphors unify when they relate unlike things. By this means everything may be related to everything else and so give poets and others the misleading impression

that "all is one" (Parmenides) that there is a universal correspondence of all things, or a universal analogy of all things. Metaphor often fuses or synthesizes the elements related. Metaphor allows us to examine behavior in various lights. If captivation by a model, expression, or slogan leads us into emotionally disturbed behavior we may reexamine and reinterpret our metaphor, if we are able, or gain the insight which other metaphors may give. Sometimes, however, a single unifying model is what is needed to clarify one's experience and emotions, and organize his life. For this purpose alone, it may not make any difference how false in other respects the model is. This may be the reason why religion, Freudianism, and cult or youth group experiences may be found so unifying. However, this theory has the drawback that the unifying view may be later seen to be unfounded and unrealistic in many respects and lead to undesirable consequences. Also a critical person may not be able to believe in such models at all or may later find he can no longer believe in them, and so see that he has been misled. Special deceptive methods must be used to become religious or Freudian. In addition, the unity gained by such belief may be gained at the expense of a more adequate unity and adjustment, one involving fewer things which could falsify it. Ecstatic states of acute schizophrenia, religious mysticism, as well as certain drug experiences, often give the feeling that all is one, that opposites are reconciled, and that there is a mystical unity of all things (*unio mystica*). It is a form of psychosis.

14. *synaesthetic metaphor* Terms applicable to one sense are applied to those of another, e.g., "bitter tears," "See how you feel," "gaiety of yellow," "high sound," "white noise", "smooth sound," "coolness of green," "hot color," "feel blue," "blue mood." In musical tone poems the listener is asked to visualize musical sounds. Drug takers report seeing sound. Some synaesthetic metaphors describe synaesthetic experiences, others only suppose such experiences. Emotions are often related to color as follows:

    red — anger, rage, joy
    orange — warmth
    yellow — cowardice, fear
    green — jealousy

blue — peaceful, calm
black — dread, sad, depression
white — peaceful, calm, guiltless
purple — rage

Psychological disorders frequently involve synaesthesia such as delusions, sense hallucinations of all types, and experiences such as "hearing one's own thoughts." "Anesthetic hallucinations" refer to sensations without sense organs or receptors to account for them, e.g., feeling that the body is rotting, burning sensation in the brain (when no physical evidence is found for it), pushing sensation in blood vessels, etc. This is not to say that neural and cortical mechanisms aren't involved.

15. *oxymoron* or *antithesis* Supposed opposites are combined, e.g., "unconscious fear," "unconscious desire," "see the sun about to grin, about to break into ice cubes," "being angry need not involve feeling angry," "O snow, my flame," "sadness gives pleasure," "past joy and present grief," "enjoy anger," "truth is falsity" (may suggest that nothing is absolutely true or false), "emotion is reason" (may suggest that the categories are artificial or that emotion may be analyzed into rational assertions and assessments), "death is life" (may suggest that death is only a concept of conscious living experiences), "to be negative is to be positive" (may suggest that one may advance knowledge by means of criticism), "irrelevance is a tool of relevance" (may suggest that one may, in Shakespeare's words, "by indirection find directions out"). Both emotions and metaphors thrive on contrasts. Because metaphor combines unlike terms it may seem like a riddle, paradox, enigma, miracle, mystery, marvel, revelation, disclosure, or a mystical transcendence. It may give the experience we call the "sublime." It does not, however, allow us to actually transcend to a new mystical or magical kind of knowledge. A number of examples of oxymoron or antithesis follow:

1) A parent smiles as if trying to look polite or kind as she scolds her child for his table manners.

2) A parent teaches manners rudely.

3) A repressed person sometimes weeps when praised. He may cry because he thinks the praise is quite undeserved.

4) Manic-depressives alternate from one extreme state to its opposite.

5) A depressed person sometimes views himself as exactly the opposite of what he is, e.g., an excellent scientist claims he is stupid.

6) A juvenile likes being bad.

7) One who fears being disliked often actually makes himself be disliked.

8) People often do the reverse of what is expected of them.

9) One may refuse to take part because of fear he will not succeed.

10) Because of feelings of insecurity one may adopt even less secure, arbitrary or mystical rules.

11) One who is afraid of people withdraws even more and becomes more afraid, thereby doing the opposite of what would be helpful.

12) Compensations, such as weak people acting strong.

13) Reaction-formation involves expressing the opposite emotion one is experiencing.

14) Negativism involves saying and doing the opposite of what is requested. This is a severe form of stubbornness, e.g., "The more one asks her to compose herself, the more excited she becomes."

15) To obtain a desired response, e.g., from a female, one must often show interest in the opposite of what is desired.

16) Double bind is holding contradictory views at the same time, e.g., feelings of guilt if one does not perform an act and feelings of guilt if one does perform the act. One may be disliked for his jealousy and at the same time be said to be inattentive if he is not jealous. One thing may be said but with intonations suggesting the reverse.

17) Conflicts and paradoxes combine opposites.

18) Ambivalence involves having opposed attitudes, views, or emotions. One may both love and hate the same person.

19) Synthesis of thesis and antithesis is a combination of opposites.

20) Metaphor is generally the combination of unlike terms or terms from unlike contexts.

21) Pleasure and pain intertwine. One may enjoy pain and dislike pleasure. Opposite emotions may combine, e.g., enjoy being hostile.

22) Split personality involves two opposed personalities such that the individual while being one type does not remember being the other type. One personality may be shy and inhibited, the other bold and aggressive.

23) Dunlap's "Beta Hypothesis" and V. Frankl's "Paradoxical Intention" involve doing the very thing which one is afraid to do but with informed assessment so as to dissipate the fear. It may involve many acts not just fear, e.g., squinting, tics, nail-biting, smoking, etc. One may also be asked to imagine things he fears or dislikes.

24) Opposites are combined so as to give insight, e.g., "Emotions are rational."

25) Stress on opposites may commit the either-or fallacy, or all-or-none fallacy. One often thinks he is either a good or a bad person, or that a statement must be either true or false.

26) Many terms combine opposites, such as, "Virgin Mary."

27) Freudians state that dying and killing, giving and receiving, and other opposites are equivalent in the unconscious. The device of interchanging opposites may take place, but psychologists and philosophical psychology usually regard the "unconscious" as a fictive entity.

28) It is often good therapy to tell those things which one fears to tell most.

29) In some cases of anxiety neurosis the patient describes hearing a voice as, for example, "silently screaming" in one's head.

30) One may say about something he loves that he hates it, because he feels others might disapprove.

31) Feminine coquetry involves alternate "yes" or promise and "no" or withdrawal. The male is rejected but never deprived of hope. This may lead to frustration for the male and indecision or even conscious hostility on the part of the female. The result: a double bind.

32) "Emotions are Rational." (V. McGill *Emotions and Reason* p. 62) (See #24)

33) Stubbornness: the more one is asked to be composed the less he or she is able to do so.

34) In chivalric love one suffers agreeably or "suffers love." Love is a "painful thrill," a "cruel love."

35) In word association tests some people almost always give antonyms or synonyms.

16. *etymological metaphor* Words are always applied to new situations thereby expanding their uses. Thus, metaphor is a principle of the development of language. "Idea" derives from the Greek word for "to see," "melancholy" from "black bile," "express" from "press out." We speak of the "sphere" of knowledge. "Person" derives from "mask," "emotion" means "commotion."

17. *visual metaphor* A mermaid is an example of this. Emblems and icons are visual representations of ideas. A lion represents courage. Poems were once regarded as paintings and it was thought that one should be able to draw or visualize an entire poem. Deviation from usual perception results in illusions, and illusion is a kind of metaphor. We see incorrectly because we have learned the wrong contextual cues. Autism involves the imagery of dreams, fantasies, delusions, hallucinations. Images often illustrate or ornament ideas making them sensuous, vivid, and persuasive.

Dunlap's "Beta Hypothesis" and V. Frankl's "Paradoxical Intention," as was mentioned, involve doing the very thing one is afraid to do. By doing these things with the proper reassessments one may cure himself of an irrational reaction. The same procedure is used with imagery. It may be called covariation of imagery. One simply imagines what he hates, but with proper assessments he imagines behaving in the desired rather than in the undesired way, or practices imagining the correct behavior. Basketball and dart skills may be improved by such methods. (See D. Beattie "The Effect of Imagery Practice on the Acquisition of a Motor Skill" M.A. Thesis, Toronto 1949) Memory of traumatic events may be dissipated in this way. Worthwhile goals may be imagined to serve as strong sources of motivation, e.g., seeing oneself as a knowledgeable philosopher, imagining oneself as having an attractive figure – as an aid to forcing oneself to diet, etc. A reassessment regarding fear of mice may be to think of mice as one does a pet cat or dog, or by personification, think of the mouse as a close friend. Visual metaphor also involves "seing-as" which was discussed earlier. A child described thunder as "the loud mouth who is playing outside." The imagist poets tried to reduce poetry to a number of juxtaposed images, e.g., "The apparition of these faces in the crowd: Petals on a wet, black bough." (Ezra Pound)

The psychologists'Rorschach test is a metaphorical reading of ink blot designs which supposedly reveals intellect and emotions. This is a visual seeing-as or metaphorical activity. Color supposedly portrays emotion, form indicates intellectual processes; shading shows anxiety or depression; movement shows originality or creativity; content shows the area of pre-occupation (cf. imagery). G. Ulett and D. Goodrich (1969) state, "The validity of the Rorschach Test as a scientific method is still questioned." (52-53) This test seems to be a farfetched use of metaphor. The test instead of being a careful measure of one's emotions and thought may be rather thought of as a test of the metaphorical ability of the patient. It is a kind of association test. For example, one patient referred to one blot as "terrestrial sex." The Rorschach suggests that perception is selective. Perception may be thought of as assessment which guides seeing. A stare is a metaphor and causes uneasiness because it departs from the way we normally look. We often have original experiences which nevertheless seem to have been had before or vice versa, e.g., "*deja vu,* strangely familiar vision; *jamais vu,* strange unfamiliarity of familiar experience; *deja extendu,* original comment is thought familiar; *deja pense,* new thought is thought familiar.

18. *personification* The inanimate is treated as animate, e.g., "It is an angry wind." One speaks of "contented" cows. EEG experiments with plants are said to show that plants have emotions. But this is a confusion. It is to overgeneralize about what is only reception of electrical impulses and merely assumes emotions. It is to personify. Dogs are said to smile. Children give inanimate things and animals human faces. Faces are carved into pumpkins. In the fable, animals are personified and speak. We speak of "unfriendly town," "a frog's desires," and we give inanimate things gender. In German, nouns are masculine, feminine, or neuter. "Love" (Liebe) is of the feminine gender, anger (Zorn) is masculine. The "state" is often personified as an organism. "Pathetic fallacy" refers to giving animals the feelings and emotions of a human. Animals and inanimate objects may be befriended because of lack of ability to get along with people. To animate is also to emotify. But what kind of facial expression is needed to imitate a praying-mantis, a caterpillar, an ant? Analogy is sometimes used to avoid anthropomorphism (making human what is not human) or personification, e.g., man's intelligence is to man as God's intelligence is to God. But even this analogy is anthropomorphic. One may also "dehumanize," or make what is animate or human, more inanimate and less human, e.g., "That clerk barks at everyone." "Depersonalization" is "identification" with objects or loss of identity or sense of self. A child schizophrenic often cannot distinguish between the animate and inanimate and has a disturbed body image such that he may not know where his feet are.

19. *therapeutic metaphor* Metaphor may be used to avoid the literal, escape from narrow or oppressive categories, avoid taboo or unacceptable language, provide release (catharsis), and give in-

direct ways of saying things. Euphemism is substitution of an agreeable word for a word we wish to avoid uttering, e.g., "stirred up" for hateful. By means of metaphor one is able to distance himself from an object, person, or situation. Language, especially metaphor, is found to play a significant role in the treatment of the so-called "emotional disturbed" patient. Schizophrenics often display actions marked by linguistic and behavioral abnormality. They appear to take language literally and that literal statement largely constitutes their emotion. Dr. W. Muncie (1937) reported, "One patient wanted to be an airplane pilot in order to get the proper perspective on the world." Richard Johnson (1964) reports that a patient may think a revolving door is a grinding mouth, and thus refuse to go through it. Such patients also use metaphors when literal language is more appropriate. One reason we say a patient is emotionally disturbed is because he speaks a "word salad," that is, disconnected and highly metaphorical language. This fact has offered the psychiatrist a clue to classifying and treating such patients. David Pavy (1968) wrote, "Deviant verbal behavior is one of the principle diagnostic indices of the syndrome of schizophrenia." Metaphor, then, may partly constitute emotion. It is one clue to what is meant by emotion and emotional disturbance. Caruth and Ekstein (1966) have expressed the view that metaphor may be used to establish communication with the schizophrenic patient because it has the emotive distance needed. A metaphor does not reveal one's true assessments and feelings indirectly because it is multi-meaning and allows for greatly diverse interpretations. Thus the patient can use it as an escape or release from holding a too emotionally disturbing literal view of reality. The escape or release is the experience of using the metaphor. The model here is not one of a dam of energy of emotion and some of it steaming out. Metaphor is a use of language different than that of literal language, and emotion is to a large extent a use of metaphor. Metaphor does not just render or allow emotion in us to be expressed or "pressed out." The experience of the metaphor is the emotion. The two are one. Each rhetorical device is like an emotion and each emotion is like a rhetorical device. This is an attempt to formulate and elaborate on the Collingwood thesis (see aesthetics section) that emotion is expression, that it is the same experience. We do not know what is behind what scenes here, what inner scenes; we let the metaphor stand out and be in the spotlight. We watch it perform its magic.

We may thus, in therapy, examine the patient's metaphors, and use metaphors to communicate with the patient in an attempt to reestablish his emotional "balance." There is poetry therapy, and poetry is largely metaphor. Jack Leedy's recent book (1969) is entitled, *Poetry Therapy: The Use of Poetry in the Treatment of Emotional Disorders.* The model "emotional balance" here may mislead. It means "linguistic balance." The escape metaphor may be thought of in terms of Freud's defense-mechanisms, e.g., "condensation." A "condensation" is at times regarded as two situations combined concisely into one on the basis of emotive likeness. This is also sometimes the very definition of a metaphor. It is a combining of two things or terms on the basis of subjective or "felt" similarity. Metaphor can provide the moving emotive experience itself. We often speak of the "tension" between the two terms of a metaphor. "Tension" is emotion. The metaphor renders emotion. Poetry is said to "move" (e + motion) the reader.

The gloss for "cognitive capacity," and "efforts to find oneself," is mainly the ability to clarify to oneself one's language, of which emotion is largely constituted. It is to clarify such expressions as "I'll show you yet," "You can't do that to me," "What would they think of me?" and "What is it all about?" Therapy also involves showing one that what he takes literally is really only metaphorical.

William Godwin in his book Enquiry Concerning Political Justice and its Influence on Morals and Happiness pointed out that positive emotions such as cheerfulness aid body health, and negative emotions such as melancholy destroy the body. Thus clear thinking which informs the emotions helps prolong life.

20. *elucidating metaphor* Metaphor is often used to clarify, to describe and name emotions which cannot otherwise be described or named, e.g., "feel heavy," "chill in my heart," "his heart moved in mine." One can always ask how an emotion feels. The reply is, for example, love is "relaxed" or "expansive," anger is "rough."

Some hold that, in fact, metaphor recaptures emotional experiences or even that it is the equivalent of a feeling. Others state that metaphors should accurately reflect emotions, implying that at times they are not identical or equivalent. Metaphors reveal fine shades and nuances of our emotions, clarify certain feelings and moods. The metaphor may serve as the "formula" for an emotion. We may think here of those who think that because works such as the Koran or the Bible are so richly metaphorical that they must be divinely inspired. They are, however, only metaphors. They may involve paradox, mystery, and mysticism which yield certain emotions. Both emotions and metaphors are somewhat mystical.

Metaphor clarifies or constitutes emotion. The music of different cultures produces a difference in behavioral patterns. A guitar may define sadness. By listening to a guitar one may become sad in a way he never did before. Travel gives an emotion. One does not just travel, he travels into the future, into hopes, dreams, and excitement.

To speak of the harmony of the four humors may make no sense literally, but metaphorically may make good sense. The same is the case with "I am nervous." Metaphor renders what a person feels but also constitutes and renders something more than just the feeling. It does this by means of new class inclusions, relating old and new, sensuous and non-sensuous, abstract and concrete, material and immaterial, perceptible and imperceptible, spiritual and non-spiritual, known and unknown, e.g., a "sleeping" leg is referred to as a "soda water" feeling, joy is referred to as "being on a cloud." Personality, emotions and most or all mental states are rendered by metaphors, e.g., "stream of consciousness," "flow of emotions," "He is a wolf," "Spread some jelly on your life," "To do that is to try to put a spider web together with your fingers," "My anger could fill this room." Metaphor is thus said to constitute emotions, describe emotions, express emotions, stimulate emotions, or to be itself emotive. Dreams are interpreted metaphorically. Metaphors also give insight or new knowledge by breaking down old categories such as mind-body, reason-emotion, etc. They allow us to develop new hypotheses and connections thus serving as a source of knowledge, discovery, disclosure, and illumination. They guide experimentation, control and guide feeling as well. Metaphor is often a brief way of saying something complex, a summary, elliptical, or a condensed statement of much experience, e.g., "He is a good egg." Personality is thus described metaphorically.

One can be confused about the nature of time, mind, self, emotions, death, grief, anxiety, etc., in such a way as to do harm to oneself, others, and one's environment. One needs then philosophical clarification, needs to find one's way about. This sort of therapy is similar to what William Sahakian (1970) calls "philosophical psychotherapy." But it is better established in the tradition of ordinary-language philosophy. In the latter tradition Wittgenstein (1968) states,

"A main cause of philosophical disease – a one-sided diet: one nourishes one's thinking with only one kind of example." (PI 593)

"The philosopher's treatment of a question is like the treatment of an illness." (PI 255)

"There is not a philosophical method, though there are indeed methods, like different therapies." (PI 133)

"What is your aim in philosophy? – To show the fly the way out of the flybottle." (PI 309)

"A philosophical problem has the form: 'I don't know my way about.' " (PI 123)

The average person may indeed have a need to constantly clarify his thinking and emotions by means of metaphor. One may explore and give insight into the nature of his emotions by metaphorical juxtaposition. For instance, to understand the nature of jealousy, imagine if one would feel as jealous if his spouse had a relation with someone of the same sex rather than of the opposite sex. The wider one's knowledge, the greater is the possibility of emotional options and choices. Even the state of depression can yield artistic or descriptive insight. Metaphor can allow for a wide diversity of interpretations of a situation and so allow greater choices of action and perspective. For people who think they cannot change their behavior the metaphorical method applies because metaphors give different perspectives and options of acting (metaphorical behavior). Metaphor allows one to take things less literally and so be less captivated by statement. For example, one may be captivated by the statement, "I must be loved by everyone," or "Others bore me," rather than juxtapose grammar to see that it is I who bore myself. Metaphor provides the shock or critical way of putting things necessary to both philosophical as well as psychiatric insight. People tend to cling to old beliefs and resist new ideas. It allows for an "expansion" of knowledge. Love and joy may be thought of as expansions, as going out expansively to others and to life. Knowledge in this sense may be thought of as love. What was often thought to be the basic emotion, love, is now seen to be basically knowledge and understanding. Such understanding is enhanced by the insight metaphor gives.

Francis Bacon once said that poets can best show the nature of emotions, how they conflict and relate. (Gardiner 1937 p. 143) Since what basically characterizes poetry is metaphor, it is this which can best give knowledge of emotions. The oxymoron, for example, has been useful to show contrasts, for example, "Love is hate." It is here that truth and beauty can unite.

Paul Simonov, a Russian psychologist, maintains that emotion allows for new insight when rational methods fail (1970):

"Our emotions appear to be a reserve mechanism for making connections between highly improbable events or events that are seldom encountered . . . . Emotional arousal . . . makes possible the bringing together of memories that are remote from one another. The new combinations are compared with reality and those associations that correspond to actual connections in the environment are selected."

R. Drake similarly states, "Strong emotions cause peculiar associations." (34) This amounts to saying that emotion allows us to create metaphor which gives insight, new hypotheses and problem-solving possibilities.

In general, in the arts as elsewhere, there is a widespread use of metaphor, a need to hear and create new metaphors for aesthetic, scientific and everyday practical reasons. One may find that he has a metaphor-hunger (i.e., be emotionally starved) which must be satisfied by writing, by the arts, by conversing with those who speak metaphorically, or by creating new scientific models and hypotheses. One may obtain increased satisfaction with a greater knowledge of the nature of metaphor. It is needed for one's well-being.

Bibliography:

Warren Shibles An Analysis of Metaphor The Hague: Mouton 1971

Warren Shibles, ed., Essays on Metaphor Whitewater, Wisconsin: The Language Press 1972

Warren Shibles Metaphor: An Annotated Bibliography and History, Whitewater, Wisconsin: The Language Press 1971

Warren Taylor Tudor Figures of Rhetoric Whitewater, Wisconsin: The Language Press 1972

Sources:

Jack Barlow "Metaphor and Insight in Psychotherapy" PhD diss. 1973

Elaine Caruth and R. Ekstein "Interpretation Within the Metaphor" American Academy of Child Psychiatry Journal 5 (1) (1965) 35-45

G. K. Chesterton "About Mad Metaphors" As I Was Saying London: Methuen 1936 pp. 1-6

Sushil De Sanskrit Poetics as a Study of Aesthetics Berkeley: University of California Press 1963

Raleigh Drake Abnormal Psychology New Jersey: Littlefield, Adams 1954

Max Eastman The Literary Mind: Its Place in an Age of Science New York: Scribner's 1932 esp. part 4, ch. 1, sec. 5-6

David Forest "Poiesis and the Language of Schizophrenia" Psychiatry 28 (1965) 1-18

Harry M. Gardiner, R. Metcalf, and J. Beebe-Center Feeling and Emotion: A History of Theories New York: American Book Co. 1937

Richard Johnson "Imaginative Sensitivity in Schizophrenia" Review of Existential Psychology and Psychiatry 4, 3 (1964) 255-264

261

Jack Leedy *Poetry Therapy: The Use of Poetry in the Treatment of Emotional Disorders* Philadelphia: Lippincott 1969

A. I. Melden *"The Conceptual Dimensions of Emotions" Human Action* T. Mischel, ed., New York: Academic Press 1969

W. Muncie (M.D.) *"The Psychopathology of Metaphor" Archives of Neurology and Psychiatry* 37 (1937) 796-804

David Pavy *"Verbal Behavior in Schizophrenia" Psychological Bulletin* 70, 3 (1968) 164-178

William Sahakian *Psychopathology Today* Illinois: Peacock Publisher 1970

Theodore Sarbin *"Anxiety: Reification of a Metaphor." Essays on Metaphor* W. Shibles, ed., Whitewater, Wisconsin: The Language Press 1972

Warren Shibles *"Ethics as Open-Context Terms" Philosophical Pictures* 2nd edition, Dubuque, Iowa: Kendall Hunt 1972

Warren Shibles *"Figurative Language" Colliers Encyclopedia* (next edition)

Warren Shibles *'Il metodo metaforico" Lingua e Stile* 8 (1973) 321-334

Warren Shibles *"Linguo-Centric Predicament," "Language as Paradox" Philosophical Pictures,* 2nd Edition, Dubuque, Iowa: Kendall-Hunt 1972

Warren Shibles *"The Metaphorical Method" Journal of Aesthetic Education* 8 (April 1974) 25-36

Warren Shibles *"Metaphor and Creativity" Communication* (forthcoming)

Warren Shibles *"Die Metaphorische Methode" Deutsche Vierteljahrschrift* 1973

Pavel Simonov *"Emotions and Creativity" Psychology Today* 4,3 (Aug. 1970) 51-55, 77

George Ulett and D. Goodrich *A Synopsis of Contemporary Psychiatry* Saint Louis: C. Mosby 1969

Harold Vetter *Language, Behavior and Psychopathology* Chicago: Rand McNally 1969; *Language Behavior in Schizophrenia* Springfield, Illinois: C. Thomas 1968

Ludwig Wittgenstein *Philosophical Investigations* 3rd edition, New York: Macmillan 1968

Informal Logical Fallacies

Formal logic and symbolic logic are metaphors based largely on, or are similar to, mathematical models. They have very little to do with clarifying thinking done in ordinary language but rather are often seen to be irrelevant to it. Their application is more with mathematical and computer systems. Benedetto Croce once wrote,

"As the science of thought, logistic is a laughable thing."

We do sometimes think in terms of syllogisms but only rarely. Syllogistic thinking may be thought of as one rhetorical device among others. The main rhetorical device is metaphor. Informal logic is a form of rhetoric and traditionally many of the devices of informal logic and formal logic were classified as rhetorical devices. Thinking in the normal, as well as the abnormal person, is rhetorical and bound up with ordinary language. Albert Ellis' list of irrational ideas comprises linguistic statements leading to psychological problems. These may be regarded as logical fallacies. If one learns formal logic, geology, chess, etc. these may serve as central metaphors and so affect our thinking. But we usually no more think in terms of logic than in terms of chess. Our main tool of all reasoning is rather the language we speak and the potential of that language. Following are some of the forms of informal fallacies. They are often regarded as fallacious in one sense but acceptable in another. Most fallacies are committed by scholars, politicians, and the average person, but they appear in extreme forms in schizophrenia and other "mental" disorders. One may become fixated or captivated by a particular fallacy. They are language-games or forms of metaphor, and may help to classify an individual's manner of thinking. If one's assessments are faulty, then his emotions become negative ones, and there is also loss of contact with reality. When one reads about these fallacies they seem obvious, when one commits them they seem unknown.

FALLACY OF HASTY GENERALIZATION

This involves concluding about all instances on the basis of a single instance. Because one woman is irrational one cannot conclude on that basis alone that all women are irrational. This involves "jumping to a conclusion" on the basis of faulty or insufficient evidence. Hasty generalization may involve synecdoche or substitution whereby one substitutes part for whole and then ignores the fact that it is only a part. On the other hand, scientists often do legitimately generalize on the basis of a single instance. For example, if one knows basic laws of physics and then tests out the movement of a single type of substance, he may tentatively conclude about all substances of that type. That is, although only one instance is encountered, past experience and laws of nature and behavior may allow one to conclude much more than is given. This, then, seems to be hasty generalization because based on a single instance but is actually well-founded because based on a lot of other prior knowledge. We may, for example, tell a good deal about a person merely by looking at him. We judge whether a book might be worth reading without ever having read it.

The fallacious hasty generalization of the average person might involve such statements as, "X is a good school because it is well-known." But seldom does one know what any of the teachers are like during any particular year, and it is found that the same teachers teach or taught in other schools. One often generalizes hastily on the basis of false inference such as "I'm no good because I failed this exam," or, because of someone's tendency to agree, one may say of him that he is a brilliant person. The schizophrenic or psychologically disordered person uses these same devices. He may, for example, think that because someone stares at him that he is trying to kill him, or that because he got one answer right he is a genius. Things may be thought to be identical merely on the basis of a single similar quality. The thinking of the psychologically disordered person is on a continuum with the "normal" person. Or, putting it differently, our political speeches, advertisements, typical everyday conversations, are paradigm cases of informal fallacy.

IGNORATIO ELENCHI

This fallacy involves refutation of a misunderstood statement, or premises which are entirely unrelated to the conclusion. The psychiatric expression, "flight of ideas," is continuous speech with the goal or subject at hand never being reached. It is a clever leap from topic to topic. Light conversations and party conversations are of this sort as is the speech of the acute manic.

GENETIC FALLACY

According to this fallacy what leads one to a view is irrelevant to the truth or falsity of the view. On the other hand, often the only way of understanding a term or statement is to try to find out how one came to hold such a view. For example, to find out what we really mean by a word we must know the context in which we learned to apply it. In psychiatry this seems especially true, although Freudians commit the genetic fallacy by deterministically relating one's adult behavior to the oral, anal, and phallic stages of early childhood. One may also confuse the cause of something with its description. Because statements in logic must be either true or false, it is thought that how one arrived at the truth or falsity is not relevant. Sometimes this may be the case, e.g., whether or not it is raining. But in dealing with human thought, how one came to think what he does can be very important and relevant. Also, human thinking involves many more categories than truth or falsity. There are doubt, possibility, ignorance, etc. "Truth" in itself is an obscure open-context term.

The semi-technical psychiatric term, "circumstantiality," is often used to describe the genetic sort of fallacy whereby the patient speaks at length of extraneous detail without immediately getting to the point.

FALLACY OF ACCIDENT

This involves arguing from a rule to a non-applicable case. The opposite fallacy is to argue from a special case to a rule. "Accident" refers to unnecessary properties. This may relate to accidental associations such as, "I am rich, therefore I am intelligent."

FALLACIES OF AMBIGUITY

a. *equivocation* Metaphysical words are perhaps the best examples of equivocation. Such words are open-context and may mean so many things that it is not clear what is meant or that the words are used in the same sense. Examples are: being, good, bad, ought, duty, right, wrong, truth, time, space, etc. "The book *is* on the table, therefore the book *exists,*" is such an equivocation. It is not clear what could be meant by "exists" other than being on the table. Metaphysicians think exist has a transcendent meaning in itself and traditionally misuse language in this way because one can say, "X is," in some metaphysical or contextless sense. "Depression" and "emotion" terms are also ambiguous terms.

b. *Amphiboly* This refers to sentences having several meanings due to misleading construction.

c. *Fallacy of division and composition* Parts and wholes are confused as may be the case with synecdoche and substitution. Psychiatric classifications of "mental" disorders usually involve naming-fallacies or faulty divisions. Cause criteria are confused with miscellaneous and incidental criteria.

FALLACY OF ACCENT

The wrong word or part of the sentence is accented resulting in a misunderstanding.

FALLACY OF SPECIAL PLEADING

Only isolated, selected, pro reasons are given rather than both pro and con. Legal judgments are of this sort. Courtroom decisions are pro and con but not based upon an adequate and complete analysis of all of the relevant factors. They are based upon only what the lawyers decide to ask for legal purposes. One may end up being guilty legally, but innocent actually. In trial a "person" is constructed by the restricted testimony and it is only this legal "person" which is tried. The person's emotional life is also fictitiously created. Testimony is often limited to specific subjects in specific periods of time thus precluding much relevant testimony. Senate hearings may construct an event more adequately than courtroom testimony. Also, that one gives only a pro-argument does not mean that he has not *thought* of and previously analyzed pro and con arguments.

CIRCULAR STATEMENTS (Petitio Principii Fallacy)

Two forms of this are a) S is true because S is true, and b) S is true because A is true, and A because B, and B because S. The latter example fits dictionary definitions most of which are circular. One word is defined in terms of another and the other in terms of the first word. (For an extended presentation see W. Shibles "Are All Statements Circular?" *Philosophical Pictures.*) "I get angry because I am an emotional person," may be circular because one knows he is emotional because he becomes angry. Tautological statements, e.g., A is A, say nothing and are meaningless. Covertly circular statements are similarly meaningless, but they become fallacies when it is thought that they are non-circular. Although nearly every statement can be seen to be circular in some respect, the circular sense should not be confused with the non-circular sense of the statement. That a statement is partly circular, and so true, may erroneously give one the impression that the non-circular part is true also. It may seem the case that one ought to do his duty until it is noticed that "duty" means "that which one ought to do." Circular statements may sometimes be used as an escape or defense-mechanism, e.g. A patient may defend his hostility by asserting, "Everyone should have what is coming to him."

COMPLEX QUESTION

An instance of this is "Who created the world?" This question leads most people to think the world was created and that it was created by someone, viz. God. Both assumptions are incorrect and the question is really two questions in one. Most certainly, no one created the world, and the world may not have been "originally" created. "Create" is misused when applied to "creation" of the world.

AD IGNORANTIAM FALLACY (Argument from ignorance)

Several forms of this are:
a) P is true because it has not been proven false.
b) P is true because it has not been proven true.

It is fallacious to argue "God exists because no one has ever proven that God does not exist." In addition, one can show that God is an obscure or meaningless term and so dissolve the question, "Does God exist?" There is all kinds of evidence showing that it makes no sense to hold that God exists. A statement may be false if proven false, but not false just because it has not been proven true. Often mystical views in religion, astrology, psychic experiences, etc. are based on the fact that we have no explanations for such experiences, i.e., they are based on the argument from ignorance. Because we don't know the explanation for something, does not give evidence for belief. Rather, such mystical phenomena seem to have quite convincing explanations in terms of psychological aberrations. Instead of mystical interpretations it would seem more honest to assert, "I do not know." Arguments against abortion are often based on this fallacy. Because they do not know whether or not to call an embryo a person some claim it is in fact a person from conception.

AD VERECUNDIAM FALLACY (Appeal to Authority)

Appeal to authority. This fallacy is used many times each day by most people. It involves appeal to "experts," logic, God, science, the dictionary, friends, one's doctorate, newspapers, one's parents, etc. Advertisements often employ this device, e.g., "Doctors say . . ." Instead of appeal to authority one might rather look objectively at the relevant facts and arguments.

ARGUMENTUM AD MISERICORDIAM

One appeals to the pity of the audience rather than to objective argument. Pity for the speaker or someone only remotely connected with the case in point, appears to be beside the argument. Pity may at times be relevant to the argument and, if so, may not result in a fallacy. On the other hand, pity or negative feelings brought on by a value assessment of something being "too bad," may well be an irrational emotion and so never be essentially relevant to any argument.

AD POPULUM FALLACY

This sort of argument appeals to the prejudices and emotions of the audience rather than to objective reasoning. What is meant by "appeal to emotions"? There are statements made which, although irrelevant to one's argument, tend to induce positive feelings in the audience. Appeal to emotions is partly an appeal to assessments. Appeal to prejudice involves uttering statements appealing to the unbounded or uncritical, superstitious or false beliefs of the audience. People tend to believe that familiar beliefs are true beliefs. Thus, this fallacy is an appeal to common beliefs rather than to objective critical argument or evidence. One tends to believe what his emotionally close friends or parents say. Appeal to emotions may also involve becoming angry if the opponent does not agree with you, or using value-laden terms such as "poor," "awful," "ridiculous," "absurd," etc.

TU QUOQUE FALLACY

This fallacy involves thinking that a thing is right to do if someone else also does it, or replying to a charge by making the same charge in return (thus *Tu Quoque,* or "you also"). That another violates a law makes one no less guilty for doing the same. But this is not always a fallacy. The fact that others perform the act also may nullify one's wrong-doing, e.g., from the perspective of an educated and informed notion of equality.

AD HOMINEM FALLACY

The person is criticized rather than the argument. One's personal life, tone of voice, age, sex, occupation, etc. may be criticized rather than the views presented. This is one of the fallacies most commonly committed. Professors are known to frequently reply to students' objections with such statements as, "I see you have a lot to learn," "That's absurd," "You had better do a lot more reading," etc., rather than answer the objections. These replies, or failure to reply by ignoring the student's questions, are very harmful to the emotions of the student and hinder inquiry. Such teachers show that they are unable to honestly inquire and would therefore have little of value to teach. Of course, students commit the fallacy also. In one sense, the *ad hominem fallacy* is not a fallacy if one's objective statement deals with the argument and at the same time takes into consideration the knowledge and background of the student. Failure to consider the total aspect of the student's thinking is a failure to objectively communicate with the student. Any college class may be enhanced by administering an attitude and emotion questionnaire before teaching the course. The *ad hominem fallacy*, is a fallacy, however, when it takes the place of an objective reply.

According to the Fallacy of Opposition, if the enemy likes something we may therefore dislike it. This appears to be a form of *ad hominem fallacy*. Some simply stubbornly oppose another's objections, on principle. In psychiatry, the schizophrenic often responds with "negativism," that is, he does and says the opposite of what is requested.

EITHER-OR FALLACY

This fallacy involves a two-valued logic of either truth or falsity rather than a many-valued logic involving probability, possibility, uncertainty, meaninglessness, or simply not knowing. One may erroneously think, "If I'm not the best, then I'm no good." The fallacy rests partly on an all-or-none view and ignores the possibility of gradation.

POST HOC FALLACY (False Cause Fallacy)

Because A happens before B does not mean A causes B. David Hume's view was that cause is merely empirical or experiential, constant, contingent conjunction. Thus there is only correlation not necessary connection. (See W. Shibles "Intention") That one event occurs before another need not mean the first event causes the second, but there may nevertheless be a high correlation between the occurrence of the two events.

Defense Mechanisms: Psychiatric Logic

Defense-mechanisms, as well as the informal fallacies, are rhetorical devices. Informal fallacies are sometimes used as defense-mechanisms or denial and escape mechanisms. Defense-mechanisms may be verbal, behavioral or perceptual. Psychic blindness helps one avoid seeing, catatonic and conversion hysteria can be thought of as forms of avoiding acting or escaping from a problem. For the most part the defense-mechanisms do not defend but are self-defeating and suicidal mechanisms. Failure to constantly learn and honestly inquire into oneself and one's environment may also be thought of as a self-defeating escape or denial mechanism. Albert Ellis states,

"Psychopathic individuals brilliantly avoid facing basic issues and evade accepting a long-range view of life." (298)

The defense-mechanisms seem to be devices by means of which the organism attempts to cope with problems it cannot otherwise deal with. They are like the emotions of anger, depression, love, etc. in this sense. Emotions may also be thought of as defense-mechanisms and each emotion could be listed here. Verbal and behavioral mechanisms may also be attempts to cope with excessive or negative emotions. It is obvious that an endless number of devices could be listed here including the different types of metaphor. The more traditional ones are given. The definitions are altered so as not to be based on Freudian theory, although the Freudian defense-mechanisms are otherwise found to be valuable devices.

273

That defense-mechanisms apply to a wide range of phenomena such as perception, behavior, dreams, language, etc., is supported by some researchers. R. Drake wrote,

"Many hallucinations are defense-mechanisms." (18)

"Stuttering (for Adler) is a defense against some deficiency." (25)

G. Ulett and D. Goodrich state,

"The defense-mechanisms serve as a basis for symptom formation (for neurosis)."

A. Freedman and H. Kaplan state that in anxiety a person develops a variety of defense-mechanisms. (162) Drake presents the view that such behaviors as tics, wrinkling one's forehead, squinting, twitching, etc. express repressed elements or conflicts and can be controlled by reassessment or attending to such behaviors. (87) Selective amnesia, confabulation (filling in past with imagined experiences), fugues (wandering away psychologically and/or physically), dissociation or thought from feeling, the alcoholic's and suicidal's self-deception, are all types of defense-mechanisms. The average person has defense-mechanisms allowing him to hold contradictory ideas, e.g., scientific method *and* at the same time superstitions or mystical views. The following account is necessarily brief but further clarification of each device is encouraged. Such clarification can only be effectively done by analyzing actual statements and behaviors. S. Cashden says,

"According to the communication theory, schizophrenic behaviors are deviant communications, that help the patient avert the interpersonal rejection he has learned to anticipate throughout his life." (73)

TRANSFERENCE

"Transference" is the translation of the Greek word for metaphor. All kinds of transferences are possible between object, word, statement, thought, behavior, people, problems, emotions, etc. One's problem may be transferred from a cognitive impasse to a physical symptom such as colitis, ulcer, paralysis, etc. Fear of, or an emotion toward, one object may be transferred to another object. An emotion toward one person may be transferred to another. Transference sometimes refers to the attachment a patient begins to feel toward the therapist.

The notion of transfer may be further clarified by relating it to the types of metaphorical transfers and types. Transference relates to learned associations, stimulus generalization, or conditioning.

FIXATION

Although this sometimes means fixation at a certain stage of development it is more useful to think of it as one's being captivated by a metaphor, linguistic statement, image, perception, or motor behavior (cf. habit). Behaviorists might refer to fixation as strongly reinforced conditioning. Psychiatric patients are often obsessed with a belief, statement, fear, persecution, etc. Even scientists and researchers in other disciplines are often captivated by or fixate on some theoretical model or metaphor, as Thomas Kuhn has pointed out in *The Structure of Scientific Revolutions*. The scientist may literally see the world in terms of his models in almost the same way as perhaps a schizophrenic sees a schizophrenic world. Supposedly, by fixation one has security and a way to cope with and organize an otherwise incoherent mass of material. But if the model fixated on is mystical, unrealistic, or confused the fixation becomes maladaptive.

Fixation may involve perseveration, repeated thought, stereotypy (repetition, for no reason, of a single phrase or behavior), recurring ideas or tunes, repetition of first reaction learned, verbigeration (the meaningless repetition of words or phrases), compulsion, obsession, echolalia, (repetition of answers in the same words questioner used).

SYMBOLIZATION

Symbolization may be a misleading and unnecessary term for association, synecdoche, transference, substitution, metaphor. It should not be used in the sense that some concrete object represents a metaphysical or "transcendent" entity. One object comes to "stand for," or represent another. But one object cannot descriptively and literally "stand for" another. It is either only stipulated that one object is to represent another or two objects have properties so similar that one suggests the other. Stars do not look like or suggest states but on a flag they might be stipulated to represent states.

In human thinking one thing or statement may similarly come to symbolize another because of stipulation or similarity of qualities or associations. Some of the associations are subjective, e.g., two things may be regarded alike because one is unfamiliar with either one, even though their qualities are entirely different.

For normal and abnormal thinking, symbolization is a common device. It allows a single image or object to represent a complex situation or series of objects or problems. A house comes to represent what happened in it, e.g., discord and conflict, a death that occurred, a traumatic experience, happiness, etc. This is partly the basis of emblems. Because of such fixed associations one may find he has to move away from the house, or greatly alter his assessments.

The specific symbols may be understood by analyzing one's assessments or associations. It is unscientific and harmful to claim there are symbols without having concrete evidence in terms of associations and assessments present. Freud commits this error in seeing every room as a womb, and every object or statement as a symbol of a childhood or traumatic experience. This turns symbol into conceit or far-fetched metaphor and commits the fallacy of taking one's metaphors literally. Also symbols cannot represent metaphysical or transcendent entities. They cannot represent more than we can concretely know.

METAPHORIZATION

One may attempt to avoid stating or facing his problems by putting them metaphorically, rather than in more literal or descriptive statement. On the other hand, metaphor may be used to describe what cannot be described effectively in any other way, and therapists can communicate with some patients only in terms of metaphor. (See chapter on metaphor.)

INTROJECTION

Someone who is feared, hated, or loved is regarded as a subject of transfer or identification. A person may internalize qualities of someone he fears losing. A non-participant may say, "We won the game." There is a subtle taking on of the qualities or attitudes of others. One may see herself as being as popular and desirable as her favorite movie star. One may fear or hate himself when it is actually someone else he hates, that is, he may direct his hate for others against himself. This may be because he does not want to hate others, or because he learned to blame himself rather than others.

IDENTIFICATION

Identity may involve taking on the properties of others or even objects, as one's own. It may be subtle and may involve role-taking, identifying with a character in a film or novel, acting like one's friends or parents, imitating, etc. The problem of identity also involves equivocation because it is not clear whether or not psychiatric, sociological, psychological, philosophical, racial, social, sexual, biological, political, power, etc. identity is referred to. One may reject racial and other identities in favor of personal identity. As a defense-mechanism one may identify with the deceased person as an attempt to compensate somehow for the loss, or identify with someone wronged to thereby punish oneself, or identify with a person who has the qualities one lacks. Identification may be a conviction that one is other than he is so as to deny one's unacceptable qualities. Knowledge of oneself, one's language, others, and the environment determines the kind of identity assumed. A person is the assessments or metaphors he has of himself.

PROJECTION

The attribution, especially of one's negative qualities, to others. An unsuccessful person may try to find fault with others in an attempt to deny his lack of success, to show that others have failed also, or to attack a quality in others and so vicariously express dislike of the quality in himself. A number of different language-games of projection are possible. They largely involve seeing the world in terms of one's own self-assessments. Projection is the attribution to objective reality of that which is subjective. Hallucinations may be thought of as projections of subjective states on reality. The scientists' models are also theoretical projections imposed on reality.

CONVERSION

A conflict or unresolvable problem so affects one's body as to result in physical malfunction or paralysis, e.g., psychic blindness, catatonia, paralysis of a limb, inability to move (as in the state of shock). Sometimes, as in conversion hysteria, when one has the physical defect the psychological problem vanishes as if replaced or transferred to the physical. One may be unable to move when in shock. Thanatomimesis involves being or pretending to be dead, or at least motionless, so as to avoid a predator.

REACTION-FORMATION

This involves doing or saying the reverse instead of what one wishes to do or say. In place of expressing hatred one may show extreme kindness as if to compensate for the desire not to hate or to attempt to keep the hatred hidden. Negativism involves responding or doing the opposite of what is requested. Reaction-formation may be thought of as the metaphorical mechanism of antithesis or oxymoron according to which opposites are combined or replaced by one another. This expands the traditional view that reaction-formation is a transformation of one "drive" into its opposite.

DISPLACEMENT

Another term for transference, symbolization, or metaphorization. An object or thought is taken out of its normal context and so displaced. Displacement may refer to the breaking of an association or connection between feeling and assessment.

DEPERSONALIZATION

A person gradually develops a feeling of unreality, self-estrangement, or multiple personality. Irrational statements and assessments lead to depersonalization. A suicidal often thinks he is not killing himself but only getting rid of his problems.

DENIAL

The problem or undesirable trait is denied. The devices of denial are too numerous to mention. Some are amnesia, failure to discuss or inquire, leaving the situation, intellectualizing, rationalizing, withdrawal, lying, etc. The alcoholic often denies that he is an alcoholic, and the angry person denies that he is angry.

ACTING OUT

Acting-out is a way of attempting to solve one's conflicts and problems by action, rather than by discussion. It is often self-defeating and may in no way alter the source of the problem. Suicide and excessive drinking may be regarded as types of acting-out. In place of such action, open communication and reassessment are preferable. In acting-out, a destructive action takes the place of talking-out the problem.

INTELLECTUALIZATION

Intellectualization involves the use of abstract or metaphysical terms, ambiguous, or over-theoretical terms unrelated to concrete experience. By the use of such language one may avoid facing his conflicts and problems. Intellectualization is also a kind of rationalization. Freudian theory is such an intellectualization. By speaking abstractly with others, meaningful communication and personal contact may be avoided.

RATIONALIZATION

Rationalization is attempting to find reasons other than the actual reasons. The reasons found may seem plausible or contrived. One rationalizes in an attempt to justify an unjustifiable act. A psychotic patient may, for example, defend his inactivity by maintaining, "It's my job to be leisurely."

REPRESSION

Repression is traditionally described as repression of ideas or emotions. This is unacceptable because it presupposes unfounded mentalistic entities. Repression may rather be described as inability to express or communicate. One may be afraid of discussing because he or she has found it painful to do so. Repression may also involve selectively forgetting painful experiences.

REGRESSION

Regression is a form of escape by acting as one did in problem-free situations such as by acting as a child or acting irresponsibly. This should not suppose that one actually becomes like a child but rather that one, as an adult deviant, acts like a child in some ways. Metaphysical definitions of regression such as, "The ego attempts to return to an earlier libidinal state," should be avoided.

SUBLIMATION

Sublimation is substitution for and distraction from a major need or desire, especially sexual desire. Intellectual and physical distraction may serve as substitutes for sexual activity, e.g., sports, dancing, alcohol, conversation, humor, motion pictures, eating, etc. Often things merely associated with sexual activity become, because socially acceptable, desired in themselves, e.g., dancing, flirting, music, etc. Sublimation is a form of metaphorical transference or substitution.

COMPENSATION

Compensation is an attempt to make up for a fault. A cruel act may be followed by extra kindness, a weak person attempts to act strong, the less intelligent as intelligent, etc.

DREAMS

Conflicts and problems are often indicated by having dreams and by dream content. Often the objects and statements uttered may be related to one's actual problems, e.g., one may dream of having failed an exam, though in fact the individual merely fears failing it. Dreams often take place on the level of images and so are often thought to be symbolic, metaphorical, or condensed. When one reports a dream he may add events which he would like to add but which did not in fact occur in the dream. Dreams involve non-mentalistic associations and may be seen to reflect the rational nature of man rather than a hidden unconscious or mystical state of man. The "irrational" is what man is not aware of. It involves the subtle associations he employs. Dreams employ a number of types of defense-mechanism. Day-dreaming is also a defense-mechanism. "Pseudologia fantastica" is a daydream which is taken as a real event and is even acted on. People having this are often thought of as being pathological liars.

HUMOR

Humor is largely based on metaphorical juxtaposition and deviation and may serve as a healthful or as a self-defeating defense-mechanism. The Ganser syndrome, or "nonsense syndrome" involves humorous replies in order to escape the seriousness of, or the facing of bad news, e.g., the doctor may be called a "nurse"; the patient if asked who he is he may reply, "A famous bull-fighter," or give obviously incorrect replies.

Sources:

S. Cashden *Abnormal Psychology* New Jersey: Prentice-Hall 1972.
Raleigh Drake *Abnormal Psychology* New Jersey: Littlefield, Adams 1954.
Albert Ellis *Reason and Emotion* New York: Lyle Stuart 1962.
Thomas Kuhn *The Structure of Scientific Revolutions* University of Chicago Press 1962.
Warren Shibles "Are All Statements Circular?" *Philosophical Pictures* 2nd Edition, Dubuque, Iowa: Kendall-Hunt 1972.
Warren Shibles "Intention" *Wittgenstein, Language and Philosophy* Dubuque, Iowa: Kendall-Hunt 1970.
G. Ulett and D. Goodrich *A Synopsis of Contemporary Psychiatry* Saint Louis: Mosby 1969.

A Critique of Psychiatric Classifications

In 1968 the second revised edition of the Diagnostic and Statistical Manual of Mental Disorders (DSM-II) was published. The manual is integrated with the classifications of the World Health Organization's International Classification of Diseases, and has been approved by the American Psychiatric Association. It has both national and, for the first time, international approval. The manual is revised from the first 1952 manual because of changing theories and clinical findings. The manual explicitly states that it attempts to provide classifications which will be acceptable to psychiatrists with widely different orientations. It is noted that although these are agreed upon classifications what constitutes each classification and what the classifications mean, is not yet agreed upon. In fact, the very term "mental" disorder is a misnomer because in terms of the prevalent view of contemporary philosophical psychology, "mind" is pseudo-psychological, fictional, and is not an entity at all. (See Ryle, Wittgenstein, Shibles.) "Dementia" also refers to "mental." A more descriptive term should be used. I would suggest "behavioral disorder" in place of "mental disorder." And behavior could be subdivided into 1) perception, 2) motor, 3) imagery, 4) language (self-talk, assessments, cognition, memory, speaking to others, etc.), 5) feelings (as reported and responses), 6) organic, hereditary, etc. aspects. These categories can then be further subdivided. (See earlier chapter on classification of emotions.) The manual is a collection of relatively ambiguous names. It concludes,

*I wish to express my appreciation to Dr. Aaron Beck for reading this chapter and offering some helpful criticisms.

"It is only an agreement to use the same sets of categories for classifying disorders. For many disorders, it is clear that clinicians in different countries will still define these categories in different ways. The next step must be to establish a common set of definitions for these categories."

This chapter attempts to revise and criticize present definitions of mental disorders and provide a few suggestions leading to new definitions based upon the cognitive theory of emotions, contemporary philosophical psychology, and the metaphorical method of assessing thought and language. Descriptions and definitions other than those of DSM-II are often added. Descriptions of various disorders where sources are not cited are based on psychiatric literature.

Aaron Beck (1967) gave a cognitive analysis of mental disorders. (269-273) He states,

"The differential diagnosis of the psychiatric disorders may be sharpened by using the cognitive content and the degree of impairment as diagnostic criteria." (274)

"A thinking disorder may be common to all types of psychopathology." (239)

"A sharp delineation of the specific content of the thinking disorder can help in making a differential diagnosis among the various psychiatric disorders." (269)

Often the descriptions of the classifications give an inadequate analysis of emotions as well as other psychological phenomena. This occurs in spite of the qualifications presented in the Psychiatric Diagnostic Manual (DSM-II) which reads:

"Inevitably some users of this Manual will read into it some general view of the nature of mental disorders. The Committee can only aver that such interpretations are, in fact, unjustified." (ix)

This statement may be challenged by considering, for example, the way in which emotions are presented. Under "296 Major affective disorders," (Affective psychoses) DSM-II states,

"This group of psychoses is characterized by a single disorder of mood, either extreme depression or elation, that dominates the mental life of the patient and is responsible for whatever loss of contact he has with his environment. The onset of the mood does not seem to be related directly to a precipitating life experience . . ." (35, 36).

Here, mood erroneously seems to be regarded as a single cause, whereas, on the cognitive theory, emotions or mood consist of both cognition, feeling, context, and assessment of the situation. For this reason also it would seem illogical to say that mood is not related immediately to a precipitating life situation. The criterion of a precipitating event may be better described in terms of a sudden event or cognition causing a change in one's emotional state. Also it is not clear how a mood dominates one's mental life or how one can so separate mood from "mental." The account appears to atomistically separate emotion-mental, emotion-reason. In any case, emotion and mental would first have to be described, but they are not. It may be suggested that by thought (mental), one means only use of language (self-talk or speaking to others), imagery and motor ability. (See W. Shibles *Philosophical Pictures* and earlier chapter on language.) S. Cashden wrote, "The growth of deviant communication patterns is synonymous with the growth of psychopathology." (70) By emotion is meant cognition (language) which precedes but may also be simultaneous with, or subsequent to feeling. That is, emotion is cognition and feeling. Emotion is not the same as feeling, and is not opposed to cognition, because it partly consists of cognition. Beck similarly attacks the classification of emotion of the earlier 1952 edition. He wrote, on the basis of extensive experimental research:

"The diagnostic manual of American Psychiatric Association (1952) defines the psychotic affective reactions in terms of 'a primary, severe disorder of mood with resultant disturbance of thought and behavior, in consonance with the affect.' Although this is a widely accepted concept, the converse would appear to be at least as plausible, viz., that there is primary disorder of thought with resultant disturbance of affect and behavior in consonance with the cognitive distortions . . . It is proposed, therefore, that the typical depressive affects are evoked by the erroneous conceptualizations: If the patient incorrectly perceives himself as inadequate, deserted or sinful, he will experience corresponding affects such as sadness, loneliness, or guilt." (239)

Thus the views of Beck and other cognitivists, such as Albert Ellis, Madga Arnold, A. I. Melden, etc., would lead to a reclassification of mental disorder more adequately based on cognition, and an assessment or cognitive view of emotions.

R. Drake (1954) in his summary of texts on abnormal psychology, wrote,

"A person who is dominated by some fixed idea, or who is unable to exercise 'normal' rational control is abnormal." (1)

"Many abnormalities are due to faulty habits of thinking, feeling, or responding." (5)

The existing classifications are, however, based on the work of Emil Kraepelin, Adolph Meyer, and Sigmund Freud. (Beck 61)

Raleigh Drake gives the following definitions:

"Psychogenic: A cluster of associated ideas forming a mental set, accompanied by characteristic feelings in the presence of its specific stimulus situation." (6)

"All functional disorders must be explained on the basis of some disorder of association . . . failure to form wholesome associations." (34)

Drake summarizes some prevalent criticisms of Freudian theory and this would suggest its inadequacy for classificatory systems of mental disorders:

"Many psychoanalytic principles are based on folklore and have no other objective basis. It is assumed that there are three kinds of mind: The conscious, unconscious, and preconscious. This division has never had the support of psychologists." (38)

"Scientific verification of [the] value of various [psychoanalytic] techniques [is] almost impossible. [There is] personification of the animistic, and fictional concepts of id, ego, super-ego, censor." (133)

Involutional melancholia, manic-depression, and psychotic depressive reaction, were all labelled "affective disorders." Schizophrenia is referred to as a cognitive disorder, except for the schizo-affective type of schizophrenia. Again the classification is arbitrary unless the nature of affect or emotion is clarified, and this objection has been supported by others such as Ulett, who states that all of these types involve both affect and cognition. (122) Ulett also seems to stress a cognitive sort of classification:

"General agreement exists in regard to the importance of therapy as a 'growing up' experience during which the patient gains a firmer grasp of the real nature of human relationships, gives up his severe distortions of the world about him, and achieves a more honest appreciation of his own latent capacities." (143)

The traditional classifications of the so-called "mental disorders," are seen to be based to some extent on naming-fallacies, category-mistakes, the metaphor-to-myth fallacy, the fallacy of taking words as things. Classifications are based on mixed psychiatric theories, mixed categories, mixed descriptions, or inadequate descriptions. The classificatory terms refer inconsistently to duration, cause, degree, possibility of cure, previous history, etc. Schizophrenia, for example, is literally "a splitting of the mind." As there is no mind it is not very descriptive. One might as well have said, "He lost his marbles." Secondly, "split" is vague. Also the term is often mistranslated or metaphorically referred to as a "split from reality."

Some of the main descriptive categories used in classifying are the following: ambulatory, traumatic, acute (referring to recent onset or lack of possibility of cure), process (referring to incurable types), organic versus functional, reactive (to outside events) versus autonomous, autocthonous (not relating to patient's history of specific conflicts), latent (lack of previous history), endogenous (inner) versus exogenous (outer) (exogenous meant toxins but now includes psychological factors), childhood type-adult type, classifications by drugs the patients respond to, circular (mood swing), involutional (physical cause such as menopause), idiosyncratic (not part of patient's culture or environment.)

A criticism of these terms is that 1) many of the terms are obscure, abstract, conceptually confused, or non-descriptive; 2) the terms are used only sometimes, and used inconsistently. The classification of mental disorders is, in many ways, as dissociated and illogical as is "schizophrenic" thinking.

The term "psychosomatic" is a misleading term because it implies a "mind-body" relationship whereas, as was stated earlier, there is no mind and so no mind-body relation. Instead of mind one should substitute mainly language use (cognition or assessment). Thus "psychosomatic" reduces to "cognition leading to feeling or body states," and this is the definition of emotion according to the cognitive theory of emotion. "Psychosomatic," then, merely refers to one kind of emotion whereby negative assessments lead to physical disorders of a certain type. The types are classified in DSM-II. By thinking of psychosomatic disorder as emotion and by becoming clear about emotion we may be in a better position to understand such disorders. Kaplan and Kaplan (1967) wrote,

"In the field of psychosomatic medicine, no single theoretical model is considered entirely satisfactory at present." (1039)

As was mentioned, the most important single indicator of mental disorders and sources for the classification of mental disorder, is language use. This includes deviations in what one says to himself silently and what he says aloud to himself or to others. The stress on language brings in a number of traditional classificatory criteria, namely, informal logic and rhetoric. Informal logic is mainly rhetoric and both can be reduced to language-games and forms of metaphor. Metaphor has recently been extensively classified and categorized such that it may help sort out abnormal speech. It may be noted that metaphor encompasses imagery and behavioral metaphor or deviation. (See chapter which relates metaphor to psychiatric categories and devices, and also W. Shibles *Metaphor*). The "metaphorical method" has also been presented as a scientific method of inquiry. It helps one gain insight in constructing hypotheses while disallowing one to become captivated by his metaphors so as to commit the metaphor-to-myth fallacy. It seems that all terms for psychological or "internal" states are metaphorical. It is often asserted that man thinks metaphorically. The basic models and metaphors which comprise the thinking of the neurotic or psychotic may give insight into how we normally think and feel. Metaphor forms a continuum between the normal and the abnormal.

"Both philosophers and poets live by metaphors." (S. Pepper.)

"All thinking is metaphorical." (Robert Frost)

"To know is merely to work with one's favorite metaphors." (Nietzsche)

"The conduct of even the plainest, most 'direct' untechnical prose is a ceaseless exercise in metaphor." (I.A. Richards.)

Following is an analysis of the DSM-II classifications. Numbers refer to these classifications. It may be noted that DSM-II encourages multiple-classifications. A patient may have several disorders at the same time. The definitions given are only meant as hypotheses for further inquiry and clarification of terms rather than as adequate descriptions. The attempt is to establish a classification on a basis of rational and philosophically sound therapy. It may be called "philosophical therapy."

300 NEUROSES

DSM-II states,

"Anxiety is the chief characteristic of the neuroses. It may be felt and expressed directly, or it may be controlled unconsciously and automatically by conversion, displacement and various other psychological mechanisms. Generally, these produce symptoms experienced as subjective distress from which the patient desires relief."

Neurosis is mainly characterized by the emotion, anxiety, but no definition of anxiety is given. Nor is it clear how anxiety relates to fear or depression. It is possible to say that there is no such thing as anxiety as such. It is not one thing. Kaplan and Kaplan (1967) define anxiety as a chronic, vague, internal threat and conflict regarding an unknown object. This is contrasted with fear which is an acute, distinct, external threat without conflict regarding a known object. (858) Beck (1967) defines depression as a disorder involving cognitive and motivational as well as feeling and physical aspects (187). He found that depression involves sadness, pessimism, failure, guilt, withdrawal and a number of other emotions. (200) On his analysis, anxiety and depression were distinguished. (201, 270-1) The terms nevertheless are obscure in their general usage and should be reduced to concrete specific paradigms. "Anxiety" is not sufficiently clear to serve as a distinguishing basis for classification. Also, as such, it seems to be a pseudo-emotion or fiction.

The "anxiety" is said to be "unconscious" or "displaced," involves additional Freudian or mentalistic and unfounded notions. It would be better to deal, here, with descriptions of specific language, imagery, and physical behavior. Beck states, "For the most part, the neuroses may be differentiated on the basis of the thought content." (269) For example, cognitive defense mechanisms precede and are connected with physical disorders. DSM-II distinguishes neurosis from psychosis in that the former shows less distortion of reality, less personality disorganization, and neurotic patients unlike most psychotic patients are aware of being disturbed. The neurotic desires relief from certain symptoms he has or imagines he has. Thus, neurosis appears to be a mild form of psychosis. Personality disorders may also, to some extent, be thought to be mild forms of neuroses. But to speak of "mild forms" ignores many qualitative distinctions. "X is not as severe as y" ignores the respect in which it is less severe.

The above definition of neurosis may be related to psychosomatic disorder, or experiences such as psychogenic pain which F. Kapp states involves a symbolic attempt to cope with conflict leading to physical pain, e.g., hallucination of pain in order to obtain love.

"Neurosis" derives from the Greek word meaning "nerve." Thus neurosis is supposedly a nervous condition. But if neurosis is a functional disorder the reference to nerves is inappropriate. In another sense, all thinking and action relate to nerves and so the name "neurosis" fails to distinguish between normal and abnormal. "Neuropsychology" is the general study of the relation between the nervous system and the psychological processes.

300.00 ANXIETY NEUROSIS

DSM-II describes this as

"anxious over-concern extending to panic and frequently associated with somatic symptoms . . . and is not restricted to specific situations. This disorder must be distinguished from normal apprehension of fear, which occurs in realistically dangerous situations."

The word "panic" here is curious since it means intense fear, and anxious supposedly does not mean fear. "Panic" derives from the Greek word meaning "fear" or "pertaining to the god Pan," i.e., fear caused by Pan. Anxiety could logically lead to fear if we were clear about these concepts and knew that in fact one "leads to" the other. But such terms are not adequate for a careful analysis.

The above definition appears only to use unrealistic, abnormal fear as the defining characteristic of anxiety neurosis. It involves the metaphorical mechanism of hyperbole. Some of the following characteristics sometimes given may be used in place of anxiety and as descriptions, but they are still not adequate descriptions.

Cognitive or emotional aspects involve excessive fear of imagined or real dangers such as fear of fainting, fear of intense feelings, fear of dying, fear of "losing one's mind," worry about body parts or organs, apprehension, mild depression, irritability especially for noise or spouse or children, insomnia, becoming confused when erotically aroused. Anxiety neurosis would seem to be a faulty relation between cognition and feeling. The whole category seems to be basically fear and conflict, and body states associated with them.

Physical and behavioral characteristics involve continuous tension, dyspnea (labored breathing), palpitation, dizziness, trembling, chest pain, headache, autonomic discharge, fidgetiness, weakness.

Insofar as texts use conceptually confused terms such as those found here, no adequate description can be presented. As much as possible complete and individual accounts of the specific disorders are needed, but again the terms of description must be satisfactory. The account must be based on an adequate theory of emotions, esp., the cognitive theory.

300.1 HYSTERICAL NEUROSIS

This encompasses the subcategories of conversion type and dissociative type but is more general and vague. DSM-II states,

"An involuntary psychogenic loss or disorder of function. Symptoms characteristically begin and end suddenly in emotionally charged situations and are symbolic of the underlying conflicts. Often they can be modified by suggestion alone."

"Psychogenic" qualifies as a naming-fallacy for reasons given earlier. The language-game involved here seems to be that partly involved in shock. That is, unresolved cognitive conflict guides negative feeling as well as motor dysfunction. A substitution or synecdoche takes place whereby the motor or sensory impairment takes the place of or follows the cognitive conflict. That cognition is central is indicated by the fact that only suggestion is usually able to correct the disorder. In the case of conversion hysteria such cure can be immediate and dramatically successful.

"Hysteria" is another naming-fallacy in the sense that it derives from the Greek word meaning "disease of the womb" because it was erroneously thought to be caused by the womb. The disorder is, however, much more prevalent with women than men. R. Drake denies the definiteness of the category and suggests a cognitive basis for hysteria:

"Today hysteria is not considered a definite disease but a means, learned to a large extent, of avoiding or controlling certain phases of the environment," (85) "The hysteric's symptoms are the result of faulty thinking and faulty adjustment to difficulties." (89)

Even so-called "normal" anger is usually used by the average person to attempt to control the environment. It too is often a self-defeating mechanism. Hysteria may result in psychic blindness or paralysis.

The deviation from reality or avoidance mechanisms used involve distrust of friendship, amnesia, dissociation of ideas, indifference (including "la belle indifference" to the psychogenic paralysis or handicap), depression, suicidal attempts, frigidity, tendency to invalidism, being ill or seeking operations, defensiveness, lack of emotional control, e.g., uncontrolled weeping or laughter. Young girls often have hysteria. The symptoms suggest that these are often confused assessments or conflicts regarding sex. Amnesia and lack of goals involve memory and intention. A clear analysis and classification of these terms remains to be given. Relevant work in philosophical psychology should be examined. (See W. Shibles "Memory," and "Intention.")

300.1 HYSTERICAL NEUROSIS, CONVERSION TYPE

DSM-II states,

"The special senses or voluntary nervous system are affected, causing such symptoms as blindness, deafness, anosmia, anaesthesias, para[n]esthesias, paralyses, ataxias akinesias, and dyskinesias."

It is supposedly not done consciously as is malingering, and is different from psychophysiologic disorders because it is not just mediated by the autonomic nervous system. This definition also appeals to an unconscious mind.

The patient may show indifference to his symptom thus making it appear that he is courageous and modest whereas he seems to have merely substituted the physical impairment for the conflict. Conversion seems to be based on a cognitive conflict leading to a malfunction of motor and sensory function. There may have been great physical stress involved such as great sexual desire which is frustrated, or a feared battle situation. An analogous reaction is that of "freezing" at the sight of a feared object. The typical nerve patterns for conversion should be specifically indicated and the sorts of cognitive conflicts more fully specified.

300.14 HYSTERICAL NEUROSIS, DISSOCIATIVE TYPE

DSM-II states,

"Alterations may occur in the patient's state of consciousness or in his identity, to produce such symptoms as amnesia, somnambulism, fugue, and multiple personality."

Here dissociation appears to suggest dissociation of ideas, but many psychotics as well as neurotics or even "normal" people suffer from such dissociation. There is no dissociation of ideas as such, however, because there is no association of ideas, because there are no "ideas" as such. "Idea" is a mentalistic survival from the age of atomism and "mental chemistry." Dissociation, here, seems also to refer to a change of speaking and acting such that one is confused about the self, fails to remember certain things. A "fugue" (literally "flight," or "escape") refers to a physical or psychological wandering away. It involves amnesia for the fugue when it is over. It may be noted that people usually forget things that are unpleasant, and psychologically and physically avoid unpleasant situations. Multiple-personality is observed daily by the various roles we play. We speak and identify ourselves differently depending upon where we are and with whom, and how many we are talking with.

According to the definition, the patient's alteration of identity is separated from alteration of consciousness. But there is no separation because identity is determined by cognition, by how one regards himself. Confusion about one's self and conflicts regarding whom he would like to be and what he would like to do may lead to hysterical neurosis. It would appear that this is basically a cognitive disorder.

300.2 PHOBIC NEUROSIS

"Phobia," from the Greek word, means fear and often refers to irrational fear thus indicating a stress on cognition. Such cognition produces certain body tensions and negative feelings or emotions. DSM-II states,

"Intense fear of an object or situation which the patient consciously recognizes as no real danger to him. His apprehension may be experienced as faintness, fatigue, palpitations, perspiration, nausea, tremor, and even panic. Phobias are generally attributed to fears displaced to the phobic object or situation from some other object of which the patient is unaware."

Irrational fear of such objects as high places, elevators, etc., seems to be based on faulty and excessive conditioning. Parents sometimes in this way induce in their children fear of mice, fear of imperfection, fear of inferiority, fear of failure, fear of high places, etc. The individual may induce such fears in himself also. Thus it would seem that phobic neurosis might include or overlap with a great many other categories and seems to lack the definite boundary usually ascribed to it. It is usually defined as only involving certain objects, places, persons, or animals, but seems rather to involve assessments which need include no objects but only linguistic formulations such as "I must be perfect." When the fear is of an object the fear may involve merely an image of the object, e.g., one falling from a high place, or a verbal statement such as "I'm going to fall." Imagery, motor behavior and perception as well as verbal assessment need revision.

These patients are often stubborn, defensive against parental threat, indecisive, overcontrolled, orderly. They strive for perfection and superiority, are overconcerned about details, and engage in escapism and avoidance.

It is not clear that phobias are merely "fear displaced to the phobic object or situation from some other object of which the patient is unaware," or that the object symbolically represents a conflict. Certainly substitution and metaphorical displacement generally form part of our thinking, but phobia seems to involve also the linguistic expressions we learn as well as other learned associations. "Displacement of fear" illegitimately treats fear as an atomistic entity and ignores the specific linguistic factors involved. To displace fear of one thing for fear of another would involve transferring a feeling about one object to another object. This transference may come about because of conflicting assessments. For example, one may fear sexual arousal because he learned that it is immoral, but yet not want to fear such arousal. As a result he may learn to attach these fear feelings to an object or situation. Knowing the specific rhetoric and language-game involved is crucial.

300.3 OBSESSIVE COMPULSIVE NEUROSIS

An obsessive idea or action cannot be inhibited although it is recognized as being irrational. The person often worries about being out of control or about being unable to complete the compulsive action. The Freudians impose the extravagant metaphor of "anal fixation" on these patients, whereas the disorder rather involves diverse cognitive fixations. The cognitive fixations may have been recently learned. They involve such statements as, "Did I pray enough?" "I must step on each crack in the sidewalk," "My hands are not clean enough." There is a compulsion to act to avoid obsessive fears.

The patient is sometimes characterized as dependent, orderly, stubborn, economical, repressed, punctual, conscientious, indecisive, controlled emotionally, having feelings of inferiority. Such factors suggest overstrict upbringing generally, not merely or strict toilet training. Repetitive actions are the basis of religious and other ritual and are, in part, superstitious attempts to control nature and to meet the demands put on one by his parents or by himself. The compulsive may say to himself, "Unless I am perfect I am no good." The cause of the disorder seems to involve learned irrational ideas such as this confusion about being "no good," "perfect," or "bad."

300.4 DEPRESSIVE NEUROSIS

Just as there was difficulty defining anxiety, "depression" is seen to be a conceptually confused emotion term. DSM-II states,

"An excessive reaction of depression due to an internal conflict or to an identifiable event such as the loss of a cherished possession. It is to be distinguished from involutional melancholia and manic-depressive illness."

It is not clear what an "internal conflict" is. It appears to be a fictitious mentalistic category. Depression, literally a "pressing down," is a metaphorical term for a certain pattern of behavior, not a literal term for an internal state. The synonymous term, "melancholy," derives from the Greek word meaning "black bile."

On the cognitive theory of emotions, depression is assessments which cause and/or maintain certain negative feelings. The cognitions could be rational or irrational. For example, one concludes that he is incompetent, inferior, or bad, or develops a negative view of the world. This leads to negative feelings and partly constitutes depression. A. Beck (1967) wrote,

"There are no specific signs or symptoms, aside from delusions, that distinguish psychotic from neurotic depressives . . . The difference . . . is quantitative rather than qualitative." (86)

He presents G. Foulds' account of the difference between twenty psychotic depressives (first frequency number) and twenty neurotic depressives (second number):

1) He is an unworthy person in his own eyes. (12-3)
2) He is a condemned person because of his sins. (12-3)
3) People are talking about him and criticizing him.
4) He is afraid to go out alone. (13-4)
5) He has said things that have injured others. (9-3)
6) He is so 'worked-up' that he paces about wringing his hands. (11-4)
7) He cannot communicate with others because he doesn't seem to be on the same 'wave-length'. (10-3)
8) There is something thought to be unusual about his

body, with one side being different from the other, or meaning something different. (6-0)
9) The future is pointless. (12-7)
10) He might do away with himself because he is no longer able to cope with his difficulties. (8-3)
11) Other people regard him as very odd. (8-3)
12) He is often bothered with pains over his heart, in his chest, or in his back. (8-3)
13) He is so low in spirits that he just sits for hours on end. (12-7)
14) When he goes to bed, he wouldn't care if he 'never woke up again.' (10-5)

300.5 NEURASTHENIC NEUROSIS (Neurasthenia)

"Neurasthenia" means literally "weakness of the nerves." In DSM-I the condition was called "Psychophysiologic nervous system reaction." The patient complains of continual physical weakness or exhaustion. The patient is distressed or depressed by his symptoms and one might call this a fixation of depression, as it supposedly is less easily cured than Anxiety neurosis.

300.6 DEPERSONALIZATION NEUROSIS

DSM-II states,

"This syndrome is dominated by a feeling of unreality and of estrangement from the self, body, or surroundings."

The feeling should be lasting rather than brief. Not too unlike the situation in Alice in Wonderland, the patient's body parts seem to greatly expand, change, or seem not to belong to him. The cause is sometimes said to be due to "inner conflict," and the syndrome a kind of (self-defeating) defense-mechanism.

300.7 HYPOCHONDRIACAL NEUROSIS

DSM-II states,

"This condition is dominated by preoccupation with the body and with fear of presumed diseases of various organs. Though the fears are not of delusional quality as in psychotic depressions, they persist despite reassurance."

These fixed "ideas" (i.e., statements) may well be found to alter by changing one's assessments but also by changing his perceptions, imagery and habits. As with the other types of neurosis a conflict or confusion in one's thinking may be found.

PSYCHOSES (NOT CAUSED BY PHYSICAL CONDITIONS)

This category should rather specify that the physical causes are not yet known. Even cognition may be thought to be a physical cause because it involves physical behavior, nerves, chemistry.

"Psychosis" comes from the Greek word meaning "a giving of life, animation" and is related to the word for "soul" and "life." It was thought that the "soul" gives the body life. But, in science, "soul" is a superstitious fiction and of no practical use in therapy or in the classification of psychological disorders. The term "psychosis" is misleading.

Beck states,

"The major difference between neurosis as a class and psychosis as a class is the presence of more pronounced cognitive impairment in the latter. The erroneous ideas are more intense, more compelling, and more impermeable. The conceptual errors (arbitrary inference, selective abstraction and overgeneralization) are more frequent and more extreme." (273)

The psychoses are usually thought to involve negative, erratic and excessive emotions, irrational and illogical speech (thought), distorted imagery, distorted behavior. There is confused thinking, amnesia, perceptual and cognitive delusions and negative views of self, future, environment.

296 MAJOR AFFECTIVE DISORDERS (Affective psychoses)

This category includes Involutional melancholia and the Manic types. DSM-II states,

"This group of psychoses is characterized by a single disorder of mood, either extreme depression or elation that dominates the mental life of the patient and is responsible for whatever loss of contact he has with his environment. The onset of the mood does not seem to be related directly to a precipitating life experience and therefore is distinguishable from Psychotic depressive reaction and Depressive neurosis."

These disorders are supposedly not due to a life experience yet Depressive neurosis was defined as being due to an "internal conflict" or "identifiable event." Certainly affective disorders would also be due to internal conflicts. "Affective" partly means cognitive, and negative emotions appear to be due to cognitive conflict or confusion or irrational ideas.

This group is supposedly characterized by a single basic mood, but nearly all neurotic and psychotic disorders involve depression or elation. Also it is not clear that depression and elation are unitary events. A more careful analysis of emotion reduces it to language statements used, perceptual, motor and imagistic deviation. To speak of "emotional disorder" is unenlightening. DSM-II also regards emotions or "mood" as being "responsible for whatever loss of contact he has with his environment." This erroneously treats emotions as a specific cause.

Also it is not clear what is meant by saying that a mood "dominates mental life." This sounds like the historical view that the intellect is the "slave" of the passions. On the cognitive view the mood is itself partly cognitive. Although the onset of the mood may not seem to be related to an immediate experience it may nevertheless be partly based on prior and long term assessments.

296.0 INVOLUTIONAL MELANCHOLIA

As was mentioned, "melancholia" is a naming-fallacy. Its literal meaning is "black bile," which is part of the medieval theory of humors. "Involutional" refers to regressive aging processes such as a decline in vigor due to menopause. DSM-II states,

301

"This is a disorder occurring in the involutional period and characterized by worry, anxiety, agitation, and severe insomnia. Feelings of guilt and somatic preoccupations are frequently present and may be of delusional proportions . . Opinion is divided as to whether this psychosis can be distinguished from the other effective disorders."

It is supposedly distinguished from Manic depressive by involving no previous attacks, from Schizophrenia because delusions are based on mood, from Psychotic depression because the depression is not caused by a life experience.

Most of the obscure terms used in this account have been previously discussed. Supposedly this disorder is due to menopause or the climacteric and glandular disturbance. A. Beck questions both this cause as well as the value of this as a separate classification. Beck wrote,

"There is no specific psychosis of the climacterium." (103) There is "strong evidence against the notion of a specific, involutional syndrome distinguishable from other depressions on the basis of the symptomatology." (105)

According to Beck there is no clear evidence that it is due to hormonal change and no more reason to label it involutional than to label it adolescent depression.

Depression supposedly due to menopause may rather be due to fears regarding what is expected at menopause and because of middleage one begins to reassess his goals, possibilities, failures, and to observe signs of aging, decline, and death. One's friends become ill and die, job opportunities diminish, one's beauty lessens, one's goals are less likely to be accomplished, there is lost hope. With proper realistic and adjustive assessments one may prevent depression during middleage or during stressful periods such as adolescence, menopause, or menstruation.

MANIC-DEPRESSIVE ILLNESSES

DSM-II states,

"These disorders are marked by severe mood swing and a tendency to remission and recurrence."

"Illness" seems to derive from the word meaning "bad." It is not descriptive but may mislead by suggesting a value term. "Disorder" or the omission of the term might be preferable. "Mania" derives from the Greek word meaning "madness, frenzy," and relates to the word "oracle" or "divination." It was once thought that while in a trance or state of madness one could determine the cure of his disease. The term "manic" seems inappropriate here. G. Zilboorg (Beck 88) states,

"Manic-depressive psychoses despite their age-long existence do not actually represent a separate clinical entity . . ."

Manic depressive illnesses generally are said to be characterized by significant changes of mood. There is often improvement and also relapse and there is said to be no precipitating event.

Again, it may be suggested that the long term cognitive irrationalities, conflicts and confusions may be the cause. Negative assessments of self and world make the depressive a candidate for suicide. R. Drake gives an aspect of such analysis when he states,

"Mania is a compensation for unpleasant inner thoughts and is an attempt to forget them by extreme activity; depression is the reaction to the failure to forget—There is remorse, 'flight from reality,' and depression." (102-103)

This is primarily a woman's disorder as about 75% of the manic-depressives are female. The disorder accounts for about 15% of mental hospital admissions (R. Drake).

On the basis of experimental and clinical findings and in accordance with his cognitive theory of emotions, A. Beck (91) offers the following comparison of manic and depressive symptoms:

MANIC	*DEPRESSIVE*

Emotional

MANIC	DEPRESSIVE
elated	depressed
increased gratification	loss of gratification
likes self	dislikes self
increased attachments	loss of attachments
increased mirth	loss of mirth

Cognitive

MANIC	DEPRESSIVE
positive self-image	negative self-image
positive expectations	negative expectations
blames others	blames self
denial of problems	exaggerates problems
arbitrary decision making	indecisive
delusions: self-enhancing	delusions: self-degrading

Motivation

MANIC	DEPRESSIVE
driven and impulsive	paralysis of will
action-oriented wishes	wishes to escape
drive for independence	increased dependent wishes
desire for self-enhancement	desire for death

Physical and Vegetative Manifestations

MANIC	DEPRESSIVE
hyperactivity	retardation/agitation
indefatigable	easily fatigued
appetite variable	loss of appetite
increased libido	loss of libido
insomnia [cannot sleep]	insomnia [wake early]

Although these are commonly found characteristics they need not all be necessary conditions. What is especially necessary for making distinctions and effecting a cure is a careful analysis of one's beliefs, statements, rhetoric, and language-games.

296.1 MANIC-DEPRESSIVE ILLNESS, MANIC TYPE

DSM-II states that this type involves only manic occurrences. If depression does occur it is brief. The manic episodes are supposedly characterized by excessive elation, irritability, talkativeness, flight of ideas, increased speech and motor activity. This account leaves out the most important characteristics, namely, the cognitive and motivational aspects, especially since they are the direct opposite of those of the depressive. Some report that intellectual functions are intact whereas others state that there is delusion, grandiosity, religiosity, excessive unwarranted generosity. As with the LSD experience, the Manic may be thrilled with a simple blade of grass. This elation may be a factor in the appreciation and sensitivity of some artists and art critics.

296.2 MANIC-DEPRESSIVE ILLNESS, DEPRESSED TYPE

DSM-II states that the disorder consists only of depressed episodes. It supposedly does not have a precipitating cause as does Psychotic depressive reaction. There is motor and mental retardation which sometimes leads to stupor.

As was mentioned earlier, the precipitating cause may have been, to a large extent, long-term irrational assessments and beliefs. The depressive has a negative view of himself and the world. He says to himself that he is no good and degrades himself. The confusion involves non-adjustive learning habits as well as lack of a clear idea of how value terms (e.g., "bad") work. Such confusions lead to negative feelings, and the emotion term "depression" covers feeling, cognition, and context. The kinds of depression possible are determined by the kinds of contexts, cognitions, and feelings possible and the relations between. Only such detailed description would be adequate for an understanding of the individual depressive person. Again, the DSM-II account leaves out such significant features except for the description of one abstract emotion in terms of another abstract emotion. That is, depression is secondarily characterized as "uneasiness, apprehension, perplexity, agitation. While DSM-II states that illusions, if present, are due to the dominant mood, it may rather be found that they are due to the dominant assessments. Even imagery and perception are to a large extent influenced by cognitive assessments.

Manic depression is often thought to be hard to diagnose. It occurs two or three times more in women than in men. The question arises whether this is only because the average personality of a woman may be closer than a man's to that of the depressive.

296.3 MANIC-DEPRESSIVE ILLNESS, CIRCULAR TYPE

DSM-II states:

"This disorder is distinguished by at least one attack of both a depressive episode *and* a manic episode . . . The current episode should be specified and coded [as circular manic or circular depressed]."

"Alternating" should perhaps be more descriptive here than "circular." The swing from one state to the other is seldom regular, e.g., every 24 hours, but this may be due to cognitive factors or fixations regarding time, which are associated with the conflict leading to the depressive and manic state. Other cycles take place every ten years. When the cycle takes place so seldom it may not be a cycle at all but rather a developmental growth change. Thus, "circular" and "cycle" may be misleading metaphors because they exclude growth change possibilities. "Circular" also irrelevantly suggests tautological thinking. If "alternating," seems to imply reversal to a previous state without allowing for growth states, the term "mixed states" may be used instead. It is quite likely that manic or depressed states change and do not remain static, because cognitions and habits change thus causing changes in feelings. Depressives, for example, often become more depressed. Self-talk becomes more fixed.

A rapid alteration of elated or happy states and crying or depressed states may indicate other disorders such as schizophrenia, adolescent depression, hysteria, or even "normal" but confused emotional behavior.

296.33 MANIC-DEPRESSIVE ILLNESS, CIRCULAR TYPE, MANIC

296.34 MANIC-DEPRESSIVE ILLNESS, CIRCULAR TYPE, DEPRESSED

These two types are to be used to specify when the patient is in the manic or depressive state of the circular type 296.3. It may be noted that these two types are used only in the United States.

295 SCHIZOPHRENIA

DSM-II states that except for the schizo-affective type, schizophrenia is a thought disorder and involves behavioral disorder.

"Disturbances in thinking are marked by alterations of concept formation which may lead to misinterpretation of reality and sometimes to delusions and hallucinations, which frequently appear psychologically self-protective."

This statement by DSM-II is almost the assessment theory definition of emotion. Cognitive distortion leads to behavioral deviation, uncontrolled or inappropriate feelings. The cognitive distortions seem to be ways of coping with confused beliefs or statements. Though they may appear to be "self-protective" or defense-mechanisms, they are usually self-defeating.

It was earlier mentioned that "schizophrenia" means literally "splitting of the mind," and that this is a misleading description because "mind" is a fiction. Some comments on the usefulness and soundness of the "schizophrenia" category follow:

"The etiology of schizophrenic conditions is today unknown." (133) (Ulett and Goodrich)

"Lacking today is a single, well-formed, and testable hypothesis." (135) (Ulett and Goodrich)

"There are no objective criteria today for the diagnosis of schizophrenia." (621) "Schizophrenia is as yet not curable." (Lehmann 649)

"So far no definite neurological abnormality [for schizophrenia] has been found." (Drake 99)

Behaviorists regard schizophrenia as being based on non-adaptive past learning. (For a critique of behaviorism see chapter "Learning Theory of Love.") On the cognitive theory of emotions such learning relates especially to one's learning of informal logical fallacies, confused concepts, faulty rhetoric, self-defeating language-games, misuse of and captivation by metaphors, lack of critical and philosophical understanding and analysis of language—especially of value terms such as "bad," "wrong," "perfect," "ought," etc. The cognitive or assessment theory is supportive of the behavioristic approach, but attempts to make the latter approach more adequate by including linguistic assessments and by giving an analysis and clarification of such assessments in terms of contemporary philosophical analyses. In a separate chapter the specific logical fallacies, defense-mechanisms, etc. have been presented and related to types of metaphorical (rhetorical) devices. This procedure offers a philosophically sound clarification of the many abstract, inconsistent, or unclarified terms now used in describing schizophrenic thinking. Such theoretical and Freudian terms as "primary process thinking," "preverbal stage," "id," "ego," "unconscious," etc. should be avoided until they can be made clearly intelligible. However, Freud's defense-mechanisms if defined as language-games or rhetorical devices are found to be useful. In place of vague and inconsistent mental categories, is put mainly language use, but also included are imagery, perception, and behavior. To know is to be able to say something. By thinking we mainly mean using language. There is epistemological primacy of language.

Some of the previous and prevalent terms describing schizophrenic thinking are as follows: "splitting of psychic functions," confusion, delusion, "primary process thinking," loss of continuity, cognitive closure (seek false but quick solutions to problems), condensation, blocking, clang associations, flight of ideas, paralogical ideas may be linked solely by grammatical form or similarity, idea fixation, senseless naming, echolalia (repeat questioner's question), holding contradictory beliefs, incoherence, "word-salad," far-fetched substitutions, stilted language, overgeneralization, inability to abstract, proverbs are taken literally, bizarre associations, (inability to pass likeness association tests), loss of self boundary so that thoughts spread to others; the patients may act like another person or like two people alternately, they may identify with an object and suffer if the object is abused, outsiders may control their thoughts, ambivalent ideas (hold opposite ideas at once), confused notion of self, private symbolism, there may be alternation between rational and irrational periods, patients may not be able to do a simple task yet be able to do a complex task; there are delusions about technology such as thinking they are controlled by x-rays, identification of things on the basis of a single even minor quality (e.g., thinking one is Napoleon because one is short), pathological symmetry, (e.g., Patricia is Kirsten's mother, therefore Kirsten is Patricia's mother), overly concrete thinking, double-bind, inappropriate diction, inability to easily detect deleted words, negativism (say and do the reverse of what is asked), verbigeration (irrational continued repetition of words), and loss of memory for recent things. These typical descriptions need careful organization and more concrete analysis. To say schizophrenics have "emotional problems," "personality disorganization," or "splitting of psychic function," is vague and unscientific. A careful consistent behavioral analysis is needed which involves philosophical clarification.

The schizophrenic may have hallucinations or delusions or mood changes which follow from bizarre cognitive associations. The hallucinations according to some accounts are usually auditory, persecutory, and involve taste or smell but seldom the visual or tactile. He may hear his own thoughts. People may seem to them to change their shape rapidly; they may hear the voice of God or the devil. With cenesthetic hallucination they may imagine states such as "brain burns." Hallucinated voices may tell the schizophrenic to do certain things or to commit suicide.

Many of the above fallacies are common errors made by the average man. For example, most people believe in reason and science yet believe in a religion which is contradictory to reason and science.

It is interesting to relate schizophrenic thinking to the thinking of the religious mystic and the LSD drug taker. A. Freedman and H. Kaplan (1972) give the following account.

"The ecstatic states occuring in acute schizophrenia are related to the ecstatic transports of religious mysticism. The mystical experience, whether religious or not, possesses certain distinguishing qualities:
1) *Ineffability*. The subject often insists that his experience is inexpressible and indescribable, that it is impossible to convey what it is like to one who has never experienced it.
2) *Noesis*. The subject has the feeling that the mystery of the universe has been plumbed, that an immense illumination or revelation has occurred. Along with this may go a curious sense of authority, the conviction that one is privileged to lead and to command. As for the revelation itself, it seems to consist of layer upon layer of truth, that, as it unfolds, may find expression in some familiar or even commonplace thought . . . The revelation may be expressed in words that are unintelligible to the speaker.
3) *Transiency*. [of the experience] Yet it is as unforgettable as it is highly treasured, and it colors all subsequent activity.
4) *Passivity* . . . There is an obeyance of the will, as if the subject were in the grip of a superior power . . .
5) *Unio mystica* . . . A sense of mystic unity with an infinite power, an oceanic feeling in which opposites are reconciled, in which there are "darknesses that dazzle" and "voices of silence." [Note relevance of metaphor] There is a quality of timelessness . . ."

Schizophrenia is sometimes said to go through the stages of depression, sudden revelation (apophany phase), and then a fragmented state (apocalyptic stage).

An analysis of the language, i.e., cognition, of the schizophrenic and a behavioral modification of this plus his behavior should be the direction of research regarding therapy in addition to work on physiological and chemotherapy approaches. Few or no drugs are found to be effective unless accompanied by psychotherapy. Some results of the cognitive approach may be indicated by the fact that elated patients are able to achieve results with seriously withdrawn or even mute schizophrenics. Aaron Beck (1967) states,

"A manic patient may have a notable effect in arousing the interest and activity of a withdrawn, mute, schizophrenic patient." (97)

"Some manic patients are unusually successful in breaking through the autistic barrier of withdrawn schizophrenics." (92)

295.0 SCHIZOPHRENIA, SIMPLE TYPE

DSM-II describes this as,

"A slow and insidious reduction of external attachments and interests and by apathy and indifference leading to impoverishment of interpersonal relations, [and] mental deterioration . . ."

According to the usual descriptions this person lacks: will power, work capacity, ability to care for himself, concern, interest in people or things, normal emotional reaction. He is withdrawn, may not eat, may take walks at two o'clock in the morning. That the disorder is "slow and insidious" may suggest that faulty long-term assessments are mainly involved rather than just short-term conflicts or confusions.

295.1 SCHIZOPHRENIA, HEBEPHRENIC TYPE

"Hebephrenia" from the Greek word means "youth mind." It refers to "adolescent insanity." It usually begins from age 12-25. DSM-II describes it as,

"Disordered thinking, shallow and inappropriate affect, unpredictable giggling, silly and regressive behavior and mannerisms, and frequent hypochondriacal complaints."

It seems inaccurate and unfounded to speak of this as "regressive" behavior even though it is characterized by clowning, angry outbursts, excessive smiling and grimacing. These patients also may renounce all activity, have dulled emotions, show sex preoccupation, and feel mentally and physically deficient. "Regression" may imply return to Freud's stages of oral, anal, and phallic fixation and this theory appears to be an extravagant metaphor taken literally rather than a descriptive, experiential finding. Also "regression" implies that one is returning to a former or childhood state, and it may be that hebephrenic behavior is in many ways unlike child behavior. That is, the average "normal" person may act more like a child than does a hebephrenic, when all things are considered.

295.2 SCHIZOPHRENIA, CATATONIC TYPE

R. Drake appears to base this disorder on a cognitive source, as he says,

"Catalepsy (muscular rigidity) [lit. "seizure"] is caused by a dominating idea which is symbolized by the posture." (32)

"Catatonic" itself derives from the Greek word meaning "stretching down" or "depression." Two types listed are "excited" and "withdrawn." (See the following two classifications.) These two are for use in the United States only. Catatonia supposedly can occur in any type of schizophrenia.

295.23 SCHIZOPHRENIA, CATATONIC TYPE, EXCITED

DSM-II says this type involves "excessive and sometimes violent motor activity and excitement," but gives practically no description of it. It is often said to involve verbal incoherence, continuous talking and shouting, destructiveness, self-injury, exhaustion from overactivity, sleeplessness, impulsive activity, cursing, self-disregard. More concrete and adequate characterizations are needed.

295.24 SCHIZOPHRENIA, CATATONIC TYPE, WITHDRAWN

DSM-II describes this as "generalized inhibition manifested by stupor, mutism, negativism, or waxy flexibility." It seems to involve, especially, difficulty with motor activity. But the schizoaffective type also involves artificial body positions. It is not clear why this type is labelled "withdrawn" rather than "depressed." "Depression" in the other categories has taken many forms and one of the main meanings of depression is "being withdrawn." Both depression and the withdrawn catatonic seem to have characteristics of appetite loss, inaction, concern with death, retardation, and the withdrawn catatonic is said to sometimes alternate between mania and melancholia or depression. The degree of withdrawal for the catatonic is excessive as it may involve stupor, failure to swallow, command automaticity, negativism (doing the opposite of that which is requested). More clarity is needed in distinguishing "withdrawn" and "depressed." "Withdrawn" seems to refer partially to motor inactivity, and partly to depression.

295.3 SCHIZOPHRENIA, PARANOID TYPE

DSM-II says this involves "persecutory or grandiose delusions, often associated with hallucinations. Excessive religiosity is sometimes seen . . . Behavior tends to be consistent with his delusions." There is said to be possibly a predominance of either hostility, grandiosity, or hallucination.

T. Sarbin (1972) seriously questions the clarity and usefulness of the term "hallucination" as well as "imagery." For him, imagery is "muted role-taking." He rejects mental phenomena, and so also images, as being pictures in our minds. An image is rather regarded as as-if, fictive, or pretense seeing. The skill involves first copying performances of others, then learning how to pretend just as we first learn to speak, then learning to mute speech in talking silently to ourselves. His view does not, however, deny the experience of imagery. It merely attempts to give a possible specific and intelligible analysis of imagery. (See chapters on imagery and perception in this book.)

Sarbin rejects the concept of hallucination because it too seems to be a pseudo-psychological entity or mentalistic concept. The therapist, he believes, should concern himself with what the patient is communicating rather than with mentalistic "hallucinations." Sarbin states that more empirical data is needed for an understanding of hallucinations, and until this is available hallucination should not serve as a criterion of "mental disorders."

In his article "The Concept of Hallucination" (1967) Sarbin presents the view that "hallucination" is a pejorative or value term used to describe people already thought to be abnormal or disturbed. If the person reporting his imagery is a schizophrenic we may say he is hallucinating, but if he is a poet we may say, "How clever." How we describe imagery is, then, partly determined by the external, biographical situation, or prior conditions. It is not just a direct report of an internal state. Thus reports of imagery may be alternatively referred to as vision, dream, fantasy, hallucination, etc. A child who plays imaginative games does not hallucinate but sees-as. One may say he acts as-if he sees things which are not there. Similarly we often say someone is a "warm" person. In so doing we do not hallucinate warmth but make metaphorical associations. Even reports of imagery by neurotics or psychotics may be mere metaphorical statements rather than literal reports of inner images. Hallucinations as reported by a patient are determined by verbal report, but the therapist need not always take the patient's word for such experiences. The patient may be lying, uttering relatively empty verbal phrases. Although one need not accept Sarbin's theory, it does seem that further specific research needs to be done regarding both imagery and hallucination before taking these categories literally.

295.4 ACUTE SCHIZOPHRENIC EPISODE

Sudden onset distinguishes this type from the gradual onset of simple schizophrenia. The episode may last only several weeks with complete recovery, or it may develop into another kind of schizophrenia. DSM-II states that it involves "confusion, perplexity, ideas of reference, emotional turmoil, dream-like dissociation, and excitement, depression, or fear." On this basis it would seem to be hard to distinguish from other types.

295.5 SCHIZOPHRENIA, LATENT TYPE

DSM-II states,

"This category is for patients having clear symptoms of schizophrenia but no history of a psychotic schizophrenic episode."

Lehman, however, states that this is a thought disorder without necessarily clear psychosis.

295.6 SCHIZOPHRENIA, RESIDUAL TYPE

DSM-II states,

"This category is for patients showing signs of schizophrenia but who, following a psychotic schizophrenic episode, are no longer psychotic."

This is sometimes referred to as "ambulatory" schizophrenia.

295.7 SCHIZOPHRENIA, SCHIZO-AFFECTIVE TYPE

DSM-II describes this as:

"For patients showing a mixture of schizophrenic symptoms and pronounced elation or depression."

The same objections apply to the use of "affective" here as applied to the category 296 "Major affective disorders." An adequate definition and analysis is needed to make this category intelligible. Beck presents a similar view and cites others who question the usefulness of this category:

"Henderson and Gillespie (1963) are dubious about the use of the term schizo-affective psychosis and offer the opinion that it has created more diagnostic difficulties than it has solved." (Beck 118)

"As Clark and Mallet (1963) have pointed out, a large proportion of psychotic patients show an admixture of schizophrenic and affective features, and it is difficult to decide whether a given case should be regarded as 'schizophrenic with affective features,' or as 'affective disorder with schizophrenia.' " (Beck 108)

This type is divided into excited and depressed (the following two categories).

295.73 SCHIZOPHRENIA, SCHIZO-AFFECTIVE TYPE, EXCITED

(No specific DSM-II description.) Some of the ecstatic states presented earlier (religious ecstasy, omnipotence feelings, feelings of oneness, etc.) apply to this type. The patient may seem happy and smile when a tragedy or death occurs. His emotional expression is sometimes said to be split from his cognition. A more careful statement would be that his assessments may be confused and so lead to unusual "motor" behavior (e.g., facial expression) and feelings. It may also be that the assessments are not coordinated in the usual accepted way with one's feelings or observable "motor" behavior. The patient appears to react with greatly inappropriate emotions.

295.74 SCHIZOPHRENIA, SCHIZO-AFFECTIVE TYPE, DEPRESSED

The concept of "depression" was analyzed earlier. This type is characterized by apathy, inactivity, covering eyes or face (as children sometimes do to try to avoid being seen or criticized), negativism, avoidance, stiffening of body, scowling, swearing, lack of emotion, waxy flexibility (tendency to maintain artificial positions). (Catatonia is characterized by this latter characteristic also.) These patients are suicidal, as are most depressives, and they may be concerned, even exclusively concerned, with death.

295.8 SCHIZOPHRENIA, CHILDHOOD TYPE

DSM-II states,

"Symptoms appear before puberty . . . Autistic, atypical, and withdrawn behavior; failure to develop identity separate from the mother's."

Characteristics sometimes given are: repetitive, stereotyped behavior; late speech development (e.g., age 5 or 6); play is abnormal; has confused body image; has need to touch people; hits head on wall; communicates poorly. It is surprising to have a category based on a childhood type when other types seem to fail to make this type distinction. Should there be childhood, adolescent, adult, elderly, senile, male, female, etc. types in each category? Is "puberty" related to the disorder and so significant that DSM-II should state,"symptoms appear before puberty..? The definition, however, does stress developmental aspects.

295.90 SCHIZOPHRENIA, CHRONIC UNDIFFERENTIATED TYPE

For mixed schizophrenic symptoms not fitting under other types.

295.99 SCHIZOPHRENIA, OTHER (AND UNSPECIFIED TYPES)

(The last five categories 295.73 to 295.99 are for use only in the United States.)

297 PARANOID STATES

DSM-II states,

"These are psychotic disorders in which a delusion, generally persecutory or grandiose, is the essential abnormality. Disturbances in mood, behavior and thinking (including hallucinations) are derived from this delusion. This distinguishes paranoid states from the affective psychoses and schizophrenias, in which mood and thought disorders, respectively, are the central abnormalities. Most authorities, however, question whether disorders in this group are distinct clinical entities and not merely variants of schizophrenia or paranoid personality."

Paranoid states may supposedly occur in nearly any psychosis. The distinguishing characteristic is basically cognitive – the faulty assessment of being persecuted. It seems to involve a narrow, fixed idea such as that of a delusion of superior ability, grandiosity, or jealousy. Otherwise the person may be normally rational. The disorder is supposedly rare (2% of mental hospital admissions) and 70% of those afflicted are male.

297.0 PARANOIA

DSM-II states,

"This extremely rare condition is characterized by gradual development of an intricate, complex, and elaborate paranoid system based on and often proceeding logically from misinterpretation of an actual event."

297.1 INVOLUTIONAL PARANOID STATE

DSM-II characterizes this as "Delusion formation with onset in the involutional period." The concept "involutional" was discussed under 296.0 Involutional melancholia.

298.0 PSYCHOTIC DEPRESSIVE REACTION
(REACTIVE DEPRESSIVE PSYCHOSIS)

This is a more severe disorder than Depressive neurosis. "Depression" has been discussed earlier. This depression is usually brought on by a specific experience.

301 PERSONALITY DISORDERS (NON-PSYCHOTIC)

DSM-II states,

"This group of disorders is characterized by deeply ingrained maladaptive patterns of behavior that are perceptibly different in quality from psychotic and neurotic symptoms."

There is, however, a question as to whether there is a qualitative difference, as stated, or rather often differences of degree of severity. Psychotic and neurotic states may give us insight into our usual ways of thinking and personality, and vice versa. It may be noted that the female tends to be a manic-depressive or involutional melancholic, whereas of the few paranoids there are, most tend to be men. The personality disorders are given names closely resembling those of psychotic and neurotic states. In general, however, clear and consistent ways of describing personality are one of the greatest needs in contemporary human research. The harm done by the personality faults of the so-called average, normal person is more violent than the usual forms of physical violence, yet "mental" violence due to anger, irritation, etc. seems to be accepted and goes uncorrected. Poor personality adjustment is partly due to previous mistaken views of the nature of emotion. It is generally still erroneously believed that emotions are feelings, cannot be changed, and are part of one's nature. The assessment or cognitive theory changes this view and rejects all three beliefs. Personality is central to one's research whether of the natural or social sciences, or of the sort of government which one should establish. It plays a part in alienation and love. A "good" personality is often the most desirable attribute one can have. The average person has serious personality problems. Extensive research should concentrate on personality clarification in keeping with contemporary views of psychology, psychiatry, and philosophical psychology. The following types of personality disorders are not adequate in this respect.

301.0 PARANOID PERSONALITY

"Hypersensitivity, rigidity, unwarranted suspicion, jealousy, envy, excessive self-importance, and a tendency to blame others and ascribe evil motives to them."

301.1 CYCLOTHYMIC PERSONALITY (AFFECTIVE PERSONALITY)

"Recurring and alternating periods of depression and elation ... not readily attributable to external circumstances."

On the assessment theory one would look for long-term irrational cognitions as well as immediate assessments. "Worry" may, for example, be a fixed though alternating assessment or approach to problems.

301.2 SCHIZOID PERSONALITY

"Shyness, oversensitivity, seclusiveness, avoidance of close or competitive relationships, and often eccentricity."

This person is often autistic, a day-dreamer, unable to express hostile feeling.

301.3 EXPLOSIVE PERSONALITY (EPILEPTOID PERSON-ALITY DISORDER) (AGGRESSIVE PERSONALITY)

Out-of-character, seemingly uncontrollable physical or verbal outbursts, excitability, over-responsive to environmental influences.

301.4 OBSESSIVE COMPULSIVE PERSONALITY (ANANKASTIC PERSONALITY)

"Excessive concern with conformity . . . rigid, over-inhibited, over-conscientious, over-dutiful, and unable to relax easily. This disorder may lead to an Obsessive compulsive neurosis."

This account suggests a continuum with neurosis.

301.5 HYSTERICAL PERSONALITY (HISTRIONIC PERSONALITY DISORDER)

"Excitability, emotional instability, over-reactivity, and self-dramatization. This self-dramatization is always attention-seeking and often seductive, whether or not the patient is aware of its purpose. These personalities are also immature, self-centered, often vain, and usually dependent on others."

301.6 ASTHENIC PERSONALITY

"Easy fatigability, low energy level, lack of enthusiasm, marked incapacity for enjoyment, and oversensitivity to physical and emotional stress."

This trait seems to relate to Neurasthenic neurosis.

301.7 ANTISOCIAL PERSONALITY

"Repeatedly into conflict with society. They are incapable of significant loyalty to individuals, groups, or social values. They are grossly selfish, callous, irresponsible, impulsive, and unable to feel guilt or to learn from experience and punishment. Frustration tolerance is low. They tend to blame others or offer plausible rationalizations for their behavior."

301.81 PASSIVE-AGGRESSIVE PERSONALITY

"The aggressiveness may be expressed passively, for example by obstructionism, pouting, procrastination, intentional inefficiency, or stubbornness."

"Aggression" needs definition and clarification here.

301.82 INADEQUATE PERSONALITY

"Ineffectual responses to emotional, social, intellectual, and physical demands . . . He does manifest inadaptability, ineptness, poor judgment, social instability, and lack of physical and emotional stamina."

It is not clear what the distinction is between this state and depression.

Psychophysiologic disorders (305) are supposedly caused by emotional factors. Again, an analysis of emotions would need to be given to make this category intelligible and useful. It appears that the cause may be basically cognitive rather than emotional, although extended activated feeling states, as with worry, may cause physical disorder.

Sources:

Magda Arnold "Human Emotion and Action" Human Action T. Mischel, ed., New York: Academic Press 1969

A. Beck Depression University of Pennsylvania 1967

Sheldon Cashden Abnormal Psychology New Jersey: Prentice Hall 1972

Diagnostic and Statistical Manual of Mental Disorders I (1952), II (1968) Washington, D.C.: American Psychiatric Association

Raleigh Drake Abnormal Psychology New Jersey: Littlefield, Adams 1954

Albert Ellis Reason and Emotion New York: Lyle Stuart 1962

Alfred Freedman & Harold Kaplan Diagnosing Mental Illness New York: Atheneum 1972 pp. 170-171

Helen Kaplan & Harold Kaplan "Current Concepts of Psychosomatic Medicine" Comprehensive Textbook of Psychiatry A. Freedman, H. Kaplan, eds., Baltimore: Williams & Wilkins 1967 pp. 1039-1044.

Fred Kapp "Psychogenic Pain" Comprehensive Textbook of Psychiatry A. Freedman, H. Kaplan eds., pp. 1105 ff.

Heinz Lehmann "Schizophrenia IV: Clinical Features" A. Freedman, H. Kaplan, eds., Psychiatry pp. 621-648

321

A. I. Melden "The Conceptual Dimensions of Emotions" Human Action T. Mischel, ed., New York: Academic Press 1969

Gilbert Ryle Concept of Mind New York: Barnes & Noble 1949

Theodore Sarbin "The Concept of Hallucination" Journal of Personality 35 (1967) 359-380

Theodore Sarbin and Joseph Juhasz "The Historical Background of the Concept of Hallucination" Journal of the History of Behavioral Sciences 3 (1967) 339-358.

Theodore Sarbin "Imaging as Muted Role-Taking: A Historical Linguistic Analysis" The Function and Nature of Imagery P. Sheehan, ed., New York: Academic Press 1972

Warren Shibles Metaphor: An Annotated Bibliography and History Whitewater, Wisconsin: The Language Press

Warren Shibles "Memory," "Intention." Wittgenstein, Language and Philosophy Dubuque, Iowa: Kendall-Hunt 1971

George Ulett and D. Goodrich A Synopsis of Contemporary Psychiatry

Ludwig Wittgenstein Philosophical Investigations 3rd edition, G. Anscombe, trans., New York: Macmillan 1958

A Critique of Sartre
Sketch for a Theory of Emotions

The *Sketch* is considered to be the best source of Sartre's theoretical views on the nature of psychology. (Warnock) Sartre's main assertions will be presented and then discussed. Sartre asserts the following:

1) James' theory of emotion as consciousness of a physiological disturbance is inadequate because a) it fails to distinguish qualitatively between emotions; b) it fails to account for the element of thought involved in emotion. One is not merely presented with a physical change. Physiological disturbance cannot explain terrorized consciousness; c) physiology cannot account for the organized character of an emotion.

2) Janet's theory is that emotion is the behavior of defeat. It consists of both mental and physical phenomena, e.g., A girl breaks down as a substitute for discussing her case with her doctor. About this theory Sartre asserts: a) It correctly introduces the notion of purposiveness but fails to account for consciousness, or the view that consciousness can support the idea of purpose. Only consciousness can confer significance upon defeat; b) His view just rests on a shift of psychic energy or tension (from greater to lesser); c) He correctly integrates psyche with physical disturbance; d) His account does not apply to types of emotion other than shock. Emotion is an organized pattern of behavior rather than merely a disturbance.

3) Denbo's theory is that emotion is a mechanical switch from a superior to an inferior way of action and so we debase ourselves. Sartre comments about this theory that it fails to include consciousness so as to allow a switch from a superior to an inferior mode of consciousness.

323

4) Psychoanalytic theory. Sartre asserts about this that:
a) It assumes an unconscious mind. This conflicts with Sartre's Cartesianism, according to which consciousness must always be aware of itself. (It is Mary Warnock's view, however, that Sartre does not define consciousness and that his view is not really Cartesian. She also finds Sartre's view that mind knows its ideas best, quite dubious.) b) Freudians overlook the intentional nature of mental acts and think there can be an inductively determined *causal* unconscious relation between my dream and some external object. Sartre's own view of intentionality is that an account of emotion must involve the conjunction of subject and object in an indissoluble synthesis. c) Sartre agrees to some extent with the Freudians that the conscious fact is symbolical. For Sartre, consciousness constitutes itself by symbolization, not causally, however.

In his discussion of these theories, Sartre concludes that they show that emotion can only be described in terms of the consciousness. Sartre's positive view of an outline of a phenomenological theory of the emotions is as follows:

1) It assumes intention. Emotion is at first a non-reflective consciousness *of* something, e.g., fear is the way the world appears. Emotion is a way of apprehending the world.

2) As emotion is intentional, it does not involve solely the causal effect of mind on matter or matter on mind.

3) Emotion is an attempt at transformation of the world due to our being unable to put up with a situation. We try to transform the situation which is determined, as if by magic, at a time when we are unable to reflect. If we cannot change the world we change ourselves (e.g., we faint) or experience emotion, and so magically annihilate the world for ourselves (magical behavior).

4) "Emotion arises when the world of the utilizable vanishes abruptly, and the world of magic appears in its place." All the apparent ways to act are barred yet one must still act. We thus act magically.

5) The magical seeing is like a seeing-as experience, e.g., looking for a familiar object disguised in the lines of a picture and then seeing, for instance, as if the lines represent a gun.

6) Behavior pure and simple is not emotion. Real emotion is accompanied by belief. Physical disorder in itself is nothing.

7) Liberation from emotion can only come from a purifying reflection or from the total disappearance of the emotional situation.

Sartre, like Melden and others, stresses the function of context for an adequate analysis of emotion, and denies that emotion is merely a term just covering feeling states.

The expression, "mental state," is an odd concept. We know what the state of a physical object is, e.g., water in a dish. The water is still, perhaps not moved by wind or vibration. It is in a state of rest. But what is "state" as applied to mind, which is a supposedly immaterial thing? And, of course, arguments for the nature and existence of mind are needed. Thus if emotion is to be a mental state it is not clear what it is. Sartre's notion of intentionality, as derived from Husserl, is given in an attempt to avoid such difficulties as these. More will be said about this later. The point is that the problem of analyzing emotions is partly the problem of dualism. Mind is held to be separate from body and the problem then is how they could possibly interact.

(Berkeley: We first raise the dust and then claim we cannot see.)

Sartre's stress on consciousness is in a sense a stress on the first person case which behaviorists have difficulty dealing with. It was argued earlier in this book that by consciousness we mainly mean language use. Thus, Sartre's obscure concept "consciousness" may be given a concrete interpretation. Behaviorists also would find it difficult to accept Sartre's view that we have a consciousness as such which is or can be aware of all our mental and emotive activities. Warnock also doubts that mind knows its ideas best and she objects to the Sartrian notion of consciousness. (Preface)

Sartre objects to psychoanalytic theory which assumes the existence of an unconscious mind. The notion of an "unconscious," conflicts with Sartre's view that consciousness must always be aware of itself. An unconscious would apply to the conscious mind also. That is, I have given a behavioral analysis or reinterpretation of consciousness as a pattern of language and behavior in a situation.

A. C. MacIntyre, in *The Unconscious*, has given a similar analysis of Freud's theory. His point is that we have no evidence for such internal hypothetical entities as id, ego, superego, unconscious, but we do observe recurrent patterns of behavior in people, e.g. Oedipus behavior. His view is that the effective results, sometimes achieved by the psychoanalyst, are due not to Freudian theory but rather to the clinician's actual concrete experience in dealing with patients. Freud himself recorded many actual experiences (case histories) with patients. Ordinary-language philosophy also stresses the language used in the concrete and actual situation. Although Sartre's theory is mainly sheer metaphysics, a close look at his concrete examples can be quite revealing of the nature of "emotion."

It was stated that emotion words do not simply name states. Sartre asserts that an emotion is an organized pattern of behavior. This avoids the difficulties involved in attempting to find a causal relation between a physical and a mental state. Put in a different way, the notion of "organized pattern" is one way of analyzing what it is to be a causal situation. It is not that I first have an "idea" and then express it in an action but rather the "thinking" and action are intentionally and synthetically unified in an organized pattern.

It would be relevant here to mention A. I. Melden's notion of action in his book, *Free Action*. (See chapter on Melden) He asserts that it is not the case that I first have a feeling or kinesthetic sensation which causes me to raise my arm. We never have access to the feeling without the raising of the arm. That is, "I raise . . ." is always followed by the description of the thing done. I do not have a feeling of raising my arm without raising my arm. We don't have a feeling of raising but only of raising something, e.g., an arm. The raising is always in terms of the action. An action is said to be not just a feeling but the total event of raising one's arm. Melden's point is that one cannot describe the cause of an event as if it were separate from the event because the cause already involves the event. Natural science notions of cause and effect do not apply to *human actions*, he thinks. For Melden, an action is a purposive organized pattern of activity. This is very much like the analysis Sartre gives. I do not wish to raise the question here of what a cause is for science or human behavior. Whether Melden is right or not, by treating an emotion as an organized pattern of behavior some of the difficulties of causal analyses are avoided and one sort of reasonably adequate concrete and actual description of emotion can be given.

Sartre's notion of "magical behavior" may perhaps be regarded as a type of seeing-as, or as a game we play, one which is largely influenced by our language. We see a situation as "horrible" and we in another context or with relearning may see that situation as not "horrible" at all. Sartre suggests this when he says that the way to avoid such emotions is to become conscious of them or, in other terms, to see that they are games we play. There seems to be little rational reason for us to get revenge. That is, by getting revenge it is not clear that revenge will keep the disliked event from occurring again, but rather getting revenge may even promote the institution of revenge. Penal institutions sometimes move from mere punishment to corrective behavior. It is not clear that getting revenge helps the situation. One may learn not to get revenge since it seems to have little rational use. Thus, by becoming conscious of the emotion games we play we may be better able to choose those which we find effective and useful.

Sources:

A. C. MacIntyre *The Unconscious* New York: Humanities 1958
Jean-Paul Sartre *Sketch for a Theory of Emotions* London: Methuen 1962
Mary Warnock *Philosophy of Sartre* New York: Barnes & Noble 1967

A Critique of LeShan
What Makes Me Feel This Way?

Good children's books on emotions are needed and Le Shan may be commended for trying to do this. There are some fine things to be said about this book and some critical things as well. She points out such important things as the following:

a) "It is easier to control a feeling if you understand it." (30)
b) Words can upset people. (25)
c) One should think about how he feels, for he often does not know he is angry. (30)
d) "As we grow up, we may find ways to give up some of our fears." (40)
e) The child should express his fear so he will no longer fear. (Although Le Shan sometimes means to suggest by this that one should become angry rather than reassess the problem.) (50)
f) Being alone is very important for our feelings. (55)
g) Often parents fail to understand or accept the fact that children cannot sit still for very long. (68)
h) "There are things we can do to make ourselves feel better about the world we live in." (71)
i) "We can influence our feelings." (73)
j) We should verbalize some aspects of the situation to ourselves. (75)

As to the critical side, the book is too long and wordy, not clear enough, and it is not clear what age group the book is intended for. It is doubtful that the average ten year old would be inter-

*A portion of this review is reprinted from *Rational Living* 8 (1973) p. 35

ested in reading the book. One would need to be at least about age ten to read it and yet the author speaks of things which often rather relate to age 5 or 6. But more unacceptable is the theory the book presents:

1. The author does not define feeling or emotion. Such clarification is needed for children as much or more than for adults. She says feelings are just "special things." (9)

2. Bodily feelings are mistakenly confused with emotions. She says, "Curiosity and boldness are feelings." (40) Emotions are not bodily feelings but are largely rational or irrational statements which guide bodily feelings. Thus it is erroneous to say "I *feel* an emotion." Emotion is partly a description of a situation or context and may not even involve any feelings at all in some cases. "I am jealous" is a report of who did what to whom in a certain situation, and is not just a report of an "inner feeling." Thus "I feel x" where "x" is an emotion is a category-mistake.

3. She states that whatever our negative emotions are we just have to accept them:

    a) "This is partly because Jerry was just born that way." (i.e., angry, etc.) (19)
    b) It is not bad or wrong to be angry. (21)
    c) "Feelings (emotions) are . . . the spice of life." (39)
    d) "Feelings (emotions) . . . are just normal." (22)
    e) "That's the way you are." (75)
    f) "It isn't necessary or even wise to try to get rid of sad or angry feelings." (77) She suggests "letting them happen, and accepting them." (77)
    g) "When a person you love dies you need to show how you feel about it. You need to be with all the other people who are also very sad." (106)
    h) "They are feelings of all human beings, and whether we always like them or not, we are stuck with them!" (15)

Thus she holds the traditional view that emotions are passive things which just happen to us or are part of our nature so all we can do is accept them. This is because she confused feelings and emotions. If it is seen that emotions are largely rational assessments it would be seen rather that one can change one's emotions by changing one's assessments. They are not just part of one's nature. It is harmful to say "Feelings are just normal." If a child often experiences great rage or fear it is not helpful to tell him to accept it, or that he is just being normal or merely as the subtitle of the book suggests, "growing up with human emotions." It would rather seem that to continuously be hateful and angry is to grow up with *inhuman* emotions. To support and continuously experience negative emotions is to be less than a full human being. It is to be a slave of one's emotions.

4. Emotions are erroneously treated as causes. Again this derives from confusing emotions with feelings. A feeling may be the object of our assessment but an emotion is already an assessment. To love is not just to have a feeling but to assess (verbal statements, self-talk, etc.) as well. An emotion is not a single feeling or entity and so is not the cause of one's doing anything. In "sham rage" the animal has the feeling or behavior of rage but does nothing. Also one may love someone and not do anything about it. One may watch injustice in the news, become angry, and feel that it is enough just to get angry without taking any further action. In the following quotes she confuses feelings with emotions, and mistakenly treats emotions as causes:

a) "Feelings of loving and hating . . . They all make us get out and do things." (39)
b) "Compassion is a feeling that makes you want to help other people." (40)

Compassion rather is itself the assessment that you want to help other people. The statement is circular.

5. The only psychiatrist mentioned is Freud (44, 83) and it would seem that Le Shan's views are somewhat Freudian. She, for example, states that we have an "unconscious mind." This leads to the view that emotions are due to magical, irrational, "unconscious forces." This leads also to telling children that they are stuck with their negative emotions and with the irrational causes of these emotions. She says, "Your mind seems to tell you one thing (all about facts) but your feelings won't change." (43)

It is the view at least in contemporary philosophical psychology that there is no evidence for "mind" or an "unconscious mind." Rather the reason why emotions are difficult to change is because of irrational beliefs or assessments and because of distorted, ingrained perceptions based on such beliefs. Because of her Freudian view of emotions as irrational, one can see why she mentions a child going to a psychologist "once a week for quite a long time." (48)

6. Again the author invokes the irrational by suggesting that the child interpret his dreams: "When we dream, we are also trying to work out our feelings. Dreams are never silly," (52) and "One thing we know is that dreaming is very important and very good." (53) One might envision a child interpreting the dream all wrong and inducing dreams to guide his activity by. Rather it may suggest that what is worked out by dreams is not so much (or at all) feelings but rather one's irrational assessments or/ beliefs. It would be more helpful to tell the child to concentrate on realistic rational assessments than to have him try to read the symbolism of his dreams. Emotional improvement comes largely with reason and being able to clarify one's irrational statements rather than with irrational magic which leads to the emotion in the first place.

Le Shan could have approached dream interpretation in a clearer way if she had simply spoken of it as metaphorical association. That is, one can use what I call the "metaphorical method." The child would be asked about something occurring in the dream: "What is it like?" This last question asks for a simile, one form of metaphor. Then the child finds what faulty or correct associations he has been making, and is helped to clarify them. He is clarifying his statements not his feelings. By clarifying his statements his negative feelings can almost vanish. Although she calls it dream analysis of feelings, this is what in effect Le Shan was doing. She advises us to ask the child to, "Tell me what it (e.g., thunder) makes you think of." The child was seen to associate thunder with a parent getting angry. And, incidentally, one sees here one of the harmful consequences of the parent's anger. It would seem that anger should not be so readily accepted as being normal as she claims it is.

7. It is suggested that as a therapeutic measure, one should express his negative emotions when they arise. (50) (cf. No. 3 above) To merely be encouraged to be angry or "blow up" may, however, rather lead to encouraging violent patterns of behavior in the child. Just expressing "feelings" does not get at the cause of emotional problems. What is needed is a change of one's irrational beliefs and assessments. One may encourage the patient to "blow up" only as an initial attempt to start him thinking about and assessing a problem he found too painful to think about. It would be irresponsible to have him express anger as an ongoing solution to his problem in place of changing his rational assessments which caused it in the first place.

8. The view is obscurely presented that people have "opposite feelings at the same time." (57ff.) Four objections may be given to this view:

a) They are not feelings but emotions.

b) They are not necessarily "opposites" but merely different.

c) They may not be natural ways of thinking so much as learned ways of thinking.

d) They need not in fact be at the exact same time but rather one may generally love someone but hate a specific act, or hate someone one minute and love him the next.

On the author's presentation, the child or adult may be confused as to how he can have feelings of love and hate at the same time. The irrational and unclear assessment may lead to emotional problems.

9. The author presents the view that life was better long ago and that the modern age is to blame for our negative emotions. This tends to support the view too many people hold that the environment, rather than oneself, is mainly responsible for one's emotions. She states that in the old days:

Children "could have many more adventures," (64) "Life at the time was about as different from ours as it could possibly be," (64) (This view would encourage feelings of there being a great generation gap.) "Many children were happier and more comfortable than some of you about going to school," (69) "Imagine that Bill was born in around 1800... and going from Virginia to Minnesota. He would have been outdoors all the time . . . A perfect life for Bill!" (71)

It is not at all clear that life was better for children long ago and, in any case, it may be seen that it is largely the individual who is responsible for his emotions, rather than the environment. In Utopia, one would still have negative emotions and he needs to know how emotions work so as to dissipate negative ones. We should not say "It bores me," but rather "I bore myself," not "It makes me angry," but "I anger myself."

10. The author states, "Nobody can ever love another person every single minute." (105) On the contrary, if emotions are not feelings but, in this case, ongoing attitudes involving assessments, one can then have a loving attitude all the time. Love is not just a feeling as is being hot or cold. It is important that a child not be discouraged from developing the emotion or attitude of ongoing love. What his particular feelings are at any one time is another matter.

In summary, just as the author feels that it is necessary to have the full range of emotions, from violent rage to positive emotions, so also this book is seen to have the full range of healthful and harmful suggestions for children.

Pleasure

Pleasure is not a feeling but an emotion. It involves assessment and context in a way feeling does not. We say "I feel a pain" but not "I feel a pleasure."

If one says "I have a sensation," nothing can as yet be assumed as to whether it is a good or bad sensation. But even in "I have a good sensation" what good means is not indicated. To say it is good is not to say what kind of sensation it is. It may be a smooth or liked, rough or warm sensation. "Please" derives from the Latin words meaning to smooth or pacify. This suggests lack of pain. Although a good sensation, as a sensation, is no different than a bad sensation, it does differ from other sensations in how it is regarded. To say "I have a good sensation" is less clear than saying it is liked. It is only potentially more, clear than saying, "I have a sensation." It is potentially less clear because "x is a good sensation" may sometimes imply "x is liked." "Pleasurable sensation" functions in the same way as "good sensation." Pleasant and pleasure, as emotion terms or as open-context ethical terms, do not name sensations. To experience a pleasant game is not to experience a certain sensation.

"I like x" may refer to a sensation such as "x tastes good" or refer to an assessment such as "I like reading," "I like her," or "I am pleased that . . ." Pleasure as a like of the sensation type may be referred to as physical pleasure, and of the assessment type, "mental" pleasure. Physical pleasure is more like mere sensation, whereas "mental" pleasure is like emotion: "Mental pleasure" may be regarded as linguistic assessment which guides feeling. Pain may be the opposite of bodily pleasure but not the

335

opposite of "mental" pleasure. Another reason that pain has no opposite is that pleasurable sensations are not so distinct as pain. Such sensations would be tastes, erotic feelings, etc. It makes no sense to ask how pleasantness feels because it is a value judgment or assessment of a feeling. Circularly put, sense pleasure always feels good. "Mental" pleasure always is good. Because pleasure is an emotion it is not an object as such but a modifier, qualifier or description of a complex experience. One cannot seek pleasure as such. It is possible to seek pleasurable sensations or pleasurable intellectual activities. We do not do a hobby for pleasure, it is the hobby which is pleasurable. It is not possible to have the pleasure of or enjoy golf without engaging in the activity of golf. The pleasure of writing is not the same as the pleasure of golfing. The pleasure of your company is not the pleasure of looking at a sunset or watching a thunderstorm. There is no smile without the Cheshire cat. The goal is not pleasure itself but the pleasure of playing golf. One could, however, be pleased merely by thinking of playing golf.

Sensations have duration, degree, number, are usually localized, are physical, usually have an organ of sensation. Emotions are not like this, even if one includes the brain, because emotions often partly describe a context and motor behavior. Pleasure as an emotion is not instantaneous, numberable, localized, physical, and has no organ of sensation. Do not ask, "Where did you enjoy playing tennis?" We do not have flashes of pleasure. "It hurts me to spank you more than it does you." Where does it hurt? (Example given by T. Penelhum) Being full of joy is not like being full of food. Joy cannot be measured as food can. How much joy do you have now? Bentham's "hedonistic calculus" works well neither with sensations nor with emotions. Feelings or sensations are like processes, whereas pleasure and emotion are like classifications. Emotions describe complex patterns of events.

Saying "I feel a pain," referring to a sensation need not imply that pain is a definite entity or "internal" state. "Pain" gains part of its meaning as a part of a language and contextual usage. Pain nevertheless is more definite as a usage regarding bodily sensations than is pleasure. Pleasure is false seems like a contradiction or conceit, but because pleasure is an emotion involving assessments there may be false or true pleasures. Put differently, if one has no beliefs he can have no emotional pleasure. Plato in *Philebus* (Book IX) says that some pleasures are false. One may be pleased about one's work until he finds that it is monotonous. Cigarettes and alcohol may be pleasurable until they are reassessed as harmful in terms of their consequences. They may still produce pleasurable sensations but even the quality of the sensations may be altered until the smoking and drinking is given up. Sensations may be somewhat altered and tastes changed in the same way that emotions are changed. Nevertheless it makes less sense to ask why one has a sensuous "like" than to ask why he has an emotion. It is merely asserted here that even likes, to some limited extent, may be altered and so be true or false likes, justifiable or unjustifiable. The above examples may be seen to be false pleasures. We are responsible for our emotional development as well as for our likes, dislikes, and sensations. Experiencing pleasure and liking can be hard work.

One reason why one cannot be happy and not know it, or be pleased and not know it, is because happiness and pleasure are emotions and involve cognition. One would not be able to have sensations or feelings either, without being aware of them. There is speculation as to whether this is the case with insects and animals. A third person perspective may involve the ascription of happiness or pleasure to someone who had never thought of such terms. At social gatherings one may be reminded, "Isn't this fun." The statements may be more suggestive than descriptive. In one respect one cannot experience pleasure or happiness, as such, if he has never learned our language. He may experience something or other but it may have no equivalent in our language-bound experience.

An action alone does not suffice to produce pleasure. The same action may be pleasurable under one description and painful under another description. Thus when a man puts his arms around a woman it may be assessed either as being an embrace or as being mauled, and the feelings experienced vary accordingly.

Mixed pleasure refers to mixed language-games. Mixed emotions involve diverse or even conflicting assessments. "Mixed emotion" may be considered as the name of a single experience on par with any other emotion. It may also refer to alternating one emotion with another.

One may enjoy the enjoyment of golf or dislike a pleasant experience, dislike the pleasure of smoking. To do so merely involves assessing an emotion, that is, assessments-plus-feelings about assessments-plus-feelings. One difficulty here is where the feelings of both types are experienced at the same time. This may also yield mixed emotions.

G. Ryle, in *Concept of Mind*, distinguishes between feelings of pleasure and the surprises, reliefs, joys, elations, amusements, glows of rapture which, though called pleasures, are moods. To want to play golf and not want to do anything else, to enjoy golf is an inclincation. Several types of pleasure mentioned by Ryle are:

1) pleasure, enjoy, and like refer to "propensity-fulfillments," e.g., golfing is one's pleasure and not a means to pleasure. We do not have pleasure in addition to the golfing.

2) pleasure, delight, transport, rapture, exultation, joy, name moods and signify agitations, e.g., "crazy with joy." The moods may involve feelings such as "thrills of pleasure." Moods are not feelings.

Sensations seem to be neutral in a way. Ryle states, "Most sensations and feelings are neither enjoyed nor disliked." (109) We can always ask if he enjoyed a particular sensation, e.g., "Did you enjoy the tickle?" The tickle may even be felt as uncomfortable. Enjoying is not a mood because one can "be in the mood to enjoy." Like, want, desire are not feelings. Pain is not the opposite of pleasure because pain is a specific sensation. The main point developed here is that pleasure and pleasure terms such as liking, joy, desire, are not internal states or feelings.

In *Dilemmas*, Ryle gives the following account of pleasure. Pleasure is not a feeling as is pain. To talk about the pleasure of reading is to talk about reading not about a feeling. The sensation theory cannot account for the fact that pleasure relates to an object. We ask if a certain sensation is pleasant or not, but not if pleasure is pleasant or not. To enjoy a game is not to do two things: 1) enjoy the game 2) enjoy special feelings. To enjoy the game one must heed or know he is enjoying. Pleasure cannot distract one from the pleasurable activity. It is a heed or attention concept. [To speak of pleasure as a heed concept is to give some support to an assessment theory of emotion.] Enjoyment and pleasure do not have duration in the way sensations do, such that one can enjoy something quickly or slowly. Enjoyment is the quality of an activity, a transitive verb. Ryle states, "We cannot conceive of enjoyment occurring on its own." To enjoy a tingle is not to have both a tingle and an enjoyment. An enjoyment does not outlast the enjoyed walk. Ryle's point is that category-mistakes result in dilemmas, pleasure is not feeling, pleasure is not the opposite of pain. It is a mistake to say that x is performed for pleasure. He states, "Dilemmas derive from wrongly imputed parities of reasoning."

1) Pleasure may sometimes refer to localizable sexual or stomach sensations.

2) "Pain" may also be used in a non-localized way, e.g., "a painful experience." (But this would be a metaphorical use.)

3) That pleasure is not like pain, does not show that it is non-episodic. Pleasure is an episode word referring to episodes but not feelings.

4) Pleasure seems to be a "state of mind" we are in when enjoying something. The term is then used derivatively to describe certain feelings. (Again, as a metaphorical use.)

5) Enjoyment is a response to stimuli. This is why it is a transitive verb. (Enjoyment cannot be just a response if it includes assessments. The stimuli may be the assessments.)

6) Penelhum rejects the view that pleasure is a dispositional heed concept because to report that someone is enjoying something we mean partly that something is occurring. (This is correct in the sense that emotion terms include reference to some feelings.)

7) Penelhum favors a private episode view of pleasure. I do know better than others if I am enjoying myself and so enjoying is logically like pain. It is not adequately explained on the disposition view. Also we cannot be mistaken about our enjoyment. (Without raising the question of what evidence we have for "private states" it would seem that pleasure does include reference to feelings and that I know my feelings and assessments in a way others do not. Thus pleasure is not adequately rendered as a disposition of behavior. On the other hand, Ryle seems to include so much under disposition that it may include the statement that if one has certain assessments then certain feelings follow. This is not to say that some character traits need be statements about feelings. Penelhum says that we cannot be mistaken about our enjoyment, but if enjoyment involves assessment and confusable linguistic categories it would rather seem that we can be mistaken about them.)

8) The dispositional theory cannot account for degrees of enjoyment. (The objection is false because dispositions are qualitative and involve assessments and diverse factors.)

9) For Ryle pleasure is the frame of mind in which we do things, thus we cannot enjoy activities of others. (This is a false objection because, for Ryle, a frame of mind involves assessments of others.)

10) Penelhum says that we cannot enjoy at will. (This is false because by changing our assessments we can induce positive feelings, and we can even learn to enjoy things. He makes the mistake of thinking that pleasure (emotion) is passive.)

11) Enjoyment does occur at a definite time and does have duration though it is not fast or slow. Pain is not fast or slow either. (Because emotion partly describes feeling, some duration may well be involved. In ordinary language emotion terms demarcate various aspects of a situation, e.g., process aspects versus completion or achievement aspects, temporal aspects, degree, etc. Thus, enjoyment is said to have duration sometimes, but not to be fast or slow. One may enjoy sensations, activities, success, etc. or be pleased that "something is the case." And this is just to say that pleasure terms involve different assessments, and that they are used in many different language-games.)

Anthony Kenny (1963) says that an action may be enjoyed as described one way but not enjoyed if described differently. For example, one may enjoy making love to a woman, but not to his mother. What is had here is something like "I enjoyed$_1$ and did not enjoy$_2$ making love to my mother," where enjoy$_1$ is mere physical enjoyment, and enjoy$_2$ involves assessment. But both types of enjoyment involve assessments which guide feelings.

Sources:

Anthony Kenny "Pleasure" Action, Emotion and Will London: Routledge and Kegan Paul 1963

T. Penelhum "The Logic of Pleasure" Essays in Philosophical Psychology D. Gustafson, ed., New York: Doubleday 1964

Gilbert Ryle "Enjoying and Wanting" The Concept of Mind New York: Barnes and Noble 1949 pp. 107-110

Gilbert Ryle "Pleasure" Dilemmas Cambridge University Press 1960 pp. 54-67

An Analysis of Love

"Only a wise man knows how to love." (Seneca)
"They do not love that do not show their love."
(Shakespeare)

Introduction

The word "love" is very familiar. This is unfortunate. It suggests that we know more about love than we really do. Everyone believes himself to be an expert on the subject. Love is said to be the most important emotion, the most worthwhile goal, the criterion for marriage, etc., yet clear and adequate definitions and analyses of love have never been given. The philosophical and scientific literature on love is meager and practically non-existent. The following statements concur with this view:

"One ought . . . to be surprised that a thing which plays throughout so important a part in human life has hitherto practically been disregarded by philosophers altogether, and lies before us as raw material." (A. Schopenhauer *The Metaphysics of the Love of Sexes* p. 338)

"Few authors define love." (R. Hazo *The Idea of Love* p. 6)

"In the interest of self-knowledge no better theme for investigation can be chosen than love, for all of human activities love is the most revelatory . . . The knowledge of persons requires cultivated skills on the order of any art or science. It is surely ironic that we readily acknowledge such prerequisites for the study of atoms, stars, or fossils, yet we do not dream of asking of ourselves a like effort toward the knowledge of persons." (D. Norton, Mary Kille *Philosophies of Love* p. 7)   .

"I think that we must begin reforming the topical ideas of this magnificent sentiment, because love is now in a very confused state." (Ortega *On Love* p. 108)

Thus the familiar word "love" should be made strange. This strange-making may be brought about by pretending we are children who hear the word "love" for the first time. Pretend we have never heard the word though we use it all the time. It is found that the most obvious questions such as "What is love?" are the most confused and most difficult to answer.

Another way of making "love" strange or giving insight into it is by use of the metaphorical method. In accordance with this method one may gain insight into the meaning of love by:

1. thinking of love in terms of a certain model or metaphor, e.g., "love is sex," "love is understanding," "love is communication," etc. and then expanding the metaphor.

2. realizing that any definition given of love is only a metaphor which is expanded and so should not be taken literally. To take one definition or metaphor literally is to be captivated by a metaphor, to commit the metaphor-to-myth fallacy, or create category-mistakes or naming-fallacies. With love there are many paradigms for use. "Love" may mean many different kinds of things. People in the past have erroneously sought to reduce them all to one type. Often they play one against the other such that if there is one type there cannot be the other. Also love in youth is not the same as love in old age, mother love is not like romantic love or love for a man. A woman may have a passion for her infant but not a romance with it. It is a category-mistake to think that love in animals is the same as love in humans, or that one can love his cat or rabbit as he loves a person. This is a "pathetic fallacy" — attributing human emotions to animals. Bunnies and women are different kinds of things.

3. substitution (synecdoche, metonymy) and juxtaposition of the metaphorical term in place of the word "love" wherever it occurs, e.g., "I love you," may become "I understand you," in order to distinguish the term love from related

terms and to gain insight into the word "love." The word may also be put in contexts which are usually quite foreign to it, e.g., "Rational love," "poet of women."

When in love one becomes emotional, speaks of the loved one in extravagant and metaphorical terms. The lover's world and he are metaphorically transformed. He perceives differently, sees a different world. This is the metaphorical device of seeing-as according to which scientists and others see the world in terms of their judgments, expectations, needs and theories. One's very perception is affected. (See W. Shibles *Metaphor*)

A few of the characterizations and types of metaphor are as given below. (See also the chapter, "The Metaphorical Method of Therapy.") Ortega spoke of a "rhetoric of love." Here the similarities between love and metaphor will be given or, put differently, love will be seen as metaphor. Both love and metaphor involve:

1. Insight-giving or disclosure value. Metaphor can give insight but love is often also regarded as a form of knowledge. Also, being in love gives a new perspective of life. We say "It is better to have loved and lost, than never to have loved at all."

2. Reciprocal metaphor whereby either term (person) may modify the other. Each lover modifies the other.

3. A combination of opposites or unlike terms. Man relates to woman, love often involves jealousy, melancholy or hate.

4. Tension metaphor produced by combining opposites or unlike terms. There is tension created between male and female also — "The battle of the sexes."

5. Paradox, mystery, wonder, marvel, puzzle, the mystical are produced by both metaphor and love. Love is thought to be mysterious and paradoxical. One has this feeling about that which he does not understand. Love in this sense may be like the feeling one has when faced with a paradoxical metaphor. Romantic love, especially, is mystical yet marvel-

ous, a frustration-induced confusion. It is something one cannot understand and have at the same time, for clarification and rational understanding might kill it.

6. Imagination. Metaphor and love are both imaginative activities or are regarded as such. It is not that there is a mentalistic "imagination" but that imagination is metaphor, is the concrete deviant activities involved in love.

7. Constitution and description of reality.

8. Constitution and description of emotion.

9. Deviating from usual diction, grammar, usual contextual or situational use of words, normal behavior, established categories, and deviation from culture, custom, habit, the expected, familiar beliefs, what is considered proper, the practical, the logical, the self-evident, the every-day, the literal, the real, the usual cause and effect order of events. Poets, lovers, and philosophers are often thought to be mad.

10. Rejuvenating one's thinking, making it alive by means of new perspective.

11. Nonsense. Both love and metaphor may be regarded as play.

12. Elliptical and suggestive statement. Love is an obscure and open-context term and metaphor may not be reduced to a single meaning, but many.

13. Ornamentation of the literal.

14. Imagery, vision, and pictorial representation.

15. Rendering a great mass of material concisely. Love, also, narrows scattered desires.

16. Shock, surprise, crisis. One "falls in love." Romantic love may be thought of as a defense mechanism against frustration.

17. Intuitive presentational immediacy. There is a passive or given aspect of certain passionate types of love as is the case with the givenness of metaphor. The poet has his muse.

18. Catharsis, escape, or therapy.

19. Double perspectives. There are two terms of a metaphor, two people in love.

20. Synthesis, fusion or unification.

21. Transgression. There is poetic license and the self-justification of love.

22. Synaesthesia. Mixing of senses is involved in the love experience as well as with metaphor.

23. Analogy and simile. Love is described and the lover seen in terms of likenesses and analogies.

24. Wit.

25. Experiences of the sublime, transformation, transcendence, transference. Both love and metaphor may produce such feelings but they do not in fact give access to the sublime. They are merely feelings of love or of the feeling of experiencing certain types of metaphor.

26. Hyperbole, conceit, farfetched and subjectively based or imagined connections.

27. The concrete. The abstract is rendered by or condensed into the concrete.

28. Euphemism, e.g. "make love."

29. Seeing-as, illusion, perceptual, or behavioral metaphor.

30. Fixation and exclusion. One may be captivated by love or metaphor thus disallowing him to see in any other way.

Now that "love" is made new and unfamiliar we can begin to see what it is like. The first way of doing this is to see how the word is used in ordinary language. About each use we may take the attitude, "How curious." How curious, for example, that sex is related to love, that one loves both ice-cream and women, that one can only love one other person, that love is thought of as if it is always the same — all love is romantic love or all love is irrational, etc.

An examination of our language suggests that "love" is an abstract and vague or open-context term. Put directly, when we talk of love we do not know what we are talking about. Consider the statement, "We must love our neighbor." The statement in itself means nothing. It is not like, "We must feed our neighbor." Giving food is not like giving love. It would be a category-mistake to think so. For the statement to have meaning a context is needed. We must know who the speaker is and what he is like. We may then only guess at the meaning. Some of the possible meanings of "We must love our neighbor," are that we must: talk with him, desire him, give him pleasure, give presents to him, not abuse him, respect him. The word "love" itself does not indicate which meanings are intended. "I love her," is not a descriptive term in the same way as "I am carrying her" is. Hazo wrote,

"Before issues about love can be discussed, it is necessary to describe the sense in which the authors who write about love are all concerned with the same subject." (*The Idea of Love* p. 38) and "Perhaps every human action has been called in one way or another – an act of love." (p.4)

T. Reik wrote,

"Love is one of the most overworked words in our vocabulary. There is hardly a field of human activity in which the word is not worked to death." (*A Psychologist Looks at Love* p. 207)

Sigmund Freud spoke of the

"casual and undifferentiated way in which the word 'love' is employed by language." (*Civilization and Its Discontents* Ch. 4)

Jung wrote,

"Thus we find ourselves in the unprofitable situation of beginning a discussion about a matter and a concept of absolutely unlimited extent and indefiniteness." (*Contributions to Analytical Psychology* p. 207)

Now it may be suggested that to use the word "love" as if it is meaningful in itself, is a naming-fallacy or category-mistake. Thus the commands "Love," and even "Love your neighbor" are in themselves empty. One does not know quite what to do. It is not clear quite what has been done when one says, "I love you."

What might be expected when this is said? We may have some vague idea – or we might be quite surprised: "I didn't know that's what you had in mind," or "The reason I punish you is because I love you." Such findings may be found to be less or more than interesting.

The person who uses the word "love," probably does not know what he means by it. Thus the word wherever it is used should be challenged. "I love you," may be followed by "What do you mean by that?" This is perhaps anti-social but still is an important strange-making procedure which can yield insight. It will be found that the lover is a stutterer, a maker of hyperbole and otherwise extravagant metaphor, in a word, a poet ("poet" means "maker"). "Love" characterizes a vagueness one experiences. Because he is not clear what he means by love it becomes an obscure term or naming-fallacy. One begins asking how he can love, or whether he loves anyone, e.g., "Of course I love you, I bought you an ice-cream didn't I?" To use the word "love" as a quality or entity meaningful in itself is no good. Love is more of a class word, a word elliptical for a number of different sorts of things in different linguistic and situational contexts. The view opposed here is that "love" stands for some special sort of metaphysical or mystical entity which cannot be reduced to concrete elements. One says, "Well what about love? That is one thing that you cannot reduce to particulars, to concrete things. It has a meaning all its own." This is said by people who do not know how to love. They cannot know how because they do not know what love is. They may ask "I wonder if I am really in love?" How can they ever find out? A method of dealing with the word "love," as with all abstract words, is to reduce it to concrete paradigms or uses. When we use the word "love" in any particular context we should be able to say what it means. In this way one would be better able to love. Thus, for example, love for another may mean that you listen attentively to him, speak honestly and openly to him, become physically close to him in a number of ways, experience certain feelings in his presence, etc. All of these paradigms are or can be made concrete. We can, then, have a theory of love. "Love" is an elliptical or open-context term standing for specific elements of this sort. It has a number of uses in our language. "I love ice-cream," means often "Ice-cream tastes good." Love is what you say, what you see and do. It is in this respect a very immediate unmysterious thing. Poets often represent love by such concreteness. Thus, love does not have a non-empirical abstract meaning. It is not a supernatural paint which we spread on our lives. God is not love, only the paradigms of our own beliefs in God constitute what we mean by love. To think that words symbolize a metaphysical realm is to be shot through with Cupid's arrow. It is a cupidity for the unknown.

Romantic Love

Love is regarded as an emotion. Emotions are not feelings or internal states. Therefore, love is not a feeling or internal state. But we know that anyway. Love involves an object, situation and language. "I love you" spoken in the usual circumstance is a use and means its use. Because "love" represents or is elliptical for these various factors it does not merely stand for or name an internal state or feeling. To be in love is to be in love with someone or something, and those objects are not internal. Feelings, on the other hand, do not have objects. One may feel pain or feel sexy. One reason why love is not merely sex is that sex is largely feeling, but love is more than just feeling although it may include feeling. The expression "fall in love," and romantic love place more stress on feeling than does "I love my country."

Like an emotion, love may be defined as judgments (or assessments) which guide feelings. The judgment may precede, be coexistant with, or follow the feeling. The experience of "falling in love" seems to be a feeling that overwhelms the lover. It is rather the case that the feeling is preceded by and involves a number of assessments. One is interested in music, has expressed a like for tall men, prefers people who speak softly and are a little shy, etc. One day after a beautiful concert she is impressed with, she stays to talk to the musicians. One of them is shy, speaks softly, etc. She "falls in love." In this case, the assessments precede the feeling and love is seen not to be merely a passionate feeling but to involve assessment. Without assessment being involved one may fall in love with a telephone pole as easily as with a person. Nevertheless "falling in love," romantic love, "love swoons," stress the case where feeling and assessment appear at the same time. "Falling in love" is largely due to the possibility of the attainment of greatly desired but hitherto lacking objects or experiences. Prominent factors are loneliness, sexual frustration, desire to communicate about common interests, desire for security or protection against society, parents, or problems. If the frustrations have been great the more likely it is that one will "fall in love" rather than just begin to love. If there are no strong desires or frustrated needs one will probably not "fall in love."

"Falling in love" with someone suggests accidental falling, passion or passivity as if one has no choice in the matter. But such love for another may be as much an expression of his own desires as it is of another's qualities. Assessment and imagination are involved and romantic love is not just passive.

Love which involves care, concern, on-going understanding would stress assessments which precede and guide feelings. It is this sort of love which may be said to be mature love, though all types of love may be desirable.

Love based on assessments of feelings may be exemplified by someone who, for example, recounts pleasurable intimate and sensual experiences with a woman and decides that he is in love. (See section on erotic love)

Romantic love may be regarded as the experience of "falling in love," or historically as a special form of courtly or chivalric love. *Webster's Dictionary* defines "romance" as:

"To exaggerate or invent detail or incident, to carry on a love affair with, something that lacks basis in fact; a passionate love affair." "Romantic" is: "impractical in conception or plan (visionary); marked by the imaginative or emotional appeal of the heroic, adventurous, remote, mysterious, or idealized." "Romanticism" is: "an emphasis on the imagination and emotions . . . an exaltation of the primitive . . . an interest in the remote, a predilection for melancholy."

Romantic love like "falling in love" involves frustration or unfulfilled desire as a necessary ingredient. It is "unfulfilled love." When one finds someone who suddenly meets such needs and desires he experiences romantic love or he "falls in love." A distinction may be made between romance based on one's needs being met, and romance based on one's desires being met. Basic needs stress the primitive the romantics extoll, or involve sexual and bodily satisfaction. Desires may be imagined and fabricated such that romance based on desire may take nearly any form such as that of chivalric and courtly love. This sort of love depends upon how one views love and what roles he has chosen or learned to play.

Romance as in the legend of Tristan and Isolde, in Romeo and Juliet, or Don Quixote involves need, desire and obstacles. The more forbidden the love, the stronger it becomes. The more social customs are threatened, the higher the wall is to climb, the more the self-sacrifice, the greater the physical and psychological distance between lovers, the greater the "passion." Don Juan even has an affair with a nun. Romantic love is a paradox, a combination of opposites, an oxymoron, or tensive metaphor. The greater the frustration, the greater the love. For romantic love one needs mainly to erect a series of endless frustrations and obstacles to prevent full consummation of the love. A student might fall in love with a married teacher, or vice versa. *"Amour"* refers especially to an illicit love affair. Both courtly and chivalric love involve chaste love. The lover seldom or never sees his love except at a distance. To fully obtain such love is to lose the romanticism involved, the feeling of hope that all of one's desires and needs will be met. When such lovers learn all about one another they find that only certain earthly and limited desires can be met. Thus romantic love requires distance. The loved one is being used as a symbol of all of one's hopes including perhaps also that of eternal life. This is one meaning of the expression "love is eternal" or "eternal love." Romantic love to be romantic must never touch down.

Courtly or chivalric love may be thought of as role behavior or ways certain members of society are expected to act. In this sense, one may be involved in courtly love without experiencing any special romantic feelings. Insomuch as courtly and chivalric love are expected or cultural ways of behaving they may differ from romantic love which involves romantic feelings. An exception to this is when the person is expected to have certain feelings also. Besides being a form of role behavior, courtly love is partly a rhetorical device, language-game, or literary conceit. Morton Hunt in *The Natural History of Love* characterizes chivalric love as follows:

1. True honor comes only from serving a lady.

2. The woman must be someone the lover cannot marry.

3. The love must involve frustrations and obstacles. The lover would do battle, go on long pilgrimages, sleep in ditches, and otherwise humiliate himself for the loved one.

4. Success in battle is attributed to the inspiring influence of the woman. The love of an idealized woman is thought to make a knight a better person as well as give him special powers as a warrior.

5. True love must be clandestine. The knight tells the woman that he has secretly been in love with her for many years, and how he has fought for her.

6. The melancholy and frustration arising from attempting to serve one's lady are greatly enjoyed. Her lack of acceptance or criticism of him makes the love even greater.

7. The knight may marry but is not expected to love his wife. His true love is for his idealized woman. It was declared in 1174 that:

> "Love cannot exert its powers between two people who are married to each other. For lovers give each other everything freely, under no compulsion of necessity, but married people are in duty bound to give to each other's desires and deny themselves to each other in nothing." (Hunt 143-144)

8. The love for the idealized woman must remain "pure." If she finally accepts the knight it is only to kiss him or be held by him and seldom or never does it involve sexual relations.

Four stages given of the relation of the knight to his mistress are: 1. *fegnedor*-asperant to love, 2. *precador*-suppliant,

3. *entendor*-recognized suitor, 4. *drut*-accepted lover. These stages suggest role-behavior.

Romantic love has a close relation to death because of its relation to hope for eternal life, but also because death ensures the ultimate in on-going or eternal frustration which romantic love thrives on. It is the ultimate obstacle and provides the ultimate love. This is an element in *Romeo and Juliet, Tristan,* and love-pact suicides such as are especially common in Japan. Even here the expected role-behavior aspect cannot be overlooked. The "life is death" and "death is life" theme is central to poetry and literature, e.g., tomb-womb poems of Dylan Thomas.

"Romanticism" was defined earlier as involving "a predilection for melancholy." In the *Anatomy of Melancholy* (1651) Robert Burton devotes several hundred pages to what he calls "love-melancholy." Melancholy would be a natural outcome of frustration. Whereas "falling in love" or passionate love involves hope and possibility, depression comes when one's hopes diminish, and when hope is vanished, there is despair. Thus romance alternates with depression and in a romance one is played against the other. In this way extremes of emotion alternate in almost a manic-depressive way with every "yes" and "no" of a woman's reply. Romantic love is the "yes" in a "no," and the "no" in a "yes." Love is simply the "yes."

In romance one goes from absolute lack or nothingness to all that can be imagined, without achieving anything but the experience of love itself. In romantic love, if the goal is achieved the love is lost. This is its madness. It must defeat itself to exist at all, violate protective laws, use clever schemes to defeat intelligence, or involve clever deception. It is "infatuation," which is defined by Webster as "to make foolish; to inspire with a foolish or extravagant love or admiration." The lover is in ecstasy, that is, outside both himself and the world.

Romantic love is nice. And it was seen how it may be induced. It may also be thought of as a defense-mechanism which, like other defense-mechanisms, does not really defend. Because thwarted drives and desires are about to be met, overwhelming feelings and apprehensions are experienced, and perception is affected. A plain and ordinary woman or man may be seen as the center, cause, and controller of the entire universe. How could this be possible?

A glass of water is a quite ordinary thing. When seen, one does not ordinarily remark about it, "Look at that! It's a glass of water!" Imagine, then, being on a hot desert for many days without water. Visions of oases and fountains begin to appear, quartz turns into fluid, clouds are milky, the desert is swampy under foot. Now describe the glass of water. It has become religious. Ortega in *On Love* wrote,

"There exists, in my opinion, a more profound similarity between falling in love and mysticism than has heretofore been observed . . . The lover tends to use religious expressions . . . Every lover calls his beloved divine . . ." (57-58)

Divine love itself is an idolatrous imaginary sort of illusory love. For this and other reasons given earlier, God is not love. Robert Frost put it this way:

"Earth's the right place for love: I don't know where it's likely to go better." (*Birches*)

In romantic love our perception and assessment are distorted, as a defense-mechanism, as an attempt to cope with our frustrated needs and desires. We imagine what we wish. Romantic love requires that we never love a real person, the person himself. Romantic love is a seeing-as, a metaphorical perspective deviating from the way in which we normally see others. "Falling in love" involves perceiving metaphorically, illusion. All is seen in terms of the loved one. She is that which metaphorically unites all things, the unity in diversity, and so everything may be predicated of her. "You are the sun, the moon, the stars, etc." "How beautiful is this tomato sandwich with the thought of loving you." By love, the grass is qualified. The unifying metaphor overreaches the self thereby dissolving distinctions between the lover and the loved. The lovers unite and become one. There is a transfer. In psychiatric terms, there is a loss of "ego boundary." All is identical with all. This is to say that love is boundless. The lover also becomes one with the world and the loved one gives birth to all things in it. In reciprocal metaphor each term qualifies the other. Juliet is the sun and the sun is Juliet. Romeo can touch her voice. Traditional logic and traditional distinctions dissolve in place of a love rhetoric. Dylan Thomas wrote,

"When logics die the secret of the soil grows through the eye and blood jumps in the sun."

"Blood" may be thought of as love, here, which has a logic of its own — the logic of love.

One's love, like metaphor, has many interpretations. Its meaning is inexhaustible. But the meanings it does have are nevertheless concrete, not abstract ones. The many meanings do not reduce to one single meaning. Love is not just feeling, or understanding, or giving. At this point the lover draws only on metaphor. He says things he has never heard before. And these things add interest to the manic pole. There are worlds here, worlds never known before — and there are no other worlds, certainly not the one known before. Why drink an ordinary glass of water when one can consume an imagined oasis? He begins to speak in flowers. Insanity or madness would ask no less. Thus romantic love was and still may be thought to be a disease.

The romantic lover by means of his defense-mechanisms largely imagines and so creates the one he loves. He idealizes and idolizes her. She allures or enchants as by charms and incantation or fascinates thereby captivating him and holding him spellbound in admiration or wonder. The lover is captivated by a metaphor which becomes for him a fixation. It works like a potion. Falling in love is like falling into metaphor and besides being a tensive combination of contradictions, metaphor involves as-if, make-believe, or fiction. Such metaphors may be connected on the basis of private or subjective associations. According to a popular song, "falling in love is just like falling in make-believe." Love and metaphor involve the surreal. People "fancy one another." This applies for sexual desire also. Ortega wrote,

"Nine-tenths of that which is attributed to sexuality is the work of our magnificent ability to imagine, which is no longer an instinct, but exactly the opposite: a creation." (*On Love* p. 103)

To "fall in love" is to fall out of the world. It is to escape the world. With escape comes release, catharsis, and a feeling of freedom. Love is freedom in this sense. It knows no bounds of traditional perception, thought, action, morality. It is "beyond good and evil." The common expression partly representing the romantic experience is, "All is fair in love and war."

Romantic love is the defense-mechanism by means of which reality is distorted and idealized in order to, as if by magic, make life suit one's desires. Everything is at stake and the lover is profoundly moved by the experience. Romantic love works like opium. In addition to being a defense-mechanism, love also involves other defense-mechanisms as well as a complex rhetoric. This is not to deny that "falling in love" is a marvelous experience and one which one may well want to continually attempt to induce. The romantic lover is a poet of women or a poet of men. What is also needed is knowledge of how to "fall out of love."

RATIONAL LOVE

Love or feelings which are guided by judgment may be rational or irrational. If the judgments are realistic and rational the love may be lasting and mature. If the judgments are unrealistic or based on psychological disturbances the love is irrational. The disturbed and irrational are incapable of rational love. Albert Ellis wrote,

> "Most neurotics have an inordinate desire to receive, and an infinitesimal ability to give, love." (*How to Live With a Neurotic* 40)

In the following, an attempt will be made to deal with both description (what love is usually) and stipulation (what love ought to be). By understanding the nature of love one will be better able to love. In this respect the following is an account of how to love.

Love like any emotion is not merely a sensation within us or an internal state. It is a category-mistake to say "I feel love," and we don't usually say this. "I feel love for you" involves an object and the word "love" partly describes the object, judgments, and situation. Although it does not just describe an internal feeling, some feelings may be present. Love is a feeling one gets when he thinks such and such, e.g., a statement of desire for a certain other person. The specific things thought determine the kind of love involved. Love is not just an unlearned response as some behaviorists say, e.g., John Watson. Some general classifications are often given as follows. Neither term need exclude the others.

   1.   Spiritual versus carnal. Spiritual love involves certain kinds of beliefs and assessments. It is not a rational kind of love, but it may be an enjoyable experience. By "spiritual" is often meant metaphysical or religious. The love would then be no more sound or justifiable than the metaphysics involved. Mysticism by definition is irrational and without justification except for the aesthetic or enjoyable feelings which may be produced. Religious love is referred to as *agape*. In many uses "spiritual" love refers to love which involves more than merely erotic attachment. In this sense only, "spiritual love" may refer to what is meant here by rational love. It is misleading to call it spiritual. To do so suggests an age gone by. "Spiritual" functions here as does "symbolic" or "abstract," but as was pointed out, all intelligible abstractions can and must be reduced to concrete paradigms. To say something is symbolic does not exempt it from reduction to concrete instances. Spiritual is contrasted with natural as though there were a supernatural realm. The belief in the supernatural may be regarded as irrational until sound arguments are forthcoming. Spiritual love may be both unrealistic and may involve consequences which are harmful to those involved. It is a disregard for concern with the world we all know, in favor of another unknown realm. If God has no desires and is not like humans, it is not clear what God's "love" could mean. Equivocation is at the basis of metaphysics.

   2.   Deliberate love versus natural tendency. Natural love, or love which takes place automatically may be based upon irrational beliefs. One may naturally love killing, or automatically be sadistic in relation to the one he "loves." Such love is

unconscious and may be regarded as unenlightened love. Because such love is grounded in one's habits and unreflective beliefs, one's choice of love and way of loving tend to reveal his character. Natural love or unconscious love tends to be undependable and to some extent arbitrary. It is not deliberate and thought-out, and it is not a conscious concern with the consequences of one's actions. It is as if one learned love as a role or habit. It thus seems to be based on cultural tradition and a large amount of self-righteousness. One loves merely because that is how he was taught to act, and that it is a traditional act seems to give justification. This commits the fallacy of argument from tradition or present practice. Unconscious love or natural love also fails to cope with new situations, circumstances or people. Natural love tends to be based on loving others because they are similar to oneself in a number of ways. Thus it is often love which comes easy rather than being benevolent concern. Love as a natural tendency is passive love, love over which one has little control. It is not, then, the case that "natural love" is the best kind. Those who love only naturally also learn to hate and get revenge naturally. Rather, it may be argued that genuine love must be conscious and deliberate, rational rather than irrational. It may be argued that it is wrong to love without knowing what is loved or why. On the other hand, rational love may become habitual and so natural and automatic. But even then, such habits must be periodically reassessed.

3.   Object love versus human love. Objects may be loved more than persons, and persons loved only insomuch as they are means to or involved with objects loved. Friends are often made by giving presents. This is one form of treating people as means rather than as ends. A thief or antique collector may be said to love objects. One may commit the category-mistake of treating people as objects and so regard them as inhuman, as things possessed, etc. It is a joke to say "She melts in your mouth," "She is nice as a juicy steak," "I love her like a hamburger," but we do say, "She is sweet as honey." To treat someone as an object is to deny that he has wishes,

desires, needs, and to ignore that person's ability to think and communicate. To fail to verbally communicate is one way of treating a person as a thing. In this case it would be more like treating him only as an animal. On the other hand, people do have physical bodies and such bodies are objects requiring care.

In order to love a person one must know what is meant by "person." The vagueness of the terms allows much equivocation. "Person" may refer to selected actions, bodily attraction, past accomplishment, racial membership, roles played, occupation, etc. A woman may express love for another by being a good cook but not give in more important ways. Love is not food and food is not a substitute for love. Thus it may be easy to confuse one factor with another, to think one loves everything about a person rather than, for example, just physical beauty, or person as an object. One may love a woman as one loves a painting. Object love may also be contrasted with non-object love, that is love of activities, intellectual interests, conversation, etc.

4. Love of self versus love of others. Love of others may involve altruism or benevolence. Love of self may involve acquisitiveness and selfishness. In one respect, everything one does is selfish insofar as all his actions relate to the self. Each act is his act. Giving and benevolence relate to the self in many complex ways. It may make one feel good to be benevolent, one may stand to benefit materially, or thereby create a friend. Perhaps no act is purely selfish or purely benevolent. A selfish act may be rather one done out of ignorance of the consequences for others. A benevolent act of risking one's life for another makes one feel worthwhile. Altruism becomes egoism. Pure benevolence seems to be an illusion, an impossibility. No act is done merely for the sake of another. We do not love another merely out of benevolence. A man may love a woman, her money, and her beauty as well. A person may be valued both as a means and an end. In love if one identifies himself with another he in effect is loving himself when he loves another. He gives the other the care he would give himself.

Benevolence need not involve self-harm or sacrifice but, in fact, this is often a factor. An act may sometimes be conceived of as benevolent only if it involves more concern for another than for oneself. But such an act may show an intelligent concern for the support of social continuance and therefore be conceived of as promoting one's own interests. It may even be unintelligent to harm oneself for the benefit of others. Helping others in society may be seen to be beneficial to oneself. It is a category-mistake to appropriate all types of benevolence to the self-sacrifice type.

Mother-love is not merely benevolent, because the mother often achieves satisfaction from her child and also she may have little choice but to take care of the child. What is done out of force is not done out of chosen benevolence.

Love for self involves knowing and understanding oneself so as not to feel inadequate. We can only love others as we are psychologically able to love ourselves. This means some will not be able to love others. "Love your neighbor as yourself," may be modified to "Love your neighbor as you would like to love yourself." It is not that a person is too selfish to love but rather not intelligent enough. In addition, "love" is a vague term so it is not clear what "love yourself" means. One who is able and has a sense of worth and well-being may be better able to induce these experiences in others.

Benevolence may be reciprocal and, as was mentioned above, it is seldom pure but perhaps always involves some advantage for oneself. Reciprocal romantic love may be difficult to find because both lovers must be and stay in a special state of frustration. It is rare to find two lovers idolizing one another, because both would have to be in special psychological states. Reciprocal rational love could be more lasting and, in addition, rational love can induce states similar to those experienced in romantic love. One may rationally do the irrational things necessary to induce romantic love. There is no necessity that love be reciprocal. It only depends on one's desires and outlook. He may say to himself that he cannot love a married woman and so find that his negative assessment is a factor contributing to the failure to love her.

In a way, love is not benevolent. Nearly everyone seeks love as the highest goal to be achieved. Paradoxically, by giving oneself to another, by surrendering to another one becomes more of an individual. By becoming less free one becomes more free. This is because by giving oneself, the other person admires him more exclusively and as an individual. The closeness of love is an intimate thing. The lover obliges the loved one if she or he wishes to continue being loved. A sign that the freedom of love is absent is that the person feels dependent rather than love. A spouse feels dependent when she or he is no longer able to love.

5. Good versus bad love. This may include gradations of love, mature versus adolescent love, or even rational versus irrational love. It is maintained here that rational love is superior to other kinds of love but that by means of assessment the various other types of love may be induced for their desirable accompanying feelings.

"Love" is defined by Webster's New Collegiate Dictionary (1965) as follows:

"affection based on admiration or benevolence; warm attachment, enthusiasm, or devotion; unselfish concern that freely accepts another in loyalty and seeks his good; the fatherly concern of God for man; brotherly concern for others; man's adoration of God, attraction based on sexual desire; the affection and tenderness felt by lovers; an amorous episode; the sexual embrace; to hold dear, take pleasure in; to like or desire actively."

The terms used in this definition are defined as follows:

affection — "a moderate feeling or emotion; tender attachment, the feeling aspect of consciousness."

admiration — "a feeling of delighted or astonished approbation."

benevolence — "disposition to do good, an act of kindness."

kind — "of a sympathetic nature, of a forbearing nature, of a pleasing nature, humaneness and interest in another's welfare, a disposition to be helpful."

enthusiasm — "strong excitement of feeling."

devote — "to give up wholly or purposefully, to center the attention or activities of (oneself)."

concern — "marked interest or regard usually arising through a personal tie or relationship."

In the first place, "love" is erroneously regarded as a feeling whereas it may be better regarded as an emotion involving assessments. Regarding love as "the feeling aspect of consciousness" or "affection (feeling) based on admiration" comes closer to an acceptable definition. Love is, then, a feeling which involves the following:

1. approbation or approval
2. doing good for another
3. sympathy and compassion
4. forbearance, patience or not asserting one's own wishes or rights
5. pleasing, giving satisfaction, being willing
6. interest in another's welfare
7. interest in another person and his activities
8. helping another
9. strong feeling
10. giving up wholly and purposefully to another
11. unselfishness
12. loyalty
13. sexual attraction
14. active desire
15. taking pleasure in another
16. being awed by another
17. idolizing or worship
18. feelings associated with No. 1 — 17.

A number of these characteristics involve value terms such as pleasure (good feeling or good thought), approval (assess as good), doing good, helping (doing good), benevolence (doing good), desire (an impulse toward the good), etc. In addition, there are actions promoting the good of another and a giving up to or obedience to the other's wishes or desires, all of which gives one great pleasure. Pleasing another instead of oneself is found to give one even greater pleasure than if he had pleased himself. As the definition mainly rests on the use of "good," and as "good" is an open-context term, the definition says very little in a concrete way about what love involves. The general characterizations are nevertheless suggestive because most people can think of concrete instances or examples of "good" as they appear in the definition. Nevertheless, it would not support an adequate analysis or clearly demarcate specific instances of love. To say that love involves giving up wholly, surrender, approval, interest, and concern for the other person is suggestive as will be seen at the end of this chapter. Love, as used here, has also to apply to love of objects. To avoid confusion it may be stipulated that love properly and literally refers to love of people, and metaphorically applies to animals, objects, and activities. It is, then, a category-mistake to confuse the following different uses of love:

> "I love Jane."
> "I love everyone."
> "I love driving."
> "I love eating."
> "I love gold."
> "I love that cat."

"Love" is thus seen to be an open-context term. "Love" has a loosely limited range of substitution instances. We only mean certain things by it. It is usually defined explicitly or covertly by means of positive value terms. If one is in love, it is expected that he will be "good" to the beloved, feel an "obligation" to her, and "accept" her. But, as was mentioned, ethical terms are also open-context terms though their usual substitution instances are different than those of "love." Both terms ultimately reduce to empirical descriptions and concrete paradigms, e.g., in terms of likes, wants, cause-effect, etc. Nothing is good or bad in itself but only in terms of consequences. (See W. Shibles "Ethics as Open-Context Terms") Thus "love" implies ethical terms and ethical terms imply concrete empirical statements. Both love and ethics rest, then, on our ability to understand and correctly and realistically assess others and ourselves in various circumstances. It takes intelligence, not just feeling to love and to be moral. Love is primarily judgments and assessments which compose and guide feeling. Ortega wrote,

"If he is not profound, how can his love be deep? As one is so is his love. For this reason, *we can find in love the most decisive symptom of what a person is.*" (p. 178)

Hazo states,

"Desire that is controlled or guided by reason is often called good love or spiritual love." (p. 469)

Plato and Aristotle both believed that the highest love is that of wisdom or knowledge. "Philosophy" means "love of wisdom." It is, then, not an original idea that genuine love includes and involves reason. To ask about love is to ask how we think.

It was mentioned that love stresses ethical notions which in turn rest on empirical and descriptive statements. The abstract term love reduces to concrete statements. Such statements are as rational as one's understanding and knowledge of cause and effect allow. Rational love is intelligent assessment which guides feeling. Socrates' statement that one never does evil except out of ignorance now applies to love: one never fails to love except out of ignorance, that is, one's ability to love depends upon one's intelligence. To love, one must find out about the other person, get to know him. Loving is also knowing how to make one's desires and goals adequate. The rhetoric, however, may take various forms and so be complex. For example, in some cases it may be preferable to think about one's desires thereby underplaying differences so as to aid love. One may need to inquire into what his desires are so as to determine what psychological or other things prevent love.

Love may be thought of in terms of rules for achieving happiness. One may ask, "What would make me truly happy?" It may be again suggested that man's love of the highest sort must be for inquiry, for knowledge. In *Symposium* Plato states,

"Love is . . . a philosopher or lover of wisdom."

Love may be thought of as a special kind of inquiry, a special realistic kind of knowledge, or deep understanding. For this kind of love and understanding both honesty and realistic, concrete, practical assessments are necessary. Those acts which are superstitious, done out of prejudice, based on faulty information or a lack of inquiry may be said to be immoral as well as dishonest love or false love. Those who fail to inquire or who accept dogma may be said to be incapable of genuine love. It may be left to the reader to decide whether buying air-polluting, high-powered automobiles, or giving money to mystical or religious organizations rather than to those who need food or life-saving organizations are moral acts or acts of love. The American Rationalist Associations, for example, point out that churches should not be tax-exempt, because many people perhaps even a majority, are not church affiliated. As in the case of abortion, metaphysical beliefs of a few may have serious harmful effects on others and on society as a whole. The issue partly rests on love of being vs. love of God vs. love of living men or persons vs. love of unborn foetuses or embryos. Much clarification is needed to sort out this complex issue. But whatever the outcome, an act of love is an act of informed intelligence. For these reasons rational love is deliberate and conscious and includes being aware of one's own feelings and of how ethical and emotion terms work.

On this view, a person who merely uncritically takes on the customs of his culture, e.g., a tribal member, cannot be said to be able to love rationally. His love is that determined by a role, by habit. No understanding, intelligence or even choice need be involved. This is like the "natural" or "natural tendency" love discussed earlier. In a sense, then, the so-called "primitive," or those who lack knowledge or awareness, cannot be said to love.

Animals are not capable of human rational love or of romantic love. They can have sexual relations but not human erotic love. This is because cats, birds, ants, etc. cannot assess the way humans do. They do not speak our language. On the other hand, we cannot love like animals do because we do not know how they think or what their "language" is. If the meaning of love is narrowed down to refer to only certain types of behavior excluding human assessments, then stuffed animals as well as animals may be said to love. There is a "smile" on the doll's face. Lewis Carroll's Cheshire cat had a "smile" on its "face." A dog's love for his master is not the same as human love. But actors also may "act as if they are in love," or a member of a social group may play the role of loving. It is a category-mistake and pathetic fallacy to speak of animals, insects, etc. as being capable of the sort of rational love speaking humans experience. Similarly, animals cannot be "friends" of humans in the same way that man is a friend of another man. Sunflowers, insects, and animals cannot rationally love, but perhaps they do not need to. Those who mystically and mistakenly believe in cosmic love, however, regard every movement and attraction as a kind of love, e.g., between iron filings and magnet.

Because people are sometimes unable to communicate with other people or have negative assessments concerning them and so are incapable of human love, they may prefer the uncritical non-human sort of animal love or even "love" of objects. Many regard money in the same way that others regard human love, e.g., it refreshes the soul, each coin is a friend, worth killing for.

The ability to genuinely love presupposes that one is not psychologically disturbed. Love takes a special form for the neurotic/psychotic. It is unrealistic or based on certain character defects such as need for dependency, need for dominance, masochism or sadism, mother or father fixations, "feelings" of inferiority or superiority, paranoia, hostility and anger, inability to cope with and avoid negative emotions. Because most people accept anger and negative emotions as natural or necessary, human relations become strained. One is unable to love others or unable to love others rationally and maturely. Hate, depression and neurotic thought blocks love. The result is alienation and inability to have intelligent friendships. Defense-mechanisms may be thought of as "defenses" against genuine love. The defense-mechanism of "projection" only allows one to imagine another in love with him and so project his love onto another.

The patient often falls in love with the analyst. The analyst has gotten to know the patient thereby providing a basis for love. People are afraid to love, afraid to become involved even with their husbands or wives. Many wives and husbands hold back and never really open up to one another. Parties and alcohol may lower inhibitions but nevertheless be regarded for the most part as artificial contexts and unacceptable for the existence or creation of mature love. Also, the irrational partner of a love relationship would prevent the existence of mature love. These are some reasons why few people can love well. We can only love as well as we can think.

We create love. Love is based on thought and so it is what we make it. It is limited only by our knowledge. We make another person love by our love; cause love in another. Love, then, is a process or activity. It stresses loving rather than being loved. It is something which requires effort. There cannot be a lazy lover. One must work at loving as he would work at his job. Love is the sort of thing which can be taught and improved. Also we can and must make love what we wish it to be as a result of our ideas of love. If love is viewed only as romantic love, mature love may be precluded. Love involves repeating to oneself realistic positive assessments and actions regarding the loved person. This sustains love. Rational love involves opening oneself up to love, making love possible, creating love. It is not something which just happens. Rational love is not to be judged by the amount of passion present (although more positive emotion would probably be present than with romantic love), but by whether the lover has helped to make the loved one a better person, helped him realize his potentialities, especially the potentiality to love.

Once love is seen as realistic knowledge of guiding feelings one can love better, and create love. Total acceptance, concern and surrender become possible. One can meaningfully promise to love another forever — as a dynamic, growing and improving relationship. The sort of experience induced by rational love is a transformation of oneself and experience onto a new level more valuable than any other experience. It is a new kind of knowing. A new person is created. Love makes one beautiful.

Surrender to another can bring about an experience not equalled by any other. Although the experience has been sometimes reported, few people seem to be able to accomplish it or even understand what the experience is. The experience is easily confused because of the number of different things which are meant by "surrender" or "becoming one with another." To surrender to another may mean to give up to an enemy, be a slave of the other, be dependent on the other. This is not what is meant by surrender here. One thing that is meant is that the usual alienating psychological and neurotic blocks to open communication with another are removed. Surrender means freely and reasonably relating to the other person without negative fear of loss of rights or of being manipulated. The assessment that one can only love someone else if the love is reciprocal is a block to surrender. Religious people often claim to love "God" even if "God" does not love back or show "His" love. A mother's love for a child is often not reciprocal. Also, we may surrender to our fellow-man rather than to a fictitious deity.

The feeling accompanying surrender involves the aesthetic experience. In the aesthetic experience one may distance himself from the usual practical, purposive perspective, thereby inducing a certain experience. Things are seen in ways not seen before. One paradigm for the experience of love is the aesthetic experience. The religious experience is also often merely the aesthetic experience. Thus there is seen to be an identity such that love is beauty or the aesthetic experience. Sensitivity training leads one to learn to aesthetically appreciate all of the things around one. In one sort of experience of surrender one similarly creates an aesthetic experience as lover. Two people relate to one another through the metaphorical perspective of love. Two straws are put in a soda, one sips the other's eyes in an immediate sensuous experience of surrender to the moment and occasion. One could call it caprice. This sort of analysis of surrender may partly distinguish some characteristics of European with American love practices. The former involves a different type of aesthetic inducing behavior. The French woman does not love in the same way as does the American woman. Some know better how to live than others.

Surrender may be divided into cases of romantic surrender and rational surrender. Romantic surrender involves the intense emotion and feeling of freeing oneself from frustration and restraint. It often involves sexual surrender. In German, the word for suitor or wooer is *Freier*, to make free. Catharsis, escape, the resolution of conflict, the release of tension may involve types of surrender. A personality change often comes for a woman (or man) after sexual surrender. She may become warmer and more honest and open generally with her partner. She may also become possesive and let the negative aspects of her personality show more easily. A man often cannot feel that he really knows a woman before having sexual relations with her.

Rational surrender involves such things as prevent alienation. Because it is not neurotic or manipulative but involves honest, open, communication, there is an experience of freedom from deceit, superstition, rejection. Defense-mechanisms, talk of total equality, selfishness, fear of possible harm, become minimized. Selfish people cannot love rationally or experience such surrender. It is an experience of letting oneself go, letting oneself become totally human in relation to another. It is an overcoming of oneself, one's fears, and involves the risk of treating another as a fully human being. It involves understanding the other person, whatever he is or does, rather than the emotions of hatred, revenge, jealousy, apathy, etc. The other person is treated as a person, as an end in himself rather than as a means. Such surrender involves acceptance of the other. Someone who is afraid to be seen with another is not capable of rational love or surrender, nor is someone who has negative emotions. Acceptance or agreement takes many forms. One form involves acceptance of diverse views. Surrender in this case involves discussing objectively rather than arguing. In German, the expression *"Wir sind uns einig,"* means "We agree," or literally, "We are one." Acceptance is needed for the experience of surrender. All parts of one's mate may seem almost equally sensuous or desirable. One can also surrender to life. This involves the acceptance of reality as it is, and oneself as part of that reality. The Zen experience moves in this direction. To have faith is to accept, to give up one's doubts. This experience has therapeutic value. If the surrender is genuine or philosophical it will be based on rational and open inquiry, if it is deceitful it will be based on superstition. A strong belief in anything may produce the experience of romantic surrender. Any cause one believes in may unify one's life, but it is not necessarily an intelligent or rational surrender. Genuine surrender to another and to life produces a sublime experience perhaps unequalled by any other. It is an experience beyond good and evil, beyond narrow bounds. It is a surrender into freedom.

"To live without loving is not really to live." (Moliere)
"To enlarge or illustrate this power and effect of love is to set a candle in the sun." Robert Burton (*Anatomy of Melancholy*)

ORTEGA ON LOVE

Several themes in Ortega's book, *On Love*, are that romantic love is madness, and true love is deliberately created and depends on the depth of our understanding. He also shows some awareness of the role of metaphor in matters of love.

ROMANTIC LOVE AS MADNESS

" 'Falling in love' is an inferior state of mind, a form of imbecility." (51)

Romantic love and "falling in love" are said to be passive things, pathological passions, things which just happen to us. They are often based on frustrated needs or desires, especially of a sexual nature. This may account for the desperateness of love. When such needs are fulfilled one falls out of love. It leads to a Don Juan type of love, a series of ever new loves and desires. Such love may be based mainly on physical attraction. "Falling in love" is an abnormal state which is like hypnosis. Like hypnosis, one's attention and thoughts are fixated on a single person or object to the exclusion of others. Our consciousness is narrowed and restricted. We may think about the loved one day and night. This, then, involves both idea, fixation, and repetition. The result is a kind of self-suggestion. The lover loses contact with reality and loses his ego-boundary with the loved one. He becomes her. The state is said to be not only like a hypnotic mania but like the mystic state. It involves fixed imagery or hallucination, and a lack of critical thinking in regard to the loved object. The lover knows no excess, will do anything for his love, and the measure of his love is often irrationally judged by the absurd sacrifices he is willing to make for the loved one. Ortega objects,

"Let us cease believing that the measure of a man's love lies in how stupid he has become or is willing to be." (178)

The ecstatic state of the lover leads to idealization, fiction, and metaphorical thinking. Stendhal's view of love as a crystalliza- tion is said to be based only on one's own imaginings and invention rather than on reality. It is, then, love as a fiction, and such love seems to be like a literary genre or fabrication. "Ecstasy," it is pointed out, means being outside of oneself and outside of reality. (69) Imagination keeps romantic love and sex going:

"Nine-tenths of that which is attributed to sexuality is the work of our magnificent ability to imagine . . . which is a creation." (103)

The supposed decreased ability of women to imagine is given as one of the reasons why women have such a lack of sex drive as compared with that of men. Kinsey and others have given evidence for this same assertion. However, the supposed lack of ability to imagine may rather be due to lack of interest in sex rather than to inability to imagine. Ortega states,

"The notorious disproportion between the sexuality of man and woman, which makes the normally spontaneous woman so conservative in 'love,' probably coincides with the fact that the human female usually enjoys less imaginative power than the male." (103)

"Falling in love" is a kind of dissociation, a dazed distrac- tion, an enchantment as if a kind of mystical magic. The lover, Ortega believes, tends to speak in religious mystical metaphors. This is a madman's "rhetoric of love." (102) Ortega in his article, *"La metáfora"* regards metaphor as a non-identity between two terms which leads to a subjective, ideal identification. The identifi- cation constitutes one's thought and perception (seeing-as).

"Love reaches out to the object in a visual expansion." (17) Metaphor is, then, the annihilation of real relations. It offers us an escape from reality. We see reality in terms of the loved one. Ortega could have noted that the lover sees the world metaphorically in terms of the loved one. The lover, then, would be seen to use more types of metaphor than merely religious metaphors.

Ortega notes that the lover has a constant image of the beloved and that, like the mystic, he may be visionary. One is reminded here of visionary courtly love whereby the image of the loved woman is a goal of conquest and of life itself. Imagery is one form of metaphor which enters into romantic or "mad" love.

Ortega seems to use a metaphorical technique in his analysis of love. He uses metaphorical substitution and juxtaposition. After developing the metaphor or model that love involves mental confusion, he substitutes this notion and states that "falling in love" is like "falling into mental contradiction." (52) Again he, by analogy and substitution, speaks of "falling in hate." (55) The "falling" suggests the unconscious passivity of the state. He concludes that passionate love limits us and makes us lose our reason and so we become love's fool, a slave of love.

In opposition to Ortega's analysis, here, it is not clear why one need avoid romantic love. It appears to be a valuable and desired experience which one may choose not only to engage in but even to rationally seek to induce. It is possible to do this and possible to sustain the state by rational means. Thus, romantic love need not be transitory unless it is kept passive.

The transcendent aspect of love may be explained by the fact that the lover escapes reality by means of metaphor. Once literal language and usual distinctions are transcended all becomes possible, love transcends death, the woman becomes all, all in all, and the world a trifle. Such transcendence, however, to a large extent, turns on hopes of wish-fulfillment and the nature of metaphor. That is, the sublime or transcendent comes about here by means of an extravagant use of metaphor. The lover deceives himself by metaphorically distorting reality and creating metaphors which suggest a mystical state, e.g., "Love conquers death," "You are eternity." Such expressions turn on unfounded metaphysical abstraction. It is talk of a "beyond" where "beyond" no longer has a use. Metaphors give us a feeling of the sublime but not new knowledge. It is only the experience of an interesting metaphor. This is the magic of love, love as a kind of magic.

Ortega himself discusses this feeling in connection with rational love as follows:

"If we love the object an indefinable flow of a warm and affirmative nature will emanate from us." (43)

An interesting observation made is that sexual love is never pure. It always involves numerous judgments and attitudes about the other person. There is no such thing as purely physical attraction. So also, other types of love involve sexual love:

"It is an absurdity to say that a man's or a woman's love for one another has nothing sexual about it." (89)

RATIONAL LOVE

What Ortega speaks of as true love or genuine love I will refer to as rational love, although I do not regard it as completely rational. Unlike romantic love, rational love is active, deliberate and consciously developed and created. Genuine love can come about only by one's own effort and can last and be maintained only in this way.

"Love is not an explosion, but a continued emanation." (14)

"Love is prolonged in time: one does not love in a series of sudden moments or disjointed instants . . . " (13, 14)

"Love is not an instinct but rather a creation." (180)

"Love itself is a transitive act." (43)

"Loving is a perennial vivification, creation and *intentional* preservation of what is loved." (18)

We love because we choose to and want to. We create it. It is not curiosity or desire, madness, or sentimental fiction, but "intense affirmation of another being, irrespective of his attitude toward us." (44) Here, however, Ortega seems to confuse romantic and genuine love. Why should we unrealistically affirm another if the other despises us? On the other hand, Ortega's view of love stresses reason and understanding. In order to love well one must be an intelligent and clear thinker:

"Love is not illogical or anti-rational." (188)

"If he is not profound, how can his love be deep? As one is so is his love." (178)

"Love in its very essence, is choice." (89)

Seneca similarly once wrote, "Only a wise man knows how to love." But Ortega thinks that there are few who seek inquiry or think deeply, and so it would follow that few are able to love well:

"Intelligence is an extremely rare event on this planet." (149)

"Nothing has instilled more melancholy in me than the discovery that the number of intelligent men is extremely small." (150)

"Love is an infrequent occurrence." (181)

Love is said to relate to our ability to think, our past choices, memory, perception, etc. If love is chosen in terms of our basic beliefs and choices it is firm.

"A love which has sprung from the roots of a person, in all likelihood cannot die." (31)

But this statement may well be false if one's beliefs are confused or irrational. Ortega, for example, erroneously thinks that the goal of love is to produce children. (37) If one is neurotic a love "sprung from the roots of a person" may still be so out of touch with reality as to be short-lived. On the other hand, if the love is based on great understanding and continual growth and sharing of new insight the love may be permanent. It may, however, be irrational to believe that love must always be long-lasting or permanent.

Whereas romantic love is a magical way of attempting to solve one's problems, rational love is an intelligent way of producing genuine creative relationships among people. Ortega's view may be expanded. If genuine love depends on intelligence, and if, as Ortega says, most people lack intelligence, then creative love may require that we help others to gain understanding. Love would partly become teaching others, being a therapist to others. In a word, or metaphor, love is therapy.

LOVE AND SITUATIONAL ETHICS

The following is a presentation and analysis of Joseph Fletcher's book, *Situation Ethics*. This is an ethics based on a principle of love and it involves the following.

Situation ethics is opposed to rule-bound legalistic statements which supposedly apply to all situations and contexts in the present and future. Thus it opposes the Ten Commandments insomuch as they are regarded as being unbreakable or fixed laws. Nothing is right or good in itself. "Nothing is worth anything in and of itself." (59) Fletcher's view may be supported by noting that ethical terms are open-context terms and as such are not meaningful in themselves. (See W. Shibles "Ethics as Open-Context Terms) His argument is based on the fact that rules do not apply equally to all situations, whereas it could have been based simply on the fact that ethical terms logically cannot be universal truths or narrowly rule-bound. That is, "x is good" has no meaning in itself but rather has many possible substitution instances. The meaning is determined by the specific context of its use. This factor gives support to Fletcher's view that right and wrong are only determined in a specific context.

Situationism uses rules but only insomuch as they are appropriate to the particular situation at the particular time. It is like the pragmatist view to the extent that the rule in a concrete situation must be evaluated for relevance by means of intelligence. The goals in the situation must also be considered. Reason and a knowledge of all the usual consequences of the total context are stressed. "Situation ethics puts a high premium on our knowing what's what when we act." (84)

This theory may be supported by the view that ethical terms, in spite of the "naturalistic fallacy" of not being able to reduce an "ought" to an "is," reduce to empirical terms, i.e., descriptions of needs, wants, and consequences. For example, "Gift-giving is good," may mean "I like gifts to be given," where "like" is an empirical description. But Fletcher changes this view in stating,

"Reason can note facts and infer relations, but it cannot find values." (48) Supposedly ethical decisions are not based on reason and cannot be right or wrong, true or false. He believes we cannot understand right or wrong cognitively. This view is false if ethical terms do reduce to empirical statement. There is no value or realm of value as such. Perhaps two reasons why he would want to hold such a view is because he is not clear about how ethical terms work and he thinks he must regard likes and wants as non-rational. Likes and wants need not be regarded as non-rational but merely as empirical and descriptive givens.

A further attempt to deal with such givens is to base right and wrong on choice and desire, as if the latter justify actions. Good seems to be based on mere choice. But choice does not justify actions, they are the basis of actions. We have likes, and ethics involves rationally assessing consequences of our actions in order to support those likes. Fletcher himself says in various places that when choosing a course of action in a situation one must consider both the immediate and long range consequences in terms of the total situation, including consequences for others. It is not mere choice alone which determines value. This view then, gives no support to existentialistic ethics.

The stress on choice rather is a stress on reason not merely the feeling or emotion one has in a situation. The decision is not made out of passion, sentimentality or desire, but with consideration and care. However, if Fletcher is maintaining that love is not emotion it is not clear what it could be. Perhaps a better way of putting it would be that love involves reason. Situation ethics is not "antinomian" or based on a completely unprincipled lawless approach as are some existentialistic approaches. Fletcher states, "Sartre refuses to admit to any *generally* valid principles at all, nothing even ordinarily valid, to say nothing of universal *laws.*" Simone de Beauvoir (*The Ethics of Ambiguity*) is also regarded as antinomian in holding that each situation is radically unique and that the world is basically incoherent.

There is, however, one rule, which, Fletcher says, is independent of all contexts. It is the principle of love. Love is rendered by the term *agape*, here, rather than as eros (erotic love). Agape is rational goodwill. He states,

> "Only one 'thing' is intrinsically good; namely, love: nothing else at all." (57)

> "Love is the highest good." (49)

> "Whatever is loving in any *particular* situation is good." (61)

He maintains that love: must be for people rather than things, transcends right and wrong, marriage and chastity; is not based on desire or emotion, is a primary word not definable in terms of something else, is non-reciprocal, is not limited to those we like or those deserving love. What Fletcher seems to have done is to substitute "love" for "good" in the utilitarian formula to yield, "One ought to produce the greatest *love* for the greatest number." It is a universal rather than a limited utilitarianism for he states that love is for all, is pluralistic, not just love for one person. This love transcends marriage and lovers. Henry Ward Beecher once said, "Love is more just than justice." Mary Baker Eddy stated, "To infinite, ever-present Love, all is Love and there is no error, no sin, sickness, nor death."

Several things are wrong with this theory. First the definition of love is none too clear. It seems to be what we ordinarily mean by reason. In that case we are only told that to be ethical one must do that which is rational in any particular context. Thus to produce good is to produce love is to produce actions meeting the needs and wants of all involved. The act must be done out of love and also produce love. To produce love would be to help make others aware and more rational so as to be more able to meet needs intelligently. Also, technically, it is not clear whether Fletcher would choose to produce a limited amount of love for six people, or more love for four, or hardly any love for all.

Love is also said to be an indefinable and non-reducible term. This is false. All abstract terms if they are to be intelligible must be reducible to concrete paradigms or instances. If this is not done confusion and equivocation is the result. And this is the result here, for we would not know what to do to produce love. Love is too vague to use as a criterion of right and wrong. "Love" is as much an open-context term as is "good." To hold that love is indefinable is to fail to understand that love is an emotion and may be defined in terms of the assessment theory of emotion. As clarified by the assessment theory love may stand a better chance of serving as a criterion of good or bad.

It is not clear why one should love everyone else, for its own sake and whether they are deserving or not. (Although it is not obvious or self-evident, my own view is that one should love everyone.) If Fletcher had seen that ethical terms reduce to concrete empirical terms he would see that love also involves concrete actions which have consequences in terms of the situation and prevailing needs and wants. He seems to want to talk both of love as indefinable and as definable in terms of reason and consequences at the same time. If "love" is indefinable it would not be clear how eros (sexual love) can be clearly separated from agape (rational love). The result is that these become mixed in the argument.

Fletcher speaks of the necessity of loving oneself in order to love others. But if love as justice is producing the greatest love for the greatest number, it isn't clear what love of oneself is. Is it merely awareness and understanding of oneself? Also he says love is non-reciprocal. If so would love of oneself be non-reciprocal?

Love supposedly does not involve liking. Then one may love himself but not like himself. In any case, it is not clear that one does have to love himself before he can love others. Why cannot one love himself after or at the same time that he loves others? But it is not clear what love means when it is stated that one must love himself.

It is not clear why Fletcher excludes eros (or sexual love) from *agape*. Why should love exclude sex especially since it is one of the most desired experiences known to man? Fletcher states that sex is all right to have anytime whatsoever just as long as love is served by it. Because love is vaguely defined the reader may get the impression that sexual love is always justified regardless of the consequences. That depends upon whether we take Fletcher's definition of love as being indefinable or as being *agape*, or rational love. He seems to stress the latter not the antinomian view, and so we may conclude that sexual love is not at all self-justificatory but only justified in terms of the reasoned-out consequences of the action. This is in opposition to existentialists and others who hold that the emotion of the moment justifies itself in the situation. On the latter view, people would be constantly looking for and creating situations which may selfishly "justify" otherwise unjustifiable acts. Resulting excuses are given such as "It just happened," "I couldn't help it," "You know how it is," "I had a passion," "An uncontrollable desire came over me," etc. But, then, these are still excuses.

In conclusion, Fletcher does not have a clear idea of the nature of ethical terms, emotional terms, or the term love, but nevertheless does give the helpful insight that there are no absolute truths in the realm of ethical behavior. Rational judgment of consequences and needs is needed in each concrete situation.

LEARNING THEORY OF LOVE

The following is a presentation and critical review of Miller and Siegel, *Loving: A Psychological Approach* (1972). First, some general cautions or criticisms of behaviorism are needed.

Criticisms of Behaviorism in General

There is a great deal of confusion about what is meant by stimulus and response and synonymous terms. In one sense, stimulus-response is just a way of talking about cause-and-effect. Thus philosophical criticisms of cause and effect apply to stimulus-response. Cause and stimulus need not be regarded as forces or as causal "efficacy." Stimulus is not a power in an object. Rather cause and stimulus should both be reduced to concrete paradigms. By cause or stimulus we mean only a certain description of a particular event. This description may then be correlated with another event, the effect, or another simultaneous or prior event. This is in keeping with Hume's definition of cause as a constant, contingent, conjunction of events based on past experience. Thus, instead of caused power, efficacy, or stimulus, one could more carefully speak of an event which one may correlate with another event.

Stimulus, insomuch as it describes a force or power, is a naming-fallacy. Instead of stimulus and response it would be more careful to speak of event 1 and event 2. They are relative terms. A stimulus also has a cause and so is at the same time a stimulus in one respect and a response in another respect. There is no stimulus as such. A stimulus is not like the word "stimulating" or "excitement." An electric shock may make, increase, or decrease blood flow but that is not what makes it a stimulus rather than a response. The shock given can be a response rather than a stimulus. We may, then, methodologically substitute every occurrence of "response" by "stimulus," and "stimulus" by "response" in learning experiments so as to be sure that the naming-fallacy aspects of such terms do not influence us. Such terms are not descriptions, but merely refer to events. It would be more careful simply to speak of events than of stimulus-response.

Cause-effect, and stimulus-response are such vague terms that they are not of much help in presenting a theory. The behaviorist often seems to think something important is being asserted when he says that behavior is learned or is fully analyzable in terms of stimulus-response, reinforcement, extinction, reward, punishment, etc. But these terms are only vague assertions that everything happens in terms of cause and effect. And certainly in this they are right. But they are right only because they themselves impose this vague model on reality. If we want to see things in terms of cause and effect or stimulus-response, we can. It is only up to us. There is no cause and effect as such in nature or reality. These terms are human interpretations of reality. It is only that we see reality that way. We could also see reality differently, e.g., as non-causal, and this is exactly how one does see it when cause is reduced to mere correlation. Correlation can also remove the temporal aspects from stimulus-response and cause-effect. Thus we need not think of cause as prior to effect, or stimulus as prior to response. The *post hoc* fallacy involves the assumption that because something happens before something else it is therefore its cause. Because someone gives another flowers and the other person then falls in love, does not mean the flowers caused the love. If there were no people in the world there would be no such thing as cause and effect.

To say that something is caused or learned says little. The paradigm for learning is based on the observation that behavior can be changed, and this is an important observation to make. This view opposes the view that one's behavior is biologically or genetically fixed or determined, that is, that one cannot basically change his behavior or that one has certain patterns of behavior from birth. The stress on learning shows that one can develop desirable patterns of behavior and extinguish undesirable ones. It is not a fatalism. Some behaviorists, such as Watson, believe that some emotions we are born with and that others are learned. Miller and Siegel believe that love is learned. This, then, allows us to learn it if we haven't, and to improve it. On the other hand, by saying it is learned is not sufficient to explain what it is or how it is learned. To say it is learned by stimulus-response methods is again too theoretical and vague.

Thus, stimulus is a partial description of an event. The stimulus may be regarded differently if described differently. It isolates all possible stimuli in a situation and picks one out as the important event. For example, what is the stimulus which causes one to attend a movie. One may say that he heard that it is a good film, but when pressed, find that there was a manifold of stimuli causing him to see it. Thus for each stimulus-response situation to be adequate a great number of stimuli and responses would have to be reported. Instead of $S \rightarrow R$ we would need $S_1, S_2, S_3 \ldots \rightarrow R_1, R_2, R_3 \ldots$ Too often the behaviorist presents a simplistic or overrestrictive account of behavior by failing to include many of the relevant factors. The most central area of inadequacy is that the behaviorist nearly always fails to include language, self-talk, and assessment in his $S \rightarrow R$ model. He states, for example, money is a stimulus making one respond in a certain way, e.g., work hard. But what is left out of the account is that it is not the money itself which is the main stimulus but rather the assessment of the money. Some people will never do certain things for money. But to find that out we must know of their assessments. Also, assessments themselves serve as stimuli. One may condition himself, as in the case of a critical philosopher. Love, for example, can be created by a person and he can respond with love to unloving people and situations. Our assessments serve to guide our behavior more than simple reactions to our environment. A behaviorism which, as in the case of man, excludes language and assessment would be inadequate. And this is one of the main errors of assuming that animal studies are sufficient to give insight into human behavior. Animals do not speak English (or any other human language). Thus the behaviorist's analyses are often found to fail to hold up. On the other hand, if behaviorism were to include linguistic assessment and imagery, a more adequate analysis could be given. This, then, is not an attack on behaviorism so much as an attempt to make it more clear and adequate.

Instead of speaking of stimuli it would be more helpful to speak of linguistic descriptions. The behaviorist often thinks that he is just correlating one description with another. He is rather correlating one description with another and the behaviorist himself is thinking by means of language. "Behavior," "observation," and "perception" are words in our language and, as such, have epistemological primacy as language. Perception and behavior are seen only through our language. Observation is not an acceptable primary criterion because it presupposes language. Thinking is language use plus some images. Then, to speak of stimuli or behavior is derivative from linguistic assessments of events. To speak of a stimulus it is not sufficient to just point to an object. There is a difference of assessment between being mauled and embraced though the physical event looks the same. Too much concentration on money or objects rather than language assessments as stimuli results in an inadequate and harmful analysis. Because of such assessments a stimulus is not a single physical event but a complex event involving all individuals studied as well as the researcher.

In summary, the basic words of the behaviorist are vague and result in simplistic analyses. He fails to see that linguistic assessment is significant in analyzing human behavior, he fails to see that his scientific method should begin not with observation and behavior but with language (a most important kind of behavior). However, the behaviorist program could be modified so as to be useful.

The first step is to reduce all abstract terms to concrete language-games or specific examples. The use of quantification and statistics is often especially unacceptable as a way of clarifying or understanding human assessments. Wittgenstein stated,

"In psychology there are experimental methods and *conceptual confusion." (Philosophical Investigations 232)*

Secondly, their method must be made adequate by accounting for linguistic assessments as regards human behavior. The above objection was to their methods used and lack of adequacy. With these qualifications behaviorism becomes critical philosophy and I know of no better method of problem solving in a concrete non-metaphysical way.

AN EXAMINATION OF MILLER AND SIEGEL *Loving: A Psychological Approach*

In the above recent book is given a behavioristic theory of love. Although they claim that their presentation is based on learning theory most of their statements seem to be based on their own assessments or judgments from their personal experience. No behaviorial evidence or support is given for such statements, e.g., "The actual change in sexual behavior during the last decade seems to be small." (60) Nevertheless, the behavioristic structure will be presented here first.

The authors state, "Love is learned," "Love is a learned response," "Love is a form of approach behavior." Like other learning, then, love may be described in terms of the basic tools: reward, punishment, stimulus, response, habit, extinction, reinforcement, stimulus generalization (transfer), and discrimination. The authors do, at least, mention "concept formation," although it is neither clarified nor developed. They say, "A concept is made up of several somewhat different stimuli that hang together as a group or class." A concept seems to be a stimulus generalization. But what is a stimulus? They seem to think it is a quality rather than a description or assessment of a quality. The notions of "generalized secondary reinforcers" and "association" (14,15) are vague. They may, however, be made concrete by reducing them to language and language games. The authors' stress is rather on regarding love as approach behavior or going toward an object or person, and hate as avoidance or going away from an object or person. This seems to stress observable physical behavior rather than the assessments people have, and so yields a simplistic analysis. Clouds "approach" each other but they do not therefore love one another. Fear is said to be an aversion or pain signal and hope is a pleasure or approach signal. (5 ff.)

In addition, the authors appear to base their theory on pleasure-pain principles and even seem to develop something like Bentham's now rejected "hedonistic calculus." According to Bentham we should produce the greatest physical pleasure for the greatest number. Mill then altered this because physical pleasure excludes thought or intellectual pleasure. But if pleasure is to include the latter no quantitive calculus is possible. Also a clarification is needed of "pleasure." Is this a want, need, or good feeling? How does pleasure motivate us? Is pleasure an entity or power in itself? Is it an object one seeks? How does pleasure relate to "good" feelings or "good" actions, that is, to ethical terms? These questions are not clarified by these learning theorists. A clarification would bring them into critical philosophy and into seeing that assessments are too diverse to simply lump them under pleasure-pain, approach-avoidance.

In spite of some errors of the above sort the authors do sometimes give token acceptance to language factors. When they do they still use antiquated and unhelpful terms, such as "in the mind," rather than clarifying them. They wrote,

"The love response is an emotion. It is an internal reaction. It is an expectancy. It is central or 'in the mind.' It is a feeling . . . It is all of these." (5ff)

Here "expectancy" may be analyzed as a linguistic assessment rather than as a mentalistic entity. It would be more accurate to say emotion involves feeling or internal reaction than to state it *is* a feeling or internal reaction. "Reaction" here may be more of a mentalistic term than "response" and may be a naming-fallacy unless qualified by stating that love is an "event." But the definition still is not adequate because it states that love involves internal brain, physical and feeling states, and a reaction to an external event. What is left out of the account is that emotion terms are also assessments, and descriptions of situations.

Other definitions given of love are:

"Love is a response to a generalized hope signal, a broad pleasurable expectance." (14, 15)

"Love is a strong generalized approach response to a stimulus that has been diversely and somewhat unpredictably associated with reward." (127)

"Love is a nonspecific expectation of pleasure." (167)

"Hope" and "expectation" may be made more concrete by thinking of them in terms of specific assessments. Then we will have concrete information as to what is meant by such terms, what kind of expectation is involved, how to induce or extinguish them. What is a "generalized approach response to a stimulus"? The abstractness of this expression is almost metaphysical. Does it mean someone often says "hello" and smiles. Approach may mean, ambiguously, physical movement or psychological (by means of assessment) closeness. One reason for talking of generalized response is that the authors believe that strong love involves arousal due to not knowing if and when one will be rewarded by the lover. This supposedly makes for a high degree of expectation and attraction due to desire for need fulfillment. But if so, love is just a kind of frustration of needs. This may be applicable to romantic and courtly love, but not to rational love. What is needed is not so much an extremely general theory about stimulus and response as an analysis of specific cases and assessments. One may, for example, *assess* that "love based on such hit-or-miss rewards is not worth having," and so the generalized response theory would fail to produce love in his case. Love does seem to involve a great many specific actions and assessments on the part of the loved and lover. Love is not an abstract metaphysical thing in itself but can be reduced to concrete specific perceptions, actions, behaviors and statements. The authors state,

"Love is a broad and relatively stable enjoyment of inter-action with the loved object, although it does not serve ex-clusively to satisfy one specific need." (4)

But, that love is vague or refers to a complex of events does not mean that one can effectively analyze love vaguely.

Love is said to be an impulse to act and motivation (5). But to speak this way treats love as an entity. What is meant by "im-pulse," and what is a motive?

Insomuch as the authors speak of approach and escape be-havior as being "mental" as well as physical they deviate from be-haviorism and fall back into metaphysical mentalism. It is also men-talistic to speak of "anxiety," "fear," etc. as if they are entities. It is stated, "Irrational fears and anxieties are found at the heart of neurosis." (87) What is an "irrational" fear or anxiety? Statements and assessments are rational or irrational, not emotions. Emotions may consist only of such statements but the authors are not clear about, nor do they present an adequate account of emotions. "Anxiety" is not a mentalistic entity or an entity of any sort. It is an abstract term which must be reduced to concrete empirical terms. The same problem applies to the term "conflict." What is it a conflict of? Behaviorists often speak of it as if it is a conflict of behaviors. But behaviors cannot conflict. Ideas cannot conflict be-cause there aren't any such mentalistic things. Statements, how-ever, can conflict. Conflict may best be represented as conflicts of language. Other perceptual, motor, etc. conflicts are possible but are not usually what we mean by conflict. One confusion which re-sults from not seeing that thinking is largely language use is the authors' view that childhood concepts of inferiority are experienced only as feelings. (17) One does not feel such statements, only bodi-ly sensation. Inferiority cannot be felt as pain can although feelings may be involved.

Nevertheless, the authors do say some intuitive things about approach and escape behavior which are interesting. Approach and escape behavior is said to be subtle. This analysis may have been more concretely put by mentioning what constitutes such subtlety. It is comprised of faulty and accurate thinking defense-mechanisms, accurate and distorted perception, etc. They note that to move toward X is to move away from Y, a helpful notion in terms of understanding certain kinds of love attractions. They also note that some attraction behavior is based on "anxiety" reduction. Such a relationship is based on a psychological defect and may well be unstable.

In regard to the learning device of extinction, e.g., where one gives up hope, one is said to be able to extinguish love. Love can be learned but also unlearned. Abnormal love is also learned. It is therapeutically helpful to point this out but a qualification may be added. The view only suggests that the learning comes from the environment, whereas one may by reassessing his statements (beliefs) also learn to love, or learn not to love. The authors even seem to adopt Freudian determinism according to which all our actions are determined by childhood experience. They state,

"Love of humanity . . . is a consequence of generalization from early experiences with people." (171, also 68)

"We have no way, as yet, of supplying the cultural learning experiences of infancy on if they have been skipped. Our first illness, the total inability to love, seems to be virtually incurable." (140)

"Jealousy as an adult is a generalization from the punishing experience of infancy." (140)

This is a fatalistic, questionable, and damaging view. The reader may erroneously conclude that if his early experiences were bad he cannot love humanity. Rather, we may love others even though our experiences with others are bad simply by noting that our attitude, not external events, determines our emotions. By reassessment of our ideas, such as seeing that people largely only do cruel or evil things out of ignorance, we may understand people better and come to love a not quite perfect mankind. The authors' statement that if one is conditioned badly he will not love mankind, seems to imply external behavioral phenomena to the exclusion of language behavior. To say we love someone who reinforces us, again suggests only external influences. Rather we may reinforce ourselves by the statements we make to ourselves. There is a great difference between being conditioned to do something and deciding to do it.

One of the consequences of treating love quantitatively in terms of stimuli is the authors' conclusion that the more stimuli there is the greater will the love be. But what has love or thought to do with vague technical terms such as "stimuli"? It is the assessment one has that is important. With proper assessment one may be very much in love though there are very few external stimuli. But, on their view, love is sometimes said to require a great number of positive stimuli, i.e., reinforcement. The more positive the stimuli the more love. But, then, this still does not account for neurotic love by normal people who have inappropriate assessments, etc. Miller and Siegel at times do note that lovers often are motivated by ideal notions. To this extent they include factors such as the influence of assessments. "Love at first sight" is correctly analyzed as seeing a person who fits our ideal. (20) It would, however, be more specific to say the person fits our assessments of an ideal lover.

In spite of the statements made according to which our behavior seems to be determined by findings concerning mice running mazes, the authors present a cognitive approach to problem-solving. The approach seems to abandon their behavioristic terms in favor of common sense ordinary language. They suggest,

1. Detail the problem.
2. Attack vagueness.
3. Vary the thought process, e.g., ask what it would be like if one had married someone else.
4. Talk it over with a friend.
5. Take a break to consider the problem.
6. Delay acting on the final decision.

Some of these criteria are mechanical and seem not to get at the cause of the problem. On the other hand, several stress language reassessment. Certainly vagueness must be conceptually clarified, including the vagueness of any behaviorial terms such as stimulus, response, etc. Statements #3 and #4 are especially interesting because they are examples of the metaphorical method of therapy. The authors intuitively make several suggestions which may be detailed and clarified by recent analyses of metaphor. Thus metaphorical methods involve substitution of one possible action for another, juxtaposing unlike things so as to gain insight, combination of opposites, substitution of part for whole, deviation from usual action, custom, belief, etc. use of metaphor to create humor, etc. One of the consequences of talking with a friend, taking a break, and so on is to gain a new perspective. Metaphor is one of the devices one may use to gain perspective more directly and immediately. It is the method scientists, philosophers and poets use, though not all are aware that they are doing so. Generalization and transference are types of metaphorical activity also. One of the limitations of the learning theory is that it employs too few such rhetorical devices. A category-mistake is taking a metaphor or unlike things literally. Although they do not mention the device, the authors intuitively employ it when they state that one may erroneously respond to one's future mate as he responded to his father or mother. That would be to confuse contexts and people. Childhood responses must be reevaluated. This is also an indirect argument against the claim that those actions and views which are natural or spontaneous are best.

In regard to love and sex the authors state, "Sex is central in the 'lover' relationship." (17) "Sexual surrender represents one of the fullest ways in which we can show acceptance of another." (58) It is stated that the extent of willingness to engage in sex shows the amount of acceptance of the other person. This may be true, other things being equal, but there are many exceptions to their rule. One may have grown up thinking sex is sinful and so not be willing, although the lover is otherwise completely accepted.

One of the interesting things about learning theory is that it allows for events once thought inseparable, to be easily relearned and separated. Thus it is asserted that it is naive to think that sex must always involve love. Rather, they should not be confused. One may love someone but not be able to have adequate sexual relationships with them and vice versa. The authors point out that often for youth today:

"Sex should be reserved for highly emotional, highly special, and of course, highly tense situations . . . This young man believes that every single sexual contact must be somehow a symphony of spectacular emotionalism." (58, 59)

The emotionalism view is one of the products of the church, romanticism, and existentialism. Emotions and passions are not self-justificatory. The passion supposedly mitigates the guilt involved in the belief that sex is wrong or bad. But if one assesses that sex is bad such dishonest emotionalism is not needed. Sex can be entered into as an act worthwhile in itself and the consequences of the act can be weighed beforehand in a rational way. Emotionalism rather leads to harmful acts, and failures in the sex act itself. The failures derive from conflict, guilt, confusion, fear of failure, etc. If sex had always to be spontaneously highly emotional, men and women would be even more frustrated than they already are.

Also, as was indicated earlier, rational love is not a passive thing but must be deliberate. Love involves a number of specific cognitions and actions. To bring love about one must actively engage in it. A passive love is no love at all. Love does not just come from the outside, and if it does it will not long remain. We must consciously attempt to make others happy.

Another consequence of the learning theory is that sex may be regarded as a habitual activity. Women may be regarded as a habit. This deviates from, but does not exclude, the view that sex is merely a "drive," "need," etc.

Yet another result of a stimulus-response analysis is that for the proper result to ensue the assessments involved must be realistic. (22) Love then involves little idealism. Romantic love and love at first sight are based on lack of realism. Infatuation is said to be an artificial relation not based on actual reinforcement. "Real" love, however, involves accurate assessment. In this way one would not become negatively reinforced or disillusioned. Rational or real love may, then, require good communication as well as honesty. It is pointed out that honest discussions minimize apprehension and turn arguments into objective discussions. (22, 23) Language is used to communicate with, rather than as a tool of manipulation. The authors even state that we should be honest and tell others if we dislike them. I think they show a great limitation here. Why should one dislike anyone? If someone is angry because he has not learned how to control his emotions I would not be angry with him but just understanding and perhaps try to correct his limitation. The authors wrote,

> "Anger is a powerful emotion and doesn't disappear because we deny its presence. If we don't express it openly . . . then it doesn't simply go away." (24)

This statement commits the error of thinking that emotions are internal states, something in us which we "express." Rather anger is a sign of confused or irrational thinking and can be prevented by reassessment and clarification. The authors have not seemed to see this possible application of their own learning theory. Emotions can be changed as well as prevented. One can learn not to dislike another but to love him instead, to love anyone — though it may not be easy at first.

The authors at times seem to imply, without citing it, Schachter's theory of emotion according to which emotion is an arbitrarily verbally labeled state of physical arousal. The important thing is supposedly that one be aroused. Then the arousal, even if produced by anger, may if assessed in a romantic setting, produce love. Miller and Siegel say,

> "If we experience fear with a potential lover, we often tend to find ourselves more strongly attracted to him afterward." (55)

Even a roller coaster ride or anger is said to arouse one sexually. But it may, on Schachter's view, be the case that such arousal could lead to hatred instead of love. Schachter's theory, however, does not explain why one was aroused in the first place, because his experiment begins with the injection of adrenaline. And the authors also state,

> "Almost anything that causes the adrenaline to flow can enhance the feeling of love." (55)

Again, however, it would seem that assessment plays more of a role than mere adrenaline release. The kind of physical response resulting may more closely follow assessment than adrenaline level.

According to this learning theory of love there may be "negative transfer" when we learn things from one situation and apply it to another. Thus a man may treat a woman with whom sex would ordinarily be permissible just as he treated and loved his mother where sex was not possible.

   • It is also correctly noted that we daily and throughout our lives restrain, deny, and practice avoiding sexual arousal. (146) This often has harmful effects on our sexual ability and leads to impotence and frigidity. Sexual dysfunction is said to be a learned activity. Language plays a role in one's assessment or attitude toward sex and other emotions: "Words possess some of the power to evoke . . . responses." (149)

   The authors say that one cannot command love, or expect that one can love humanity by being told to. (171, 172) We supposedly just love people who reward us. (174) Again this appears to be based on the prejudice that we are not self-conditioners or self-motivators. Rather, because emotions are assessments which guide feelings we can love by command merely by changing our assessments. In addition, we can do so without external reward and punishment. We may do it by rationally considering the issue. We may, for example, conclude that it is to everyone's advantage to love everyone else and then to a significant extent do so.

   The authors erroneously assume that marriage need be boring and repetitive. (91) Again this may be the case if one thinks only of an unchanging physical circumstance. If one adds the possibility of communicating, changing people and changing assessments the situation may become the reverse of boring. In marriage there may also be the security, need satisfaction and mutual enhancement which may allow for more intellectual growth and stimulation than would otherwise be possible. In such a marriage the honeymoon is never over. It is harmful to think that marriage is boring, because one assessment needed to make or create marital love is that marriage is a good institution. One's love and marriage are partly determined by how one assesses love and marriage themselves. It is for these reasons harmful for the authors to state, "Very young marriages stand a very poor chance of success." (100) It suggests that it is because they are young that such marriages do not last as long as others. Rather, should the lovers have a knowledge of how emotions work, such marriages may be more successful than any others.

EROTIC LOVE

*"Love lack'd a dwelling, and made him her
place,
And when in his fair parts she did abide,
She was new lodged and newly deified."
(Shakespeare A Lover's Complaint)*

Love may lead to sexual arousal, coexist with it, follow it, or there may be a mixture of these. Love may exist without sexual involvement, although it may be no more adequate than sex without love or assessment involvement.

The confusion between love and sex and the question as to whether one is necessary for the other may be clarified by distinguishing between feeling, sex, and love. By love is meant judgment which guides feeling. Feeling is bodily feeling or sensation. Sex is a general category and stresses bodily feeling but nevertheless involves assessment. It is possible to have sex without much positive feeling and such is the case with frigidity. But one does not have pure sex, or sex "neat." It always involves assessment and a great many associations of all sorts. Ortega wrote,

"Sexual instinct, strictly speaking, practically does not exist in man, but is almost always found to be indissolubly united, at least, with fantasy." (*On Love* 102)

If a woman hates her husband, sexual feelings may be slight. Sex cannot be regarded as merely physical. One reason for saying that one must be in love in order to have sexual relations, is that for the experience to be enjoyable there must be a cognitive understanding. But all types of understanding are possible. A woman may find from a man the security she needs, or she may just assess sex itself as a marvelous experience. Excellent sexual relations are possible without love but not without the proper assessments. This is in addition to the fact that certain physical methods are more effective than others. Dr. David Reuben (1969) reports that a woman usually incapable of orgasm may be brought

394

to orgasm effectively by a vibrator and after this, orgasm during intercourse may be more easily achieved. But physical response is in turn dependent on cognitive factors. The woman must want and allow herself to enjoy sex. Dr. Reuben states,

"Since all sexual feelings are gathered and organized by the brain, gaining even a little control over this organ can make everyone capable of abundant gratification." (59)

Before discussing how assessment relates to sex it is important to describe erotic differences of desire in the male and the female. According to Kinsey's report, females object to having coitus as much as their husbands desire it. Thirty percent of the females tested in one survey were found to be more or less sexually unresponsive. (HM 209) Kinsey states,

"As for college-bred males, a great majority of them are utterly ineffective in securing intercourse from any girl whom they have not dated for long periods of time and at considerable expense." (HM 607)

Albert Ellis states,

"It takes a major campaign to get younger women to bed. Even after this campaign is won, they are only intermittently available and enthusiastic. They continue to demand gigantic nonsexual attentions and rewards for relatively little put-out. They may well be temperamental and mean . . . Their efforts to please sexually are rare or nonexistent." (CC 198)

The issue is stated very clearly by the Kinsey study:

"The restraint of the wife constantly lowers the frequencies [of intercourse] in all segments of the population, but chiefly among better educated groups. A great many husbands wish their coitus were more frequent, and believe it would be if their wives were more interested . . . A large number of wives . . . report that they consider their coital frequencies already too high and wish that their husbands did not desire intercourse so often. A very few wives wish for more frequent coitus. Only a very few husbands wish their wives were not so desirous. These differences in interest inevitably cause difficulties in marital adjustment, and there is no sexual factor which causes more difficulty at upper social levels." (HM 571)

The Margaret Sanger Research Bureau reports that generally women are as sexually responsive as the average 70 year old male. (Hunt 391) Dr. Julia Sherman in *On the Psychology of Women* even has a chapter entitled, "Male Sex Drive Stronger." The female is reported to be able to go for long periods of time without sexual activity, to desire sex less frequently than husbands, to regard sex as often so secondary that it is used only to obtain other goals or objects. Sherman states,

"Husbands desire significantly more coitus than do their wives." (148)

"There is considerable evidence that sex drive (motivation to seek and initiate sexual activity) is greater among men than among women . . . " (167)

But no surveys need be done to know that the male drive is stronger. If a male propositions females he will rarely receive an affirmative reply, whereas if a female propositions males she will find very few refusals. The result is one of the most significant and explosive power imbalances and inequalities in our society. The result is a frustrated male population, and a pressured female population. Because sex is such a significant part of a person's needs and often one's most important want, it is an important power to have. Woman holds this sexual power. It is this power which is part of the reason why men are expected to work to support her rather than the other way around. The purpose of marriage is not merely that of having children. One may ask himself the question, "If sex were as available as soda how often would you have it?" There are many reasons for marriage but one of the most significant involves sexual relations. Kinsey wrote,

"Sexual factors are very important in a marriage." (HM 544) "Sexual maladjustments contribute in perhaps three-quarters of [6000 cases] of the upper level marriages that end in separation or divorce . . . " (HM 544)

Kinsey wrote that the family unit is the most stable and important social institution and one of its main purposes is to provide sexual satisfaction. Masters and Johnson (1970) wrote,

"The ultimate level in marital-unit communication is sexual intercourse . . . Very few marriages can exist as effective, complete, and ongoing entities without a comfortable component of sexual exchange." (15)

Barbara Seaman states,

"Many people, *most* people, are disappointed in their marriages." (20)

Furthermore, Kinsey states that by a woman's failing to satisfy her husband "she is encouraging him to find extra-marital relations." (HF 590) It is found that sixty-nine percent of white males at some time have sexual experience with prostitutes. (HM 597) Albert Ellis presents the estimate that sixty percent of males and forty percent of females had extra-marital relations in 1968. (cc 2) The picture created is that of a sexually inadequate female. Although women, generally, seem to accept their low sex drive some are beginning to feel frustrated because it is no stronger than it is. The liberationist often seeks increased sexual satisfaction although she sometimes merely denounces sex and men altogether or favors self-stimulation or lesbianism. Midge Decter in *The New Chastity,* states,

"Women's Liberation represents a demand for the return to female chastity." (101)

It is often the woman's negative attitude toward sex which helps to cause impotence in men. Discussions about the female orgasm reveal similar results. Kinsey reports,

"Persistent failure of the female to reach orgasm in her marital coitus, or even to respond with fair frequency, may do considerable damage to a marriage." (HF 371)

It was also found that forty-four percent of the females not having had orgasm prior to marriage did not have orgasm in the first year of marriage. (HF 324) Women typically have had great difficulty in achieving orgasm. This fact relates to their low sex drive. Dr. Julia Sherman (1971) cited Dr. Paul Gebhard's finding that,

"The percentage of women who have orgasm correlated with the extremes of happy and unhappy marriage . . . Among the extremely happy marriages only four percent of the wives were not experiencing orgasm."

The conclusion to be drawn is not that of the liberationist that the institution of marriage is inadequate, but rather that women and men do not understand how emotions work. With a knowledge of emotions, how assessment relates to sexual activity and with open, honest, communication marriage can be perhaps the most desirable and successful social unit. But without such knowledge even non-marital relations will suffer. The problem is not with the institution of marriage but with our knowledge of emotions. Albert Ellis wrote,

"When [married] people engage in non-marital sex, as they frequently do, they can resort only to masturbation or to adultery."

But he nevertheless emphasizes the attempt to work within marriage:

"The desire to work at . . . a successful monogamous mating is one of the very best high-level games that many couples are likely to find." (224)

A marital or exclusive one to one male-female relationship allows both partners to feel free, thus allowing them time for inquiry, and other accomplishments without constant anxiety and concern about relations with the opposite sex. Also a monogamous relationship may be the best condition for the creation of a total and sublime form of complete surrender and love. A major technical aspect is that a one-one relationship prevents mentally and physically crippling diseases such as syphilis. Complete and total love is hard or almost impossible to find but when two are in love neither lover wants to lose the other in any way. Having sexual relations outside of their relation is thought to be undesirable and absurd.

The greatest obstacles to marriage or male-female relationships are inability to communicate, lack of understanding of how emotions work, failure to satisfy each other sexually, and lack of inquiry, intelligence, or rationality. If one mate is irrational the other may be unable to successfully make the relationship work. The price of irrationality is divorce, extra-marital relations, or an unhappy relationship.

The nature of the orgasm in the female has been found to be difficult to describe. Some refer to a vaginal versus a clitoral orgasm, but then it may be pointed out that the vagina always or almost always also effects movement in the clitoris. To speak of a clitoral orgasm may stress the fact that the clitoris is being more directly rather than more indirectly stimulated. Masters and Johnson state,

> "Rarely do women, when masturbating, manipulate the clitoral glans directly." (302)

Reports vary. Frequently women seem to have difficulty determining whether or not they had an orgasm or merely a pleasant feeling, and often cannot tell whether it was a vaginal or clitoral orgasm. Even an orgasm achieved by means of the clitoris may be felt as a vaginal orgasm. A "total orgasm" may be felt throughout the body.

Although the American female is seen to generally lack sex drive and be sexually inadequate she nevertheless appears to greatly exceed man in her sexual capacity when it can be aroused. Dr. Julia Sherman stated that women have less sex drive than men, but more capacity. Masters and Johnson found that women are able to experience five to fifty orgasms consecutively by means of a vibrator or similar method. A few women can enjoy sexual relations satisfying at least twenty-five men consecutively. Whether many or most women are capable of this is yet to be determined. Also, after a woman's inhibitions are overcome, such as after many years of marriage, her sex drive is found to increase. This suggests that women may be utilizing only a small fraction of their capacity for the enjoyment of sex. Masters and Johnson state,

> "Her physiological capacity for sexual response infinitely surpasses that of man." (219)

They also point out that this capacity contrasts with actual performance and desire which is often represented by "the time-worn cry of 'I don't feel anything.'" (223) A sexually unsatisfied woman may develop nervousness, headaches, backaches, and depression or hostility. David Reuben (1969) states,

> "Everybody has the capacity for full sexual enjoyment." (59)

Once satisfaction or orgasm is achieved women report, "I feel the ecstasy of being a woman at last," or "I didn't know it would mean that much to me." The experience usually seems to alter her entire life — it is a birth into life. She melts. A glow and optimism prevail.

The picture which emerges is that men are sexually frustrated and women, though they may have greater capacity than men, nevertheless have less desire. The result is that both men and women are frustrated, male-female relations are strained, and marriage is difficult to maintain. There are countless women (and some men) who have never passionately kissed their spouse. Frigidity may be a disease worse than venereal disease. Both require cure. In terms of the existing situation, men should have mistresses as is the practice in many countries. There is, then, a sound basis for the existing "double standard" according to which men can have extra-marital sex but women cannot. On the other hand, because man desires more frequent coitus, and woman has the capacity, one logical solution, which may be preferred, is to determine how she may function at levels closer to her supposed superior capacity. What is it that blocks her capacity and prevents her from experiencing erotic emotion and orgasm?

On the assessment theory, the cause of sexual failure of physically normal men and women is confused, or irrational assessments leading to fear, hostility, apprehension, etc., thus preventing erotic feelings from being experienced. It is a paradigm of a "psychosomatic" phenomenon. The body does not respond or responds adversely if the assessments are negative. Men become impotent and women become frigid due to faulty assessment. Psychological factors may also influence menstruation. It is ironic that in those few cases when the woman is sexually aggressive the man may become fearful leading to his impotence.

One such case is the great difficulty many or most women, and a few men, have in "letting go," or "abandon." One is afraid to love sexually, afraid to "give her (or his) all" to the other, afraid to surrender or "become one" with the other and so achieve a sublime sexual experience, or orgasm. As with rational love, few people are able to experience the surrender necessary for erotic love. There is too much concern with the self, fear about what might go wrong, neurotic or irrational blocks. Kinsey speaks of "failure of the female to participate with the abandon which is necessary for the successful consumation of any sexual relation." (HM 544)

One assessment which may be of great help is to assess the sexual experience as valuable in itself rather than as a reward for attention or for love. One block to sexual satisfaction is the notion that the mate must romantically or rationally love you before you can have sex with him or her. If such were required few people would have adequate sexual relations and there is a great deal of evidence that this is, in fact, the case. On the other hand, if sex were regarded as a desirable experience in itself and independent of other factors those factors would not serve to inhibit as they usually do. Albert Ellis wrote,

"Remember that it is *nice* but not *necessary* for you to put sex within the context of a total relationship . . . *In the meantime* you can frequently enjoy sex for its own sake . . ." (SP 188)

Masters and Johnson (1970) state,

"The crucial factors most often missing in the sexual value system of the nonorgasmic woman are the pleasure in, the honoring of, and the privilege to express need for the sexual experience." (198)

Barbara Seaman (1972) speaks of "the kinds of punitive power games that sexually frustrated women are wont to play," and the fear they have of "letting go" . . (33, 107) She wrote,

"Many women have poor sex experiences because they are too worried over the impression they are making, too aware of the other in the *wrong* sort of way." (210)

She also believes that love is not necessary for good sexual relations. (215) Masters and Johnson (1970) state,

"Fear of adequacy is the greatest known deterrent to effective sexual functioning, simply because it so completely distracts the fearful individual from his or her natural responsivity." (12,13)

But this is one among many irrational or self-defeating ideas frequently held. Culture and religious teaching have imposed values which greatly inhibit successful sexual relations. Often a woman overcomes her inhibitions solely by means of alcohol or tranquilizers. Masters and Johnson (1970) wrote,

"The factor of religious orthodoxy still remains of major import in primary orgasmic dysfunction as in almost every form of human sexual inadequacy." (229)

But culture or religion cannot be solely blamed for inhibiting ideas, because one need not accept such ideas. Critical thinking involves reassessing prevalent values. Ultimately, the individual alone is to blame for his irrational and self-defeating ideas. It is the individual who is mainly responsible for his inability to achieve satisfactory sexual (or other emotional) relations. Ellis states,

"*You*, today, are your worst sexual enemy; your *background* is not!" (SP 189)

"The vast majority of problems of sexual 'inadequacy' are caused by crooked thinking!" (SP 206)

The irrational ideas held are as vast as defense-mechanisms, logical fallacies, metaphors, and rhetorical language-games. A few of the inhibiting, irrational, and self-defeating assessments are the following:

1. The man is responsible for getting the woman sexually ready (or vice versa).

2. The man is to blame for the woman's faulty sexual relations (or vice versa).

3. The culture or religion is to blame for one's inhibitions. (It is irrational to fix blame on oneself or others.)

4. "I'm not in the mood." (Irrational because one can by proper assessment change one's mood.)

5. "He (she) must love me first."

6. "Perhaps it won't work."

7. "Sex is animal and degrading or sinful."

8. "I just can't."

9. "Sex is only for reproduction."

10. "Sex is only for man's pleasure."

11. "He (she) should not touch my sexual parts."

12. (Fears of pregnancy, disease, failure, of being treated poorly afterwards, of being used, etc.)

13. (Rigid or intolerant views about how sex is to be performed and under what conditions. *The Sensuous Woman* by "J" is an attempt to loosen such rigidity.)

14. "If I do this I will be a 'loose' woman or a 'prostitute.'"

15. "He (she) is just trying to please himself (herself)."

16. "I can only enjoy sex if our total relationship is perfect."

17. "She/he is too young/old for me."

18. "He/she must say, 'I love you' first."

19. "It is abnormal or wrong for him/her to desire and have sex so much (e.g., daily)."

20. "I must have an orgasm each time I have sex."

21. "The other person must do everything which I like."

22. "I cannot give sexually because society and people do not treat me as I wish to be treated."

23. "I am too preoccupied with other things to be able to enjoy sex."

24. "If men are sexually frustrated that is only their problem not the woman's problem."

25. "I cannot be honest or open about my thoughts and feelings."

26. "There is only one proper sexual position and time for sex."

27. "His/her body-build is not perfect."

28. "Sex is just mechanical." (cf. "Eating is just mechanical.")

29. "Man is not an animal with animal desires."

30. "Using a vibrator to begin to arouse a previously sexually unresponsive body is wrong, repulsive or degrading."

31. "Love is just spontaneous, it is not created by me."

32. "There is no need to learn the mechanics of sexual arousal and technique because sex should be a spiritual thing."

In place of such negative assessments one might instead say:

1. "Intercourse can be a beautiful experience in itself as well as with love."

2. "Total surrender to another can be an act of rational love, a way of becoming close and being concerned for another human being."

3. "I will attempt to make the sexual experience as full as possible by treating the other person as a total person."

4. "I will give myself unselfishly and completely and without fear to the other person."

5. "By giving to the other totally both of us may receive total human satisfaction."

6. "Sexual relations are not always successful so there is no point in expecting them all to be, or worrying that they will fail."

7. "It is irrational to become angry, fearful, blame oneself or others, be intolerant, or experience any other negative emotion."

8. "The fault of failure would be mainly due to my lack of knowledge of what is involved and my irrational assessments.

9. "I can be honest and open about my thoughts and feelings."

10. "Sexual relations can produce a love of life and of others nearly unequal to any other experience."

11. "Love is created by me."

Negative or irrational assessments appear to be the cause of our inability to achieve sexual satisfaction. These assessments bring about motor, perceptual, and sensory incapacities. Inexperienced brides and husbands need therapy and instruction before suddenly engaging in sexual relations. More is needed than rational love. One's past irrational ideas about sex need revision and one's perceptual and physical behavior need gradual alteration. Kinsey states:

"When there are long years of abstinence and restraint . . . before marriage, acquired inhibitions may do such damage to the capacity to respond that it may take some years to get rid of them after marriage, if indeed they are ever dissipated." (HP 330)

Dr. Reuben (1969) is quite correct in seeing that the brain is the important organ in successful sexual relations. However, his statements about emotions are often unclear or harmful. Albert Ellis has provided needed correction and criticism of Reuben's book in *The Sensuous Person*. Nevertheless, Reuben seems correct in a rough, perhaps overstated, way when he asserts,

"The only thing that stands between any woman and an unlimited number of orgasmic experiences is . . . the brain. The decision to have a sexual climax is not made in the vagina." (49)

"The basic problem in orgasmic impairment is that the brain and vagina are not reliably connected to each other." (126)

Thus Reuben, "J" (Joan Garrity, author of *The Sensuous Woman*), Masters and Johnson, and others recommend the use of a vibrator to arouse repressed sexual feelings. Such methods allow physical and perceptual response change which may be needed in addition to positive assessments.

The range of sexual disorders is as diverse as metaphors, and language-games. There is a rhetoric of sex. Some can only respond sexually if their attention is diverted away from their guilt emotions by alcohol or punishment. If a person has hostile emotions about the opposite sex, sexual frigidity and impotence may result. Some men thus have erections only when there is no possibility of having sex, and when there is a possibility, they become impotent. Some can only enjoy sex with a stranger or someone of a lower class because sex is regarded as degrading or because they fear failure with a friend, etc. A "nympho" may achieve orgasm only with a different partner each time because she may fear failure when she is expected to have orgasm with the same partner. Some learn to respond sexually only to a certain person. Masochism and homosexuality may be explained largely in terms of one's assessments, although it is still a question as to whether there is partly a chemical cause of homosexuality. To avoid irrational assessments what is needed is inquiry, some technical knowledge, and open communication with one's mate.

One factor in the low sexual drive of the average female is her supposed incapacity to have sexual fantasies. It may rather be that women do not respond to sexual imagery because they are not too interested in sex, rather than due to the fact that they are unable to have imagery. That is, a sexually capable female may experience as much imagery as the average male. Unlike males, some women can even fantasize themselves to orgasm. Kinsey states,

"Most females are not psychologically stimulated, as males are, by objects which are associated with sex."

"There may be a third of the females in the population who are as frequently affected by psychologic stimuli as the average of the males." (HF 688)

Females seldom respond to erotic pictures of males or viewing the penis, whereas males usually respond to erotic pictures of females. In fact, females tend to be repulsed by such objects. Kinsey claims that women have little psychologic stimulation to maintain arousal and are easily distracted from it. It is believed that women thus need more bodily stimulation and foreplay than do men. (641) Such stimulation is usually preferred in parts of the body other than the main sexual areas. (658) This may be due to restrictive upbringing and leftover assessments of guilt or the idea that sex is bad. It is as if she must be aroused in spite of herself. The Kinsey study concludes,

"These differences [in sex fantasy] account for the male's desire for frequent sexual contact, his difficulty in getting along without regular sexual contact, and his disturbance when he fails to secure the contact which he has sought. The differences often account for the female's inability to comprehend why her husband finds it difficult to get along with less frequent sexual contacts, or to abandon his plans for coitus when household duties or social activities interfere." (HF 641 ff.)

Barbara Seaman (1972) appears to agree with the above analysis. She states,

> "The fantasy-life of women, even women who are highly sexual, is less intense and varied than the fantasy life of many men." (151)

> "Men might be disappointed if they knew how pale the fantasies of most of their women actually are." (152)

But, as was mentioned, the lack of imagery may be due to lack of interest in sex rather than inability to imagine.

Language, metaphor, and imagery are especially important and involved in the sexual experience. One's beliefs and imagery lead to feelings, and feelings in turn involve or lead to further imagery and assessments. Perception and thinking involve numerous associations and preferences. We call certain objects or letters more feminine or masculine than others on the basis of subtle associations which we may not ourselves fully understand or be aware of. The sound of the letter "r" is often thought to be more masculine than the letter "o." So also, we build up certain associations with sex on the basis of past experience. Thus a great diversity of objects and events become regarded as sexually stimulating. It need not be that such items are aphrodisiacs but only that one has developed or learned certain subjective associations. Of course, there are some drugs which do increase sexual desire. Some objects which people have regarded as being erotic are champagne, cleanliness, cucumbers, dark or blue eyes, tall people, candlelight, breasts, those characteristics which differentiate the sexes, smooth soft voices, football players, long hair, the color red — but the list is endless. Anything can be symbolically related to sex. Freud gave a possible sexual connotation to every object, e.g., a room is a womb, a pole is a phallus, etc. Any object may be regarded metaphorically in this way. It is one way of substituting an object for the actual forbidden or unattainable sex object desired. This may be regarded as what is meant by sublimation or symbolization. Sublimation may involve dancing, art, increased activity, talking, flirting, etc. Sublimation is a defense-mechanism which is to a large extent self-deceptive and self-defeating. It is one of the devices central to courtly love, a love which is never consummated.

One may suddenly find he is in love, only to later find that it had a lot to do with the associations or "atmosphere" rather than the specific person he was with. There was a moon, it was still, the lake glistened, she spoke softly, put her hand in his, etc. Prior assessments determine many of these associations. One who generally prefers tall girls may tend to fall in love with tall girls. But associations may be negative as well. Women who do not especially like sex tend to be repulsed by male sexual objects. Even when they learn to enjoy sex they may still carry over these negative associations. Fears and phobias often involve subtle associations.

Assessment plays a part in "pillow-talk," and foreplay. People are often so inhibited and preoccupied that foreplay is almost impossible. They are unable to be affectionate generally and are not at present capable of rational love. It seems likely that one who is not capable of rational love would tend not to be consistently capable of erotic love either. Certainly this would be the case where a total experience of oneness is involved. Such love is said usually to occur only a few times in a person's life. Reuben states,

"Most people will experience this combination less than a dozen times in their life span." (77)

By means of the assessment theory of emotion this experience may well become commonplace. Assessment must, of course, be accompanied by good health and care of the body. Regular sex before marriage or while young is advocated as a means of preventing negative assessments in regard to sex. Women without premarital orgasm and experience were frequently not able to make adequate sexual adjustments during marriage. In addition, sexual responsiveness depends upon use. If little sex is engaged in, the sexual organs degenerate especially after menopause. Masters and Johnson wrote in this regard,

"There is a tremendous physiological and, of course, psychological value in continuity of sexual exposure, as expressed by the physical efficiency of vaginal response to sexual stimulation. To a significant degree, regularity of sexual exposure will overcome the influence of sex-steroid inadequacy in the female pelvis. (341)

Barbara Seaman puts this more emphatically,

"One of the nicest things Masters and Johnson have found is that frequent intercourse helps keep the vagina youthful." (87)

This is not surprising since daily exercise is needed to keep the body healthy. And sexual intercourse is often recommended as a pleasant way of keeping the entire body and mind healthy. Erotic love seems to be an everyday affair.

Menopause is not necessarily merely due to a sudden change in the body chemistry. It was just indicated that an adequate sex life is possible if sex is frequent enough. Thus it is a faulty assessment, which may lead to depression, to think that one's erotic life is over at menopause. Menopause depression and emotion, as menstrual depression, may have more to do with negative or unrealistic assessments than with chemical changes. At menopause one may fear loss of beauty, oncoming old age, fear of loss of love, etc. It is these fears which may mainly bring on the emotions experienced during menopause. A preventive assessment would be to accept what one is and will realistically potentially be. And, as it happens, women at any age (and more than men) are sexually desirable. They hold an enviable position, the realization of which may help prevent negative menopausal assessments. Elderly women will still be loved and desired more than men and they will live longer than men do. Dr. Julia Sherman (1971) wrote,

"The evidence at this time is not sufficient to clarify how much of the symptoms of the menopausal period and later life are attributable to situational difficulties, neurotic attitudes, identity crises, and/or hormonal deficiencies." (236-237)

"There is no doubt that many women of menopausal age are depressed simply because of their troubles." (232)

Sources:

Albert Ellis The Civilized Couple's Guide to Extramarital Adventure New York: Peter Wyden 1972

Albert Ellis The Sensuous Person: Critique and Corrections New Jersey: Lyle Stuart 1972

Morton Hunt The Natural History of Love New York: Knopf 1959

Alfred Kinsey, et al. *Sexual Behavior in the Human Female* New York: Simon & Schuster 1965 (1953)

Alfred Kinsey, et al. *Sexual Behavior in the Human Male* Philadelphia: Saunders 1948

William Masters and Virginia Johnson *Human Sexual Adequacy* Boston: Little Brown 1970

Jose Ortega *On Love* New York: World 1972

David Reuben *Everything You Always Wanted to Know About Sex* New York: David McKay 1969

Barbara Seaman *Free and Female* Conn.: Fawcett 1972

Julia Sherman *On the Psychology of Women* Illinois: C. Thomas 1971

A CRITIQUE OF LIBERATIONISM

The liberationist attempt to reassess the role of the female in society is in certain respects valuable as is her attempt to achieve greater sexual and emotional satisfaction and correct various inequalities. However, because there has been general confusion as to the nature of emotions, progress has been hampered. A way for the liberationist to attain her goals more quickly and certainly is to employ the assessment or cognitive theory of emotions in order to understand and solve some of her most central problems. This account is sympathetic to the problems of the liberationist but is not sympathetic to a desire for sheer power. A critique of a typical liberationist book follows:

Mrs. (or Ms) Seaman in *Free and Female* is quite correct in asserting that women may achieve a more satisfactory erotic life. However, her arguments for this view are not so satisfactory. She believes that woman has a great capacity for sex and can have an orgasm anytime. (19) Women should engage in sex anytime for its own sake and without regard to promiscuity. (19) This statement is irresponsible if it violates agreements made between married or other individuals or if the consequences are harmful. Otherwise it may be a healthful assessment to make. She later modifies this statement by suggesting that the liberated woman would be better able to marry for love. However, it is not indicated what is meant by love — whether it is rational love or simply agreement as to notions of equality and financial arrangements. Her statement that unrepressed eroticism in itself will make woman more creative (24) lacks foundation, although it is supported in the sense that women could devote less time to worrying about sex and more to their creative work. Sex itself may be thought of as aesthetic creativity of the highest sort. In any case, women need spend almost no time in attaining a sexual partner whereas for men it usually takes a great deal of time and expense. Women usually already have free time for creativity. They have chosen to spend that time knitting, having children, in music, gardening, making ceramics, doing church work, etc.

Seaman, like other liberationists, establishes that women are sexually inadequate. She asserts that since they have more internal organs they take longer to be aroused. (32) This statement seems extremely hypothetical. Assessment may have much more to do with it than the number of blood vessels, that is, if women had fewer negative beliefs they could respond more quickly. She correctly points out that women often merely endure sex rather than try to find out how to enjoy it. They "think of England" during intercourse instead. (34) She states,

"But women — especially women — have been afraid to think for themselves about their own sexual tastes and pleasures." (62)

Dana Densmore in "On Celibacy" wrote,

"Sex is actually a minor need . . . We must come to realize that we don't need sex . . . And if despite all this, genital tensions persist you can still masturbate. Isn't that a lot easier anyway?" (359, 360)

Seaman's argument is that men and society are to blame for the sexual inadequacy of most women. It is an error for the liberationist to blame men, society, or even herself for her problems. This is irrational because it is self-defeating and solves no problem to blame or say someone or something is bad or bad in itself. Such thinking leads to unfounded inferiority complexes. Blame, or attributing badness, is an open-context use or misuse of ethical terms. Nothing is bad in itself.

It is also irrational to blame others for one's own negative emotions, because the cause of negative emotions is one's own irrational assessments. One causes himself to be hostile and angry and these are self-defeating emotions to have. The liberationist causes herself to have her negative emotions. This does not mean that society and male-female relations should not be reassessed and improved. But the best way of improving such relations is by means of communication and a knowledge of the assessment theory of emotions. In addition, blaming others leads to escapism or avoidance of one's problems. Liberationists often seek to escape from marital love, sexual and many other kinds of bonds. Freedom becomes escapism. Lisa Hobbs wrote,

"The feminists wallow in *Weltschmerz*, heartsick that the world is the way it is, that they were born confined to women's bodies . . . " (167) "There is nothing so ego-satisfying as to pass off one's own failings to an all-powerful, evil conspiracy." (166)

Seaman states that men repress women, force women to be what they are (18), cause women to have sexual and mental failure (32), are afraid to stimulate their wives for fear it will make them too sexy (33), are to blame for female frigidity (48 ff), are to blame for the myths women have about sex (215 ff). She states,

"Sexually and in every other way, we were forced to become what men wanted us to be." (75)

The resulting picture created is that women have been unable to think critically about what they are told or about cultural patterns of behavior. It is as if they are not only sexually inadequate but unable to think for themselves as well:

"Women's Liberation has intoned a seemingly endless and various litany of women's incapacities." (Midge Decter 1972)

"It has been men, not women, who have written all the romantic literature and poetry in all civilizations." (Hobbs 24, 25)

"Every institution which dominates our lives — state, church, marriage, education, the military, etc. — was created by . . . the males." (Hobbs 20) (Though more women than men are religious.)

"Rare is the woman who can come up with more than one alternative to a problem. And so woman falls back on her intuition for she is incapable of analysis, incapable of constructing a realistic alternative." (Lisa Hobbs 65)

Men and society are blamed for women's failures. She even blames women at times. One woman stated, "I think it's the woman's fault too." (102)

Seaman writes,

"Should we then just lie back and wait for our lovers to push the right button? I think not." (67) "Many women have poor sex experiences because they are too worried over the impression they are making, too aware of the other in the wrong sort of way." (210)

But some of these statements are not so much blaming statements as healthful suggestions for overcoming irrational assessments. She stresses the need for open, honest communication between the sexes (67). Instead of blaming oneself or others or attacking the institution of marriage or society, the problem of female sexual frustration may be overcome by understanding how emotions work and then changing the assessments so they can lead to positive rather than negative feelings. Liberationists by blaming and by concentrating on external causes are in effect doing women more harm than good. A woman who blames and hates men may find she cannot enjoy sexual relations with them. The liberationist thus often stresses masturbation or lesbianism. Seaman attacks the liberationist view that orgasm being clitoral, the vagina and men are not needed for adequate sex. (59) She rejects the view that the vaginal orgasm is a myth. The vagina is rather seen to play a large part in sexual fulfillment. However, some women do fixate on the clitoris. (76) On her view, orgasms are more or less the same but are only assessed differently. (67 ff)

Seaman states,

"Feminists . . . want to educate men, not eliminate them." (76, 77)

It is certainly the case that especially impotent or inconsiderate men should be educated. But the education will not be successful unless Seaman's analysis is extended to include an understanding of how emotions work. Her analysis often focuses on notions of equality and money:

> "The economic liberation of women will probably make for better sex, for all." (211)

She says that marriage cannot be good unless there is economic equality for women. (215) This especially is an irrational, irrelevant, and self-defeating idea. If one believes it then it may well lead to poor sexual relations. Here is a woman-created myth which tends to repress women. It may be granted that men and women are not treated equally in some respects, but that does not mean all or any social problems must be solved before sex or even marriage can be enjoyed. Should one, for example, say, "I cannot enjoy sex until the children behave better, or until the war is ended, or until I get a better job, or . . ."? If she did, she would wait forever. There is not total equality. Women's salaries have in many cases been lower than men's, women have sexual power over men, and men have given their lives in battle while women stayed home. Should only women fight in war for the next thousand years to make things equal? She does suggest that for equality women should not accept alimony or child support. (215 ff) The divorce laws of the United States are perhaps the most unjust and sexist laws to be found anywhere. They are almost without exception completely favorable to the wife at the expense of the husband. Men are practically never able to obtain custody of the children. The divorced husband is expected to support his ex-wife for life but there seems to be no justification for this. She may have done a useful job at home although it probably in no way compares to the work the husband does. But even if her work were more difficult there is no reason why she should be paid alimony or supported for the rest of her life. Why shouldn't she rather pay him alimony and support him while he stays at home? The husband has almost no rights in divorce but all responsibility. While married a woman can if she wishes obtain more education and training than the husband can because he is always having to earn a living thus leaving him little time or energy for further education. Why should not a divorced wife also help pay for child support? Women receive alimony checks and then go into retirement without ever having worked or having to work, while their divorced husband often has to pay more in alimony than he earns. Lawyers frequently quote the old saying that unless you are rich you cannot afford to get a divorce. No matter how horribly the wife is to her husband he would still be forced to stay with her because he cannot afford to do otherwise. The German magazine *Simplicissimus* had a cartoon with the caption, "Oh, you are getting married Olga — so you must have the alimony payments all worked out." Childless women who were married less than a month have managed to obtain alimony payments for life in amounts larger than most men earn in a lifetime. Now, only a few states even allow no-fault divorce though often both parties are at fault. The judge has neither the training nor the time or staff to properly determine who is at fault and fault partly determines the amount of alimony paid.

The lawyer often tells the wife not to work so that she may obtain more alimony. She is encouraged by the system never to work. But it often doesn't matter because even if she earns $10,000 a year he often still pays so much in alimony that he hardly has enough to live on. If he loses his job he may have to take two or three jobs just to pay alimony. Furthermore, the divorced husband is not legally allowed to remarry because his earnings after alimony are too meager. Few laws are more outdated or unfair than our divorce laws and they favor the wife at the expense of the husband. Divorced men and everyone should be encouraged to protest this injustice and have divorce laws changed. The liberationist can be highly praised for opposing alimony payments.

Another reason given for failure of the woman to surrender sexually is that she may feel dependent. (215 ff) This is a prevalent but strange argument. She is being supported without having to do the sort of unpleasant demanding labor required of her husband. Lucianne Goldberg and Jeannie Sakol in *Purr, Baby, Purr* state,

"They (liberationists) believe that marriage was created by males for the exploitation of female labor. Common sense would indicate it's the other way around." (109)

"One would think that it is the husband who is the wage slave to the wife." (115)

416

Woman is not dependent but rather taken care of. A man receives retirement which he works for all his life, woman receives it all along. A woman because of her sexual power and because she can be supported in marriage need never work a day in her lifetime. Men would enjoy having the sort of option for dependency the liberationist complains of. Should her man fail to support her, she may receive alimony or simply find another man who will support her. Due to her sexual advantage it would not be difficult to do so, regardless of her age. It is irrational for her to complain of the gift of dependency. This is especially the case if, as Seaman states, women tend to marry someone who will be a good provider. (210) It is the man who depends on the woman for sexual fulfillment. She has sexual power over the male. In many marriages, the husband returns home exhausted from work only to find a frigid, hostile, or liberationist wife who then expects him to do the dishes, help clean house, take care of the children. Women in America sexually intimidate and humiliate men because of women's sex power over men — because man's sex drive is stronger than theirs. Men must beg for sex. This is reflected in advertising and courtship customs. Men consequently become bitter or learn to hate women. Thus it is common to hear "Woman is man's downfall." Women do not humanely contribute their part to the male-female relationship. They are usually selfish, spoiled, complaining, demanding and frigid. This is what most men know. It does not serve inquiry to pretend things are otherwise. Mirrors are made for women. They will be angry by reading this for anger and sex are their manipulating weapons. Women oppress men. America has a sexually sick society. On the other hand, a few women work extremely hard, do not abuse their sexual advantage, and enjoy their role as wives.

One reason the wife may condemn dependency is because she dislikes being obliged to have sex with her husband and she, as Seaman states, is sexually inadequate. The solution is to help her to become sexually adequate rather than independent or free. Sexual adequacy is freedom. Independence is especially attractive to the female because outside of marriage her sexual power advantage is even greater than within marriage. In any case, it is irrational to think one can't enjoy sex because one is dependent. A man is dependent upon woman for sex and it would be a double bind to believe that he cannot enjoy sex because he is dependent. This is a double bind in which men are often caught. Both men and women need to understand how emotions work, and not blame each other or society. Social institutions do need to be constantly reevaluated but it is irrational to create emotional disorder and hostility to do such reevaluation. Such negative emotions can be worse than the social problems themselves.

It is strange that Seaman should speak of women as being sexually repressed when it is man who has been traditionally frustrated. Woman has sexual power and so she is the one who represses men. Thus it is strange that Seaman wants woman to copy men's sexual behavior. (18) If women do copy such behavior they will find themselves as frustrated as men are and driven to take the risks of their lives and jobs for the sake of sexual satisfaction.

In regard to the quest for equality Dr. Julia Sherman (1971) wrote,

"Equality of the sexes has . . . been presented in the form of . . . equality in the sense of sameness. Differences between the sexes have been minimized. A review of the evidence indicates that sexual equality in this sense is a pure myth." (244, 245)

"It seems likely that most women have sensed what the evidence showed — that there is considerable hypocrisy, if not simply unwitting inconsistency, about the ideal of the equality of the sexes . . . Quite possibly, many women . . . concluded that pursuing male careers is rarely worth the cost." (242)

Seaman states that sexual morality is a private matter. (299) But the sexual inadequacy of women and sexual frustration of men is a social problem as well. One must be sympathetic with the frustration of both men and women. Also the liberationist is typically hostile, angry or otherwise a slave of her emotions. Lisa Hobbs in *Love and Liberation* states,

"There is no possibility (of good male-female relationships) if the female continues to blame the male for every frustration she suffers as a woman. To use hate as a working philosophy can only draw energies and attention away from a real liberation." (113)

What is needed instead is a liberation from being a slave of our emotions. The liberationist needs to be liberated from herself. Midge Decter (*The New Chastity*) states,

"In general, however, the new liberators of women give no evidence of a feeling of obligation to alter themselves." (55)

A few of the many questionable or faulty ideas of the liberationists are:

1. Women are superior to men. (Seaman 22) (cf. #23)
2. Men are afraid to erotically arouse their women.
3. Women should have complete control of all aspects of our social system.
4. "All women are oppressed and exploited sexually." (Bosmajian, 285)
5. Women are the same as men.
6. One must love himself before he can love others; that is, love of others is based on selfishness.
7. Marriage is only for the purpose of reproduction.
8. Men are the cause of women's failure to respond sexually.
9. Women should be equal to men in every way possible.

Should this rule for equality (of different people) for its own sake prevail it would lead to absurd or unjust consequences. For example, women alone could be required to fight and give their lives on the battlefield for the next several thousand years until the number of women killed equals the number of men who have been killed in past wars. Also perhaps women would only be allowed to live as long as men. But, in addition, equality in every respect would mean equal rights in every respect. Women often want fifty-percent of employees in each institution to be women. This leads also to requiring fifty-percent of each race, body type, degree of intelligence, etc. to be employed in each institution.

10. Women are not paid for their work.

But women own over half of the cash, two-thirds of the savings accounts, 57 percent of the listed securities and three-fourths of the suburban homes, and do less work than men according to L. Goldberg and J. Sakol (142). She is protected by divorce laws, and because men die at an earlier age she inherits great sums of money.

11. Sex is unnecessary and a new chastity is needed.
12. The vaginal orgasm is a myth. Thus women do not need men.

In spite of this view, women do and will continue to have orgasms by means of vaginal intercourse. It is usually preferred to clitoral manipulation. Also, vaginal movement involves the clitoris anyway.

13. It is degrading to be a wife.
14. It is degrading to do housework.
15. All or even many women would be happy if they had work outside the home.
16. Love and erotic emotion are and should be just natural and spontaneous. (For refutation of this see chapter "An Analysis of Love.")
17. Promiscuous women but not promiscuous men are frowned on.
18. The husband's sex techniques are bad. (Rather it is often the women who will not discuss sex or try to find out how to improve. Her dislike of sex may easily contribute to male impotence.)
19. "The instant you become 'a wife' you are no longer 'a woman.' " (Hobbs 8)
20. "Woman is not expected to make any substantial advance in her skills (as wife, etc.)."
21. Women should begin working at the best jobs.
22. The way to achieve the liberationist goal is to be angry and bitter, otherwise nothing will get done.
23. Woman is inferior.
24. Woman is a slave.
25. Marriage, sex, and men must be perfect.
26. Relations between men and women should be legislated so that there is perfect equality.
27. The problem is not with the individual, only with the environment and one's past learning.
28. Women are forced to buy objects which keep them beautiful.

29. The fact that there is rape shows how men oppress women. (Rape may also be seen as psychological disturbance and a sign that men are sexually frustrated by women.)
30. Men have double standards regarding sex. (If women were sexually adequate the double standard would not be necessary.)
31. Women were originally repressed to provide a better balance between the sexes. (Why would men repress them so much as to make them sexually inadequate?)
32. Only women know about and can write about women.
33. Women must live vicariously through men.
34. Women do what they do because they are forced rather than out of choice.
35. Men only love other men not women as equals.
36. Women cannot have good sex relations with men unless they are regarded as equals.
37. Men do not like large vaginas.(Greer *The Female Eunuch* p.33)
38. Females have no voice and are not listened to by men.
39. Men refuse to talk to women about anything important or philosophical.
40. Men are taught to think abstractly but women are not.
41. Men are taught to be super-active sexually.
42. Men are not sensitive to other's needs.
43. Consideration for others is only a feminine trait.
44. Women have been taught from birth that they are stupid, unable to analyze, intuitive, passive, physically weak, hysterical, too emotional, dependent, only fit to be a wife or sex object.
45. Men make women feel like a thing or sex object only. (Men would like to feel like a sex object rather than as merely a provider or as frustrated.)
46. When women are alone at home they are nothing and unimportant.
47. Nothing that a housewife does is important or matters.
48. Women are taught to fail at most things.
49. Women are always being laughed at.
50. Women are taught to serve others but not themselves.
51. Women are made stupid by the roles they are forced to take.
52. It is awful to be a woman.
53. All work in the USA is alienating.

54. Marxism is the best solution to social change. (A common assertion in some but not all liberationist literature.)
55. Men in our society cannot experience sex as transcendent.
56. A woman is expected to be passive and not initiate sexual activity with her mate. (Rather men usually complain that their wives are not aggressive with them.)
57. Husbands dominate wives but wives do not dominate husbands.
58. One should feel depressed as a wife because she can no longer date the men she used to date. (The husband is similarly restricted, but both presumably by choice.)
59. Women do not themselves choose to have and care for children.
60. In addition to their full-time jobs men must help with housework, house repairs and taking care of the children.
61. Wives must spend all of their time caring for their husbands and children. (Many do not have children. When children are in school, women are largely free to do as they wish.)

Nevertheless there are specific abuses which both men and women could and ought to reassess. An attempt to make more careful and responsible statements than have thus far usually been made, would do much for the cause of the liberationist. Hopefully, both men and women will learn to treat each other as fully human beings. The assessment theory of emotions is an attempt to bring this about in support of the genuine problems which underlie the liberationist cause.
Sources:

Hamaida & Haig Bosmajian This Great Argument: The Rights of Women *Mass.: Addison-Wesley 1972*

Midge Decter The New Chastity and Other Arguments Against Women's Liberation *New York: Coward, McCann 1972*

Dana Densmore "On Celibacy" Up Against the Wall Mother *Elsie Adams and Mary Briscoe, California: Glencoe 1971 pp. 358-361*

Lucianne Goldberg and Jeannie Sakol Purr, Baby, Purr *New York: Hawthorne 1971*

Lisa Hobbs Love and Liberation *New York: McGraw-Hill 1970*

Barbara Seaman Free and Female *Conn: Fawcett 1972*

Julia Sherman On the Psychology of Women *Illinois: C. Thomas 1971*

JEALOUSY

"No true love there can be without it's dread penalty — jealousy." Owen Meredith

"They are not even jealous for the cause, but jealous for they are jealous: 'tis a monster begot upon itself, born on itself." *Othello* 3, 3 (Iago)

Jealousy involves a threat of loss of something one regards as his, or desire for something he would like to have but which someone else has. The latter case is like envy. Envy involves wanting something someone else has, and jealousy fearing the loss of something one already possesses. The terms are often interchangeable as in "I am jealous (or envious) of your having such a beautiful house." "Envy" is from the Latin *invidia*, meaning "envy or jealousy." The root of the word means "to look askance at, look maliciously at, grudge, cast an evil eye upon."

Webster's Collegiate defines envy as,

"painful or resentful awareness of an advantage enjoyed by another joined with a desire to possess the same advantage." "an object of envious notice or feeling," and "to feel or show envy."

It is a category-mistake to say that one feels envy, because envy is an emotion not a feeling. Jealousy is defined as,

"intolerant of rivalry or unfaithfulness: apprehensive of the loss of another's exclusive devotion; hostile toward a rival or one believed to enjoy an advantage; vigilant in guarding a possession."

Jealousy is defined circularly as "a jealous disposition, attitude or feeling." Again, emotions should not be regarded as feelings. Thus, the jealous person cannot stand the occurrence of certain events. If, in fact, jealousy is intolerance it would seem to be an irrational emotion to have. Insomuch as apprehension, hostility and fear are involved jealousy would also be irrational.

422

The objects of jealousy here are rivalry, unfaithfulness, superiority of another, loss of mate or object, desire for exclusive possession. It is rational to attempt to maintain that which belongs to one, try to be as able as possible, or even — if it is mutually agreed upon — to expect exclusive possession. What is irrational is to worry, experience fear, or become angry over such things. The stoics put it forward that one can only do what is within one's power. There is no point in compounding adversity by imposing negative emotions on oneself and others regarding that which is not within one's power. In this sense, jealousy is an irrational emotion and so it would seem desirable to prevent it and eliminate it. In order to do this the assessments involved in jealousy need clarification.

In the first place, because jealousy is not a feeling it can be changed and controlled and is not a necessary or fixed part of human character. Some relevant considerations are the following:

1) One may be jealous because he fears the mate is having an affair or the affair is an actuality. Insomuch as it is out of one's control one cannot do anything about the affair. To become angry about it is to try to change the event as if by magic. To be angry about something one has no control of serves no purpose. At the moment of learning of the affair one can attempt to discuss the matter with the mate and then determine what action to take. One of the reasons affairs seem shocking is because certain rules of behavior were implicitly or explicitly agreed upon which are now suddenly broken without warning. If the mate had discussed the matter in advance of the affair no jealousy need have arisen. And if, even after the affair, a separation is decided upon one need not be jealous but rather pleased that a more fulfilling relationship has been found. After divorce one tends not to be jealous of the mate but rather angry. This suggests that jealousy partly involves possession. If the rules for behavior were agreed upon there would be little problem with jealousy. The fact that jealousy is not necessary does not mean one is free to violate his commitments and responsibilities to his mate.

424

2) One may be jealous of the spouse even when there is no love between them. The jealousy may be due to thinking of the spouse as owned, as a possession, such that it is only the possession of property aspect which is defended. A possession often seems desirable only when it is being taken away. It is irrational and unrealistic to think of people as property possessions. To do so ignores the human context of thought, desire, choice, etc. For a person to be jealous there must be at least some one thing which one likes about that person. Jealousy based on possession is a poor ground of jealousy. Once it is realized that human agents cannot be possessed jealousy becomes envy.

3) One is often jealous of someone of the same sex but not of the opposite sex. A man may be jealous of his wife's affair with another man but not so much of her affair with a woman. He may be jealous of her sexual activity but not of her intellectual activity. One may be more jealous of a lover younger than himself than one older. What one is jealous of indicates the sort of love which is had between two people. It is important then to know what these ties are so as not to be jealous merely because someone else would be jealous in such a circumstance. Thus the particular ties should be assessed so as to avoid jealousy. Often jealousy and revenge are merely learned and adopted from the culture. One is expected to be jealous or revengeful even when it makes no sense to do so. He may wish to avoid being called "cuckold." Jealousy is often the experience of being unable to cope with a potential loss without being clear about just what it is that is being lost. One says vaguely "I am jealous of her," or "I am jealous of him."

4) It is often thought bad to be a jealous person. Jealousy is thus an ineffective means of achieving what one wants to achieve. Sometimes it is erroneously used as proof of affection. A woman may feel unloved if her husband is never jealous of her. The man is then caught in a double-bind: He is disliked if he is jealous and disliked if he is not jealous.

5) Jealousy is often unrealistic because it involves an inadequate assessment of other people's behavior. Because one greatly fears something will happen or because it could happen he

imagines that it has already happened. A single man may even imagine that he has a wife, then imagine she is unfaithful, and then experience actual jealousy. The fact that women have sexual superiority over men serves as a constant ground of possible insecurity on the part of the male. A woman may have no inclinations whatsoever to have an affair but the fact that she has more potential than the male to do so creates a jealousy-producing situation. To this may be added the fact that women and men are not always clear and rational about their commitments and responsibilities.

6) People seem to be mainly jealous about sexual matters. This is because few have adequate sex lives. If such needs were met it would eliminate the major cause of jealousy between the sexes. The existence of jealousy is a sign or symptom of an unresolved social problem regarding sexual fulfillment. The desire for exclusive sexual rights is partly based on the need for sexual fulfillment. If one had unlimited availability of sexual fulfillment, sexual relations might be far less exclusive than they now are.

7) Jealousy is not a feeling and so alcohol, drugs, acting-out, etc. are not effective in eliminating it. When one says he is jealous, he is not merely reporting a feeling within himself. If it were, a pill or chemical might ease the pain. We do not ask, "When did you first notice it?" "What does it feel like?" Jealousy involves present, past, and future. If one tries to think of a situation in which he was jealous and then tries to think just of the feelings involved he would reduce the jealousy by more than half. When someone says he is jealous we ask him to tell us about the situation, about what happened or how he sees his relationships with others. The cure involves discussing, clarifying, and assessing the situation.

8) Jealousy may be based on an irrational like or desire and so be eliminated by reassessment. If the attraction of a person to another is merely financial the person is a means rather than an end, and so what that person does may be no ground for jealousy except insofar as money is related. Jealousy relates to romantic love in a different way than it relates to rational love and erotic love. Love is used rather generally in this account.

9) Jealousy is often based on the view that it would be terrible or bad if one's mate did a certain thing. One who believes this is thereby limited or enslaved. A mistreated woman feared being separated from her husband until she realized that there was really nothing "bad" about being separated and that a separation can even help a marriage.

10) Jealousy may involve equality. One may be jealous merely because someone else can do things he cannot do. The interest could be in equality for its own sake, equality in every aspect of one's life. It is an irrational and unrealistic demand to seek total equality. Men make poor women. There are individual differences and contextual differences. Instead of equality of isolated items for the sake of equality alone, a balanced equality in terms of an intelligent assessment of the total situation and diverse needs and interests would seem preferable. Because a man generally desires or needs sexual satisfaction more than a woman does, she should not be jealous about this. To be one with another person may produce more freedom and satisfaction than having equal legal rights with another.

11) Jealousy is often due to the assessment that because the agreements between two people are unilaterally broken the violater no longer cares about the consequences of his actions. The violation is then felt as an insult. If it is an insult then it is not jealousy. An insult is a critical attack by another. This is only a statement that someone else is bad. One cannot be insulted if he does not wish to be. If the criticism or insult is just he acts on it, if it is not just he ignores it. No negative emotion or feeling need be involved. A person then need never be insulted or jealous.

12) A person may be put in a jealous situation by being unfairly taken advantage of. Although jealousy would still be an irrational emotion if it does occur, it may be justified. A neighbor may play on the weaknesses, difficulties, or confusions of a wife, for example, in order to obtain sexual gratification or for quite limited purposes without concern for the husband and without full concern for the desired wife. The husband's role would have to involve an attempt to discuss and clarify the situation with the wife rather than to become jealous, angry or envious.

13) Jealousy may be caused by personality defect, lack of understanding of how emotions work, unclear assessments and goals, failure to communicate one's needs and desires, making irresponsible or false statements. Especially crucial are relationships where communication is poor, or where one is rational and the spouse is irrational or neurotic. Sibling rivalry or jealousy comes about when a child's demands are great but assessments unclear. Bringing home a newborn child may seem to the older brother like a husband's bringing home another wife would seem to a wife.

Regarding the notion of trust and faithfulness the average person is usually not stable and clear enough about how emotions work, to be counted on in any exclusive way. Kinsey's statistics on extra-marital relations bear this out.

14) Is love possible without jealousy or jealousy possible without love? Lack of jealousy improves the ability to love, and rational and genuine love may not be possible with jealousy. For love, jealousy-producing situations must be resolved by reevaluation and open communication. One may openly appeal to one's mate to help in overcoming jealousy. Jealousy is possible without love because it may involve loss or fear of loss of anything at all.

Certainly one does not want to lose someone he loves but a relationship based upon jealousy is not an adequate relationship. In terms of rational love, loss may be desired if it benefits the friend, loved person, or society.

BIBLIOGRAPHY ON LOVE

Adler, Alfred "Love is a Recent Invention" *Journal of Individual Psychology* 27 (2) (Nov. 1971)

Ard, Ben "How to Avoid Destructive Jealousy" *Sexology* 34 (1962) 346-348

Beaty, Frederick *Love in British Romantic Literature* DeKalb: Northern Illinois University Press 1971

Beigel, Hugo "Romantic Love" *American Sociological Review* Vol. 16 (1951)

Betz, Joseph "The Relation Between Love and Justice: A Survey of the Five Possible Positions." *Journal of Value Inquiry* 4 (Fall 1970) 181-203

Bloom, M. "Toward a Developmental Concept of Love" *Journal of Human Relations* 15 (1967) 246-273

Brennan, Joseph "Morals and Love" *Ethics and Morals* New York: Harper & Row 1973

Burton, Robert *The Anatomy of Melancholy* New York: Tudor 1927 Part Three, "Love-Melancholy"

Capellanus, Andreas *The Art of Courtly Love* J. Parry, trans., New York: Ungar 1959

Cassanova, Giacomo *History of My Life* 4 vols., New York: Harcourt-Brace 1967

Cicero, Marcus *On Friendship* Cambridge: Harvard University Press 1953

Ehman, Robert "Personal Love" *Personalist* 49 (Winter 1968) 116-141

Fisher, Marlene ed. *The Theme of Love* Dubuque, Iowa: Brown 1969

Fletcher, Joseph *Situation Ethics: The New Morality* Philadelphia: Westminster Press 1966

Fromm, Erich *The Art of Loving* New York: Harper 1956

Goode, W. "The Theoretical Importance of Love" *American Sociological Review* 24 (1959) 38-47

Gratton, C. "Selected Bibliography on Love" *Humanitus* 2 (1966) 215-221

Harlow, H. "The Nature of Love" *American Psychologist* 13 (1958) 673-685

Hazo, Robert *The Idea of Love* New York: Praeger 1967

Hobbs, Lisa *Love and Liberation* New York: McGraw-Hill 1970

Hunt, Morton *The Natural History of Love* New York: Knopf 1959

Kahn, Samuel *The Psychology of Love* New York: Philosophical Library 1968

Kephart, W. "Some Correlates of Romantic Love" *Journal of Marriage and the Family* 29 (1967) 470-474

Kinney, Arthur, et al., eds. *Symposium on Love* New York: Houghton-Mifflin 1970

Krich, Aron, ed. *The Anatomy of Love* New York: Dell 1960

Lawlor, John, ed. *Patterns of Love and Courtesy* London: Arnold 1966

Lepp, Ignace *The Psychology of Loving* B. Gilligan, trans. New York: New American Library 1963

Lindenauer, G. "A Matter of Respect: The Importance of Communicating Love" *Journal of Emotional Education* 8 (1968) 68-75

"Love" *Great Books of Western World* Syntopicon

Lowen, A. *Love and Orgasm* New York: Macmillan 1965

Maslow, Abraham "Love" *Motivation and Personality* 2nd edition New York: Harper & Row 1970 chapter 8

Maslow, Abraham *Toward a Psychology of Being* New York: Van Nostrand Reinhold 1968

May, Rollo *Love and Will* New York: W. Norton 1969

Menninger, Karl *Love Against Hate* New York: Harcourt 1942 (1970)

Miller, Howard and P. Siegel *Loving: A Psychological Approach* New York: John Wiley 1972

Montagu, M. *The Direction of Human Development* New York: Harper 1955

Moore, John *Love in Twelfth Century France* University of Alabama Press 1972

Murstein, Bernard, ed. *Theories of Attraction and Love* New York: Springer 1971

Nataraj, P. "Perception of Love by the Married and Unmarried Woman" *Psychology Annual* 1 (1966-67)

Nelson, John *Renaissance Theory of Love* New York: Columbia University Press 1958

Newman, F. *The Meaning of Courtly Love* Albany: State University of New York Press 1968

Norton, David and Mary Kille *Philosophies of Love* San Francisco: Chandler 1971

Ortega y Gasset, Jose *On Love* Toby Talbot, trans. New York: Meridian Books 1958

Otto, Herbert, ed. *Love Today* New York: Association Press 1972

Ovid *The Art of Love* R. Humphries, trans., Bloomington: Indiana University Press 1957

Reik, Theodor *Of Love and Lust* New York: Grove Press 1959

Rougemont, Denis de *Love Declared* New York: Random House 1963

Rougemont Denis de *Love in the Western World* M. Belgion, trans., New York: Pantheon 1956

Rougemont, Denis de *Passion and Society* London: Faber and Faber 1956

Rubin, Z. "The Measurement of Romantic Love" *Journal of Personality and Social Psychology* Sept. 16, 1970 pp. 265-273

Stendhal, Marie-Henri Beyle *On Love* New York: Liveright 1947

Swensen, C. "Love: A Self-Report Analysis With College Students" *Journal of Individual Psychology* 17 (1961) 167-171

Verene, D., ed. *Sexual Love and Western Morality: A Philosophical Anthology* New York: Harper & Row 1972

Appendix I Emotion Questionnaire

PART I

DO YOU EXPERIENCE:
(Use symbols   N=never, S=seldom, U=usually,
F=frequently, A=always)

1. extreme violent anger
2. anger involving shouting
3. subdued anger
4. unexpressed anger
5. irritation at others' behavior
6. irritation at yourself.
7. speaking in an irritated tone of voice
8. intolerance of others' behavior
9. disgust with others
10. disgust with situations or environment
11. loathing
12. boredom
13. ecstasy
14. grief
15. sadness
16. apprehension
17. fear
18. terror
19. hate
20. hate of yourself
21. hate of others
22. hate of certain things
23. fear of mice
24. fear of facing the day
25. fear of failure
26. fear of death
27. fear of being embarrassed
28. fear of criticism
29. fear of not being loved
30. fear of not being listened to
31. fear of being rejected
32. fear of not having your own way
33. contentment
34. happiness

431

35. joy
36. surrender of whole being to another
37. timidity
38. boredom
39. acceptance of everyone
40. acceptance of self for the most part
41. guilt
42. misery
43. cynicism
44. stubborness
45. delight
46. submission
47. modesty
48. embarrassment
49. disappointment
50. shame
51. pessimism
52. optimism
53. courage
54. conceit
55. outrage
56. anxiety
57. distrust
58. envy
59. sullenness
60. masochism
61. resentment
62. pleasure
63. being sarcastic
64. being cruel
65. being rebellious
66. depression
67. sadness
68. loneliness
69. carrying a grudge
70. worry
71. sulking
72. brooding
73. erotic love
74. love of self
75. love of another
76. love of others
77. being whining
78. mocking others
79. being annoyed at inequality
80. being annoyed at unfairness
81. talking back to those who criticize you
82. feeling inferior to others
83. feeling superior to others
84. getting upset over trivial things

85. anxiousness
86. anxiety
87. being uptight
88. tension
89. nervousness
90. hate of certain types of people
91. hate of degrading environment
92. lack of respect
93. crying easily
94. wishing someone were dead
95. wanting to kill someone
96. wishing you were dead
97. wanting to kill yourself
98. feeling alienated from people
99. feeling alienated from the world
100. being oppressed by the modern age
101. being oppressed by pollution
102. being irritated at atheists
103. being irritated at religion or religious people
104. being irritated with your job.
105. frustration at being a mother
106. frustration at being a wife
107. frustration with your present situation
108. frustration with being a student
109. sexual frustration
110. frustration with your present occupation
111. dread
112. jealousy
113. helplessness
114. self-pity
115. uncontrollability
116. silliness

(Where relevant use symbols above (N, S, U, F, A,)

1. Do you have emotional problems you cannot solve?
2. Do you feel crippled because of your emotions?
3. Have you thought of not getting angry at all?
4. Have you mentally practiced not to get angry.
5. Do you work at turning bad situations into good ones?
6. Do you use humor as a means of avoiding negative emotions?
7. Do you swear? (how often?)
8. Do you think you should be very rational?
9. Are you emotional?
10. Are you rational?
11. Are negative emotions necessary?
12. Are they part of one's nature?
13. Can one's emotions be very greatly changed?
14. Do you accept all of your physical qualities?
15. Do you accept all of your mental qualities?

16. Do you act as you would like to?
17. Do you pretend to be other than you are so people will like you?
18. Do you have confidence?
19. Are you leading the life you wish to lead?
20. Does life seem worthless?
21. Are you living up to your abilities?
22. Are you living up to your goals?
23. Do emotions give you headache, upset stomach, ulcer? (Specify)
24. Are you genuinely interested in inquiry and gaining rational knowledge?
25. Are you a mystic?
26. Do you belong to a religion?
27. Do you believe in God?
28. Do you believe in astrology?
29. Do you believe in a soul?
30. Are you literally appalled at injustice?
31. Are you literally appalled at inequality?
32. Do you think you are treated unfairly?
33. Should everyone be treated equally?
34. Does injustice, inequality or, unfairness actually upset you?
35. Do you have a good sense of humor?
36. Can you write well?
37. Are you a clear thinker?
38. Do you enjoy deep or philosophical discussions?
39. Are you able to converse well with your mate?
40. Do you express yourself well?
41. Are you good with language?
42. Do you like objective discussions?
43. Do you get angry at what others say?
44. Do you get easily irritated at what others say?
45. Do you get easily irritated at what your spouse says?
46. Do you feel unimportant?
47. Do you get angry if others are angry at you?
48. Do you get irritated if others are irritated with you?
49. Are women less rational than men?
50. Should a woman accept herself as being irrational
    a) because women are irrational?
    b) because she is menstruating?
51. Do women often have very illogical arguments?
52. Are you afraid you will fail?
53. Are you afraid of being laughed at?
54. Do you make fun of others?
55. Do you get upset if someone calls you a bad name?
56. Does it bother you a lot if people do not like you?
57. Does it bother you a lot to think people say bad things about you?
58. Can you make decisions easily?

59. Do you become upset if you cannot come to a decision?
60. Do you think the environment is largely to blame for the faults you have?
61. Are your feelings easily hurt?
62. Can you laugh at your shortcomings?
63. Can you communicate all of your true thoughts and feelings to others?
64. Do you usually take things too seriously?
65. Do you think you are manly/womanly enough?
66. Would you prefer to be a man?
67. Would you prefer to be a woman?
68. Do you often have unresolved conflicts?
69. Are you an unlucky person?
70. Do you get upset if things do not go as scheduled?
71. Do you get upset if things do not go as you would like?
72. Do you feel unappreciated?
73. Do you think you should be getting more attention than you are getting?
74. Do you feel that people usually avoid you?
75. Do you feel dependent on anyone?
76. Do you wish to be more independent?
77. Can you be honest and open with others?
78. Can you surrender your complete love to another?
79. Do you think you can basically change your emotions?
80. Do you think critically and examine whatever people say to you?
81. Do you think one need almost never get angry?
82. Do you react emotionally to objective statements?
83. Do you argue?
84. Do you accept criticism easily?
85. Do you deal with what others say objectively?
86. Do you think you are intelligent?
87. Are you afraid you are becoming less intelligent?
88. Do you try by reading or writing to improve your intelligence?
89. Are you afraid you will lose control of yourself?
90. Do you consider carefully the consequences of each of your actions?
91. Do you brood about problems or things?
92. Are you doing what you wish to do?
93. Do you tend to just take on the goals of those around you?
94. Do you tend to just take on the values of those around you?
95. Have you thought about your goals carefully and thoroughly?
96. Are you deliberate in your thought?
97. Are you deliberate in your action?
98. Do you think you are a failure?
99. Do you become very emotional if you fail?
100. Do you think people must like you before you can be happy?
101. Do you think you must be successful in the eyes of others before you can be happy?

102. Are some things absolutely right or wrong?
103. Is the environment the main cause of your emotional problems?
104. Can you solve your emotional problems easily?
105. Is reason inadequate to deal with emotional problems?
106. Do you tend to "collect injustices"?
107. Do things around you usually have to be just right, or in excellent order?
108. Do you think that at the time you are emotionally upset you can be rational?
109. Do you think your feelings are more important for self understanding than your thoughts?
110. Do you think it is others who make you angry or yourself?
111. Do you feel bad because you make yourself feel bad?
112. Do you think you must and can master your own emotions?
113. Do you think there is only one fair way to do things?
114. Do you think that basically it is you who are to blame for your own emotional problems?
115. Are situations and objects often the cause of your emotional experiences?
116. Do you think you lack confidence?
117. Do you reject yourself?
118. Are you to some extent a bad person?
119. Do you think that you are responsible for your emotions?
120. What behavior do you now have which you would like not to have?
121. What behavior would you like to have which you do not now have?
122. What ideas and emotion would you like to change?
123. Do you avoid responsibility?
124. Act unfair to others?
125. Lack discipline?
126. Eat too much?
127. Sleep too much?
128. Clean too much?
129. Drink too much?
130. Smoke too much?
131. Withdraw from social activity?
132. Procrastinate a lot?
133. Arrive late for appointments?
134. Can you concentrate easily on reading and read for long periods of time?
135. Are your thoughts and actions deliberate?
136. Are you almost completely able to put yourself in the other person's shoes?
137. Do people tell you you are angry when you do not think you are?
138. Do you find it hard to get to sleep?

IN THE FOLLOWING SUBSTITUTE "MATE" IF NOT MARRIED:

1. Are you married?
2. Is your marriage perfect?
3. Is your marriage a happy one?
4. Do you think it can improve? (how much?)
5. Can you converse easily and openly with your spouse?
6. Is present communication with your spouse acceptable to you?
7. Does your spouse become irritated easily?
8. Does your spouse criticize you too much?
9. Does your spouse nag you?
10. Does your spouse become angry with you?
11. Do you or would you like to find someone with whom you can communicate better than with your spouse?
12. Do you do or say things to your spouse which may lead him/her to find another mate?
13. Does your spouse value things more than people?
14. Are you proud to be a wife/husband?
15. Do you feel used?
16. Do you often contemplate separation or divorce?
17. Do you feel oppressed by your spouse?
18. Does your spouse surrender completely to you?
19. Do you spend most of your time with your spouse talking of problems?
20. Does your spouse often talk about his or her rights in marriage?
21. Are you afraid to discuss your sexual relations?
    a. with your spouse?
    b. with others?
22. How often do you think the average husband desires sex?
23. Does your spouse desire sex more often than you do?
24. How often do you have sex?
25. Can you get in the mood for sex anytime?
26. Do you think that your desire for sex is largely due to emotional or rational factors?
27. Have you ever wanted to have extra-marital sexual relations?
28. Do you feel sexually adequate?
29. Are your sexual relations adequate?
30. Can women obtain a sexual partner easier than men?
31. Do you enjoy sex?
32. Does your spouse often make you jealous?
33. Do you think the emotions of your spouse should be changed?
34. Do you think your spouse really loves you?
35. Do you think you should have more freedom in your marriage?
36. Does your spouse understand you?
37. Do you work hard at trying to be an especially good wife/husband?

38. Do you sometimes like to show you are more intelligent than your spouse?
39. Do you sometimes like to laugh at your spouse?
40. Do your children irritate you or get you angry?
41. Do you feel trapped at home by your husband and/or children?
42. Are you happy with the way you are handling your children?
43. Do you yell at your children? (How often?)
44. Have you studied and made a great effort to find ways of eliminating anger and irritation?
45. Were you successful?
46. Do you need to be in love with someone in order to have sex with them?
47. Are you opposed to marriage?
48. Is there as much happiness in your home as in others?
49. Do sexual things disgust you?
50. Do you avoid sexy shows if you can?
51. Does your spouse hold out on you in a number of ways?
52. Is it difficult for you to become sexually aroused?
53. When your spouse suggests something to you that he or she would like do you try to follow the suggestion?
54. Is your spouse relaxed with you or do you make him nervous?
55. Does your spouse often avoid you because you are tense or have too many problems for him or her?
56. Do you think it is mainly the man's job to get the woman sexually ready?
57. Do you think about sex in advance so you will be more sexually ready?
58. Do you make it easy for your spouse to have sex with you?
59. Do you pull away sharply or in disgust at the affectionate advances or movements of your spouse?
60. Do you let your spouse touch your sexual parts freely?
61. Would you make love with a stranger?
62. Are you a homosexual?
63. How often, if ever, do you have orgasm during sex?
64. If a female, describe your orgasm as being vaginal, clitoral, both or just a general feeling?
65. If female, how often do you not feel much of anything during sex?
66. Do you masturbate? If so how often?

PART II

1. How often can you adequately face your problems?
2. Are you outgoing or reserved socially?
3. What is your emotion toward conceited people?
4. How often do you talk about your emotions?
5. How often do you feel guilty?
6. Is it more important for people to agree about something than to inquire into it?
7. Are you disgusted with fat or sloppy people?
8. Do you think you are an interesting speaker?
9. Do you think you are an interesting person?
10. What are your major interests in school?
11. What were your major interests in school?
12. Out of school my major interests are?
13. Do you keep your things especially well organized?
14. When people get angry with you do you also become angry?
15. Are you more of an individual or a joiner?
16. Would you rather enjoy life quietly or be admired for your achievements?
17. Do you think you are quite mature in things you do?
18. Do you research most things out carefully before you do them?
19. Do you prefer: a) small gatherings, or b) large parties?
20. What types of books do you prefer to read?
21. Are you bossy?
22. Do you get more out of reading or talking usually?
23. Do you require more praise and compliments than you receive?
24. Do you mingle among different kinds of people easily?
25. Do you prefer a big wedding?
26. Do you prefer a big funeral?
27. Do you anger quickly?
28. How much do you talk about the past?
29. Do you like poetry?
30. Do you almost always prefer company rather than going places alone?
31. Do you have images?
32. Do you hallucinate?
33. Have you seen a vision?
34. Do you have a good memory usually?
35. When in groups do you do things you would not ordinarily wish to do?
36. Do you believe people have fixed natures?
37. Do you think you have a pre-established purpose?
38. Does your education come mainly from others or yourself?
39. Are you flighty?
40. Is the best way of doing things the natural way?
41. Are you energetic and always keep busy?
42. Are you a very enthusiastic person?

43. Are you interested in everything around you?
44. Do you curse people out? (How often?)
45. Do you ever feel nauseous? (How often?)
46. Is your stomach upset due to emotional problems?
47. Do you usually keep your mind on your work?
48. Do you often cough?
49. Have you had bad sex experiences?
50. Do you purposely destroy or smash things?
51. Do you often have a hard time getting going?
52. Do you often fail to obey the rules?
53. Is disease caused by sin?
54. Are you like most people?
55. Do you live right?
56. Do you hear or see strange things?
57. Are you easily downed in an argument?
58. Do you believe there are absolute truths?
59. Would you like to live in a commune?
60. How often do you go to church?
61. How often do you quarrel?
62. Do you like loud parties?
63. When you are emotionally upset do you take an alcoholic drink?
64. Would you like to escape from society?
65. Are you happy most of the time?
66. Do you believe in an afterlife?
67. Do you believe in eternity?
68. Are you often grouchy without knowing why?
69. Are you irritated when people interrupt you?
70. Do you often have headaches? Dizziness?
71. Are you often afraid you will not get enough sex?
72. Do you have asthma?
73. Do you like to flirt?
74. Do you do anything compulsively? (specify)
75. Do you like to hunt?
76. Would you as a soldier kill people?
77. Do you gossip?
78. Do your friends have habits which annoy you?
79. Have you had traumatic love experiences?
80. Are you jealous of anyone? (whom?)
81. Is life usually a strain for you?
82. Are some subjects too touchy to speak of? (specify which)
83. Do you have a lot of patience?
84. Do you often flit from one topic to the next?
85. Did you have a very strict upbringing?
86. Do you believe in magic or miracles?
87. Does your future seem hopeless?
88. The person(s) to whom you are or were most attached are (child, spouse, mother, father,_____)?
89. Do you have a bad reputation?

90. Do you find it hard to make friends?
91. Do you think that some things should just not be talked about?
92. Does your spouse think you are really trying to make him/her happy?
93. Do you think you are attractive?
    a) In what way?
    b) How much?
94. Describe any nervous traits you have.
95. Do you sometimes hate and love the same people?
96. Do you feel that you are getting too old?
97. Do you mind if people disagree with you?
98. Do you have as much energy as others?
99. Do you often crave excitement?
100. Do you fear giving speeches?
101. Do you daydream a lot?
102. Do your moods change rapidly?
103. You do not understand how people can get so interested in their activities?
104. Are you so concerned about the future that you fail to enjoy the present?
105. Are you moody?
106. Are you cheerful most of the time?
107. If someone wrongs you do you try right away to discuss it with him?
108. Are you more interested in athletics than intellectual things?
109. Do you think people should mind their own business?
110. Do you keep up with the latest clothing styles?
111. When you are justifiably criticized do you correct your mistakes?
112. Is your family really proud of you?
113. Do they fully accept you?
114. Are you always trying to improve yourself?
115. Do you spend a great deal of time following or watching sports?
116. Do you think people can read minds?
117. Do you almost always try to be aggressively kind, warm and understanding with people?
118. Do you often tell your troubles to others?
119. Do you dislike prostitutes?
120. Do you like prostitutes?
121. Do you dislike nuns?
122. Do you dislike college people?
123. Do you dislike average townspeople?
124. Who taught you the most?
125. Who would you most like to be like?
126. Do you have more problems than most people?
127. Do you like school?
128. Was your childhood homelife happy?
129. Should you treat your parents as good as friends even if you dislike them?

130. I am never mean to others. (T or F)
131. Do you have colitis?
132. Do you feel as if people don't want you around? (If so, how often?)
133. Are you sometimes afraid to go home?
134. Do you have evidence for immortality?
135. Do you think life is absurd?
136. Do you think you can be punished for sins after death?
137. Are you tense to be around?
138. How often do you speak in a severe or intolerant tone of voice?
139. Do you always try to treat people as ends rather than means?
140. Do you think that each person is important in his own right?
141. Do you become angry at others because of your own problems?
142. Do you fear deliberately going out to meet members of the opposite sex?
143. Do you teach politeness rudely?
144. Are you ever sarcastic?
145. Do you ever seriously say "Who do you think you are, anyway?"
146.   "What's the matter with you, anyhow?"
147.   "You are stupid."
148.   "I think you're really crazy."
149.   "Where were you brought up anyway?"
150.   "I have told you over and over."
151.   "How many times must I tell you?"
152. Do you impose your will on others?
153. Do you think a child's feelings should be taken seriously even though the situation itself is not very serious?
154. Do you give up being rational with children because it doesn't work?
155. Do you get angry with one person because he does not adequately deal with the emotions of another person?
156. Are you sympathetic with each of your child's emotions?
157. Do you state for them what you think is bothering them?
158. Do you try to correct the behavior of a child while he is in the midst of an emotion?
159. Do you show your child you understand his pain and embarrassment?
160. Do you think that we become negatively emotional often because we are not understood?
161. Do you think of children as immature?
162. Do your problems with children or other things keep you from being closer to your spouse?
163. Do you sometimes feel humiliated?
164. Do you spank your children?
165. Do you worry about eternity?
166. Is life good to you?
167. Do people not take enough time to learn of and listen to your problems?

168. One must be very good in at least one thing in order to have self-respect? (T or F)
169. Are you disturbed if you are not praised for your good work?
170. Are you hurt at being criticized?
171. Do you become angry if you just miss getting a good grade, catching a bus, etc.?
172. Do you feel that no one loves you?
173. Does change to a new town or job upset you?
174. Do you become upset with other peoples' problems?
175. Does it annoy you to hear people criticize religion?
176. Does it disturb you greatly if you are not accepted or listened to at a party?
177. Do you become upset if things do not go the way they should?
178. Do you get annoyed if you make a mistake?
179. Are you a sensitive person?
180. Are your feelings easily hurt?
181. Do you think there is a generation gap making it hard for younger people to understand older people?
182. Does self-respect come from the approval of others?
183. Do you feel you must be accepted by other people?
184. Should people be blamed for their wrong actions?
185. Are some men perverse by nature?
186. Are some men evil or wicked?
187. Do you worry about the future?
188. What I visually see is partly determined by my beliefs?
189. What I visually see is partly determined by my past habits?
190. Do you think your happiness is determined mainly by you?
191. Do you think you could completely rid yourself of religious faith?
192. Are you almost always successful?
193. Do you think of children as immature adults?
194. Do you have an identity problem?

PART III (Essay Questions)

1. Describe your dreams and your attitude toward them.

2. What do you dream about? Give details.

3. What are the most valuable things in your life?

4. List physical defects which may be relevant to your self-image, emotional life, sex life.

5. List the actual statements you usually make to your children when you are irritated with them.

6. Describe in detail several things you literally hate?

7. Describe someone you hate telling why you hate that person.

8. I fear most_____. (List 6 things, the most important first)

9. I am frustrated with_____. (List 6 — most important first)

10. I prefer a spouse who has these qualities (List 6 things — most important first)

11. List your long term negative emotional sentiments or traits (e.g., dislike modern society, hate criticism.)

12. What is your feeling about your father and mother?

13. How do you think others think about you?

14. How do you think of yourself?

15. Give your own definition of love. Be as complete as possible.

16. What do you think is the best way of becoming clear about your emotions?

17. What are your immediate and long term goals? Are they really adequate for you?

18. Describe the bad emotional experiences you have had. Indicate if you are completely over them. If they are still problems state specifically what bothers you about them.

19. What are the shortcomings of your spouse or mate?

20. Please add additional questions you think should have been asked.

21. Your remarks.

22. (Self-analysis question)
    What emotional problems do you now have? Include also any recent emotional incidents.
    a) Objectively describe the problem.
    b) Write the actual statements you think and say about the problem.
    c) Criticize rationally each statement in b) indicating what you should rather have said and done about the problem.

Appendix II

Imagery and Visual Perception

"We find certain things about seeing puzzling, because
we do not find the whole business of seeing puzzling enough."
Wittgenstein (PI 212)

Introduction

It was mentioned that, in addition to language, imagery and
perception play a part in constituting thinking and assessment.
Such assessment constitutes emotion and leads to feeling. Imagery
and perception, then, are involved with emotion. As was mentioned
in the chapter on psychiatric disorders, some patients are classified
on the basis of having hallucinations or imagery. The average person
imagines that certain events are taking place, or imagines a goal for
himself. He can, for example, see himself as an executive with a
large house, expensive car, etc. Imagery may be motivating and
serve as a goal in this way. Also, patients who have certain fears,
e.g., of mice, can learn to replace their imagery of running from
the feared object by imagery of staying and calmly coping with it.
It is a method of changing one's emotions by means of changing
one's imagery. One imagines himself doing things as he would like
to do them. It is also possible and useful to practice imagery just
as does a blind person in developing new clues to behavior. Basketball players, dart throwers, musicians, typists, etc. practice with
their eyes closed. In this way, new imagery is developed and improved. Such imagery ties in closely with assessment, language, and

445

metaphor. The imagist poets explicitly juxtaposed images in order to give insight. The psychotic may create and be captivated by such metaphors as "My brain is rotting," "silent screaming," etc. Here the imagery or metaphors are taken literally. (See chapter on metaphor.) It need not be the case that the psychotic actually has hallucinations or senses the imagery he reports, but rather that he believes the reported language-bound experience, e.g., "I hear a silent scream." The experience may be partly a language disorder of "images." As will be seen, images are not merely pictures in the mind, but involve language and assessment. Wittgenstein wrote,

"When someone says the word 'cube' to me, for example, I know what it means. But can the whole *use* of the word come before my mind, when I understand it in this way?" (PI 139)

To understand emotions and to achieve effective therapy it is necessary to be clear about the nature of perception and imagery. Since about 1930, psychologists have avoided the subject because it seemed to involve mentalism. Francis Galton in 1880 reported that some see no images at all. (See "image," "imagery," "metaphor as image," "synaesthesia," W. Shibles *Metaphor: An Annotated Bibliography and History.*) But this may be because it was not clear what was meant by an image. William James also said he did not have visual imagery. The behaviorist, John Watson, rejected the notion of mental images. Little work has been done on synaesthesia. A few distinctions have been made but without much clarity. Some types of imagery are "preservation imagery" (imagery from looking at something for a long time), autism, after-image (on which much research of a certain sort has been done), hypnagogic imagery (longer lasting than the former), *deja vu* experiences, voluntary and involuntary imagery (drugs may make imagery involuntary), eidetic imagery (Purkinje 1819), etc. Dreams are special types of imagery and much work remains to be done in clarifying them. (See N. Malcolm *Dreaming*) Freudian interpretations of dreams are only as sound as Freudian theory. Dreams need to be reanalyzed in terms of contemporary theory. Metaphor and symbolization play large roles in dream analysis and recent work in these areas is relevant. Dreams may be consciously invoked or induced as well as merely assessed. Improper or mystical interpretations and preoccupations with dreams may be harmful. Memory is another area involving imagery. (See W. Shibles "Memory and Remembering" *Wittgenstein, Language and Philosophy*.)

Although little work was done since 1930, within the last two years psychologists have again begun to treat imagery as a legitimate subject for research. Peter Sheehan edited a recent work, *The Function and Nature of Imagery* (1972), philosophical views are discussed by Alastair Hannay *Mental Images: A Defense* (1971), Allan Paivio wrote, *Imagery and Verbal Processes* (1971), and several other books on imagery have recently appeared. Paivio's theory, incidentally, is that:

"Images and verbal processes are viewed as alternative coding systems, or modes of symbolic representation, which are developmentally linked to experiences with concrete objects and events as well as with language." (8)

The philosophers J. Shorter, Ryle, and Wittgenstein oppose mental imagery and treat it as linguistic depicting or as a seeing-as. The power of imagination is largely a language-game power. It may also be suggested that just as assessment guides feeling to constitute emotion, assessment guides sensation to constitute perception. One may imagine she or he has a lover, or hallucinate one. Imagery may be explored as an adaptive or defense-mechanism activity which fits in with one's total thought, i.e., linguistic assessment and needs. The following is an analysis of perception which may serve as a basis for further research.

Seeing and Knowing

Knowing is often thought of as a mental activity, as thinking or having ideas. Knowledge is often thought of as a storehouse of ideas. We have no evidence for there being ideas or thought as such. They are pseudo-psychological entities. Knowing is not having thoughts or ideas. "I have knowledge" can thus be a naming-fallacy if "knowledge" is used in the language-game of description. There are many uses of knowledge which are acceptable other than that of describing a mental entity, e.g., "I know this is a piece of paper" as meaning that I can touch it. By "knowing," we mainly, in fact, refer to what we say or do. To know something is to be able to describe it. One may also know how to do something, e.g., swim.

"To know is to see." But one may say, "I know I am seeing." This would mean, "I see I am seeing," which appears false. It is not adequate to rest knowledge on seeing or observation as an epistemological starting point of inquiry because seeing presupposes language. To assert that one just sees is an assertion. A theory or statement cannot be made by seeing alone. Other senses than seeing are involved in language. We see and hear language. We say that and so presuppose language. We may say "But seeing names an experience." Again we *say* that. Which experience does it name and how do we describe such an experience? It is inadequate to say that to know is to see, in spite of the fact that scientific method often bases its evidence on observation. If not all knowing is seeing perhaps seeing is a kind of knowing.

"To see is to know." This is often phrased "Seeing is believing." Is seeing knowing? An electric eye may be said to see but not know. An ant is said to see but it is not clear what knowing would be for the ant. An ant cannot know because it does not speak English and does not have the word "know." In neither the case of the ant nor the human do we have evidence that seeing is a mentalistic phenomenon. To say we see, erroneously implies that seeing is a mental process. In any case, seeing is not in these ways usually identified with knowing. "See the evidence," is circular in the sense that "evidence" derives from the word "to see." "See the evidence," becomes "See what you see." All things which see do not necessarily know. Nor is it clear what knowing or seeing is for an insect or animal. We often say, "To see is not necessarily to know; to see is to sense."

In the case of humans, what part of knowing is seeing? How is seeing a kind of knowing? "I know that there is a chair in this room." This is to know that something is the case. It is to know in the sense of a linguistic description. One cannot literally see that there is a chair in this room, though one might be able to see a chair and a room. A dog cannot see that there is a chair in a room, because dogs do not speak our language. Nevertheless seeing is related to the statement. One of the tests for there being a chair in the room is that one sees a chair and a room. (One could, of course, have touched both objects instead.) But this is not quite adequate. To know that is a chair is to be able to say there is a chair there. One test for knowing is being able to understand and speak the language. One cannot see a chair in a room without knowing there is a chair in the room and without being able to describe it. Even the description "see a chair" depends on language. Seeing seems to necessarily involve our ability with language but language does not necessarily involve our ability with seeing.

Seeing does not have epistemological primacy. Seeing already includes linguistic knowledge. Thus to say, "I see the chair," already includes knowledge and not just seeing. The mistake is that of thinking that there can be seeing in itself, that one can just see, that seeing is atomistic and can take place independent of other experience. That is, seeing in itself is not knowing and there can be no pure seeing or seeing in itself. Seeing involves language and other abilities and so involves knowing. In this sense, to see is to know. It may be equally true to say, "I know the chair is there because I see it," as to say, "I see the chair is there because I know how to use my language." Seeing is bound up inseparably with knowing. One cannot just see, have unrelated seeing. The Kantian view that there is no conception without sensation and no sensation without conception is relevant. It is for this reason that seeing is not just sensation plus interpretation. This is why the duck-rabbit ambiguous figure is not just a seeing plus an interpretation. By "conception" here is meant largely language use. This is also one reason why perception is not immediate or direct. To see direct may mean simply that one is not looking through a glass. Seeing involves relations and language and so already involves reasoning or interpretation. That further interpretations of observations are often given, may erroneously suggest that there was no original interpretation involved in seeing. "I perceive that," is often a synonym for "I think that." It is no good to say "We organize perception unconsciously," unless we know what an unconscious mind is. We do not.

Because seeing already involves interpretation it can be false. We may see falsely. Perceptions can be corrected. We may learn how and what to see in aesthetics, philosophy, art, etc.

Webster's Collegiate Dictionary defines perception as "physical sensation interpreted in the light of experience," and "a capacity for comprehension." *The Century Dictionary and Cyclopedia* defines it as the faculty of "gaining knowledge by virtue of a real action of an object upon the mind," and "an immediate judgement founded on sense . . . " Perception is bound up with knowledge. Words involving knowing often or usually derive from words for seeing, e.g., evidence, advice, revise, supervise, survey, idea (from "to see"), insight, enlighten, outlook, reflect, introspect, illusory, illuminate, obscure, enlighten, clarify, observe, notice, see that, glimmer of truth, clouded thinking, blind alley, bright person, "I see what you mean," a thought flashed through his mind. Thus, knowing is rendered by means of metaphors. It was mentioned above that the usual metaphors for mental entities are unfounded. Instead of "a thought flashed through his mind," one would be more correct in saying "He uttered a sentence to himself" (not aloud).

SEEING-AS

Insomuch as seeing involves cognition or language, we see things in terms of our beliefs. Seeing involves seeing things as something. It is seeing-as. We see *that* something is the case, see *what* people do, see *how* something looks, see *differences*, see chairs, tables, etc. Statements about seeing are often elliptical or metaphorical, e.g., "The water *looks* wet," where wet is a felt not a seen quality; "Ice *looks* cold," "I hear a car," when actually a noise is heard, "He spoke *bitter* words," where bitter is a taste, "The surface *looks* rough," where rough is a tactile quality. Color and pitch are metaphorically said to be high or low. The voice is described as neutral, white, hard, brown, red, majestic, thoughtful, cutting, trailing, broken. Vowels are light, dark, sharp, thin, wide, feminine, masculine, hard, strong, fine, high, deep.

The philosopher of science, Norwood Hanson (1969), elaborates the notion of seeing-as into a significant feature of science. He says that we see in terms of our beliefs and theories. We do not just all see the same things. Thus a 13th century astronomer literally sees differently than does a 20th century astronomer. Seeing is partly determined by cognition and all seeing is perspectival. Seeing involves seeing-as. Hanson wrote,

> "We usually *see* through spectacles made of our past experience, our knowledge, and tinted and mottled by the logical forms of our special languages and notations. Seeing is what I call a 'theory laden' operation . . . " (149)

Seeing is not merely pure sensation, or given directly somehow without cognitive association. There is not pure seeing.

> "A visual sensation of a brilliant yellow-white disc is not itself a seeing of the sun . . . " (82)

And without language we would not see even a "yellow-white disc." It is not clear what we would "see." We "see" through or in terms of our language. Seeing and seeing-as are language-games.

> "Unless there were a linguistic component to seeing, nothing that we saw, observed, witnessed, etc. would have the slightest relevance to our knowledge, scientific or otherwise." (125)

> "It might be that our language in the form of what we know puts an indelible stamp on what we see . . . " (183)

Hanson also points out that our language, because of its structure, partly determines what we see. If the language were different we might say things such as "the sun rounds," "lawns square," "grass greens," "sun yellows." (179) This is a restatement of the Whorf-Sapir Hypothesis according to which we perceive the world through the categories and limitations of our language. It is also Wittgenstein's view that the limits of our language are the limtis of the world.

Hanson's view of seeing-as derives from statements made by Wittgenstein. The latter gives the example of an ambiguous duck-rabbit figure to illustrate seeing-as :

(There is also hearing-as, touching-as, tasting-as, smelling-as, feeling as, etc.) The figure may be seen as a duck or as a rabbit. We see only one figure at a time. The figure seems to shift from the one aspect to the other, to click from one to the other. In one sense, seeing-as refers only to the experience of the changing of the aspect from duck to rabbit or vice versa. We no more see the duck as a rabbit, than the rabbit as a duck. The object seen is no more a duck that a rabbit. There is no single interpretation of an object but rather many perspectives. The duck-rabbit figure may, for example, be seen as mere lines on paper. We learn these different descriptions. Nor is the difference in what is seen a shift in a mental interpretation. He rejects mental entities. On the other hand, the seeing itself is not pure but already involves language and cognition. He states,

" 'Seeing as . . .' is not a part of perception. And for that reason it is like seeing and again not like." (PI p. 197)

This could mean merely that seeing-as *is* perception and not just a *part of* perception, and also that seeing-as is not just perception, not just sensation. Seeing is a contextual language-game not reducible to pure seeing plus a separate mental interpretation. Nor is seeing-as comparing mental-images. Seeing is a given, bed-rock experience, a technique not an interpretation.

To be able to see the figure as a duck requires that we have learned about ducks. In some unpublished notes Wittgenstein gave the diagram:

This may be seen-as a soldier and a dog going through a door. Wittgenstein states that it is important here to know that the soldier is in red and blue. That is, the rifle seems to be of a certain antique type.

Seeing-as is a different language-game than seeing, and the one should not be confused with the other. One may be able to see an aspect but not notice it or see-as. An "aspect-blind" person may not be able to see the duck, but only the rabbit.

It is clear that Wittgenstein's notion of seeing-as is that it is a given language-game or "form of life" not to be confused with others. Taking it in this sense, O. K. Bouwsma (1965) has given one application of Wittgenstein's view. Wittgenstein said,

"The epithet 'sad,' as applied for example to the outline face, characterizes the grouping of lines in a circle," (PI p. 209) and "In aesthetic matters we often say, 'You have to see it like *this.*' " (PI p. 202)

Bouwsma considers the expression, "The music is sad." His main point is that difficulty arises with such a statement which we normally make only when we think of other language-games or "forms of life." We should not think that the music is sad in the same way that Cassie is sad. We are *seeing* the music *as* sad, not seeing the music in terms of or through Cassie's sort of sadness. The puzzlement about "The music is sad" vanishes when we realize that the puzzlement arose from misleading analogies. The music *is* sad, it is not *seen-as* sad. The duck is a duck and is not seen-as a duck. But also there is the different experience of seeing-as.

The difficulty with taking "The music is sad" as not a puzzling statement, is where one does not have that experience. This is what was called aspect-blindness. One may say, "The music is delicious," and it is not clear that this would be an acceptable usage unless several people concur. Artists may attempt to show people such aspects, to get them to *see* the music *as* delicious. But when they do they can only point to or repeat the music. A picture of a red, juicy apple will not help. The function of the critic, then, is to experience the art object (*see* it *as*), and then he can only point in various ways to the object and hope the public will see the aspects also. There will not be one aspect that will define the particular work of art.

Hanson's view (1958), like that of Wittgenstein, is that our theories and knowledge actually become a part of our seeing: "The knowledge is there in the seeing and not an adjunct of it." (22) Hanson's statement, "So too the interpretation of a piece of music is there in the music," is in agreement with Bouwsma's views.

Hanson did distinguish between 1) phenomenal seeing, and 2) seeing in terms of a theory. One may get the impression from Hanson that if one has a new theory one visually sees differently. I think the case is rather that seeing-as is not seeing in terms of a theory or an interpretation. To say that the theory is built into the seeing needs clarification. It may mean only that seeing and seeing-as are language-games. I think this is what Hanson means for he says seeing-as is an amalgam of pictures and language. In any case, a distinction should be made here regarding 1) visually seeing-as, and 2) non-visually seeing-as.

Wittgenstein gives several types of seeing-as: a) seeing aspects of an ambiguous figure such as a duck-rabbit, b) seeing a picture which is interpreted in various ways in a text, e.g., a square regarded as an open box, a glass, a cube, a wire frame, etc. A child playing may regard a box as a house. (PI p. 206) This distinction is referred to by Burlingame (1965) as 1) the perceptual sense, and 2) the non-perceptual sense, respectively.

Coplestone (1954) confuses visually and non-visually seeing-as when he states that one can by reflection notice being and existence just as one can *see* the landscape and then *notice* (or not notice) its beauty. Seeing-as in the one case need not be like seeing-as in the other. Also some things cannot be seen and so not seen-as. We cannot see, for example, the form of a leaf "in general." (Wittgenstein, PI 74)

G. Vesey (1956) argues that all seeing is seeing-as. He argues as follows, "I saw it, but I didn't see it as anything," seems self-contradictory. If a person sees something it must look like something to him. Vesey thinks that a judgment is involved in our seeing something. This judgment is different from the judgment of what the object looks like. The look of a thing is phenomenal, given.

This view again falls into the danger of confusing all seeing with seeing-as and all types of seeing-as with each other. If, however, we take Vesey to be merely stating that there are many language-games one can play, that there is no single way of seeing in the visual or in the non-visual sense, then his view would be consistent with Wittgenstein's. And it is this that I do take him to be asserting. Thus all seeing is seeing-as. Hanson (1958) seems to agree and to agree also about the number of possible ways of seeing. Hanson stated that there are an infinite number of ways a constellation of lines, etc., may be seen.

Sources:

O.K. Bouwsma *"The Expression Theory of Art"* Philosophical Essays University of Nebraska Press 1965

Charles Burlingame *"On the Logic of the 'Seeing-As' Locution"* PhD. Diss., University of Virginia 1965

F. Copleston *"On Seeing and Noticing"* Philosophy 29 (109) (April 1954) 152-159

Norwood Hanson Patterns of Discovery Cambridge University Press 1958

Norwood Hanson Perception and Discovery San Francisco: Freeman, Cooper 1969

G. Vesey *"Seeing and Seeing As"* Aristotelian Society Proceedings N.S. 56 (1956) 109-124

Ludwig Wittgenstein The Blue and Brown Books New York: Harper 1958 162-182

Ludwig Wittgenstein Philosophical Investigations 3rd edition New York: Macmillan 1968 (1953)

ILLUSION AS METAPHOR

"Illusions are like metaphors."
Colin Turbayne (*The Language of Vision*)

"What you see is an illusion not a real object." Buildings are painted on a large canvas for a stage setting so that they "look real." But the canvas is real. There may not even be buildings which correspond to the picture. The buildings the picture represents may be unreal. Something is really seen but it may be labeled or described as a painted canvas, or as a building. To say it is illusory and not a real building is only to say the viewer has not identified it in the usual way or in a certain expected way: "I thought it was a building but now I see it is a canvas." Here an illusion is something one sees which he mistakes for something else. He does not see an illusory object but a "real object," a canvas.

What is meant by a real object is an object which can be seen, touched or sensed in the usual ways. All of its aspects are equally "real" and so no aspects are "real." The object is simply sensed or not sensed. "Real" means nothing more here. To be real is simply to be an object. By the same reasoning no aspects are unreal. "The object looks different than it really is," is misleading. The object can only look as it looks, though our description of it may differ.

Thus, it is unacceptable to speak of objects as being real as such. If by real we mean "perceived," as in the belief that "to be is to be perceived," then it may raise the question as to whether an object can be real or exist unperceived. The problem vanishes when it is seen that there are no such objects. What we mean by an object is that it can be directly or indirectly perceived. "Does an unperceived tree in a forest exist?" In the first place, this statement assumes there is a tree there. If it is there and we know that, then it exists. "To be is to be perceived," here only means that one has perceived it or has evidence that the tree can be perceived, e.g., one may leave a moving camera focused on the tree, count its rings, note how large it is or how much it has grown, etc. There is a consistency of these sorts involved in perception. Thus nothing exists which is neither directly nor indirectly perceived. Indirect perception, e.g., by cameras, tape recorders, etc. is actually one sort of direct perception. If the tree in the forest is in no way perceived then it does not exist. To argue that there are some things which exist which we can but have not yet perceived is inadequate because we do now have perceptual evidence that such things do exist. For example, I walk in a forest I have never been in before and perhaps see trees or plants which have never been seen before. I have not seen my heart but I perceive it. I have not seen the inside of the pen I am using but its insides would cohere with my other perceptions if I were to look inside the pen. "Exist" only means things of this sort.

"But trees not perceived still do exist." Then this is because of a misuse of the word "not." It was said that it is a contradiction to speak of "unperceived objects," and so unperceived trees cannot exist. Exist refers to perception. Not existing means not perceived. We could not, then, know something does not exist. To say there is "no" tree means there is a perceived configuration of events of a certain sort. It does not mean that there is an absolute negation. Also, to say trees are not perceived is still to refer to a perceptual configuration. One must perceive that a tree is not perceived. There is nothing which is not perceived. "Not perceived," is not an absolute negation but a statement about a certain sort of perception. "The tree is not perceived," is a report of a certain perceptual configuration. Similarly to say there is no beer in the refrigerator is to report a certain perceived configuration. It is a positive not a negative statement. Perhaps all uses of not are positive assertions and there are no negations as such. Do not think that nothing is really no thing. Similarly, the statement, "An illusion is not a real object," is misleading. That which is "not real" is as real as that which is. An illusion is a real, positive, perceived, configuration of events.

In a sense, hallucinations are more immediate than are physical objects. But both involve context and coherence only. Hallucinations involve not cohering with other objects in a certain way.

"A coin seen at an angle looks elliptical, but is really round." An object is seen. This is almost tautological. An object cannot look round or elliptical as such for the same reason that it cannot look pure as such. "Round," "elliptical," "pure" are descriptive, linguistic assessments and are not things which can be seen as such. There are paradigms for them which can be seen. We may see that there are no particles in a sample of water and so assert that in this sense it is pure. We do not see the pure, however. Also we do not see the round of a coin, but only a certain outline, circle, or type of line.

To say a coin is really round only means that if one looks at a flat coin from above, it is seen to have a certain shape, "What is *the* shape of the coin?" is a many-question fallacy. It assumes that it has a single shape, and it does not. The coin is not just round, but if looked at from the end it is flat, if looked at from an angle it is elliptical. We have chosen one out of several aspects of a coin, to say that shape is the real shape. It is, of course, convenient to do so, since if looked at from the side many different shapes would go undetected. It would be hard to tell a round object from a square one. If looked at from an angle, rather than from directly overhead, it is hard to determine a specific angle, e.g., 35 degrees. The coin is not "really" round but only round by agreed upon convention. It is also "really" flat and elliptical. Thus it is false and misleading to say, "A coin seen at an angle looks elliptical but is really round." In one respect the round coin never does look elliptical if one sees one edge as farther away than the other. Looking at a round coin at an angle is not like looking at an elliptical coin from above. It is no illusion though one might make a mistake and think one is looking at the coin from above instead of from an angle. This mistake is an error in interpretation, not an error in seeing. To substitute one aspect of a coin for all of the aspects of a coin is a form of metaphor, namely synecdoche. To say "The coin is round," is a metaphor.

"A stick put halfway in water looks bent and so is an illusion." The same argument applies here as above. It is not an illusion but an actual stick seen in water. One cannot see a stick look bent. He can see a bent stick or a stick in water and relate the two experiences. He may even mistake one description for the other, but the description or the mistake is not in what is seen. To say the stick "looks bent" is to admit one knows it is not bent. We do not see "looks." To say the stick looks bent is to assert an analogy or comparison between what is seen when a stick is put halfway in water and what is seen when looking at a bent stick. What is seen is different but nevertheless similar. Illusion is based on a faulty analogy and on a confusion of two separate contexts. The one context or aspect is no more "real" than the other. To confuse the contexts is a category-mistake. To say the stick is really straight implies that that is its only literal shape, and all other shapes would then be metaphorical: "See that illusory bent stick, it looks like a straight stick in water." What we regard as metaphorical and so illusory, largely depends upon deviations from what we are used to seeing. Illusions are metaphors.

"The same object cannot be both round and elliptical, or straight and bent." This is now seen to be false. In fact what we mean by an object is that it has all of its aspects and is seen differently from different perspectives.

"The object appears larger than it is." The object is a constant size but I judge that it is large or small. Again to say it is larger than it is is to mix contexts. It may be seen or judged as large in one context and small in another. Its "real" size is relative. The real size is the size we are used to and most familiar with. All other sizes tend to be regarded as metaphorical or as deviations from the normal.

Seeing an object as larger than it is, is due to faulty perspective clues due to a confusion of contexts or lack of experience with a certain context. We ordinarily see objects in certain ways for certain practical purposes. We learn to judge the size of an object in the distance by certain clues. In most situations these compensating clues work but in some cases they are found to be misleading. The following are some traditional illusions (cf. *Scientific American* 225 (Dec. 1971) (63-71):

1. Small objects feel heavier than larger objects of the same weight. This may be because we expect small things to be lighter and so over-compensate.

2. The moving blades of a windmill seem to reverse their direction.

3. The Necar cube may be seen with an ambiguous near or far edge. The context allows us to see the object equally well both ways. Shadows or other depth perception clues could fix the figure in one way or the other. That the figure is ambigious is due to an inadequate or incomplete context.

One may similarly ask which way this line is going: _____ Back? Left? Right?

4. A vertical line looks longer than a horizontal line of equal length.

5. M. Ponzo Illusion: If two bars of equal size are placed at different places on a picture of a vanishing railroad track one bar looks larger than does the other:

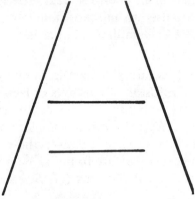

The clue that the closer the bar is to the vanishing point the larger the object really is, is misleading here because the bars are simply superimposed on the picture.

6. E. Hering Illusion. Two parallel lines appear bowed where lines radiate from a point between them.

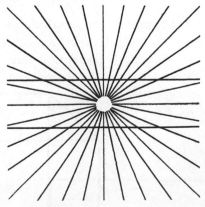

7. W. Wundt's Converse of Hering Illusion. The parallel lines are made to seem narrow by superimposing contextual lines:

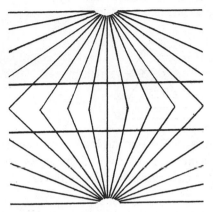

8. Muller-Lyer Illusion. Two straight lines of equal length are made to seem unequal.

The contextual difference seems to account for this.

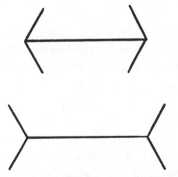

9. J. Poggendorff Illusion. A diagonal line behind a long rectangular bar seems to be offset.

We are not used to a line broken up this way and find it hard to imagine it being continuous.

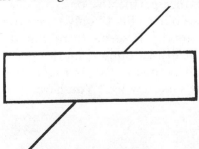

10. Penrose Impossible Triangle Illusion. The sides of a triangle do not actually meet but are photographed so that they seem to meet, thus creating a paradoxical figure.

The distortion is due to our having correct perspective clues but failing to realize that perhaps two of the sides do not actually meet. It is a metaphorical figure in that it deviates from what is normally expected.

11. Size Constancy. An object is seen as large as another although it is far away and looks small. This is an illusion only when we mistake the distance or the size. The distant object is in fact seen as small. We merely have learned to compensate for its small appearance.

12. Moon Illusion. The moon directly overhead is seen to look smaller than does the moon on the horizon. We have few comparison and perspectival clues when looking at the moon in a clear sky. Faintness is one clue. The horizon moon, however, is related to objects on the landscape and involves perspective clues and contextual comparisons. When the sky is cloudy, or the moon is seen overhead but between tall buildings the overhead moon is seen as larger than when it is alone in the sky. Some people learn to see the overhead and horizon moon as being the same size.

"I seem to see a coin."

"Seems," here, may suggest that we do not "really" see a coin. But we do "really" see something. What "seems" refers to is the fact that from another perspective or in another context what is seen might not be a coin. "Might" only refers to what might be seen in a different context. "It seems to be round from this perspective," is to say it really is round from this perspective. To say the coin is really round is to say that its round aspect is taken as being its description. It's like saying, "You haven't really seen New

York until you have seen Fifth Avenue." One could also say you haven't really seen New York until you have seen Greenwich Village, Chinatown or the Bowery. We may of course interpret it in various ways but to do so is only to indicate how the coin would look or feel in another context. To seem to see is a genuine experience of seeing as much as is just seeing the object up close. A law may be formulated to govern this and similar experiences: A further experience or a different contextual experience is not a substitute for or explanation of the original experience. The same law applies to attempts to formulate the original experience of seeing in terms of derived notions of physiology, and physics.

Here "X seems to be Y," or "The elliptical object seems to be a round object." But the X or elliptical object is already seen as elliptical and cannot from that perspective be round. To say the elliptical object is round is only to say that from one perspective it is elliptical and from another perspective it is round. The formula "X seems to be Y," clearly suggests that X is already experienced as X.

"We see appearances not reality." That is, "X appears to be Y." "Appears" is merely a synonym for "seems" and so the above arguments are applicable here also. Appearances are as real as so-called real objects. Appearances are real. Some reasons one may want to speak of artificial rather than real may be illustrated as follows. "Is that a real tiger?" "No, it is a stuffed tiger." One then does not go on to ask if it is a real stuffed tiger. What could be meant by such a question? "Is that a real stuffed tiger?" Perhaps the reply might be "It is a toy tiger, made out of velvet." Similarly one may refer to a "real observation," or a "faulty observation," an "exploratory observation" (a "toy observation").

To say "X appears to be Y," is like "X is like Y." It is a metaphor or simile relating one context to another. It is not to identify two different experiences or perspectives. There are other "appear" or "seem" words. "Artificial cream," or "artificial perception," refer to a real kind of cream and a real kind of perception and relate them to other kinds of cream and perception. "Synthetic cream" is real chemically produced cream and is similar to dairy cream.

"All we see are appearances." To say this only means that what one sees can be seen differently from a different perspective. It does not mean that one never sees "real" objects. We usually say a coin is round and to do so is not to say it is round no matter how one looks at it. We may call its elliptical look an appearance. But suppose we call *all* aspects of the coin appearances. All aspects of the coin are not the "real" aspects. What could this mean? It may mean that perhaps with some special microscope someone could see the coin in a different way and that we would like to let that be the standard way of seeing the coin. Physicists sometimes do this when they say "This table only appears to be solid. It is really a collection of moving atoms with spaces between them." But, in this case, there is a "real" way of looking at the table and all else is regarded as appearance. And this is only to say again that "real," "seems," "appears," are relative not absolute terms. "All we see are appearances," makes no sense because it assumes there can be appearance without "reality." One cannot have "artificial" cream if one does not have real cream, one cannot "seem to see" a coin if one cannot see a coin. To see all the appearances of the coin is to see the real coin. There is no correct way of seeing a coin. The traditional problem is, "If all we can see is appearances, how can we know there is a reality behind them?" The solution is to show that the question is wrongly constructed. Not all of New York is Fifth Avenue nor is all of it hidden subways. Compare: "I will show you the real New York," with "I cannot show you the real New York. It can't be seen."

"Maybe everything we see is a dream, mere illusion." This is based on a false analogy. A dream is like our waking perception. If our waking perception is really dream, what waking perception would that be like? We wake up from dreams and are conscious of them. How could we wake up from our conscious state? What would it be like? Then, if all is dream nothing is dream, and we would never know we are dreaming. But, more important, to dream would make no sense. To say all may be a dream is another matter. That is to say that it may be that in the future we will have an entirely different way of seeing.

It is also a misleading analogy to say, "The image is blurred." This implies that an image could be clear and distinct. What it seems rather to mean is that the image is blurred as an object is blurred when it is in fog or when one has excess water in his eyes. Even then, "being blurred" is not an illusion. One really sees blur. It makes sense to say, "I see the blur very clearly." One reason for speaking of blurred objects as not being real objects is that clear sight coheres better with touch than does blurred sight. This problem does not arise with images for we cannot touch an image. An image is not touched but is supposed to be a representation — a representation of something which is not there.

DOES SEEING WORK LIKE A CAMERA?

"An image is not a picture."
Wittgenstein (PI 301)

"The eye is like a camera." Light comes into the eye as it comes into the lens of the camera, and by looking into the eye an image can be seen on the back of the retina as it can be seen on film in a camera. But the camera cannot see its image or picture, and in this significant respect is unlike the eye. Perception is not a ghost inside the camera of the eye. The camera model does not explain how we see, it only suggests that there is an image on the retina. The question remains as to how we see.

The camera model suggests that we see the image on the retina, and this is true — but only when we are looking inside the retina. We do not see the image on our retinas when we see. To do so would require eyes behind our eyes. Rather, our retinas have images on them. An image on a retina is not a mental image. An image on a retina is a physiological event. The camera model misleads us into thinking that because we see a picture on the film we also see our own retinas from the inside. But do you see your retinal image from the inside? You do not see your retinal image, you see "objects." You may never have learned that you have a retina and never even seen one.

That an image on film or retina is so distinct may mislead us into thinking that an image is exactly what we see. A picture is fixed and remains stationary and static. But our eyes are always moving and produce a number of "images" not a single one. Nor will it do to say that the eye is like a motion picture camera. The camera still does not see its images and we do not just see images in our eyes. The camera does not see and our eyes do not themselves see.

We do not see everything within view but only certain selected things. If one looks at a scene and then describes what he saw he would miss very many, if not most, details. A policeman learns to look for certain things the average person would not notice. We tend to see things in terms of our needs, wants, and in terms of our knowledge and interests. A dancer or musician can notice things unobserved by others. We see differently when we are in love. A photograph taken of the scene reported would reveal many details the eyes overlook. In this sense also, the eye is unlike a camera.

"You must have seen it because it was within your field of vision." This is fallacious reasoning because it is based on the camera model. The camera does capture all within its view. Man's visual system, however, is selective. One often looks at an object directly in front of him without seeing it. Vision does not copy objects like a camera copies.

To think that seeing works like a camera suggests that seeing is a separate thing from knowing and using language. It suggests that there is seeing as such. This seems not to be the case. Seeing is not one single unitary experience. It is not just the image on a film or the opening of lenses. Vision is not silent or mute as a camera is. A motion picture with a sound track would not bridge the gap.

The view that we have a "photographic memory" is derived from the camera metaphor. It suggests that memory is a storehouse of images and that images are like pictures. The image on the retina is upside down yet we see the object as right side up. We do not have to read books upside down. Seeing in this way also deviates from the camera model.

The camera model leads us to think there is just a copying process, that the image is a copy of the object and the image in the eye is copied in the brain where we see it. It is not the case that the retina, the brain, or the mind copy the object. Also, with seeing regarded as a copying process, one is lead to think there must be an original. But when one has an experience of seeing it is not clear why he would look for an original experience of seeing, or how he would find one. We need not ask how what we see compares with the "real" original object. They cannot be compared. What we see are originals not copies. We see objects. If perceiving were copying one could only perceive the copy and not the original and so never be able to find the original anyway. If all is appearance there is no (original) reality, and if all is reality there is no appearance.

IMAGES

How can vision be internal? What is it internal to? It is not inside the body as we saw. Inside the body there are only more external objects. It looks as though we have a misleading analogy as follows:

vision: external objects :: inside a room: external to a room.

vision (inside a body): external objects :: inside a room: external objects

But we do not know what could be meant by saying vision is inside. What is it inside of? Is vision an internal object? It seems that external object is spoken of where it makes no sense to talk of internal object. Isn't this like a circle which has an outside but no inside? What sense could it make to talk of external object if it makes no sense to talk of internal object? If there are no internal objects there are no external objects. There are just objects. If there is no external there is no internal.

"But aren't images internal?" What can one say to this now? We do say images are internal or that they are internal objects. People have wondered for a long time about what kind of objects images are. Why would we want to say images are internal?

For one thing, if I see a cup of tea I can touch it, I can pick it up and drink from it. But some things I can see but cannot touch and pick up. Such things are not usual objects. So we may call them internal images. Because they don't relate to other objects in the usual way we say they are images or internal.

To say such experiences, as that of seeing something without being able to touch it, are internal seems to be to describe something. They do not. There is nothing to be internal to. All that internal means, for example, is that some things can be seen but not touched. "Internal" seems to but does not mean "something inner." That is, it is a naming-fallacy.

One reason why it seems safe to call such things as images internal is that by so doing we put off our questioner. By making them internal we put them out of reach. How could anyone question them then? And who would dare? To say images are internal is to dodge the question about their status. It is like saying, "I don't know where they are?" Since one doesn't know where they are he says they are internal.

"But certainly images seem to be internal." Isn't that because we call them "images?" An image is said to be a mental picture formed in the imagination. Because there is no evidence for a mind it will not do to speak of "mental picture." There is no imagination for the same reason that there is no mind. Are there images? Why would we say that there are? We look into a pool of water and see an image of ourselves. We see the water and we see the face. Both are there. The face, however, is also somewhere other than on the surface of the water and the water is nowhere else than with its face. Now it is clear which is the real face. Water does not speak and if one puts his hand in the water the face goes away. This does not happen with real faces. So we say that the face in the water is a reflection, or copy of a real face. It is an image of a real face.

Because there are mirror or reflection images one is led to think that there are "mental images." We see a face and a pool reflection of a face. The face and reflection are different but are both seen as external objects. This is not the case with "mental images." A "mental image" is thought of as an internal reflection or copy of an external object. But what evidence is there that it is internal? How could an internal image be a reflection of an external object?

    external reflection: external object:: internal reflection: external object.

The evidence that we have "internal images" seems to be based on the model of external reflections or mirrors. It is not evidence of there being "internal images." The face on the water is not an "internal image." We can look again at it or take a picture of it. This is not the case with an "internal image." They are different kinds of things. To argue that we have "internal images" because there are reflections, is to argue with mirrors, to be captivated by false analogies. Image is a naming-fallacy.

Another analogy leading us to think that we have images is that we see an external image on the inside of the retina. Because it is on the "inside" of the retina may lead us to think it is an "inner mental picture." This does not follow. Neither does it follow that because an image is on the retina that there is also a "mental image." We are misled by thinking that we are like cameras. The film records the flat static image which enters the camera. The retina is not flat and not static, but always in motion. The eye also is selectively sensitive and not a mere passive recipient. Thus there is no fixed picture or image coming in from the retina. There is no single simple picture as in the case of a camera. A motion picture camera might seem to be a better analogy but again it yields external images not internal ones. And also the pictures are still atomistic, flat, and static.

Because water images are easily destroyed we might think that "mental images" because they too are too easily destroyed, are like water images. However, vagueness and transitoriness does not establish an image as an "internal image."

There seems to be no evidence thus far for there being internal images. This means that it makes no sense to speak of objects as external for if there is no internal there is no external.

"Mirror images are reflections of real objects." Is it the case that mirror images seem to be real but are not? Such images are as real as the objects they reflect. Instead of "real objects" it would be more precise to say "different objects." A mirror image is one kind of object and the reflected object is another kind. Both are real. The image is no more illusion of the reflected object, than the reflected object is an illusion of the mirror image. One could say, "Look, that table is an illusion of the mirror image," or "Mirror images are real, reflected objects not illusory." The problem only comes up when we see a mirror image or reflection, and think that it is the reflected object. We then speak of illusion. But the illusion may work both ways. We may see a mirror image and think it is the reflected object, or see a reflected object and think it is a mirror image.

"Real" is seen to be merely a relative term. "We do not perceive things as they really are." How are they really? I may see a face. Suppose someone asks, "Is the face you see in front of you real?" What kind of answer would he want? He may wonder if the face is made of wax. We touch the face and determine that it is not. He may wonder if the face is similar to those he is used to. We speak to the person whose face is in question and find that the lips move normally, and that the expressions are usual. Now, if one should ask, "But is the face real?" he is asking another question. He is asking, perhaps, "Does the face exist?" Here "real" and "exist" are vague open-context terms and since no specific question is asked no specific answer can be given. "Is it really real?" or "Does it really exist?" are unintelligible questions as such, and instead of seeking answers one may simply see that the question is unanswerable and so dissolve the question.

Thus we may be misled by such questions as, "Do we perceive things as they really are?" In one sense we do, and in another sense we do not. We do perceive things or at least we know how to use these words. On the other hand, when we see things in one way we do not at the same time see them in another way. The reflection is not the object. To ask if we perceive things as they really are is to ask if perhaps some new aspect or way of seeing will be found which we will find more useful or interesting than the ways in which we now see. It is not that we will find the new way in itself more "real." Some think that earth is more physical and more real than air. But this only means that one does not trip over air as one may trip over a stone. "Real" and "exist," if they are to make sense, must be reduced to concrete examples, comparisons, and contexts.

Because we may have been misled into thinking, "Mirror images are reflections of real objects," so we may think that images are not real or that they have some kind of illusory existence. It was found that we do not have evidence to assert that inner images are reflections of external objects. Now it may be added that inner or mental images are not illusions of some real thing. "Idea" derives from the Greek ἰδεῖν which means see, form, the look or semblance as opposed to reality.

"Images are private objects." Suppose I have some private papers. They are private but could be made public. "Mental images" are said to be private, but cannot be made public. If they cannot be public it makes no sense to say they are private.

"Images are private because no one else can have my images." One might say no one else has your ideas or your mind either. But there is no evidence for idea or mind as such, as entities in themselves, and these are seen to be pseudo-psychological categories. Similarly, we lack evidence for the existence of images as pictures in the mind. Because others cannot have my experiences, it may be thought that others cannot have my ideas or images. But this presupposes that there are such things as ideas or images.

"I just know directly that I have images." That one "knows" seems certain but what is knowledge? Knowledge is that for which we have evidence. "Evidence" derives from the Latin e + videre meaning literally, "to see." Images are seen things. The statement that "I know I have images," reduces to "I see that I have seen things." But the question here is what is seeing and what is an image? It is circular reasoning to assume seeing in examining seeing. The method used, viz., observing, is the very object of investigation, viz. seeing. Of course evidence and knowing may not be merely seeing. Seeing is, however, prominent in a number of words:

advice - appear to, revise - to look again, supervise - oversee, provide - see ahead, survey - look over.

Perception seems to be an implied criterion for knowledge in the German word for perception, *Die Wahrnehmung*, which means literally, "take for true."

"I see my images." We do not see images as we see objects. To say we see images as we see objects is to commit a category-mistake. The error is avoided by putting single quotes around 'see' when it is used to refer to images. If we fail to note these two different uses of "see" we may think there is as much evidence for seeing objects as for 'seeing' images. And the fact that 'seeing' is now put in quotes may suggest a special or questionable status of images. If we were to see images rather than 'see' images we might be led to think that there are images of images of images, etc. The fact that I 'see' images does not serve as evidence that they are private, nor does it establish them as objects in the realm of seen things.

"An image is a thing or object." It is not an object we 'see' as it is an object we see. In this case, it may be better to say an image is an 'object' we 'see.' Then, the evidence for and status of images as 'objects' is in question. We know in ordinary usage what an object is, we see a table and put a book on it. Now we may think that because we do this there is also a new kind of object — a mental 'object' or inner image. It seems misleading to think so, because image refers to an experience rather than a thing. To think of image as a thing seems to be a naming-fallacy. This is not to say that one cannot describe a process of imaging.

"I can ask someone to have an image and he understands what I mean, e.g., 'Imagine a building.' " One reply might be "Yes, I know what you are saying." This case does not seem significantly in favor of an image theory. One may understand both of the following commands without reporting any imagery: 1. Avoid contradictions, 2. Imagine a building. One understands "Have an image of a building," as one understands, "Have an idea of a building." To understand these last sentences does not require that there be either ideas as such or images as such. One could even in some cases substitute one sentence for the other without loss of meaning.

We often do say "Think of a building," rather than, "Have an image of a building." The sentence has a use in terms of a linguistic and situational context, but to think that ideas, thoughts, or images describe or name distinct objects may be a naming-fallacy. It is not immediately clear that "image" names or describes an entity.

"The evidence for an image is that one can draw it." How does "it" function here? What is it that I draw? Certainly I draw something. I can scribble also. That I scribble does not mean I have a scribble image I am drawing. I do know what to do if someone asks me to scribble. If someone asks me to draw my images I am not sure what could be drawn. We do not usually say "Draw your images," or "Draw all that you are now imagining." We could, however, ask someone to draw an object such as a chair or a cow. That he draws an object may suggest to him that he is drawing his image. But drawing an image on paper is not like drawing an image in the imagination. It is not clear how the latter may be sketched out.

We may say, 1. Draw a cow, or 2. Draw your image of a cow. How would the sketches differ? Would you say, "This picture is my image of a cow, and that picture is a drawing of a cow?" We do say "Draw it from memory," and this might suggest that we are drawing our image of the cow, but it is not clear that we are. As I now think of a cow I construct certain things, an ear, four legs, a tail, horns, the udder. I do not visualize every line before I draw it. One can draw a house by putting the lines down without visualizing anything. He has learned which lines to put where. That one draws a picture does not mean he visualized it. He cannot visualize what he draws until he draws it and he cannot see what is not in front of him at the time. Drawing an object is a complex activity, not merely having a photograph-like picture in one's head. That one draws something is not clear evidence that he had an image of what he drew.

If I understand the use of the word "cow," I have all I need. I have a description of the cow and can depict it. According to Webster's Dictionary, "depict" means "1. to represent by a picture, 2. to portray in words." It derives from the Latin *depictus*, to paint.

Instead of depict one may also say "depicture" or simply "picture." To picture is a verb meaning "form a mental image," or "describe graphically in words." Both "picture" and "depict" refer to verbal descriptions. If I understand the use of the word "cow," I have all I need because I can then portray or describe "cow" in words. Perhaps, often, what is meant by having an image, is having a verbal description. I may describe a cow. But to describe a cow is not the same as describing a visual image of a cow. That one knows the description of a cow does not serve as evidence that he has an image of a cow.

When we describe an image we describe it in words. Words are marks or sounds which relate to other marks or objects. In describing images in words, then, we find that we are bringing in a number of associations other than that of merely relating a mark to an "internal image." We speak of images in terms of some purpose or goal. The purpose of an image is not usually merely to try to have an image or "inner picture" in itself. Our images do not come in full detail but certain things are selected. If I am to imagine a raging rooster, then I may concentrate on a pecking beak, flapping wings, and scratching feet. I do not visualize the belly or back. As I mention these parts we may try to visualize them. And this suggests that the image does not come alone, but in conjunction with words. The words or marks have a great many associations. Because we know these associations we may let one of them stand for the others. The image may involve just one or two associations of the object visualized. The experiencing of an image is, then, inseparable from the experiencing of a word. Wittgenstein wrote,

> Suppose, however, that someone were to draw while he had an image . . . It is quite as if he had given a verbal description: and such a description can also simply take the place of the image." (Philosophical Investigations p. 177)

The reason for this is that language, rather than thought, has epistemological primacy. Ideas and thoughts are pseudopsychological entities for which we do not have evidence. On the other hand, by "thought" and "ideas" we refer to various abilities but mainly language ability. To think is largely to speak or write to oneself or others. There is no mentalistic thinking as such. To know is largely to be able to say or write something, although we say metaphorically he "knows" how to swim. We do not know what thinking would be if we had never learned a language. We now have a language and cannot dismiss that fact. We do not know how a dog or ant thinks or even what kind of language, if any, they have. Dogs and ants cannot see or know they are seeing, as we can. The reason is that they do not speak our language. It is not clear what awareness is for an ant or what it is aware of. We cannot simply impose our linguistic categories on other animals. We can say "The ant sees," but the ant can't say that. We cannot say that without language we would think in images. If we never learned a language "image" would be unintelligible. One might say, "We may not see 'images' but we would see something or other." But without language we would not even see "something or other." Wittgenstein wrote,

When someone says the word 'cube' to me, for example, I know what it means. But can the whole use of the word come before my mind, when I understand it in this way?" *Philosophical Investigations* No. 139)

Someone utters the word "rooster" and then, as we would say, we may have an "image" of a rooster. The word and image seem to come together.

"But we can imagine a rooster without saying 'rooster' aloud." This is because we can say "rooster" to ourselves rather than aloud. If we did not have a language it is not clear what an image of a rooster would be like. What is the image ants have really like? Is it an image as we think of images? It is questionable whether we can have an image of a rooster without the word "rooster" because part of what is meant by an image of a rooster is the meaning of the word, that is, the associations involved with the marks "rooster."

An image is always of something. It involves language and description. One does not have an image in itself. What would it mean to say, "I have an image but it is not an image of anything?"

Images in various ways fit into a linguistic context. I cannot have an image of a rooster without the word "rooster," that is, without language and description.

The word "image" itself induces a picture of some sort. It has certain associations. When I think of the word I have certain experiences. In this respect one cannot have an "image" without language. A dog does not see an "image" because he does not speak English. The word "image" seems to suggest something which might not otherwise be suggested. The present investigation is intended to specify the sort of picture or suggestion "image" produces.

Now it is possible to say meaningfully "I have images," if the cautions mentioned above are taken into consideration. One of the simplest ways to show this is to describe one and compare it to the perception of an object: "I have an image of a building, but the image is not fixed. It changes as I consider it. I do not just 'see' that there are a certain number of windows. I could see it equally as having one or ten windows. It depends on what I want to see. The details seem missing. I am not sure what color to make it, but I could make it of a certain color. The textural and other details seem to be missing, etc." The word "image," then, does have an acceptable use and to determine that use one must refer to the various contexts of its use. It means here that certain descriptions can be given and intersubjectively understood. However, to think that "image" names a fixed entity, or internal state is simplistic and involves naming-fallacies and category-mistakes. Of the various uses of "image," the use in the language-game of description is highly questionable. This is not to say there are no images. It is to say that the analysis of them is more complex than is usually thought.

Comprehensive Bibliography on Emotions

Abelson, R. and M. Rosenberg. "Symbolic Psychologic: A Model of Attitudinal Cognition" *Behavioral Science* 3(1958) 1-13.

Ahumada, Rodolfo. "Emotion, Knowledge and Belief" *Personalist* 50(1969) 371-382.

Alexander, F. "The Logic of Emotions" *International Journal of Psycho-Analysis* 1935.

Alexander, F. and T. Szasz. "The Psychosomatic Approach in Medicine" *Dynamic Psychiatry* F. Alexander and H. Ross, eds., Univ. of Chicago Press 1952.

Allerand, A. "Remembrance of Feelings Past: A study of Phenomenological Genetics" PhD diss. Columbia University 1967.

Allers, R. "Cognitive Aspect of Emotion" *Thomist* 4(1942) 589-648.

Allin, A. "On Laughter" *Psychological Review* 10(1903) 306-315.

Alston, William. "Dispositions and Occurrences" *Canadian Journal of Philosophy* 1(2) (1971).

Alston, William. "Emotion and Feeling," "Emotive Meaning" *Encyclopedia of Philosophy* New York: Macmillan 1967, vol. 6, pp. 341-347.

Alston, William. "Expressing" *Philosophy in America* Max Black, ed. London: George Allen and Unwin 1965.

Alston, William. "Pleasure" *Encyclopedia of Philosophy* New York: Macmillan 1967.

Andrew, R. "The Origins of Facial Expressions" *Scientific American* 213 (1965) 88-92.

Angell, J. "Recent Discussion of Feeling" *Journal of Philosophy* 3(1906) 169-174.

Angell, J. "A Reconsideration of James' Theory of Emotion in the Light of Recent Criticisms" *Psychological Review* 23(1916) 251-261.

Angier, R. "The Conflict Theory of Emotion" *American Journal of Psychology* 39(1927) 390-401.

Anscombe, G. "On the Grammar of 'Enjoy'" *Journal of Philosophy* (Oct. 5, 1967) 607-614.

Arieti, S. "Cognition and Feeling" *Feelings and Emotions* M. Arnold, ed., New York: Academic Press 1970.

Arieti, S. "Studies of Thought Processes in Contemporary Psychiatry" *American Journal of Psychiatry* 120 (1963) 58-64.

Aristotle. "Character and Emotion" *The Rhetoric of Aristotle* L. Cooper, ed. New York: Appleton 1932.

Arnheim, R. "Emotion and Feeling in Psychology and Art" *Confin. Psychiat.* 1958.

Arnold, Magda. "Emotion" *New Catholic Encyclopedia* vol. 5 New York: McGraw-Hill 1967 pp. 308-317.

Arnold, Magda. *Emotion and Personality* 2 vols. New York: Columbia Univ. Press 1960.

Arnold, Magda, ed. *Feelings and Emotion* New York: Academic Press 1970

Arnold, Magda. "Human Emotion and Action" *Human Action* T. Mischel, ed.

Arnold, Magda, ed. *Nature of Emotion* Baltimore, Maryland: Penguin 1971.

Arnold, Magda. "Physiological Differentiation of Emotional States" *Psychological Review* 52(1945) 35-48.

Arnold, Magda. "The Status of Emotion in Contemporary Psychology" *Present-Day Psychology* A. Roback, ed. New York: Philosophical Library 1955 pp. 135-188.

Aune, Bruce. "Feelings, Moods, and Introspection" *Mind* 72(April 1963) 187-208.

Austin, John. *Philosophical Papers* 2nd ed, Oxford: Clarendon Press 1970, esp. "Pretending," "Other Minds."

Ax, A. "The Physiological Differentiation Between Fear and Anger" *Psychosomatic Medicine* 15(1953) 433-42.

Babb, Lawrence. *The Elizabethan Malady: A Study of Melancholia in English Literature from 1580-1642* East Lansing, Michigan 1951.

Bacon, F. "Of Anger" *Essays* New York: Peter Pauper Press 1968.

Baier, Kurt. "The Place of Pain" *Philosophical Quarterly* 14(1964) 138-151.

Bain, A. *Emotions and Will* London 1859.

Baldwin, J. "Origin of Emotional Expression" *Psychological Review* 1(1894) 610-23.

Balken, E. "Psychological Researches in Schizophrenic Language and Thought in a Test of Imagination" *Journal of Psychology* 16(1943) ca. p. 133.

Balken, E. and J. Masserman. "The Language of Phantasy" (in anxiety states, etc.) *Journal of Psychology* 10(1940) ca. p. 75.

Banham, K. "Senescence and the Emotions" *Pedagogical Seminary Quarterly* 78(June 1951) 175-183.

Barnett, Samuel. "The 'Expression of the Emotions' " *New Biology* 22 Penguin Books 1957.

Bartlett, B. "Feeling, Imaging and Thinking" *British Journal of Psychology* 16(1925) 16-29.

Beck, Aaron. *Depression* University of Pennsylvania 1972.

Becker, Howard. "Some Forms of Sympathy: A Phenomenological Analysis" *Journal of Abnormal and Social Psychology* 26 (April 1931) 58-68.

Bedford, E. "Emotions" *Essays in Philosophical Psychology* D. Gustafson, ed., New York: Doubleday 1964.

Bedford, E. "The Emotive Theory of Ethics" Proceedings of the XIth International Congress of Philosophy X-Xi, Amsterdam (1953) 124-129.

Beebe-Center, J. "Feeling and Emotion" *Theoretical Foundations of Psychology* H. Helson, ed., New York: Van Nostrand (1951) Chapt. 6, pp. 254-317.

Beebe-Center, J. *The Psychology of Pleasantness and Unpleasantness* New York: Van Nostrand 1932.

Benn, A. "Aristotle's Theory of Tragic Emotion" *Mind* 23(N.S) (1914) 84-90.

Benson, John. "Emotion and Expression" *Philosophical Review* 76 (3) (1967) 335-57.

Berndtson, Arthur. *Art Expression and Beauty* New York: Holt, Rinehart and Winston, 1969. Ch. 4 "Emotion" pp. 59-84, Ch. 8 "Emotion and Expression" pp. 150-154.

Bindra, D. "Organization in Emotional and Motivated Behavior" *Canadian Journal of Psychology* 1955.

Black, Max. "Some Questions About Emotive Meaning" (Symposium) *Philosophical Quarterly* 57(1948) 111-57.

Blandford, G. "On the Nature of Emotion" *Fortnightly Review* 12(1869) 103-15.

Block, Jack. "Studies in the Phenomenology of Emotions" *Journal of Nervous and Mental Disorders* 1947.

Bonheim, Helmut. "Changing Emotions and Behavior in Literature" Paper read at the Modern Language Association Meeting, Dec., 1971.

Bosanquet, B. "On the Nature of Aesthetic Emotion" *Mind* 3 (N.S) (1894) 153-66.

Bousfield, W., and W. Orbison. "Ontogenesis of Emotional Behavior" *Psychological Review* 1952.

Bouwsma, O. K. "The Expression Theory of Art" *Philosophical Essays* University of Nebraska Press 1965 pp. 21-50.

Bowles, M. "Emotions of Deaf Children" *Pedag. Sem.* 3 (1895) 330-4.

Bowra, C. *Inspiration and Poetry* London 1955.

Brady, J. "Emotional Behavior" *Handbook of Physiology* (Neurophysiology) Vol. III, J. Field, H. Magoun and V. Hall, eds., Baltimore, Maryland: Waverly Press, Section 1 (1960) 1529-1552.

Brandt, Richard. "The Emotive Theory of Ethics" *Philosophical Review* 59(1950) 535-540.

Bray, C. *Education of the Feelings and Affections* London 1867.

Breton. *Melancholike Humours* G. Harrison, ed., London: Scholastic Press 1929.

Bridges, K. "A Genetic Theory of the Emotions" *Journal of Genetic Psychology* 37(1930) 514-27.

Brierley, M. "Affect in Theory and Practice" *International Journal of Psycho-Analysis* 1937.

Bright, Timothy. *Treatise of Melancholy* London 1586.

Britan, H. *The Affective Consciousness* New York 1931.

Britton, K. "Feelings and Their Expressions" *Philosophy* 32(1957) 97-111.

Broad, C. D. "Emotion and Sentiment" *Journal of Aesthetics and Art Criticism* 13(Dec., 1954) 203-14.

Brown, J. "The Methods of Kurt Lewin in the Psychology of Action and Affection" *Psychological Review* 36(1929) 200-201.

Brown, J. and I. Farber. "Emotions Conceptualized as Intervening Variables" *Psychological Bulletin* 48(1951) 465-495.

Browning, Robert. "Broad's Theory of Emotion" *The Philosophy of C. D. Broad* Paul Schlipp, ed., New York: Tudor pp. 613-708.

Bruner, J., J. Goodnow, and G. Austin. *A Study of Thinking* New York: Wiley 1956.

Bruner, I and L. Postman. "Emotional Selectivity in Perception and Reaction" *Journal of Personality* 16(1947) 69-77.

Bryant, Sophie. "Prof. James on the Emotions" *Proceedings of the Aristotelian Society* 3(1896) 52-64.

Bull, Nina. "The Attitude Theory of Emotion" *Nervous and Mental Disease Monographs* New York: no. 81, 1951.

Bull, Nina. "Toward a Clarification of the Concept of Emotion" *Psychosomatic Medicine* 7(1945) ca. p. 210.

Bull, Nina and B. Pasquarelli. "Experimental Investigation of the Mind-Body Continuum in Affective States" *Journal of Nervous and Mental Disorders* 113(1951) 512-21.

Bullough, E. "Psychical Distance as a Factor in Art and an Aesthetic Principle" *British Journal of Psychology* 5(1912-13) 87-118.

Burton, Robert. *Anatomy of Melancholy* New York: Tudor 1951(1621).

Byrne, O. "The Evolution of the Theory and Research on Emotions" M.A. Thesis, Columbia University, New York 1927.

Caldecott, Alfred. "Emotionality: A Method of its Unifunction" *Proceedings of the Aristotelian Society* N.S. 11(1910-1911) 206-20.

Callwood, June. *Love, Hate, Anger and the Other Lively Emotions* New York: Doubleday 1964.

Campbell, C. "Are There 'Degrees' of the Moral Emotion" *Mind* 45 (N.S.) (1936) 492-97.

Candland, D., ed. *Emotion* New Jersey: Van Nostrand 1962.

Cannon, W. *Bodily Changes in Pain, Hunger, Fear and Rage* New York: Appleton-Century 1934.

Cannon, W. "Recent Studies of Bodily Effects of Fear, Rage and Pain" *Journal of Philosophy* 11(1914) 162-65.

Cannon, W. "The Role of Emotion in Disease" *American Journal of Internal Medicine* May 1936.

Carmichael, L., ed. *Manual of Child Psychology* New York: Wiley 1946, esp. pp. 752-90.

Carroll, R. *The Emotions, Their Nature and Influence Upon Human Conduct* Washington, D.C.|: Daylion 1937.

Carus, Paul. "Feeling and Emotion" *Open Court* 4(1890) 2424-6, 2435-7.

480

Cassin, Chrystine. "Emotions and Evaluations" *Personalist* 49(Fall 1968) 563-71.

Charleton, W. *Natural History of the Passions* London 1674.

Chisholm, Roderick. "Brentano's Theory of Correct and Incorrect Emotion" *Revue Internationale de Philosophie* 20(1966) 395-415.

Cicero. *Tusculan Disputations* III-IV. *Basic Works* M. Hadas, ed., New York: Modern Library 1951.

Cobb, Stanley. *Emotions and Clinical Medicine* New York: Norton 1950.

Cobbe, F. "Education of the Emotions" *Fortnightly Review* 49(1888) 223-236.

Coeffeteau, F. *A Table of Humane Passions* E. Grimeston, trans. 1621.

Coleman, J. "Facial Expressions of Emotions" *Psychological Monographs* 63(1949).

Collingwood, R. *Principles of Art* Oxford: Clarendon 1938. pp. 109-119, 308-18, 323-24.

Comfort, Alex. "A Technology of the Emotion?" *The Human Context* Vol. I.

Comte, Auguste. *System of Positive Polity* Vol. IV "Theory of the Future of Man" Ch. 2.

Cowan, L. *Pleasure and Pain* London: Macmillan 1968.

Crile, G. *The Origin and Nature of the Emotions* Philadelphia: W. Saunders 1915.

Croce, Benedetto. *Aesthetic* New York: Farrar, Straus and Giroux 1922.

Crosland, H. "Objective Measurements of Emotion" University of Oregon Series in Psychology (1931) 179-96.

Dana, C. "The Anatomic Seat of the Emotions: A Discussion of the James-Lange Theory" *Arch. Neurol. Psychiat.* 6(1921) 634-39.

Darwin, Charles. *Expression of the Emotions in Man and Animals* London: Murray 1904.

Das, Bhagavan. *The Science of the Emotions* Madras: Theosophical Publ. 1924 (London 1900).

Dashiell, J. "Are There Any Native Emotions?" *Psychological Review* 35(1928) 319-27.

Davitz, Joel. *Language of Emotion* New York: Academic Press 1969.

Davitz, Joel and M. Beldock. *Communication of Emotional Meaning* New York: McGraw-Hill 1964. esp. "The Communication of Emotional Meaning by Metaphor" (Davitz and S. Mattis) pp. 157-176.

Dejean, R. *L'emotion* Paris 1933.

Delgado, Jose. *Emotions* Dubuque, Iowa: W. C. Brown 1966.

Delgado, Jose. "Emotional Behavior in Animals and Humans" *Psychiatric Research Rep.* 12(1960) 259-71.

Denison, J. *Emotion as the Basis of Civilization* London: Scribner's 1928.

de Rivera, Joseph. "A Decision Theory of the Emotions" *Dissertation Abstracts* 23(1) (1963) 296-97.

Descartes, R. *The Passions of the Soul*

Dewey, John. "The Theory of Emotion" *Psychological Review* 1(1894) 553-69; 2(1894) 13-22.

Diagnostic and Statistical Manual of Mental Disorders (DSM-II) 2nd edition, American Psychiatric Assoc. 1968.

Dietl, Paul. "Hume on the Passions" *Philosophy and Phenomenological Research* 28(4) (1967-1968) 554-566.

Dillman, I. "An Examination of Sartre's Theory of Emotions" *Ratio* 5(2) (1960-1963) 190-212.

Dittmann, Allen. *Interpersonal Messages of Emotion* New York: Springer 1972.

Donnellan, Keith. "Causes, Objects, and Producers of the Emotions" *Journal of Philosophy* 67(1970) 947-50.

Dorner, A. "Emotions" *Encyclopedia of Religion and Ethics* J. Hastings, ed. Vol. 5, 1912 pp. 283-292.

481

Duffy, E. "Emotion: An Example of the Need for Reorientation in Psychology" *Psychological Review* 41(1934) 184-98.

Duffy, E. "An Explanation of 'Emotional' Phenomenon Without the Use of the Concept 'Emotion' " *Journal of General Psychology* 25(1941) 283-93.

Duffy, E. "Leeper's Motivational Theory of Emotion" *Psychological Review* 55(1948) 324-29.

Dunbar, Flanders. *Emotions and Bodily Changes: A Survey of Literature on Psychosomatic Interrelationships* 1910-1953 New York: Columbia Univ. Press 4th ed. (1954) 1192 pages.

Dunker, Karl. "On Pleasure, Emotion and Striving" *Philosophy and Phenomenological Research* 1(1940) 391-430.

Dunlap, K., ed. *The Emotions* Baltimore: Williams & Wilkins 1922.

Dunlap, K. "Thought, Content, and Feeling" *Psychological Review* 23(1916) 49-70.

Ekman, P., et al. *Emotions in the Human Face* New York: Pergamon 1972.

Eldred, S. and D. Price. "A Linguistic Evaluation of Feeling States in Psychotherapy" *Psychiatry* 21(1958) 115-121.

Ellis, A. "Causes and Objects of Emotions" *Analysis* 30(6) (April 1971) 201-205.

Ellis, Albert. "An Operational Reformation of Some of the Basic Principles of Psychoanalysis" *Psychoanalytic Review* 43(1956) 163-180.

Ellis, Albert. "New Approaches to Psychotherapy Techniques" *Journal of Clinical Psychology* Monograph Supplement no. 11, Brandon, Vermont 1955.

Ellis, Albert. "Psychotherapy Techniques for Use With Psychotics" *American Journal of Psychotherapy* 9(1955) 452-76.

Ellis, Albert. "Rational Psychotherapy" *Journal of General Psychology* 59(1958) 35-49. Paper presented at the American Psychological Association, August 31, 1956.

Ellis, Albert. *Reason and Emotion in Psychotherapy* New York: Lyle Stuart, 1962.

"Emotion" *Great Books Syntopicon* Chapt. 20 pp. 413-36.

Engel, George. "Is Grief a Disease?" *Psychosomatic Medicine* 23(1961) 18-22.

Epstein, S. "The Nature of Anxiety" *Anxiety* C. Spielberger, New York: Academic Press 1972.

Ewing, A. C. "The Justification of Emotion" *Proceedings of the Aristotelian Society* Suppl. vol. 31(1957) 59-74.

Fabry, J. *The Pursuit of Meaning: Logotherapy Applied to Life* Boston: Beacon 1968.

Farber, I. and L. West. "Conceptual Problems of Research on Emotions" *Explorations in the Physiology of Emotions* Psychiatric Research Report no. 12, L. West and M. Greenblatt, eds., Washington, D. C.: American Psychiatric Association 1960 pp. 1-7.

Farrell, W. "Man's Emotional Life" *Cross Crown* 6(1954) 178-98.

Feinstein, Howard. "William James on the Emotions" *Journal of the History of Ideas* 31(Jan.-March 1970) 133-42.

Feleky, Antoinette. "The Expression of Emotions" *Psychological Review* 21(1914) 33-41.

Feleky, Antoinette. *Feelings and Emotions* New York: Pioneer 1922.

Fell, Joseph. *Emotion in the Thought of Sartre* New York: Columbia Univ. Press 1965.

Fenichel, O. "The Ego and the Affects" *Psychoanalytic Review* 1941.

Fere, Ch. "Emotions and Infection" *Popular Science Monthly* 44 (1894) 342-6.

Fere, Ch. *The Pathology of Emotions* London 1899.

Festinger, Leon. *A Theory of Cognitive Dissonance* Stanford University Press 1957.

Festinger, Leon. *Conflict, Decision, and Dissonance* Stanford University Press 1964.

Flint, R. "On Some Alleged Distinctions Between Thought and Feeling" *Mind* 2(1877) 112-118.

Flugel, C. *Studies in Feeling and Desire* London 1935.

Fortenbough, William. "Aristotle's Rhetoric on Emotions" *Archiv fur Geschichte der Philosophie* 52(1970) 40-70.

Fraad, Lewis. "Emotion and Illness in the Adolescent" *Diseases of the Nervous System* 28(1967) 40-43.

Frank, L. *Feelings and Emotions* New York: Doubleday 1954.

Freedman, Alfred and H. Kaplan, eds. *Comprehensive Textbook of Psychiatry* Baltimore: Williams and Wilkins 1967.

Fremont-Smith, F. "The Influence of Emotion in Precipitating Convulsions" *American Journal of Psychiatry* 13(1934) ca. 717.

Freud, Sigmund. *Complete Works* J. Strachey, ed. London: Hogarth Press.

Gamls, Ian. "Indian Aesthetics and the Nature of Dramatic Emotions" *British Journal of Aesthetics* 9(Oct. 1969) 372-386.

Gardiner, Harry. "Recent Discussion of Emotion" *Philosophical Review* 5(1896) 102-112.

Gardiner, Harry., R. Metcalf, and J. Beebe-Center. *Feeling and Emotion: A History of Theories* New York: American Book Co. 1937; Westport, Conn.. Greenwood 1971.

Gaylin, W. *The Meaning of Despair* New York: Science House 1968.

Geldard, Frank. *Fundamentals of Psychology* New York: John Wiley 1962, Ch. 3 "Emotions as Drives" pp. 33-51.

Gellert, Bridget. "Three Literary Treatments of Melancholy: Marston, Shakespeare, and Burton" Columbia University 1967.

Gellhorn, Ernst. *Biological Foundations of Emotion* Illinois: Scott, Foresman 1968.

Gellhorn, Ernst. "Prolegomena to a Theory of Emotions" *Perspectives in Biology and Medicine* Univ. of Chicago Press 4(4) (1961) 403-436.

Gellhorn, Ernst and G. Loofbourrow. *Emotions and Emotional Disorders: A Neurophysiological Study* New York: Harper & Row 1963.

Gitelson, M. "The Emotional Problems of Elderly People" *Geriatrics* 3(1948).

Glass, D. *Neurophysiology and Emotion* New York: Rockefeller University Press 1967.

Goldberg, Bruce. "The Linguistic Expression of Feeling" *American Philosophical Quarterly* 8(1971) 86-92.

Goldman, Alvin. *A Theory of Human Action* New Jersey: Prentice-Hall 1970.

Goldstein, Jeffrey. *Psychology of Humor* New York: Academic Press 1972.

Goldstein, Kurt. "On Emotions: Considerations from the Organismic Point of View" *Journal of Psychology* 31(1951) 37-49.

Gombrich, E. "Art and the Language of Emotions" *Proceedings of the Aristotelian Society* Suppl. 36 (1962) 215-235.

Goodenough, Florence. "Expression of the Emotions in a Blind-Deaf Child" *Journal of Abnormal and Social Psychology* 27(1932) 328-333.

Gordon, K. "Imagination and Emotion" *Journal of Psychology* 1937.

Gordon, Kate. "Feelings as the Object of Thought" *Journal of Philosophy* 3(1906) 123-27.

Gordon, Robert. "Emotions and Knowledge" *Journal of Philosophy* 66(July 3, 1969) 408-13.

Gordon, Robert "Judgmental Emotions" *Analysis* 34 (1973) 40-48.

Goshen, Charles. "A Systematic Classification of the Phenomenology of Emotions" *Psychiatric Quarterly* 41(1967) 483-495.

Goslin, Justin. "Mental Causes and Fear" *Mind* 71(July, 1962) 289-306.

Gosling, J. "Emotion and Object" *Philosophical Review* 74(1965) 486-503.

Gotlind, Erik. *Three Theories of Emotion: Some View on Philosophical Method* Lund: Gleerup 1958. (See Alan White review)

Gray, J. *The Psychology of Fear and Stress* New York: McGraw-Hill 1971.

Gray, S. "An Objective Theory of Emotion" *Psychological Review* 42(1935) 108-16.

Green, O. "The Expression of Emotion" *Mind* 79(1970) 551-568.

Grierson, F. "Feeling and Intellect" *Critic* 48(1906) 264-6.

Grimberg, L. *Emotion and Delinquency* London: Kegan, Paul 1928.

Gruner, O. "Emotional States as a Basis of Occult Phenomena" *The Canon of Medicine of Avicenna* London: Luzac 1930.

Guilford, J. "There is System in Color Preferences" *Journal of the Optical Society of America* 30(1940) 455-59.

Gurney, Edmund. "What is an Emotion?" *Mind* 9(1884) 421-6.

Hall, C. "Inheritance of Emotionality" *Sigma Xi Quarterly* 26(1938) 17-27.

Hamilton, W. *Lectures on Metaphysics and Logic* Vol. 1, pp. 41-46.

Hampshire, Stuart. "Feeling and Expression" Inaugural Lecture, University College, London, Oct. 25, 1960.

"Happiness" *Great Books Syntopicon* M. Adler, ed. Chicago: *Encyclopaedia Britannica* 1955 Chapt. 33, pp. 684-710.

Harlow, H. and R. Stagner. *Psychology of Feelings and Emotions* "Theory of Feelings" *Psychological Review* 39(1932) 570-89; "Theory of Emotions" *Psychological Review* 40 (1933) 184-95.

Harms, E. "Second International Symposium on Feelings and Emotions" *School & Society* 69(April 23, 1949) 301.

Hartshorne, Charles. *The Philosophy and Psychology of Sensation* University of Chicago Press 1934.

Harvey, O. "Emotions and Belief" *American Philosophical Quarterly* Vol. 9, pp. 24-40.

Harvey, O., D. Hunt and H. Schroeder. *Conceptual Systems and Personality Organization* New York: Wiley 1961.

Hebb, D. "Emotion in Man and Animal: An analysis of the intuitive processes of recognition" *Psychological Review* 53(1946) 88-106.

Hegel, G. *The Phenomenology of Mind* IV, B (3).

Herbst, W. "Jealousy" *New Catholic Encyclopedia* New York: McGraw-Hill 7(1967) 860.

Hill, D. "The Communication of Emotions by Facial Expressions in the Light of a New Theory" M.A. Thesis, Hofstra College, New York 1955.

Hillman, J. *Emotion, a comprehensive phenomenology of theories and their meanings for therapy* Northwestern University Press 1961 (Based on his Ph.D dissertation).

Hocart, A. "Ritual and Emotion" *The Life-Giving Myth* London: Methuen 1952.

Hodge, F. "The Emotions in a New Role" *Psychological Review* 42(1935) 555-65.

Hodgson, S. "Fact, Idea and Emotion" *Proceedings of the Aristotelian Society* 7(1906-1907) 112-158.

Holborow, L. "Taylor on Pain Location" *Philosophical Quarterly* 16(63) (1966) 151-59.

Honeywell, J. "Poetic Theory of Visvanatha" *Journal of Aesthetics and Art Criticism* 28(Winter 1969) 165-76.

Huarte, Juan *The Examination of Men's Wits* R. Carew, trans. 1594.

Hume, David. "Dissertation on the Passions," "Of the Delicacy of Taste and Passion" *Essays, Moral, Political and Literary* Vol. II.

Hume, David. *Treatise of Human Nature* Oxford: Clarendon Press 1960 (1888) Book II "Of the Passions."

Hunt, W. "Ambiguity of Descriptive Terms for Feeling and Emotion" *American Journal of Psychology* 47(1935) 165-166.

Hunt, W. "A Critical Review of Current Approaches to Affectivity" *Psychological Bulletin* 36(1939) 807-28.

Hunt, W. "Recent Developments in the Field of Emotion" *Psychological Bulletin* 38(1941) 249-76.

Hunt, W. "The Reliability of Introspection in Emotion" *American Journal of Psychology* 49(1937) 650-53.

Hutcheson, F. *An Essay on the Nature and Conduct of the Passions and Affections* London 1728.

Hutschnecker, A. "Love and Hate in Human Nature" (Review) *New Republic* 133(July 18, 1955) 19-20.

Irons, J. "Descartes and Modern Theories of Emotion" *Philosophical Review* 4(1895) 291-302.

Irons, J. "The Nature of Emotion" *Philosophical Review* 6(1897) 242-56, 471-96.

Irons, J. "Physical Basis of Emotion" *Mind* 4(N.S.) 10(1895) 92-99.

Irons, J. "The Primary Emotions" *Philosophical Review* 6(1897) 626-45, 7(1898) 298-9.

Irons, J. "Prof. James' Theory of Emotion" *Mind* 3(N.S) (1894) 77-97.

Irons, J. "Recent Developments in the Theory of Emotion" *Psychological Review* 2(1895) 279-84.

Izard, Carroll. *The Face of Emotion* New York: Appleton-Century-Crofts 1971.

Izard, Carroll. *Patterns of Emotions: A New Analysis of Anxiety and Depression* New York: Academic Press 1972.

Jacobson, E. *Biology of Emotions* Illinois: C. Thomas 1967.

Jacobson, E. "Problems in the Psychoanalytic Theory of Affects" *Psychoanalytic Quarterly* 21(1952) 459-60.

James, William. "The Physical Basis of Emotions" *Psychological Review* 1(1911) 516-609.

James, William. "What is an Emotion" *Mind* 9(O.S.) (1884) 188-205.

James, William and G. Lange. *The Emotions* Baltimore: Williams and Wilkins 1922.

Jeness, A. "The Recognition of Facial Expressions of Emotion" *Psychological Bulletin* 1932.

Johnston, C. "Ribot's Theory of the Passions" *Journal of Philosophy* 5(1908) 197-207.

Jonas, H. "Motility and Emotion" *Actes de XI eme Congres International de Philosophie* VII (Bruxelles 1953) Amsterdam and Louvain.

Journal of Emotional Education

Kamler, Howard. "Emotional Feelings" *Philosophia* 3(Oct. 1973).

Kantor, J. "An Attempt Toward a Naturalistic Description of the Emotions" *Psychological Review* 28(1921) 19-42, 120-140.

Kelly, G. *The Psychology of Personal Constructs* Vol. I New York: Norton 1955.

Kenny, A. *Action, Emotion and Will* London: Routledge & Kegan Paul 1963.

Kety, S. "Neurological Aspects of Emotional Behavior" *Physiological Correlates of Emotion* P. Black, ed. New York: Academic Press 1970.

Klineberg, O. "Emotional Expression in Chinese Literature" *Journal of Abnormal and Social Psychology* 33(1938) 517-20.

Knapp, P., ed., *Expression of the Emotions in Man* New York: International Universities Press 1963.

Koffka, Kurt. *Principles of Gestalt Psychology* New York: Harcourt 1935 "Emotions" pp. 400-416.

Kronegger, Maria. "Changing Emotions and Behavior: Literary Impressionism" Paper read at the Modern Language Association, Dec. 1971.

Landauer, K. "Affects, Passions and Temperament" *International Journal of Psycho-Analysis* 1938.

Landis, C. "An Attempt to Measure Emotional Traits in Juvenile Delinquency" *Studies in the Dynamics of Behavior* K. Lashley, ed., Chicago: Univ. of Chicago Press 1932.

Landis, C. "The Interpretation of Facial Expression in Emotion" *Journal of General Psychology* 1929.

Landis, C. "Studies of Emotional Reactions: II. General Behavior and Facial Expression" *Journal of Comparative Psychology* 4(1924) 447-501.

Lange, C. *The Emotions* Denmark 1885.

Langer, Susanne. *Feeling and Form* New York: Scribner 1953.

Lazarus, R. and J. Averill. "Emotion and Cognition" *Anxiety* C. Spielberger, ed., New York: Academic Press 1972.

Lazarus, R. *Psychological Stress and the Coping Process* New York: McGraw-Hill 1966.

Lazarus, R., J. Averill and E. Opton. "Cross-Cultural Studies of Psychophysiological Responses During Stress and Emotion" *International Journal of Psychology* 4(1969) 83-102.

Lazarus, R., J. Averill and E. Opton. "Towards a Cognitive Theory of Emotion" *Feelings and Emotions* M. Arnold, ed., New York: Academic Press 1970.

Leedy, Jack. *Poetry Therapy* Philadelphia: Lippincott 1969.

Leeper, R. "A Motivational Theory of Emotion to Replace 'Emotion as Disorganized Response' " *Psychological Review* 55(1948) 5-21.

Lehman, Heinze. "Emotional Basis of Illness" *Diseases of the Nervous System* 28(July 1967) 12-19.

Leiber, Justin. "Aesthetic Emotion" *Southern Journal of Philosophy* 6(Winter 1968) 215-23.

Lemnius. *The Touchstone of Complexions* T. Newton, trans. 1581(1565).

Lerner, Laurence. "Emotion" *Encyclopedia of Poetry and Poetics* A. Preminger, ed., Princeton University Press 1965 pp. 217-21.

Levi, Anthony. *French Moralists: The Theory of Passions* Oxford Univ. Press 1964.

London, I. "Treatment of Emotions in Contemporary Soviet Psychology" *Journal of General Psychology* 41(1949) 89-100.

"Love" *Great Books Syntopicon* M. Adler, ed., Chicago: Britannica 1955. Chapt. 50, pp. 1051-1082. (See also bibliography on love in this book.)

Lund, F. *Emotions of Men* New York: McGraw-Hill 1930.

Lund, F. *Emotions: Their Psychological, Physiological, and Educative Implications* New York: Ronald 1939.

Luria, A. *The Nature of Human Conflicts, or Emotions, Conflict and Will* New York: Liveright 1932.

MacCurdy, J. *The Psychology of Emotion* New York 1925.

MacLennan, S. "Emotion, Desire and Interest" *Psychological Review* 2(1895) 462-74.

MacMurray, J. *Reason and Emotion* New York 1936.

Madow, Leo. *Anger* New York: Scribner's 1972.

Malmud, R. "Poetry and the Emotions" *Journal of Abnormal and Social Psychology* 1927-8.

Mandler, G. "Emotion" *New Directions in Psychology I* R. Brown, et al., eds., New York: Holt, Rinehart and Winston 1962, pp. 267-339.

Margolis, Joseph. "Awareness of Sensations and of the Location of Sensations" *Analysis* (Oct. 1966) (Reply in *Analysis* 27 no. 5 (April 1967) 174-76 by G. Vesey.)

Markert, Christopher. *Test Your Emotions* New York: Dell 1971.

Marshall, H. "Emotions versus pleasure-pain" *Mind* 4(N.S.) 20(1895) 180-94.

Marshall, H. "Pleasure-Pain and Emotion" *Psychological Review* 2(1895) 57-64.

Marshall, H. "What is an Emotion?" *Mind* 9(O.S.) (1884) 615-17.

Marston, W. "Analysis of Emotions" *Encyclopaedia Britannica* 14th ed. 1929.

Marston, W. *Emotions of Normal People* London: Paul, Trench 1928.

Maultsby, Maxie. *Handbook of Rational Self-Counseling* Associated Rational Thinkers, University of Kentucky Medical College, Lexington, Kentucky 1971 (Publishes series of articles on Rational Emotive Therapy)

May, Helen. "A Study of Emotional Expression Among Chinese and Americans" M.A. Thesis, Columbia University 1938.

McClintock, Thomas. "Relativism and Affective Reaction Theories" *Journal of Value Inquiry* 5,2(1971) 90-104.

McCosh, James. "Elements Involved in Emotions" *Mind* 2(1877) 413-5.

McCosh, James. *The Emotions* London 1880 (cf. *Rev. Philos.* vol. 6, 551-6; *Nation* Vol. 30, 196-7)

McDonald, Margaret. "Reply to Mr. MacIver" *Analysis* 4(1937) 77-81.

McDougall, William. *An Introduction to Social Psychology* Boston: Luce 1923.

McDougall, William, A. Shand, and G. Stout. Symposium: "Instinct and Emotion" *Proceedings of the Aristotelian Society* N.S. 15(1914-1915) 22-100.

McGill, Vivian. *Emotions and Reason* Springfield, Illinois: C. Thomas 1954.

McGinnies, E. "Emotionality and Perceptual Defense" *Psychological Review* 56(1949) 244-52.

McIntyre, J. "Value Feelings and Judgments of Value" *Proceedings of the Aristotelian Society* N.S. 5(1904-1905) 53-74.

McKinney, J. "What Shall We Choose to Call Emotion?" *Journal of Nervous and Mental Disease* 72(1930) 46-64.

McLaughlin, Blaine. "Emotional Problems in Adolescents" *Diseases of the Nervous System* 28(1967) 50-52.

Meinong, Alexius. *On Emotional Presentation* M. Kalsi, trans., Northwestern University Press 1972.

Melden, A. "The Conceptual Dimension of Emotions" *Human Action* T. Mischel, ed., New York: Academic Press 1969.

Mercier, Charles. "A Classification of Feelings" *Mind* 9(1884) 325-348; 509-530; 10 (1885) 1-26.

Metfessel, M. "The All-or-None Nature of Emotional Thinking" *Journal of Psychology* 9(1940) 323-26.

Meyer, M. "That Whale Among the Fishes–The Theory of Emotions" *Psychological Review* 40(1933) 292-300.

Meyers, R. "The N.S. and General Semantics IV. The Fiction of the Thalamus as the Neural Center of Emotions, etc." *ETC* 7(1950) 104-27.

Miles, Josephine. *Wordsworth and the Vocabulary of Emotion* New York: Octagon 1965.

Miller, R. "Non-Verbal Communication of Affect" *Journal of Clinical Psychology* 15(April 1959) 155-8.

Mischel, Theodore, ed., *Human Action* New York: Academic Press 1969.

More, J. "The Emotions" *Lancet* 2(1872) 112-4.

Morgan, Clifford. *Physiological Psychology* 3rd ed., New York: McGraw-Hill 1965, Chapt. 11 "Emotion" pp. 306-38.

Mullane, Harvey. "Unconscious Emotion" *Theoria* 31(3) (1965) 181-90.

Myers, C. "Experimentation on Emotion" *Mind* 10(N.S.) (1901) 114-15.

Myers, Gerald. "Feelings into Words" *Journal of Philosophy* 60(Dec. 1963) 801-11.

Myers, Gerald. "Motives and Wants" *Mind* 73(April 1964) 173-85.

Myers, Gerald. *Self* New York: Pegasus 1969.

Myers, Gerald. "William James' Theory of Emotion" *Transactions of the Charles S. Peirce Society* 5(Spring 1969) 67-89.

Nahm, Milton. "The Philosophical Implications of Some Theories of Emotion" *Philosophy of Science* 6(1939) 458-86.

Nemesius. *The Nature of Man* G. Wither, trans. 1636.

Nony, C. "The Biological and Social Significance of the Expression of the Emotions" *British Journal of Psychology* 13(July 1922) 76-92.

Norris, E. "Feeling" *Journal of Philosophy* 3(1906) 467-69.

Novey, S. "A Clinical View of Affect Theory in Psycho-analysis" *International Journal of Psycho-Analysis* 1959.

O'Brien, P. *Emotions and Morals* New York 1950.

Ochs, C. "The Sensitive Term Pain" *Philosophy and Phenomenological Research* 27(2) (1966-67) 255-60.

Olds, J. "Pleasure Centers in the Brain" *Scientific American* 195(1956) 105-116.

Onians, R. *The Origins of European Thought, About the Body, the Mind, the Soul, the World, Time and Fate* Cambridge University Press 1951.

"The Orator's Treatment of Emotion" *Great Books Syntopicon* M. Adler, ed., Chicago: Britannica 1955 Chapt. 81, Section 4, pp. 654, 660.

Ostow, Mortimer. "Current Theories of Emotion" American Psychological Association Meeting, Cincinnati 1959.

Oswald, F. "The Influence of Emotion" *Modern Medicine and Bacter. Review* 6(1897) 28-31.

Parsons, Kathryn. "Mistaking Sensations" *Philosophical Review* 79(April 1970) 201-13.

Paulhan, F. *The Laws of Feeling* C. Ogden, trans. New York: Harcourt Brace 1930.

Paulhan, Fr. "Sur l' emotion esthetique" *Rev. Philos* . 19(1885) 652-67.

Penelhum, Terence. "The Logic of Pleasure" *Philosophy and Phenomenological Research* 17(1956-57) 488-503.

Penelhum, Terence. "Symposium on Pleasure and Falsity" *Philosophical Quarterly* 1(2) (April 1964) 81-91.

Pepper, Stephen. *Aesthetic Quality* New York: Scribners 1937, pp. 89-113.

Perkins, Moreland. "Emotion and Feelings" *Philosophical Quarterly* 75(2) (1966) 139-60.

Perkins, Moreland. "Seeing and Hearing Emotions" *Analysis* 26(6) (N.S.) (1966) 193-97.

Perls, F. *Ego, Hunger and Aggression* New York: Random House 1969(1947) Ch. 13 "Emotional Resistances"

Perry, D. *The Concept of Pleasure* The Hague: Mouton 1967.

Peters, Richard. *The Concept of Motivation* London: Kegan Paul 1958.

Peters, Richard. "Emotions, Passivity and the Place of Freud's Theory in Psychology" *Scientific Psychology* B. Wolman & E. Nagel, eds., New York: Basic Books 1965.

Peters, Richard. "Motivation, Emotion, and the Conceptual Schemes of Common Sense" *Human Action* T. Mischel, ed., New York: Academic Press 1969.

Peters, Richard, and C. Mace. "Emotions and the Category of Passivity" *Proceedings of the Aristotelian Society* 62(1961-1962) 117- 43.

Phelan, G. *Feeling Experience and Its Modalities* London: Kegan 1925.

Phillips, Claude. *Emotion in Art* M. Brockwell, ed., New York: Books for Libraries Press 1968(1925).

Phillips, M. *The Education of the Emotions thru Sentiment Development* London 1937.

Pitcher, George. "Emotion" *Mind* 74(N.S.) (1965) 326-47.

Pitcher, George. "Pain Perception" *Philosophical Quarterly* 79(3) (1970) 368-94.

"Pleasure and Pain" *Great Books Syntopicon* Chapt. 68, pp. 377-99.

Pleydell-Pearce, A. "Freedom, Emotion and Choice in the Philosophy of Jean-Paul Sartre" *Journal of the British Society for Phenomenology* 1(May 1970) 35-46.

Plutchik, Robert. *The Emotions* New York: Random House 1962.

Plutchik, Robert. "The Multi-Factor-Analytic Theory of Emotion" *Journal of Psychology* 50(1960) 153-171.

Plutchik, Robert. "Some Problems for a Theory of Emotions" *Psychosomatic Medicine* 1955.

"Poetry and Emotion" *Great Books Syntopicon* Chapt. 69, pp. 409, 414.

Porta, J. Baptista. *De Humana Physiognomia* Naples 1589.

Prescott, D. *Emotion and the Educative Process* Washington, D.C.: American Council on Education 1938.

Pribram, Karl. "The New Neurology and Biology of Emotion" *American Psychologist* 22(10) (1967) 830-838.

Prick, J. *Human Moods, Feelings & Emotions* Philadelphia: Davis 1968.

Ramsay, G. *Analysis and Theory of Emotions* London 1848

Rapaport, David. *Emotions and Memory* New York: International Univ. Press 1959.

Rapaport, David. "On the Psycho-analytic Theory of Affects" *International Journal of Psycho-Analysis* 1953.

Redl, F. "Group Emotion and Leadership" *Psychiatry* 5(1942).

Reid, L. "Instinct, Emotion and the Higher Life" *British Journal of Psychology* 14(1923) 78-94.

Reid, T. *Essays on the Active Powers of the Human Mind* Edinburgh 1788 III, part II, Ch. 3-7.

Reymert, M., ed. *Feelings and Emotions: The Wittenberg Symposium* Worchester, Mass: Clark University Press 1928.

Reymert, M., ed. *Feelings and Emotions* Moosehead Symposium, New York: McGraw-Hill 1950.

Reynoldes, Edward. *A Treatise of the Passions and Faculties of the Soul of Man* 1640.

Ribot, Theodule. *The Psychology of the Emotions* London 1897.

Richardson, R. *The Psychology and Pedagogy of Anger* Baltimore: Warwick and York 1918.

Rist, J. "Zeno and Chrysippus on Human Action and Emotion" *Stoic Philosophy* Cambridge, England: Cambridge University Press 1969, 22-36.

Robbe-Grillet, Alain. *Jealousy* New York: Grove Press 1965.

Robinson, Richard, H. Paton, and R. Cross. "The Emotive Theory of Ethics" (Symposium) *Proceedings of the Aristotelian Society* Supp. 22(1948) 79-127.

Rome, H. "The Dynamics of Emotions" *Minnesota Med.* 1953.

Rosenberg, Milton. *Attitude Organization and Change* New Haven: Yale University Press 1960 pp. 15-64, 112-163.

Rosenberg, Milton. "Cognitive Structure and Attitudinal Affect" *Journal of Abnormal and Social Psychology* 53(1956) 367-372.

Rosensohn, William. "A logical method for making a classification of emotions, using Wilhelm Wundt's theory of emotion formation" *Journal of Psychology* 55,1(1963) 175-82.

Rosenzweig, N. "The Affect System: Foresight and Fantasy" *Journal of Nervous and Mental Disease* 1958.

Rosthal, Robert. "Emotions and Incorrigibility" (Abstract for American Philosophical Association, Eastern Division, Dec. 27-29, 1968) *Journal of Philosophy* 65,(21) (Nov. 7, 1968) 701-2.

Ruckmick, C. "A Preliminary Study of the Emotions" *Psychological Monographs* 30, (3) (1921) 30-35.

Ruckmick, C. *The Psychology of Feeling and Emotion* New York: McGraw-Hill 1936.

Russell, Bertrand. *The Analysis of Mind* New York: Macmillan 1921, "Emotions and Will" pp. 279-86.

Ruthven, K. *The Conceit* London: Methuen 1969 (See section on extravagance and jealousy.)

Ryle, Gilbert. *Concept of Mind* New York: Barnes and Noble 1949, Ch. 4 "Emotions" pp. 83-115; 107-110.

Ryle, Gilbert. "Feelings" *Philosophical Quarterly* 1(1951) 193-205.

Ryle, Gilbert. "Pleasure" *Dilemmas* Cambridge University Press (1960) 54-67.

Sahakian, William. *Psychopathology Today* Itasca, Illinois: Peacock Pub. 1970.

Sahakian, William. "Stoic Philosophical Psychotherapy" *Journal of Individual Psychology* 25 (1969) 32-35.

Sankowski, Edward. "Emotion and Norm" PhD diss. Cornell Univ. 1972.

Sarbin, T., R. Taft and D. Bailey. *Clinical Inference and Cognitive Theory* New York: Holt 1960.

Sartre, Jean-Paul. *Sketch for a Theory of Emotions* London: Methuen 1962.

Schachter, Stanley. *Emotion, Obesity, and Crime* New York: Academic Press 1971.

Schachter, Stanley. "The Interaction of Cognitive and Physiological Determinants of Emotional States" *Psychobiological Approaches to Social Behavior* P. Leiderman and D. Schapiro, eds., Stanford Univ. Press 1964.

Schachter, Stanley and J. Singer. "Cognitive, Social, and Physiological Determinants of Emotional State" *Psychological Review* 69 (5) (Sept. 1962) 379-400.

Schaller, Jean-Pierre. *Our Emotions and the Moral Act* M. Bouchard, trans. New York: Alba House 1968.

Scheler, M. *The Nature of Sympathy* P. Heath, trans., London: Routledge 1954.

Schlosberg, H. "Three Dimensions of Emotion" *Psychological Review* 61 (1954) 81-88.

Schmale, A. "Relationship of Separation and Depression to Disease" *Psychosomatic Medicine* 20(1958) 259 ff.

Schramm, G. "A Periodic Table of Emotional Phases" *Journal of Abnormal and Social Psychology* 31(1936) 87-98.

Schwab, S. "The Heart in Emotional Conflicts" *American Heart Journal* 2(1926-1927) 166-172.

Seligman, David. *Bodily Feelings* (unpublished manuscript based on PhD Diss. Duke University 1967)

Senault, J. *The Use of the Passions* London 1649.

Seneca. (On Anger)

Shagass, Charles, ed. *Theories of the Mind* Glencoe, New York: Free Press 1962.

Shand, Alexander. "Character and the Emotions" *Mind* 5(N.S.) (1896) 203-26.

Shand, Alexander. "Emotion and Value" *Proceedings of the Aristotelian Society* N.S. 19(1918-1919) 208-236.

Shand, Alexander. "Feeling and Thought" *Mind* 23(N.S. 7) (1898) 477-505.

Shand, Alexander. *The Foundations of Character* London: Macmillan 1914.

Shand, Alexander. "Of Impulse, Emotion and Instinct" *Proceedings of the Aristotelian Society* N.S. 20(1919-1920) 79-89.

Shand, Alexander. "M. Ribot's Theory of the Passions" *Mind* 16(N.S.) (1907) 477-505.

Shevach, David. "Emotion and the Unconscious" PhD dissertation, Univ. of California 1971.

Shibles, Warren. "Death and Emotions" Paper presented at "Philosophical Aspects of Death" Symposium, Columbia University College of Physicians and Surgeons, and Foundation of Thanatology, May 1973.

Shibles, Warren. "Emotion, Metaphor and Therapy" *Nuovo 75: metodologia, scienza* 9,1973; 10,1974.

Shibles, Warren. "Metaphor as constituting emotions," etc. *Metaphor: An Annotated Bibliography and History* Whitewater, Wisconsin: The Language Press 1971 pp. 380-81.

Shibles, Warren. "Review of LeShan *What Makes Me Feel This Way?*" *Rational Living* 8(1973) 35.

Simon, A., C. Herbert and R. Straus. *The Physiology of Emotion* Springfield, Illinois: Charles Thomas 1961.

Simonov, Pavel. "Dynamical Stereotype and Physiology of Emotions" International Congress of Psychology, Symposium 1966 pp. 104-110.

Simonov, Pavel. "Emotions and Creativity" *Psychology Today* 4(3) (Aug. 1970).

Simonov, Pavel. "Studies of Emotional Behavior of Humans and Animals by Soviet Physiologists" *Experimental Approaches to the Study of Emotional Behavior* vol. 159, art. 3, Annals of New York Academy of Sciences 1969.

Sircello, Guy. "Emotive-Expression, Expressive Qualities of Ordinary Language" *Mind* 76(1967) 548-555.

Skinner, B. F. *The Behavior of Organisms* New York: Appleton-Century 1938, 406-609.

Skinner, B. F. *Science and Human Behavior* New York: Macmillan 1953.

Smith, Adam. *Theory of the Moral Sentiments* London 1759.

Smith, J. "On Feeling" *Proceedings of the Aristotelian Society* N.S. 14 (1913-1914) 49-76.

Smith, W. *The Measurement of Emotion* London 1922.

Solomon, M. "The Mechanism of the Emotions" *British Journal of Medical Psychology* 1927.

Spencer, Herbert. "Emotion in the Primitive Man" *Popular Science Monthly* 6(1875) 331-9. (See his other works also.)

Spielberger, C. *Anxiety* New York: Academic Press 1972.

Stankiewicz, E. "Problems of Emotive Language" *Approaches to Semiotics* The Hague pp. 239-64.

Stanley, Hiram. "Feeling and Emotion" *Mind* (1886) 66-75.

Stanley, Hiram. "Remarks on Tickling and Laughing" *American Journal of Psychology* 9(1898) 235-40.

Stanley, Hiram. *Studies in Evolutionary Psychology of Feeling* London 1895.

Stein, Edith. *On the Problem of Empathy* The Hague: Nijhoff 1970.

Stevens, S. S., ed. *Handbook of Experimental Psychology* New York: Wiley 1951.

Stevenson, Charles. "Brandt's Questions About Emotive Ethics" *Philosophical Review* 59(1950) 528-34.

Stevenson, Charles. "The Emotive Concept of Ethics and its Cognitive Implications" *Philosophical Review* 59(1950) 291-304.

Stout, G.; J. Brough, and A. Bain. "Is the Distinction of Feeling, Cognition, and Conation Valid as the Ultimate Distinction of the Mental Functions?" *Proceedings of the Aristotelian Society* 1(3) (1888-1891) 142-54.

Stratton, G. "The Function of Emotion as Shown Particularly in Excitement" *Psychological Review* 35(Sept. 1928) 351-366.

Stratton, G. "The Sensations are not the Emotions" *Psychological Review* 2(1895) 173-4.

Sully, James. "Prolegomena to a Theory of Laughter" *Philosophical Review* 9(1900) 365-83.

Sully, James. "The Laughter of Savages" *International Monthly* 4(1901) 379-402.

Szasz, Thomas. "A Contribution to the Psychology of Bodily Feelings" *Psychoanalytic Quarterly* 26(1957) 25-49.

Szasz, Thomas. *Pain and Pleasure: A Study of Bodily Feelings* New York: Basic Books 1957.

Taylor, C. "Pleasure" *Analysis* 23(1963).

Taylor, D. "The Location of Pain" *Philosophical Quarterly* 15(58) (1965) 53-63.

Taylor, Warren. *Tudor Figures of Rhetoric* Whitewater, Wisc.: The Language Press 1972 "Emotions Expressed or Aroused" indexed pp. 152-153.

Thalberg, Irving. "Constituents and Causes of Emotion and Action" *Philosophical Quarterly* 23(90) (1973) 1-13.

Thalberg, Irving. "Emotion and Thought" *American Philosophical Quarterly* (Jan. 1964) 45-55. Reprinted in *Philosophy of Mind* Stuart Hampshire, ed., New York: Harper 1966. Reviewed by W. Carter "On Thalberg's Condition for Cause" *Mind* 79(316) (Oct. 1970) 597-599.

Thalberg, Irving "Evidence and Causes of Emotion" *MIND* 88 (1974) 108-110.

Thalberg, Irving. "False Pleasures" *Journal of Philosophy* 59(1962) 65-74.

Thalberg, Irving. "Natural Expressions of Emotions" *Philosophy and Phenomenological Research* 22(3) (1962) 387-92.

Thalbitzer, S. *Emotion and Insanity* M. Beard, trans. New York 1926.

Tilghman, B. "Emotions and Some Psychologists" *Southern Journal of Philosophy* 3(2) (Summer 1965) 63-69.

Tilghman, B. *The Expression of Emotion in the Visual Arts* The Hague: Nijhoff 1970.

Titchener, Edward. "An Historical Note on the James-Lange Theory of Emotion" *American Journal of Psychology* 1914.

Titchener, Edward. *Lectures on the Elementary Psychology of Feeling and Attention* New York: Macmillan 1909.

Titchener, Edward. *An Outline of Psychology* New York: Macmillan 1896, esp. chapters 5,9.

Tolman, E. "A Behavioristic Account of the Emotions" *Behavior and Psychological Man* University of California 1958. Also *Psychological Review* 30(1923) 217-227.

Tolman, E. *Purposive Behavior in Animals and Men* New York 1932.

Tolstoy, Leo. "The Communication of Emotion" *A Modern Book of Esthetics* Melvin Rader, ed., New York: Holt 1960 pp. 62-71.

Tomkins, S. *Affect, Imagery, Consciousness* 2 vols., New York: Springer 1962.

Trebilcot, Joyce. "Dr. Kenny's Perceptions" *Mind* 79(1970) 142-3.

Trigg, Roger. *Pain and Emotion* Oxford: Clarendon Press 1970.

Troland, L. "A System for Explaining Affective Phenomena" *Journal of Abnormal Psychology* 1920.

Tuttle, H. "Emotion as a Substitute Response" *Journal of General Psychology* 1940.

Tyson, R. "Feelings and Emotions" *Journal of Clinical Psychology* 7(1951) 17-24.

Urban, W. "The Problem of a Logic of the Emotions and Affective Memory" *Psychological Review* 8(1901) 262-78, 360-70.

Vauhkonen, Kauko. "On the Pathogenesis of Morbid Jealousy" Copenhagen: Munksgaard 1968.

Veith, I. "Non-Western Concepts of Psychic Function" *The History and Philosophy of Knowledge of the Brain and its Functions* F. Poynter, ed., Oxford 1958.

Veron, Eugene. "Art as the Expression of Emotion" *A Modern Book of Esthetics* Melvin Rader, ed., New York: Holt 1960 pp. 53-61.

Vesey, G. "Being and Feeling" *Proceedings of the Aristotelian Society* 69(1968-1969) 133-87.

Voltaire. "Passions" *A Philosophical Dictionary* Haskell 1971 (1764).

Vygotskii, L. "Spinoza's Theory of the Emotions in Light of Contemporary Psychoneurology" *Soviet Studies in Philosophy* 1972.

Walker, Jeremy. "Imagination and Passion" *Philosophy and Phenomenological Research* 29(1968-1969) 575-88.

Waller, A. "Concerning Emotive Phenomena" *Proceedings of the Royal Society* Series B, 1920.

Walter, Edward. "The Logic of Emotions" *Southern Journal of Philosophy* 10(1) (1972) 71-78.

Warnock, Mary and A. Ewing. (Symposium) "The Justification of Emotions" *Proceedings of the Aristotelian Society* Suppl. 31 (1957) 43-59, 59-74.

Washburn, M. "Feeling and Emotion" *Psychological Bulletin* 24(1927). 573-95.

492

Washburn, M. "The Term Feeling" *Journal of Philosophy* 3(1906) 62-65.

Waters, R. and D. Blackwood. "The Applicability of Motivational Criteria to Emotions" *Psychological Review* 56(1949) 351-56.

Watson, John. *Behaviorism* University of Chicago Press 1930 esp. chapts. 7 & 8.

Watson, J; and R. Raynor. "Conditioned Emotional Reactions" *Journal of Experimental Psychology* 3(1920) ca.1.

Webb, W. "A Motivational Theory of Emotions" *Psychological Review* 55(1948) 329-35.

Weber, A. and D. Rapaport. "Teleology and Emotions" *Philosophy of Science* 8(1941) 69-82.

Wells, Henry. *Traditional Chinese Humor* Indiana University Press 1971.

Wenar, et al. *Origin of Psychosomatic and Emotional Disturbances* New York: Harper and Row 1962.

Wenger, M. "Mechanical Emotion" *Journal of Psychology* 29(1950) 101-108.

Wenger, W. "Prof. Boring's Robot Becomes Emotional" *American Psychologist* 3(1948) ca. 339.

White, Alan. "Feeling" *The Philosophy of Mind* New York: Random House 1967 Ch. 5, pp. 104-130.

White, Alan. "Review of Gotlind *Three Theories of Emotion*" *Philosophical Quarterly* 10(1960) 380-81.

Whitehorn, J. "Concerning Emotion as Impulsion and Instinct as Orientation" *American Journal Psychiatry* 1932.

Williams, B. "Pleasure and Belief" *Proceedings of the Aristotelian Society* Suppl. 33(1959) 57-72.

Wilson, J. *Emotion and Object* Cambridge University Press 1972.

Wittgenstein, Ludwig. *The Blue and Brown Books* R. Rhees, ed., Oxford: Blackwell 1958.

Wittgenstein, Ludwig, *Philosophical Investigations* G. Anscombe, trans., 3rd ed., New York: Macmillan 1958.

Wittgenstein, Ludwig. *Zettel* G. Anscombe, trans., London: Blackwell 1966.

Woodworth, Robert. *Experimental Psychology* New York: Holt 1971.

Woolston, H. "Religious Emotion" *American Journal of Psychology* 13(1902) 62-79.

Wright, T. *The Passions of the Minde in Generall* London 1604.

Wundt, W. *Outlines of Psychology* C. Judd, trans., Leipzig: W. Engelman 1897.

Young, Paul. "By What Criteria Can Emotion Be Defined?" *Psychological Bulletin* 38(1941) 713.

Young, Paul. "Emotion as Disorganized Response—a reply to Prof. Leeper" *Psychological Review* 56(1949) 184-91.

Young, Paul. *Emotion in Man and Animal* revised edition, New York; R. Krieger 1973.

Zachry, C. and M. Lightly. *Emotion and Conduct in Adolescence* New York: Appleton 1940.

Zangwill, D. "The Theory of Emotion: A Correspondence Between J. MacCurdy and Morton Prince" *British Journal of Psychology* 39(1948) 1-11.

Zilboorg, G. "The Emotional Problem and the Therapeutic Role of Insight" *Yearbook of Psychoanalysis* 9(1953) New York.

Zilboorg, G. *A History of Medical Psychology* New York: Norton 1967.